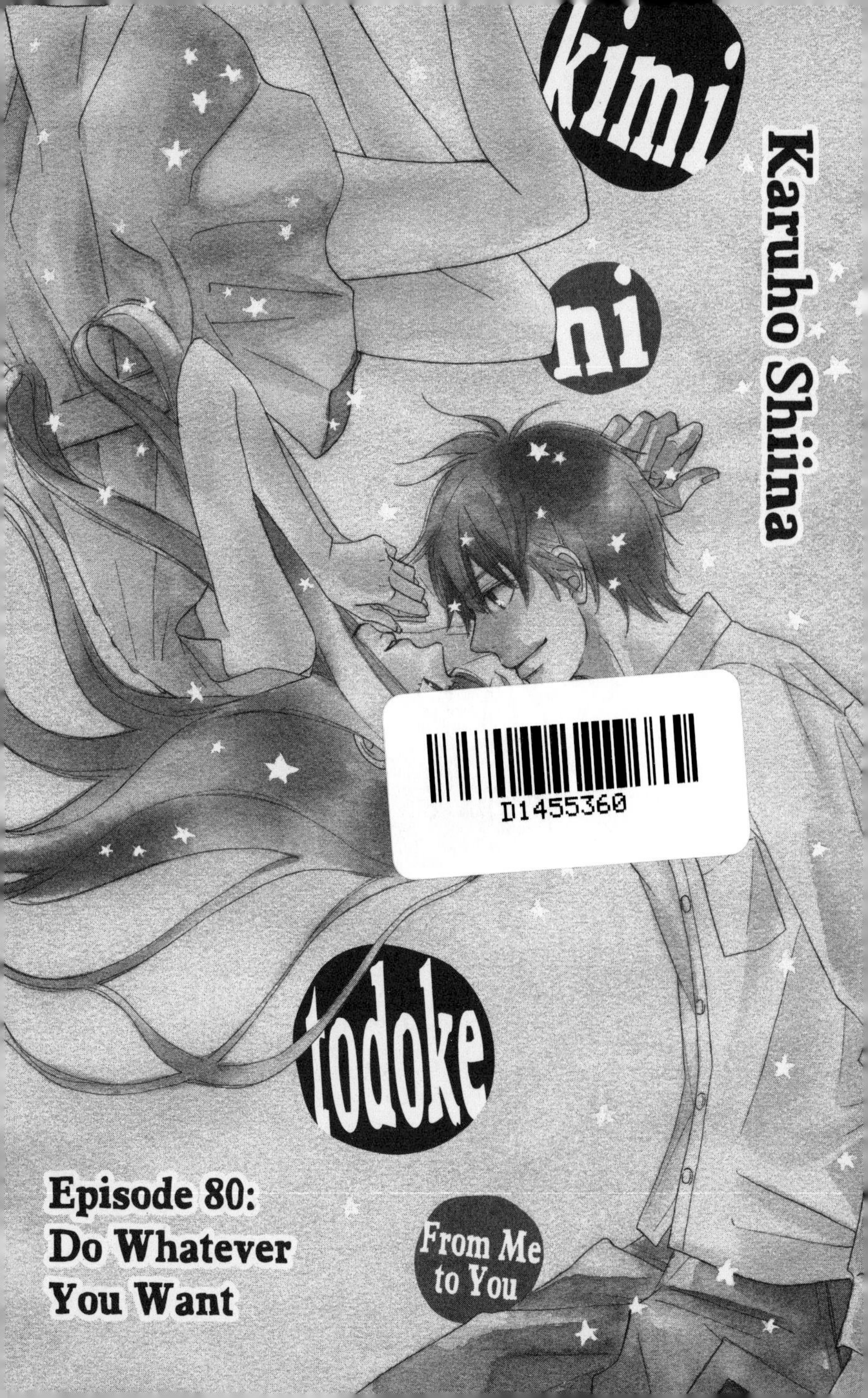
kimi ni todoke
Karuho Shiina
Episode 80:
Do Whatever You Want
From Me to You

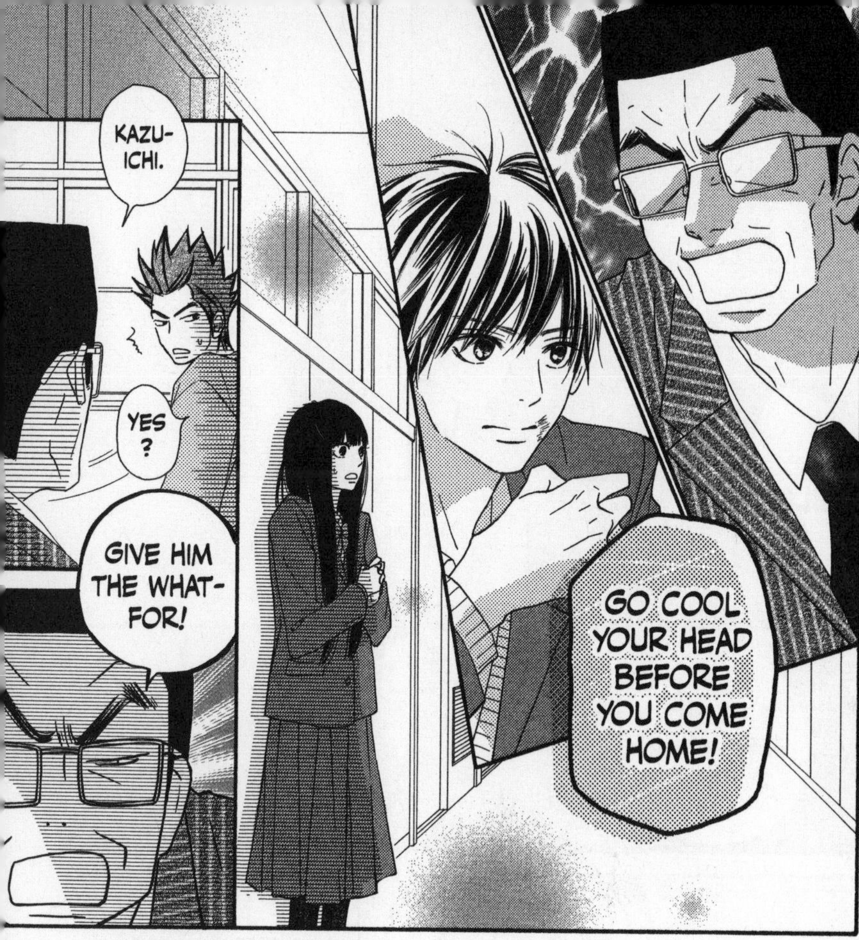
GO COOL YOUR HEAD BEFORE YOU COME HOME!
KAZU-ICHI.
YES?
GIVE HIM THE WHAT-FOR!

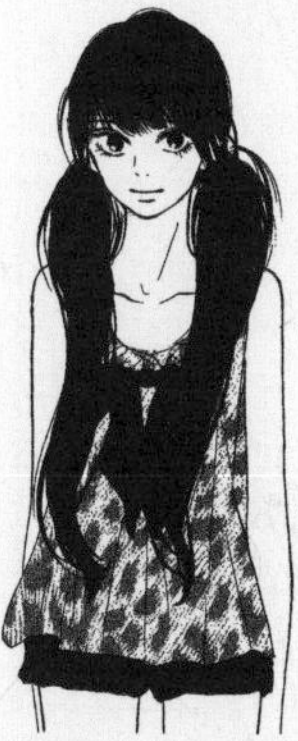

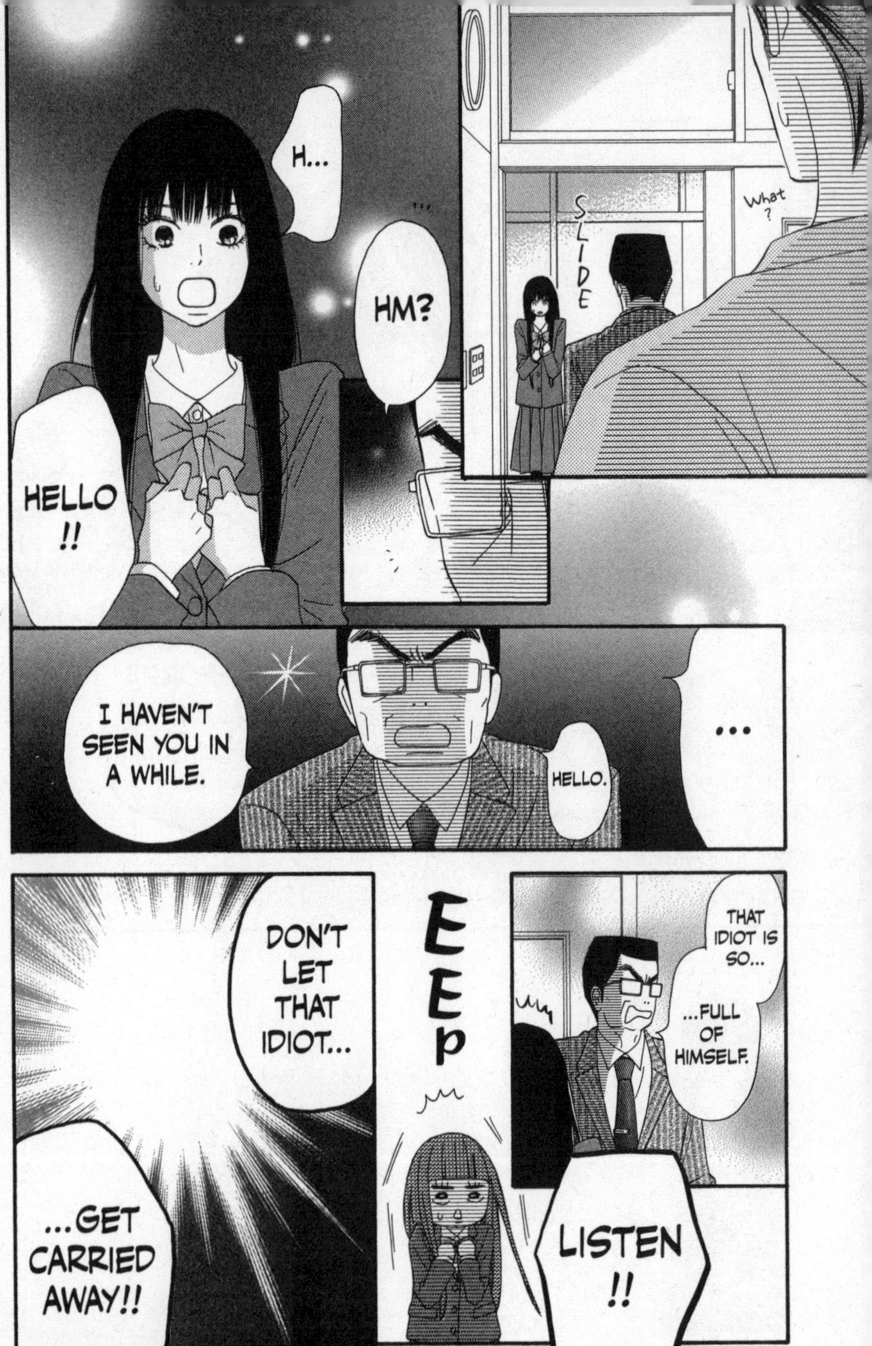
SLIDE
What ?
H...
HELLO !!
...
HM?
...
HELLO.
I HAVEN'T SEEN YOU IN A WHILE.
THAT IDIOT IS SO...
...FULL OF HIMSELF.
LISTEN !!
EEP
DON'T LET THAT IDIOT...
...GET CARRIED AWAY!!

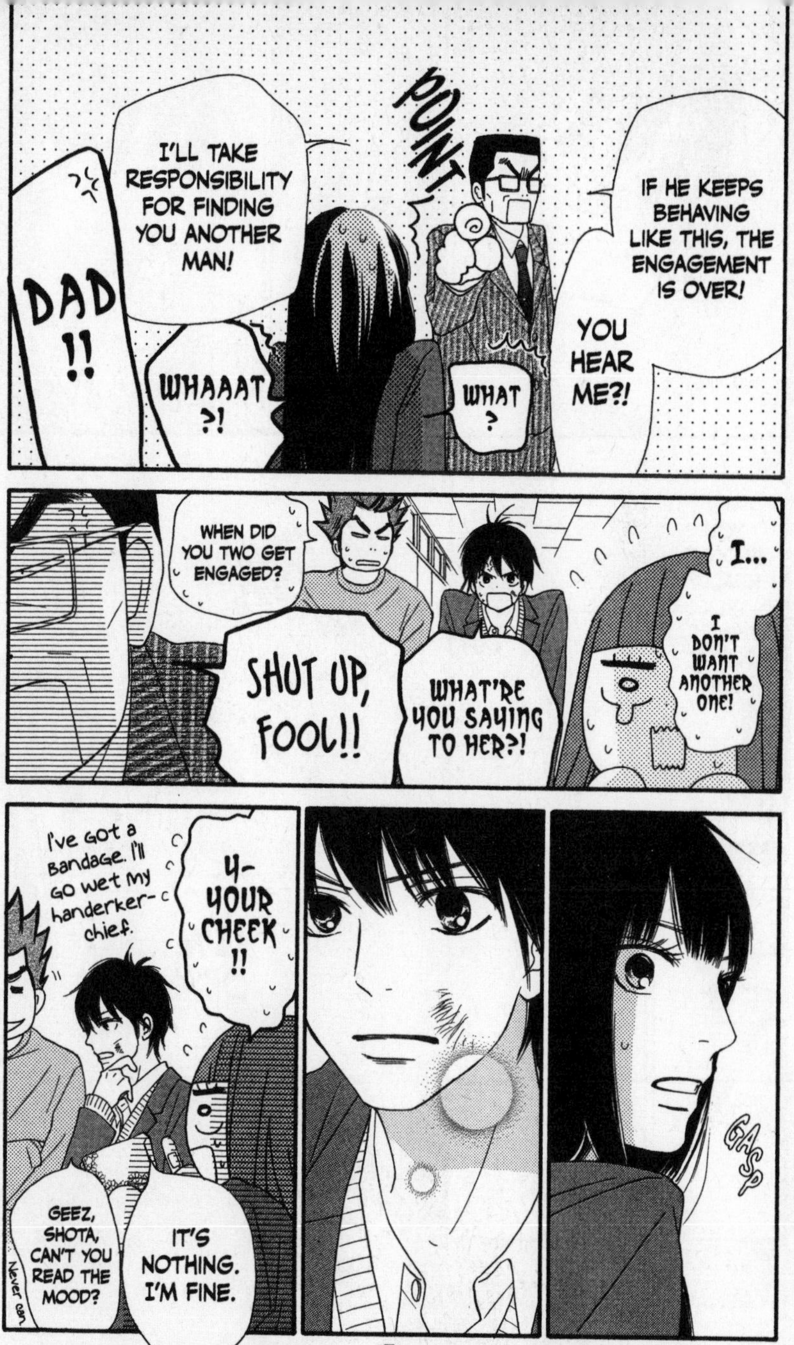
IF HE KEEPS BEHAVING LIKE THIS, THE ENGAGEMENT IS OVER!
YOU HEAR ME?!
POINT
I'LL TAKE RESPONSIBILITY FOR FINDING YOU ANOTHER MAN!
WHAT ?
WHAAAT ?!
DAD !!
I...
I DON'T WANT ANOTHER ONE!
WHAT'RE YOU SAYING TO HER?!
WHEN DID YOU TWO GET ENGAGED?
SHUT UP, FOOL!!
GASP
Y-YOUR CHEEK !!
I've got a bandage. I'll go wet my handerker-chief.
IT'S NOTHING. I'M FINE.
GEEZ, SHOTA, CAN'T YOU READ THE MOOD?
Never can

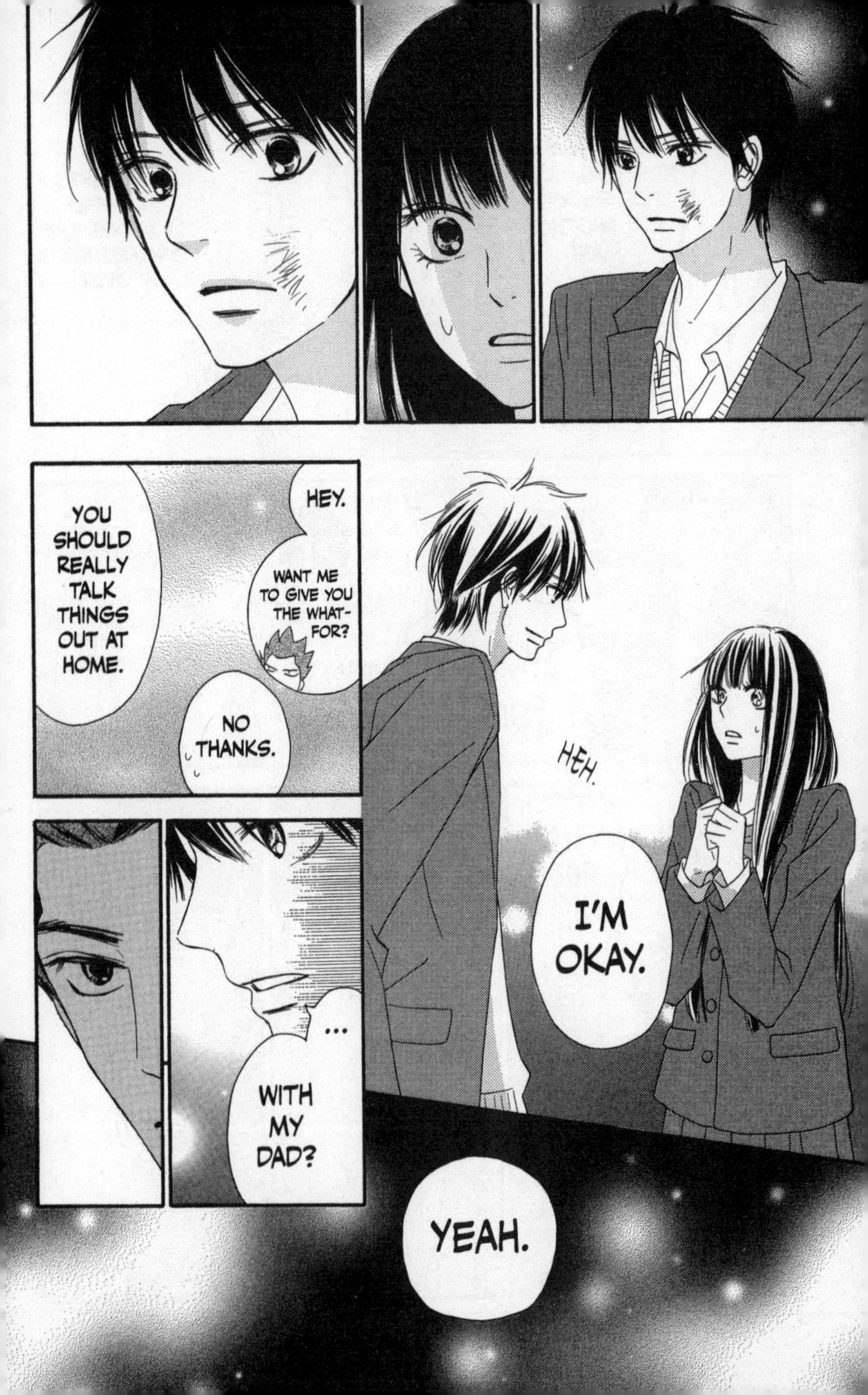
HEH.
I'M OKAY.
HEY.
WANT ME TO GIVE YOU THE WHAT-FOR?
NO THANKS.
YOU SHOULD REALLY TALK THINGS OUT AT HOME.
... WITH MY DAD?
YEAH.

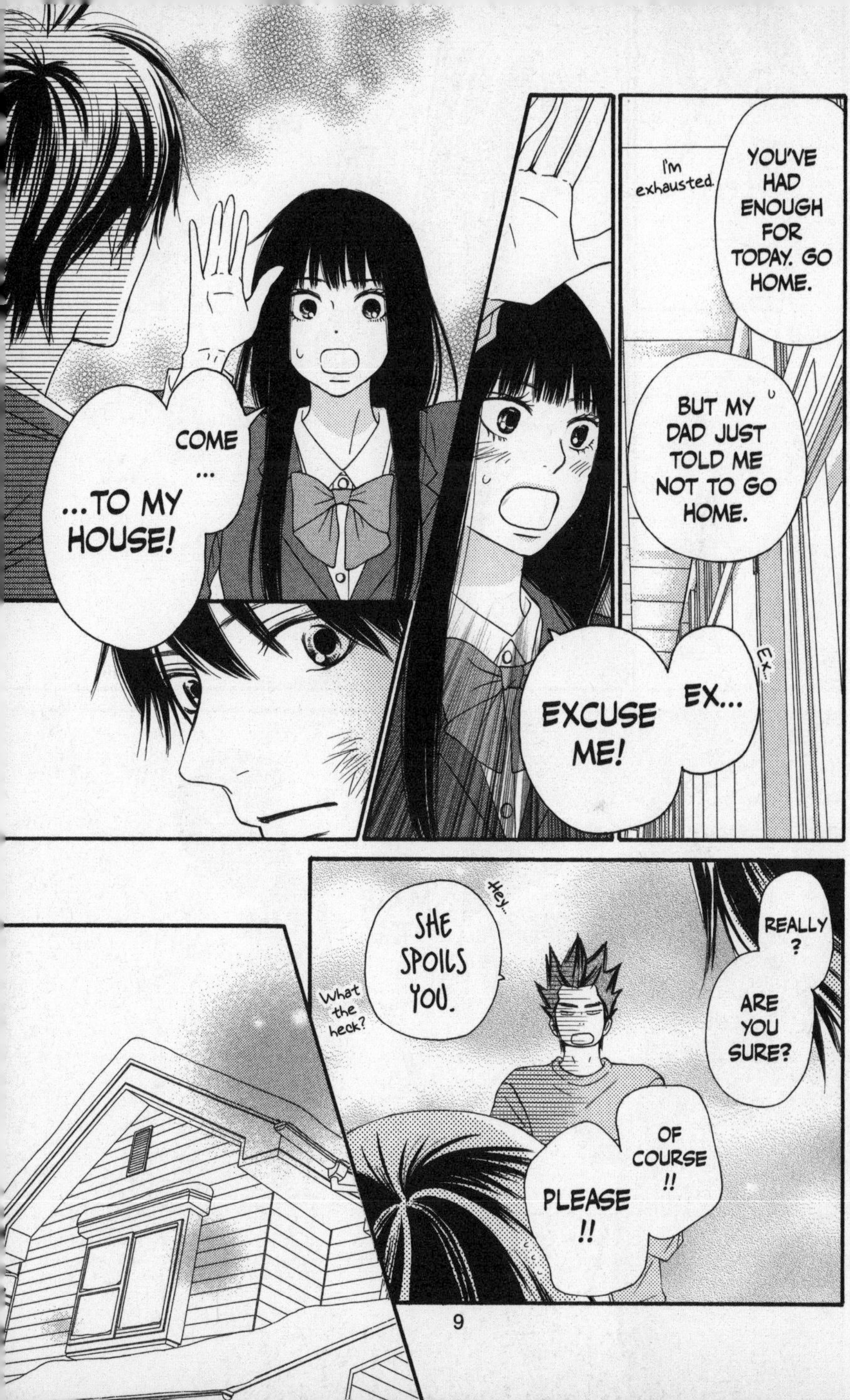

YOU'VE HAD ENOUGH FOR TODAY. GO HOME.
I'm exhausted.
BUT MY DAD JUST TOLD ME NOT TO GO HOME.
Ex...
EX...
EXCUSE ME!
COME...
...TO MY HOUSE!
REALLY? ARE YOU SURE?
Hey...
SHE SPOILS YOU.
What the heck?
OF COURSE!! PLEASE!!

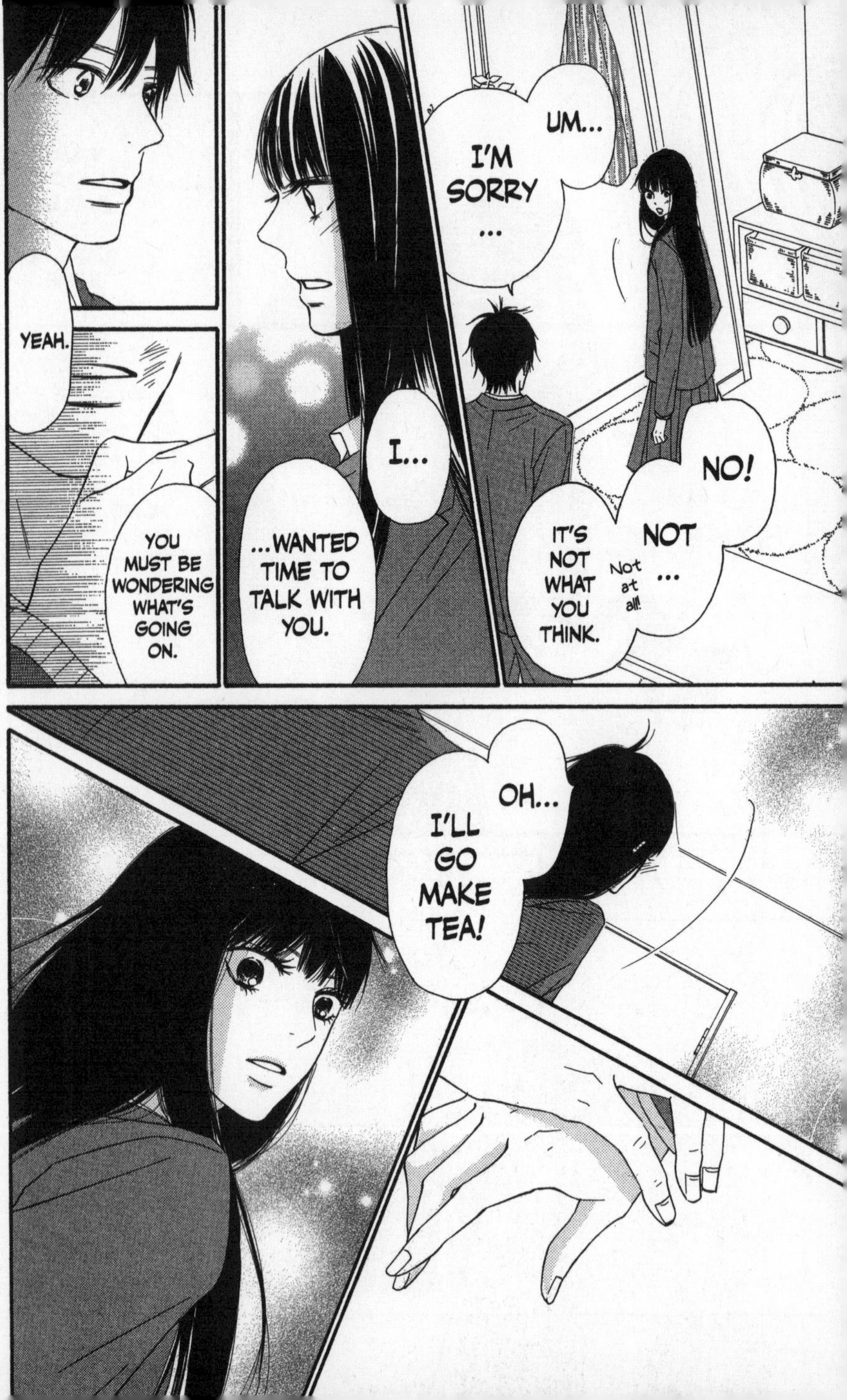
UM...
I'M SORRY ...
NO!
NOT ...
IT'S NOT WHAT YOU THINK.
Not at all!
I...
...WANTED TIME TO TALK WITH YOU.
YEAH.
YOU MUST BE WONDERING WHAT'S GOING ON.
OH...
I'LL GO MAKE TEA!

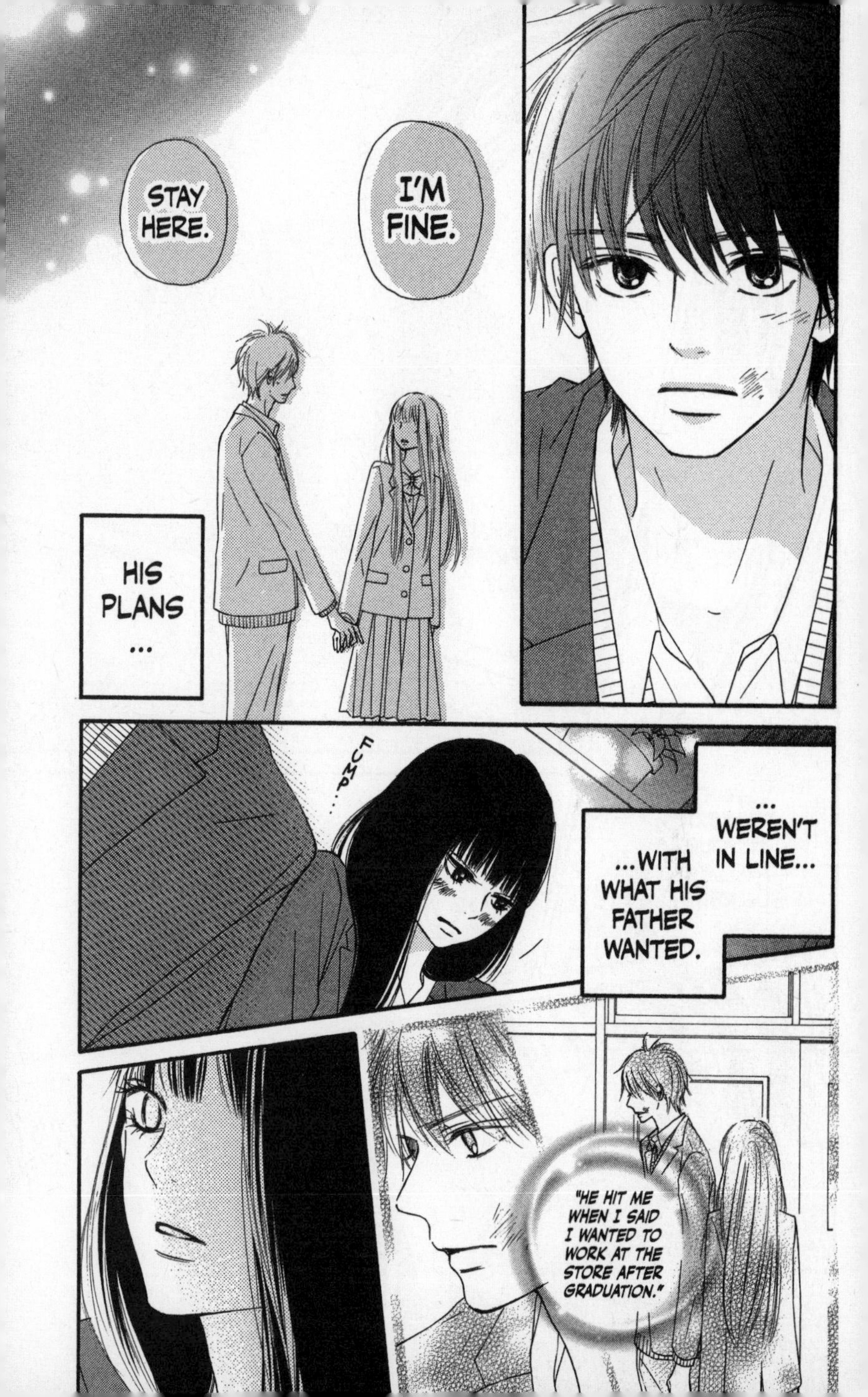
I'M FINE.
STAY HERE.
HIS PLANS ...
... WEREN'T IN LINE...
...WITH WHAT HIS FATHER WANTED.
TUMP...
"HE HIT ME WHEN I SAID I WANTED TO WORK AT THE STORE AFTER GRADUATION."

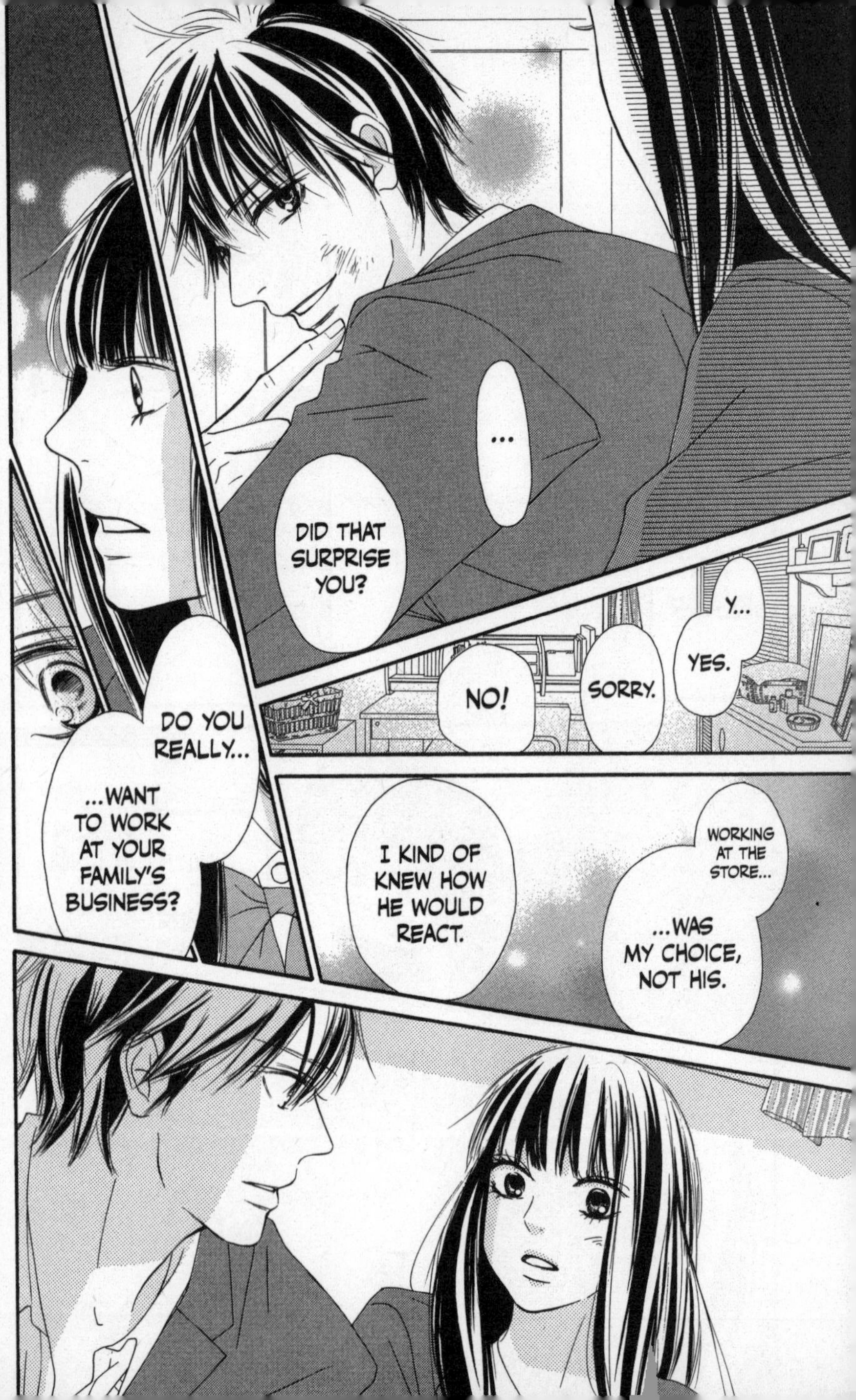
...
DID THAT SURPRISE YOU?
Y...
YES.
SORRY.
NO!
DO YOU REALLY...
...WANT TO WORK AT YOUR FAMILY'S BUSINESS?
WORKING AT THE STORE...
...WAS MY CHOICE, NOT HIS.
I KIND OF KNEW HOW HE WOULD REACT.

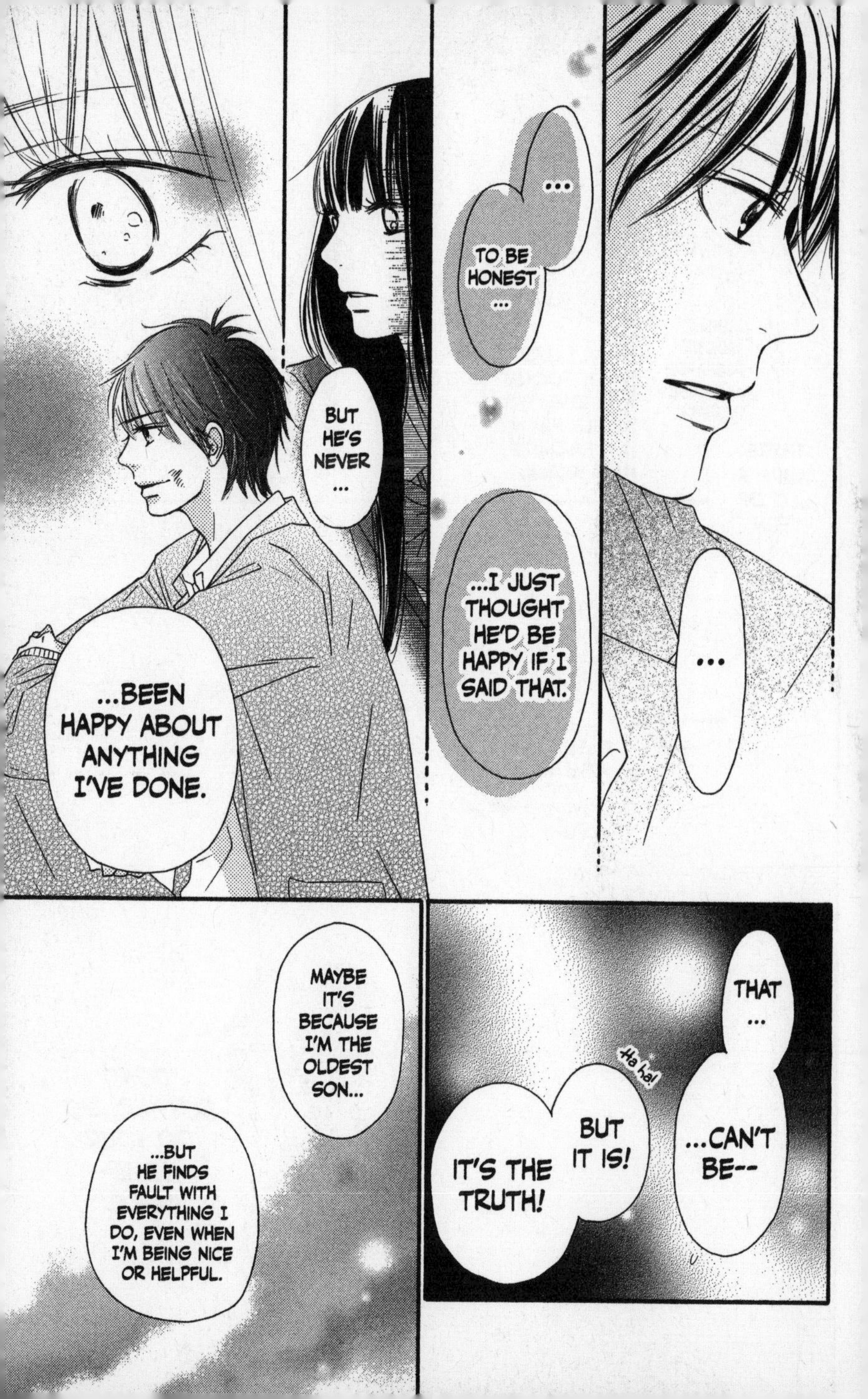
...
...
TO BE HONEST ...
...I JUST THOUGHT HE'D BE HAPPY IF I SAID THAT.
BUT HE'S NEVER ...
...BEEN HAPPY ABOUT ANYTHING I'VE DONE.
THAT ...
...CAN'T BE--
Ha ha!
BUT IT IS!
IT'S THE TRUTH!
MAYBE IT'S BECAUSE I'M THE OLDEST SON...
...BUT HE FINDS FAULT WITH EVERYTHING I DO, EVEN WHEN I'M BEING NICE OR HELPFUL.

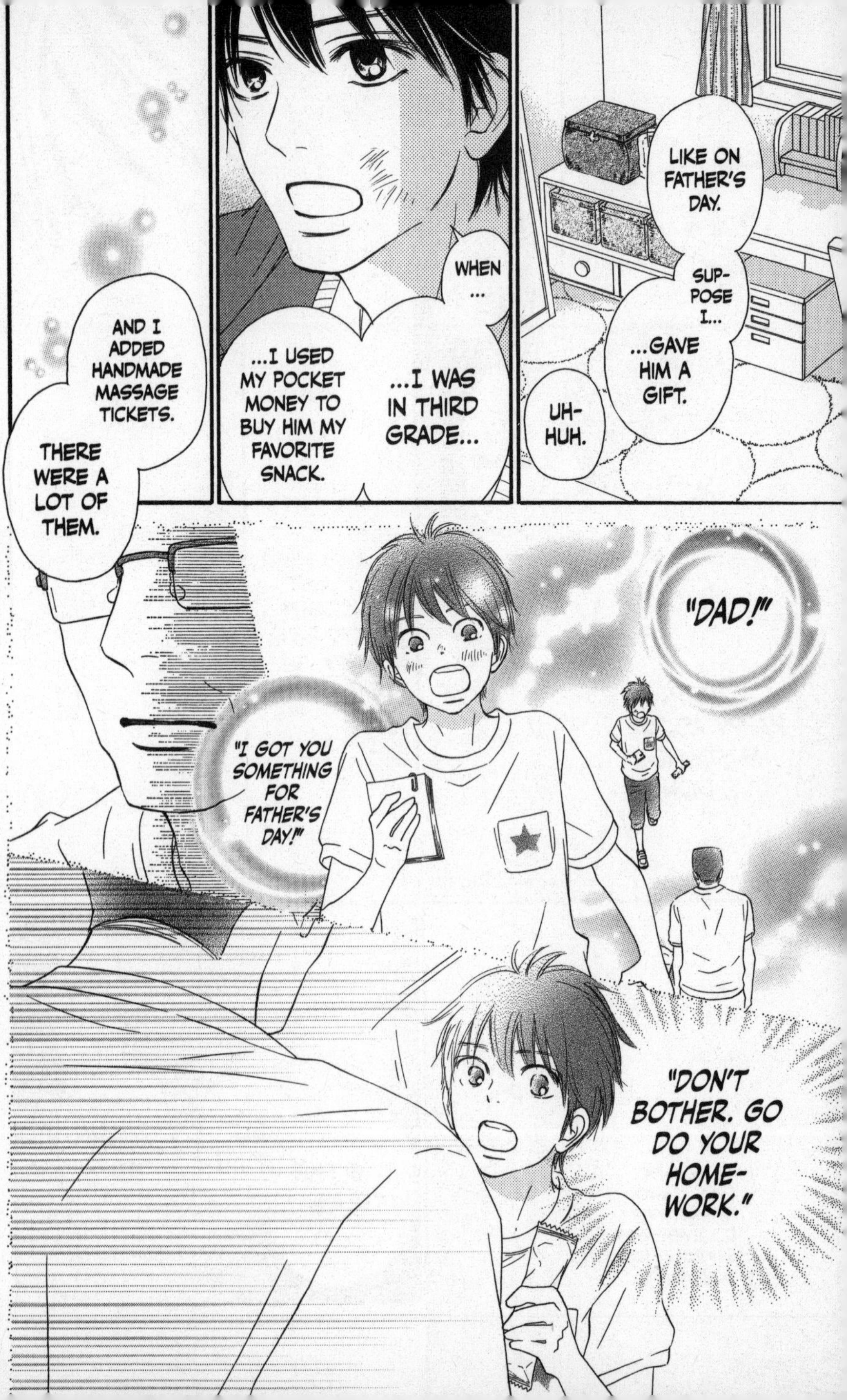
LIKE ON FATHER'S DAY.
SUP-POSE I...
...GAVE HIM A GIFT.
UH-HUH.
WHEN ...
...I WAS IN THIRD GRADE...
...I USED MY POCKET MONEY TO BUY HIM MY FAVORITE SNACK.
AND I ADDED HANDMADE MASSAGE TICKETS.
THERE WERE A LOT OF THEM.
"DAD!"
"I GOT YOU SOMETHING FOR FATHER'S DAY!"
"DON'T BOTHER. GO DO YOUR HOME-WORK."

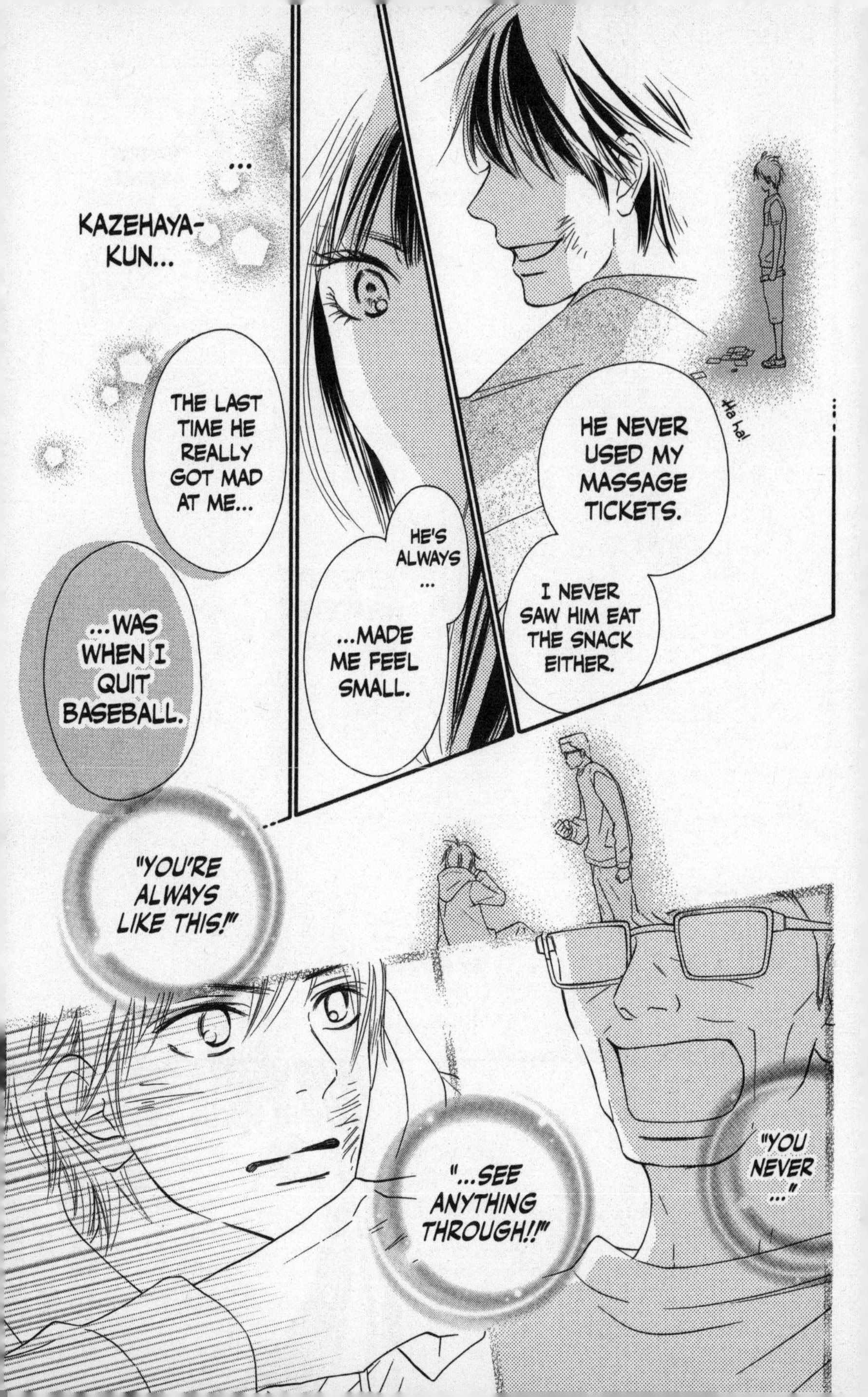
Ha ha!
HE NEVER USED MY MASSAGE TICKETS.
I NEVER SAW HIM EAT THE SNACK EITHER.
HE'S ALWAYS ...
...MADE ME FEEL SMALL.
...
KAZEHAYA-KUN...
THE LAST TIME HE REALLY GOT MAD AT ME...
...WAS WHEN I QUIT BASEBALL.
"YOU'RE ALWAYS LIKE THIS!"
"YOU NEVER ..."
"...SEE ANYTHING THROUGH!!"

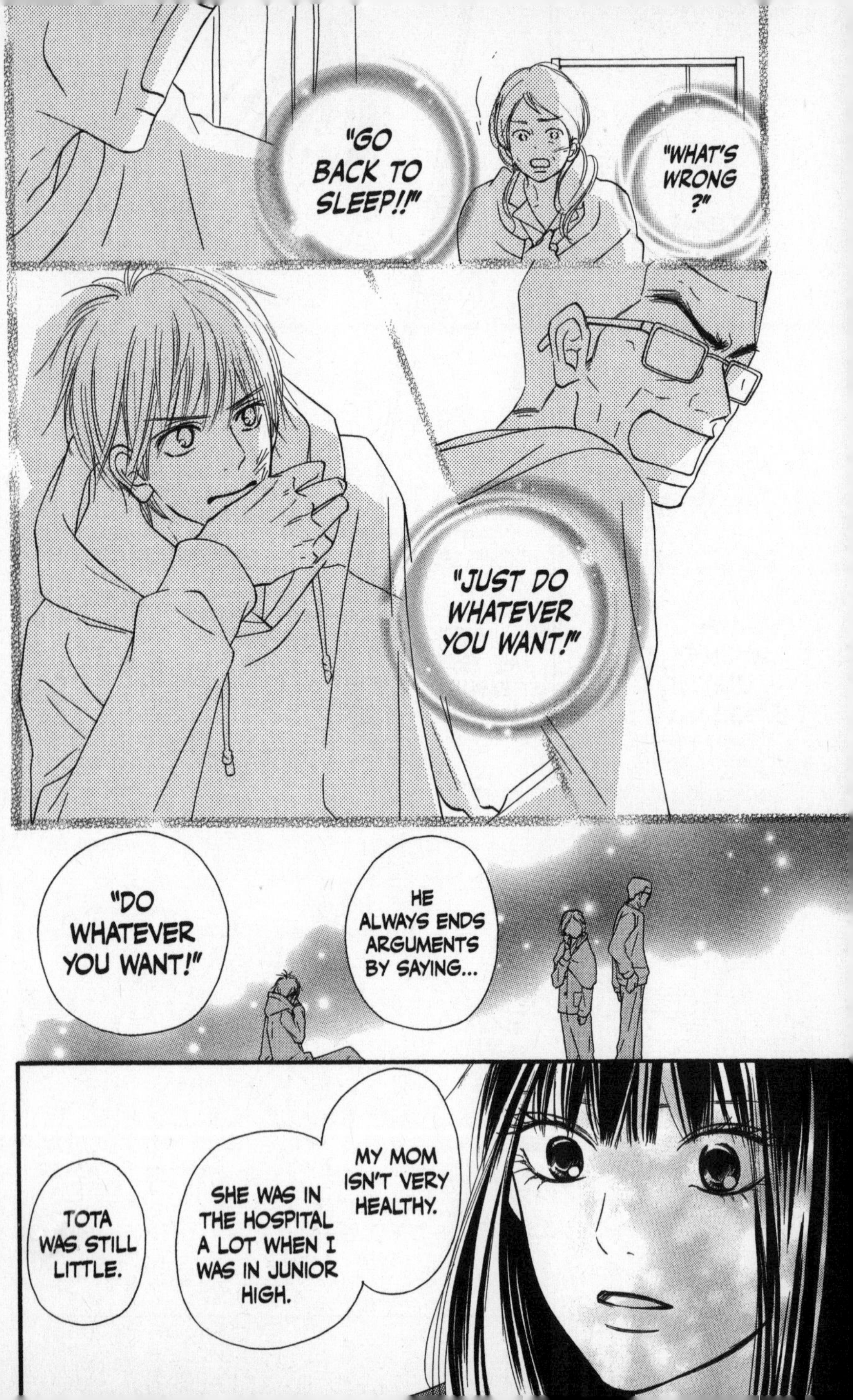
"WHAT'S WRONG?"
"GO BACK TO SLEEP!!"
"JUST DO WHATEVER YOU WANT!"
HE ALWAYS ENDS ARGUMENTS BY SAYING...
"DO WHATEVER YOU WANT!"
MY MOM ISN'T VERY HEALTHY.
SHE WAS IN THE HOSPITAL A LOT WHEN I WAS IN JUNIOR HIGH.
TOTA WAS STILL LITTLE.

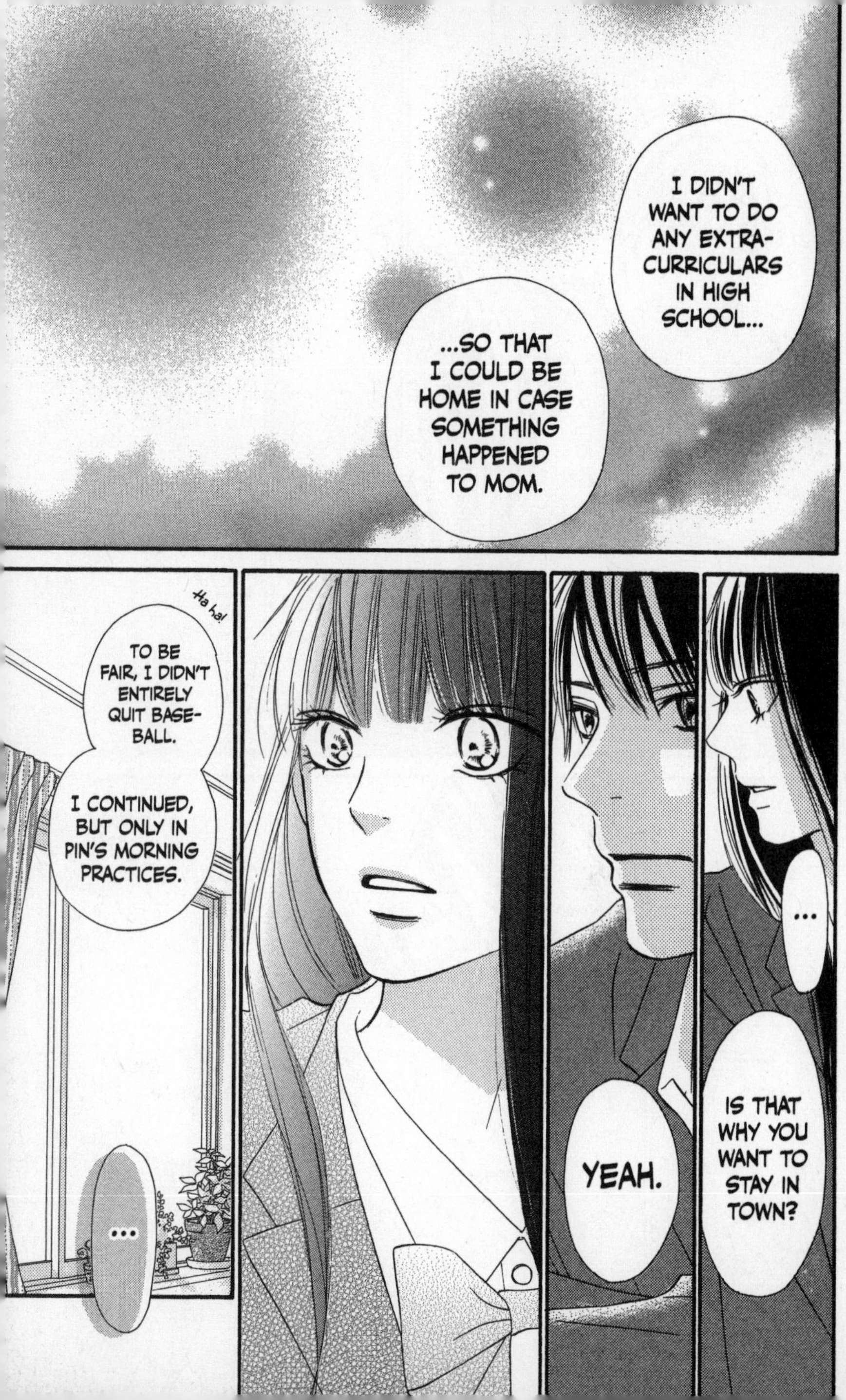
I DIDN'T WANT TO DO ANY EXTRA-CURRICULARS IN HIGH SCHOOL...
...SO THAT I COULD BE HOME IN CASE SOMETHING HAPPENED TO MOM.
...
IS THAT WHY YOU WANT TO STAY IN TOWN?
YEAH.
Ha ha!
TO BE FAIR, I DIDN'T ENTIRELY QUIT BASE-BALL.
I CONTINUED, BUT ONLY IN PIN'S MORNING PRACTICES.
...

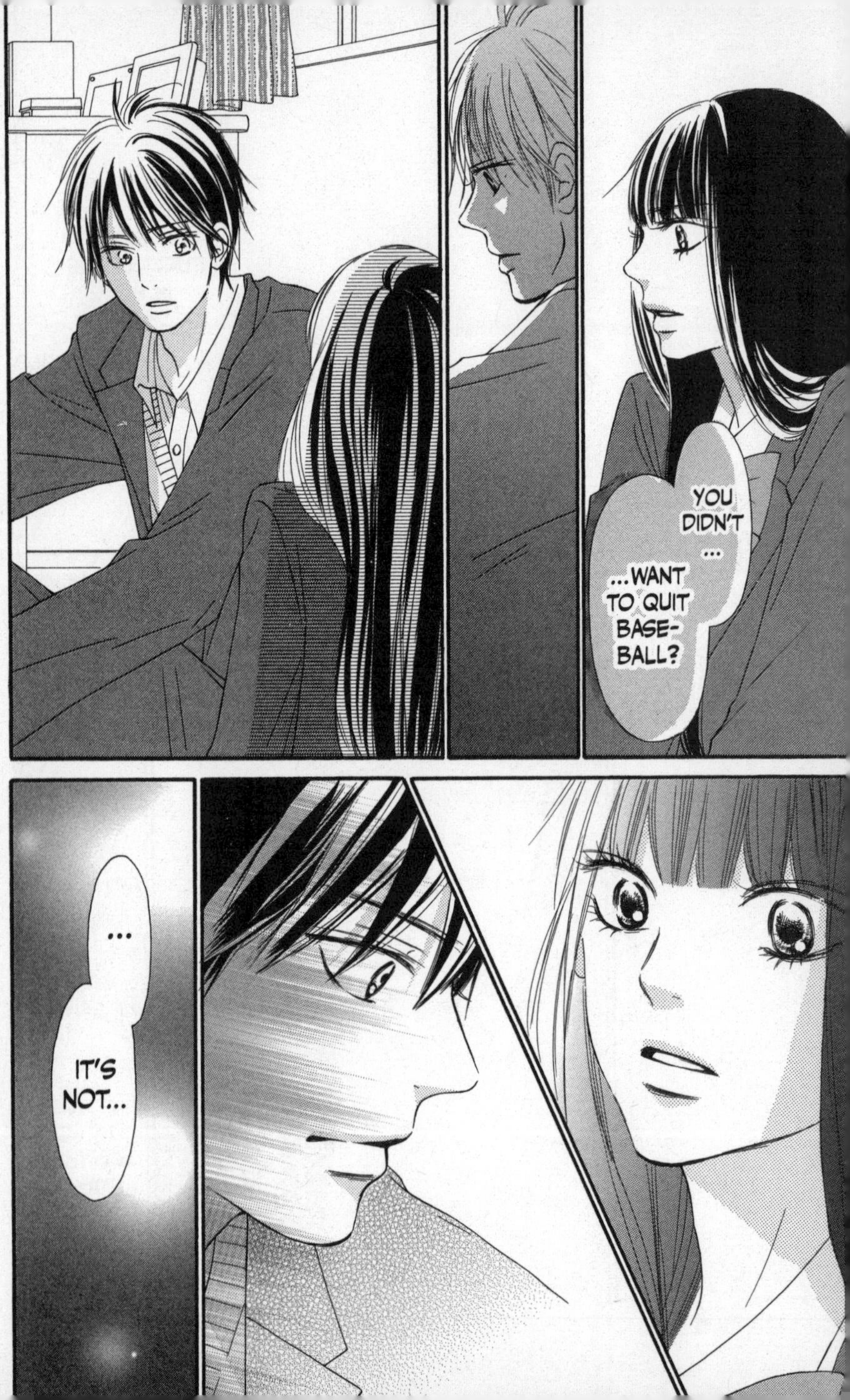
YOU DIDN'T ...
...WANT TO QUIT BASE-BALL?
... IT'S NOT...

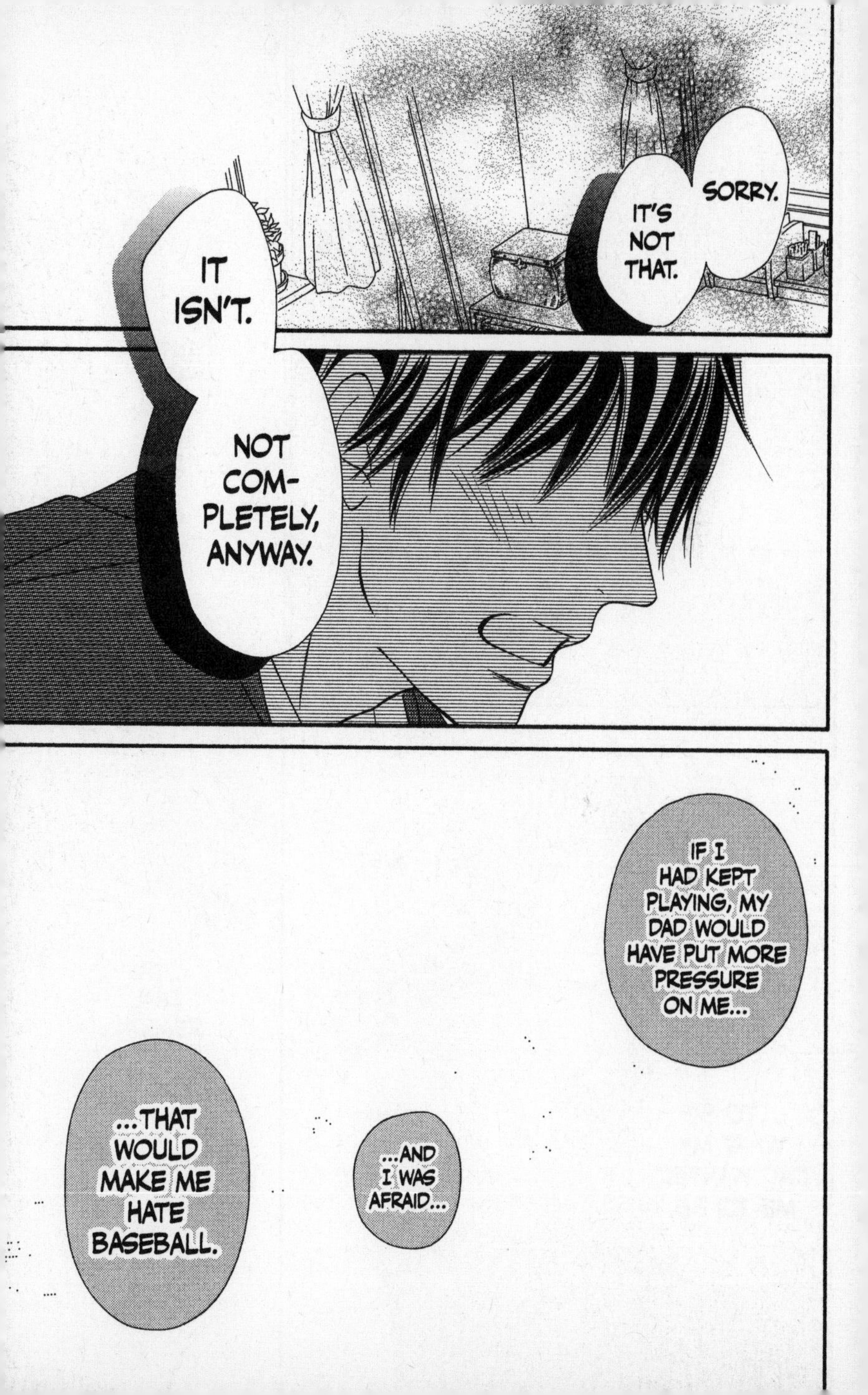
SORRY.
IT'S NOT THAT.
IT ISN'T.
NOT COM-PLETELY, ANYWAY.
IF I HAD KEPT PLAYING, MY DAD WOULD HAVE PUT MORE PRESSURE ON ME...
...AND I WAS AFRAID...
...THAT WOULD MAKE ME HATE BASEBALL.

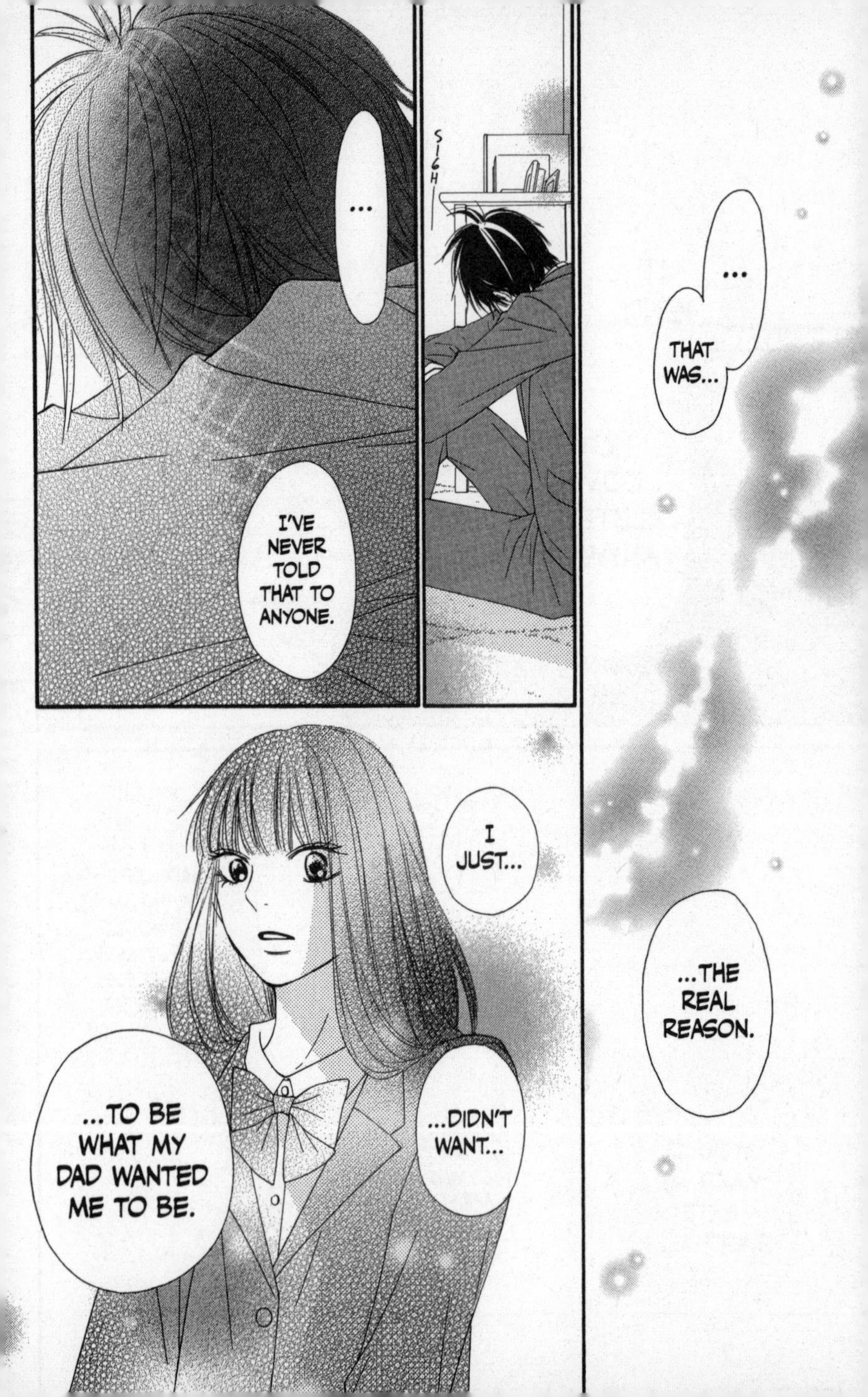
...
THAT WAS...
...THE REAL REASON.
SIGH
...
I'VE NEVER TOLD THAT TO ANYONE.
I JUST...
...DIDN'T WANT...
...TO BE WHAT MY DAD WANTED ME TO BE.

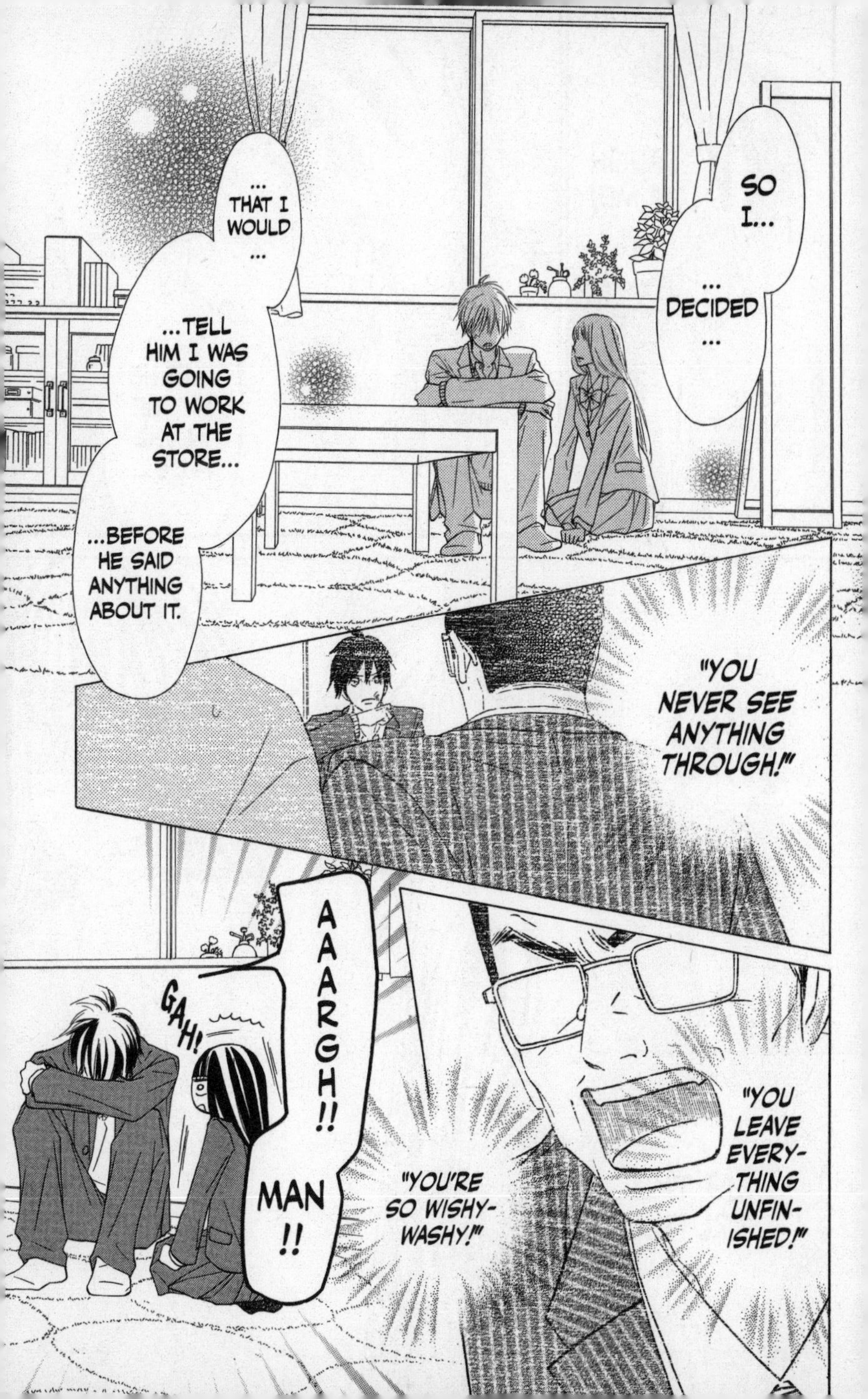
SO I...
...DECIDED...
...THAT I WOULD...
...TELL HIM I WAS GOING TO WORK AT THE STORE...
...BEFORE HE SAID ANYTHING ABOUT IT.
"YOU NEVER SEE ANYTHING THROUGH!"
"YOU LEAVE EVERY-THING UNFIN-ISHED!"
"YOU'RE SO WISHY-WASHY!"
AAAARGH!! MAN!!
GAH!

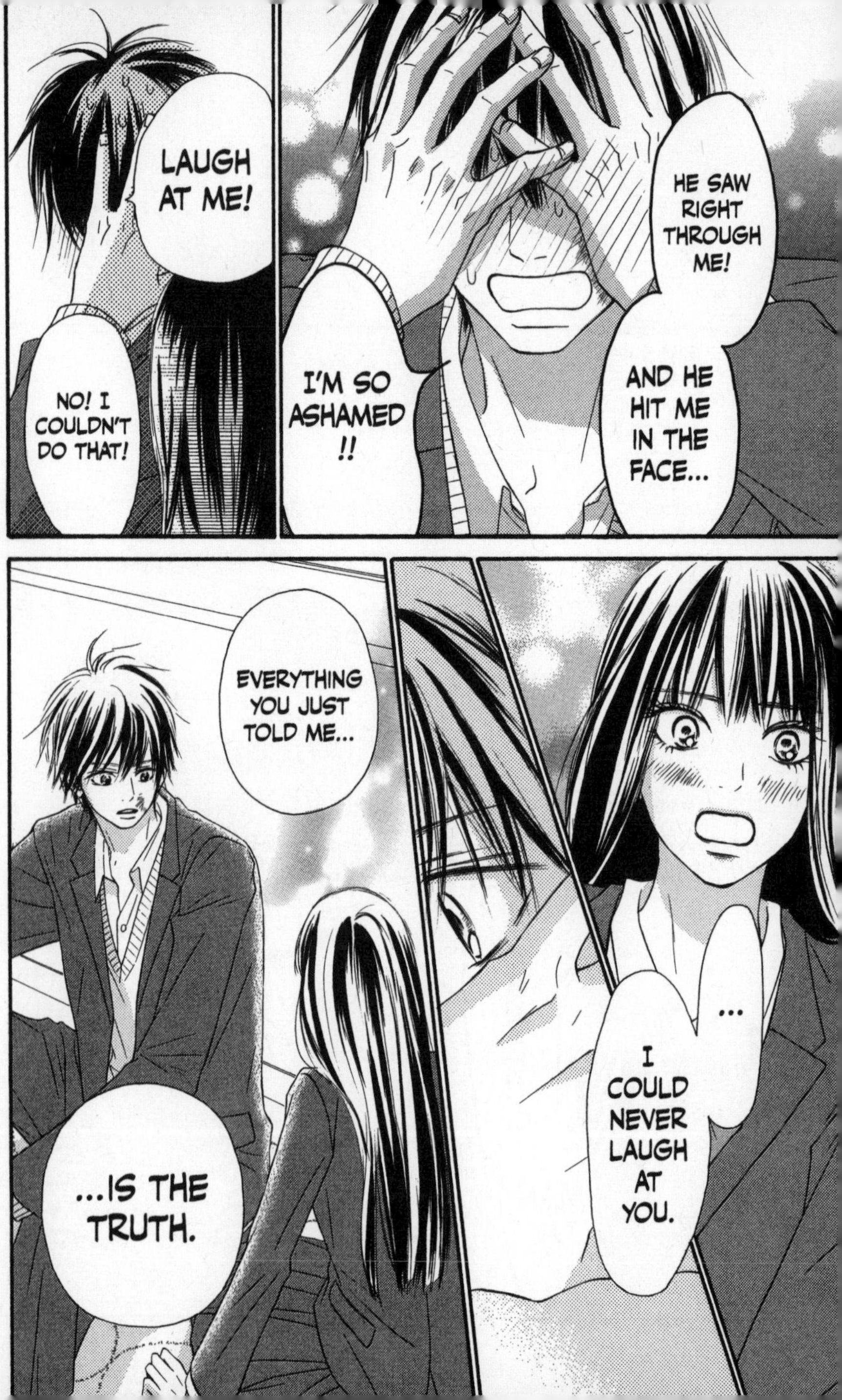
HE SAW RIGHT THROUGH ME!
AND HE HIT ME IN THE FACE...
I'M SO ASHAMED !!
LAUGH AT ME!
NO! I COULDN'T DO THAT!
...
I COULD NEVER LAUGH AT YOU.
EVERYTHING YOU JUST TOLD ME...
...IS THE TRUTH.

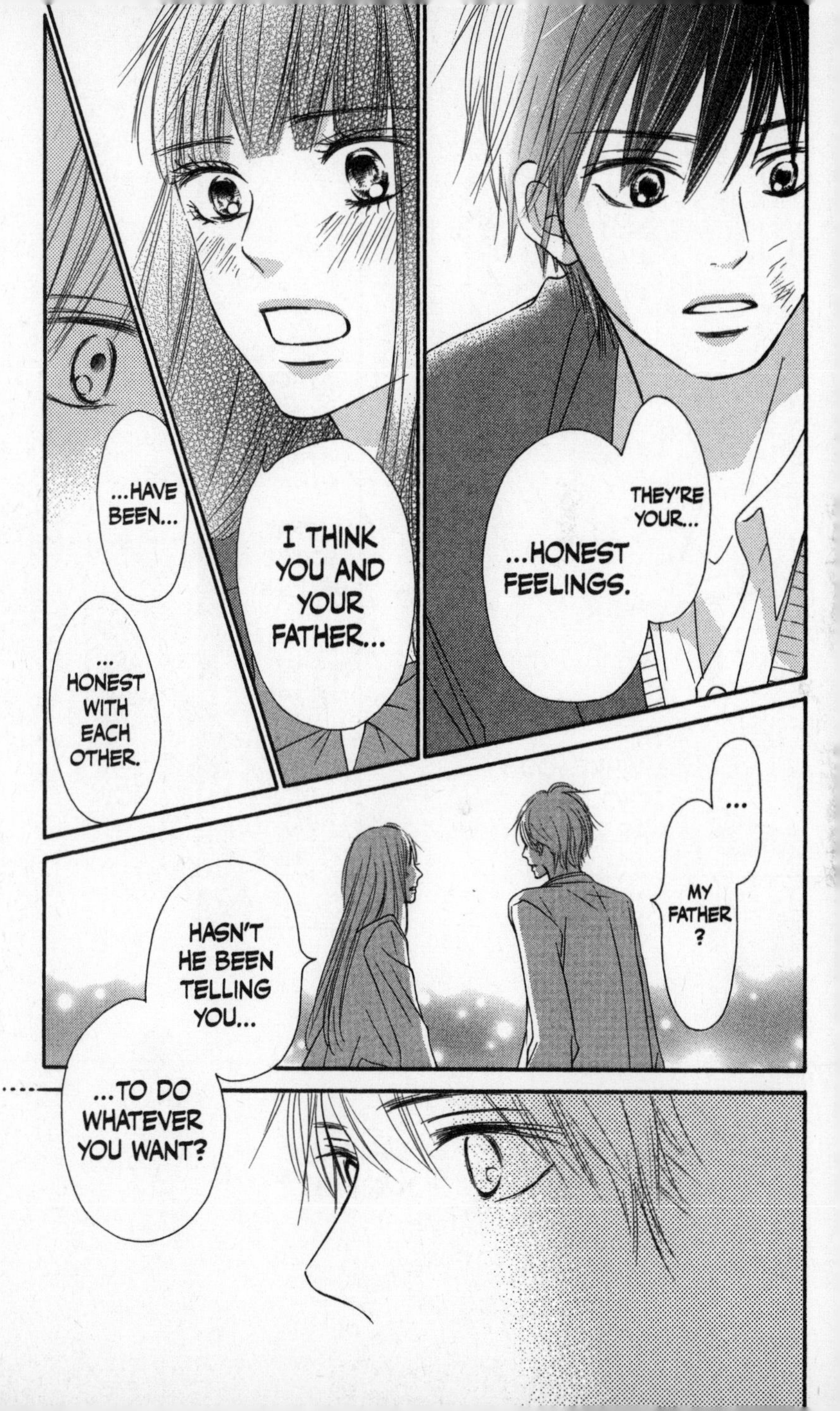
THEY'RE YOUR...
...HONEST FEELINGS.
I THINK YOU AND YOUR FATHER...
...HAVE BEEN...
... HONEST WITH EACH OTHER.
...
MY FATHER ?
HASN'T HE BEEN TELLING YOU...
...TO DO WHATEVER YOU WANT?
....—

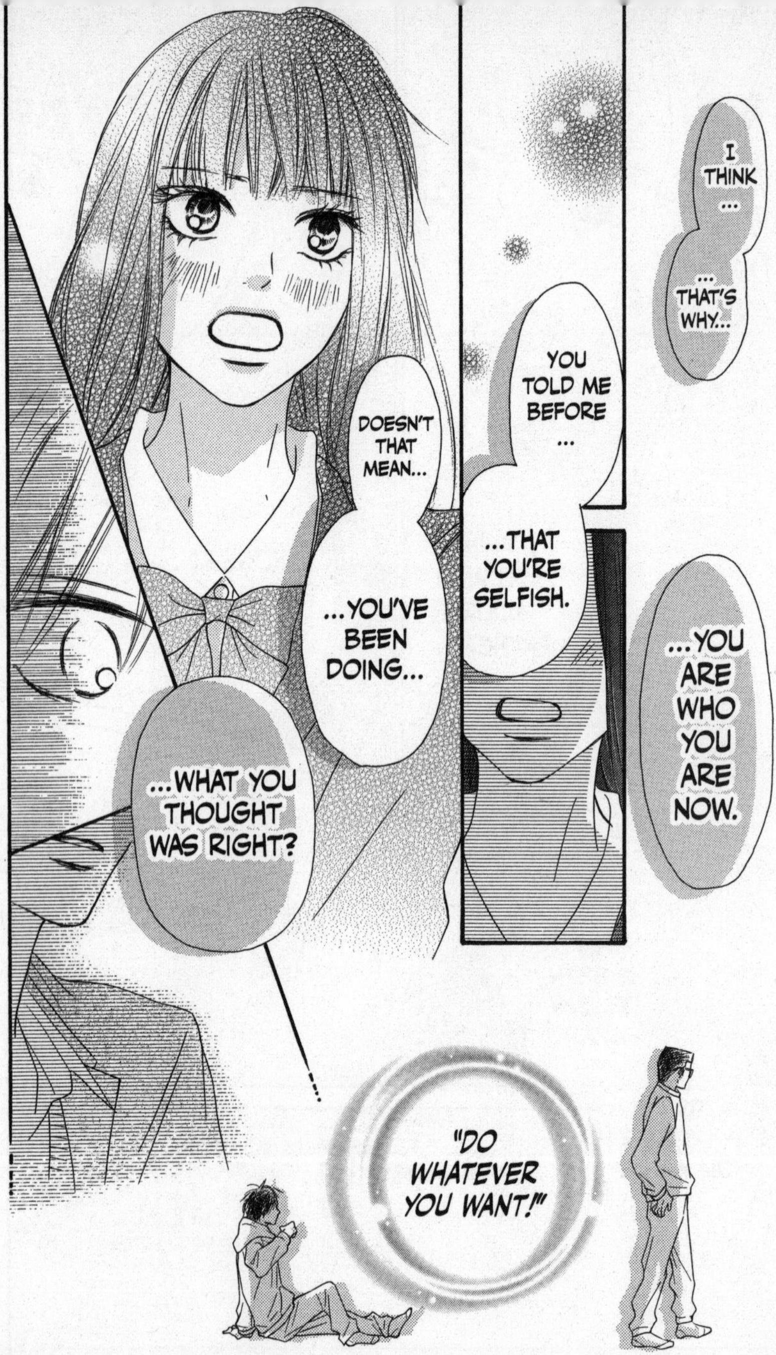
I THINK ...
... THAT'S WHY...
YOU TOLD ME BEFORE ...
...THAT YOU'RE SELFISH.
...YOU ARE WHO YOU ARE NOW.
DOESN'T THAT MEAN...
...YOU'VE BEEN DOING...
...WHAT YOU THOUGHT WAS RIGHT?
!!
"DO WHATEVER YOU WANT!"

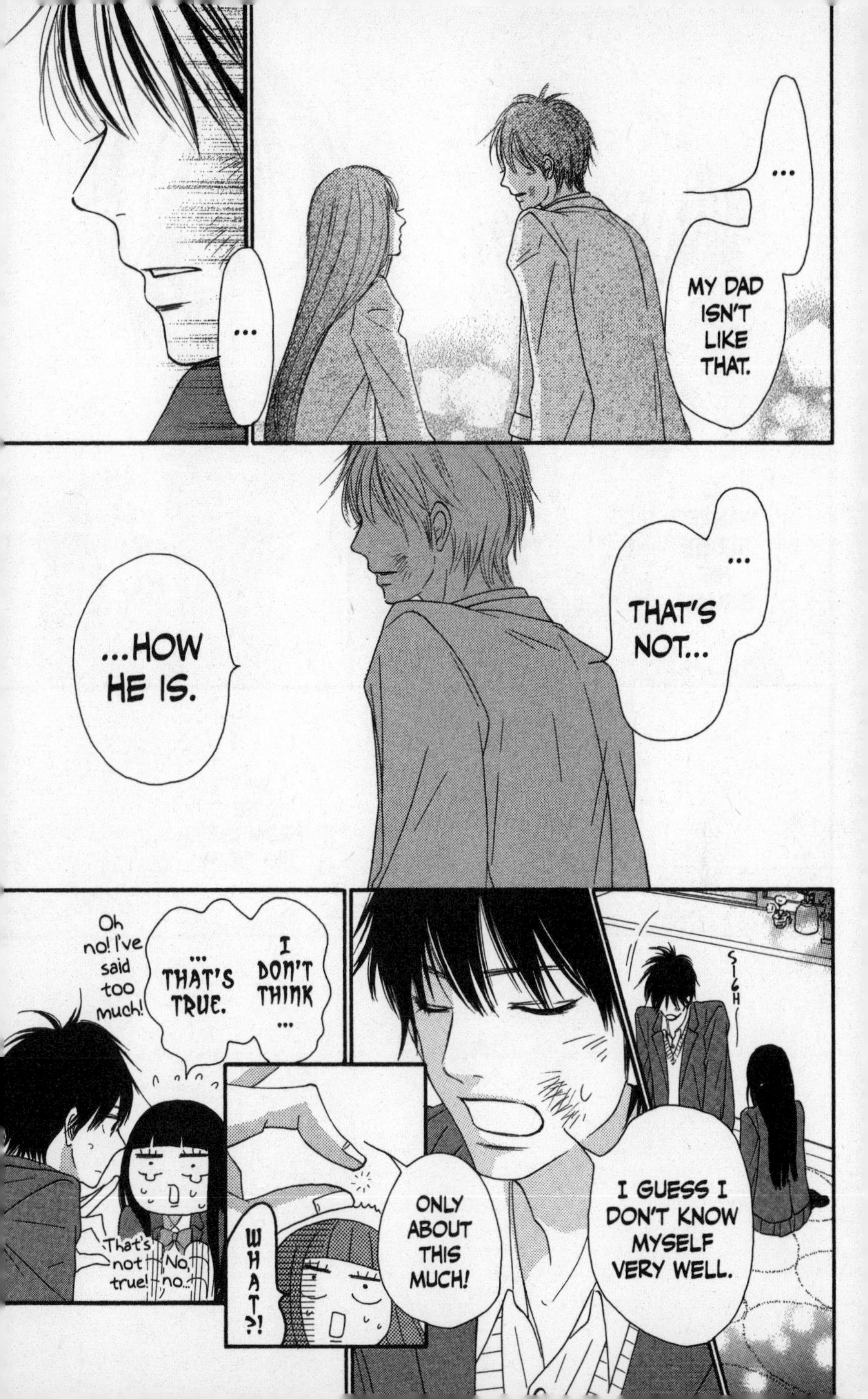
...
MY DAD ISN'T LIKE THAT.
...
... THAT'S NOT...
...HOW HE IS.
SIGH
I GUESS I DON'T KNOW MYSELF VERY WELL.
ONLY ABOUT THIS MUCH!
WHAT?!
I DON'T THINK ... ... THAT'S TRUE.
Oh no! I've said too much!
No, no...
That's not true!

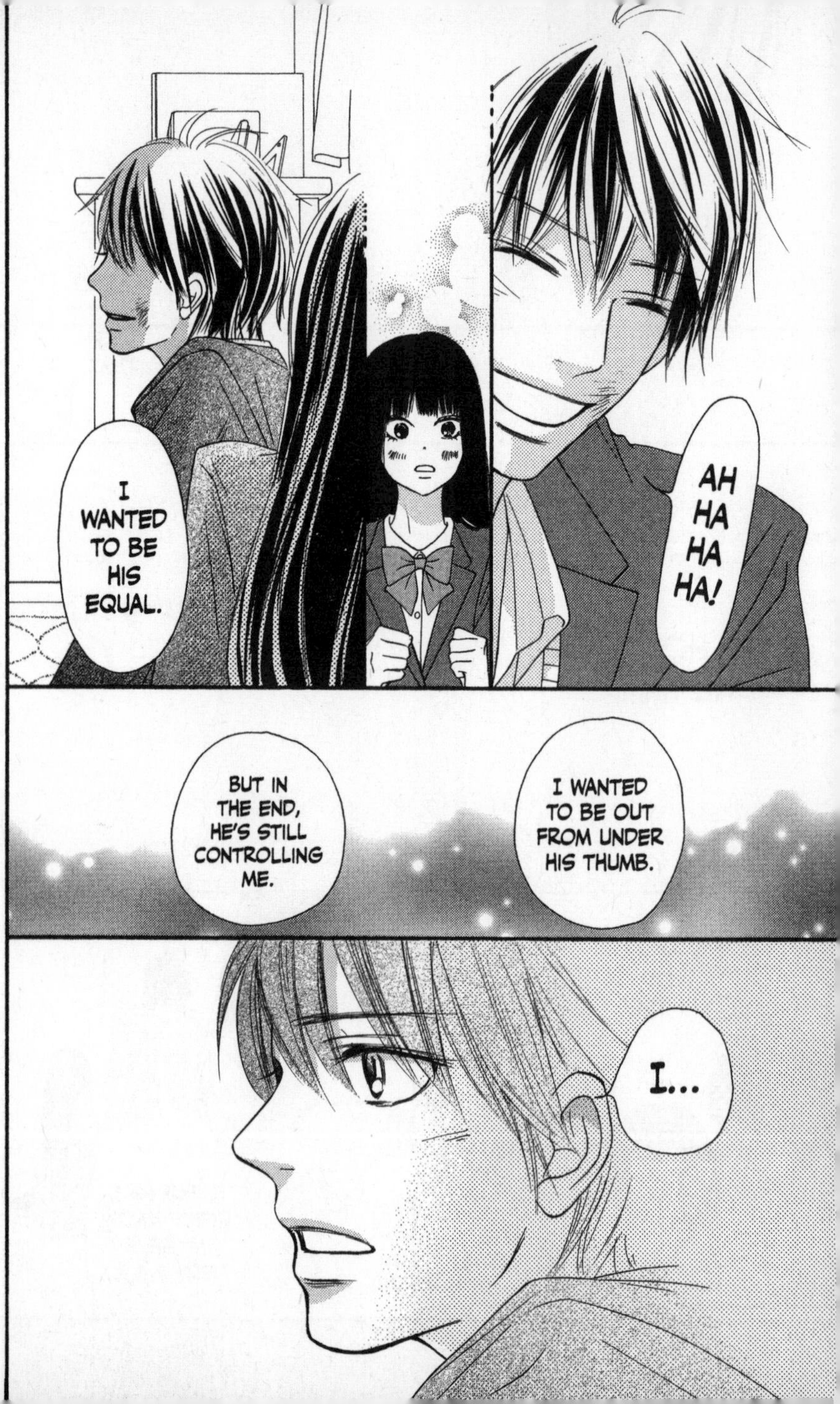
AH HA HA HA!
I WANTED TO BE HIS EQUAL.
I WANTED TO BE OUT FROM UNDER HIS THUMB.
BUT IN THE END, HE'S STILL CONTROLLING ME.
I...

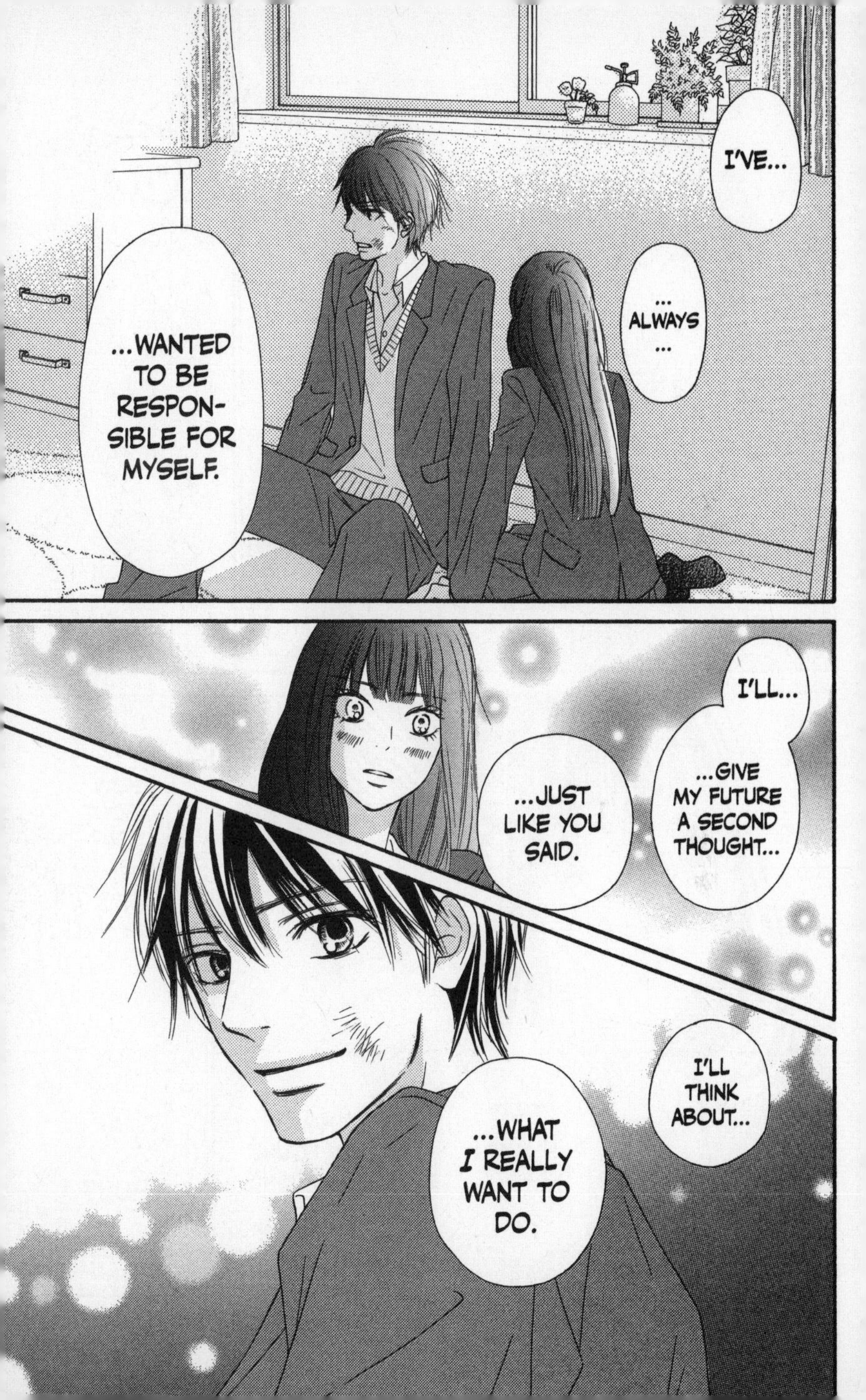
I'VE...
...ALWAYS...
...WANTED TO BE RESPON-SIBLE FOR MYSELF.
I'LL...
...GIVE MY FUTURE A SECOND THOUGHT...
...JUST LIKE YOU SAID.
I'LL THINK ABOUT...
...WHAT *I* REALLY WANT TO DO.

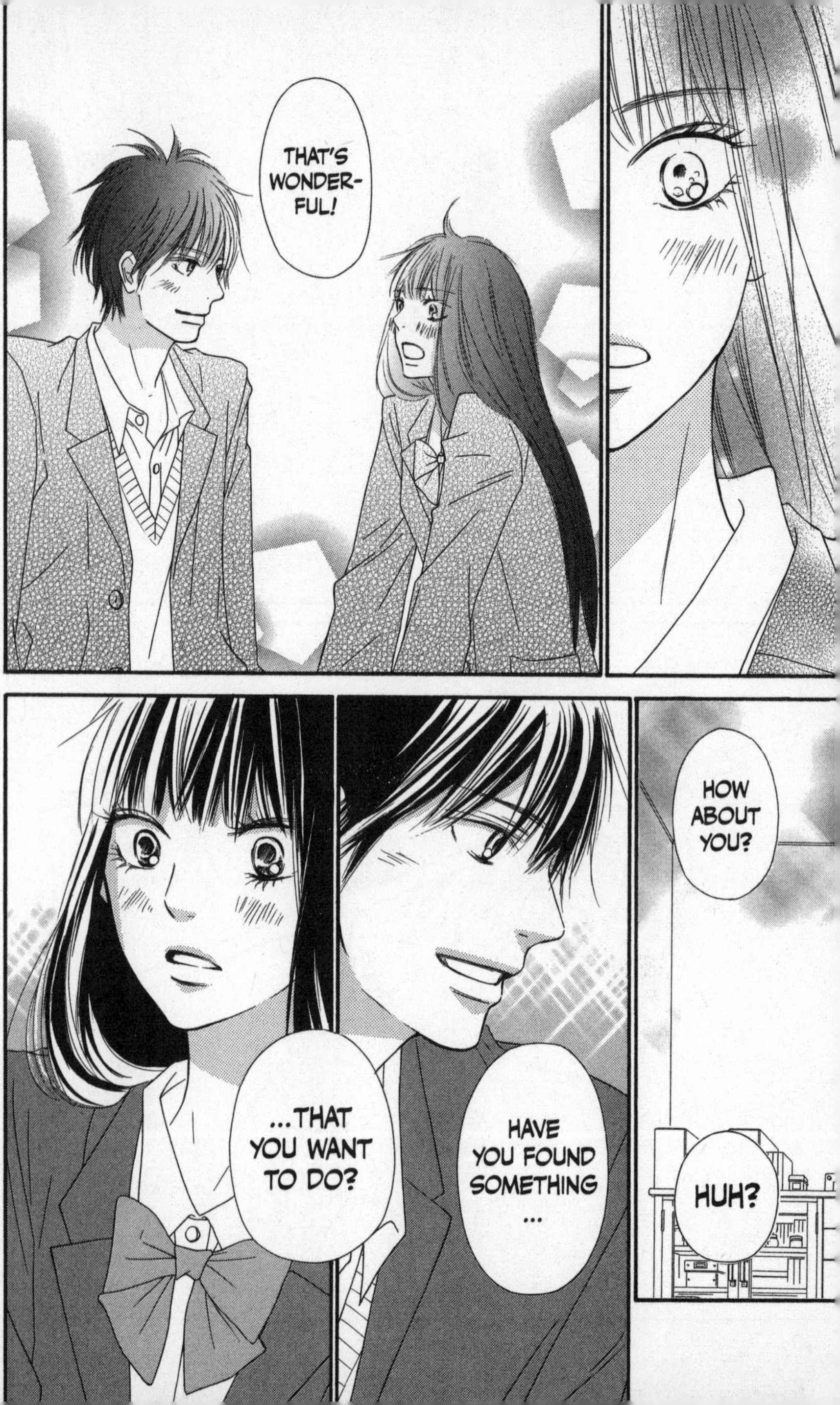
THAT'S WONDERFUL!
HOW ABOUT YOU?
HUH?
HAVE YOU FOUND SOMETHING ...
...THAT YOU WANT TO DO?

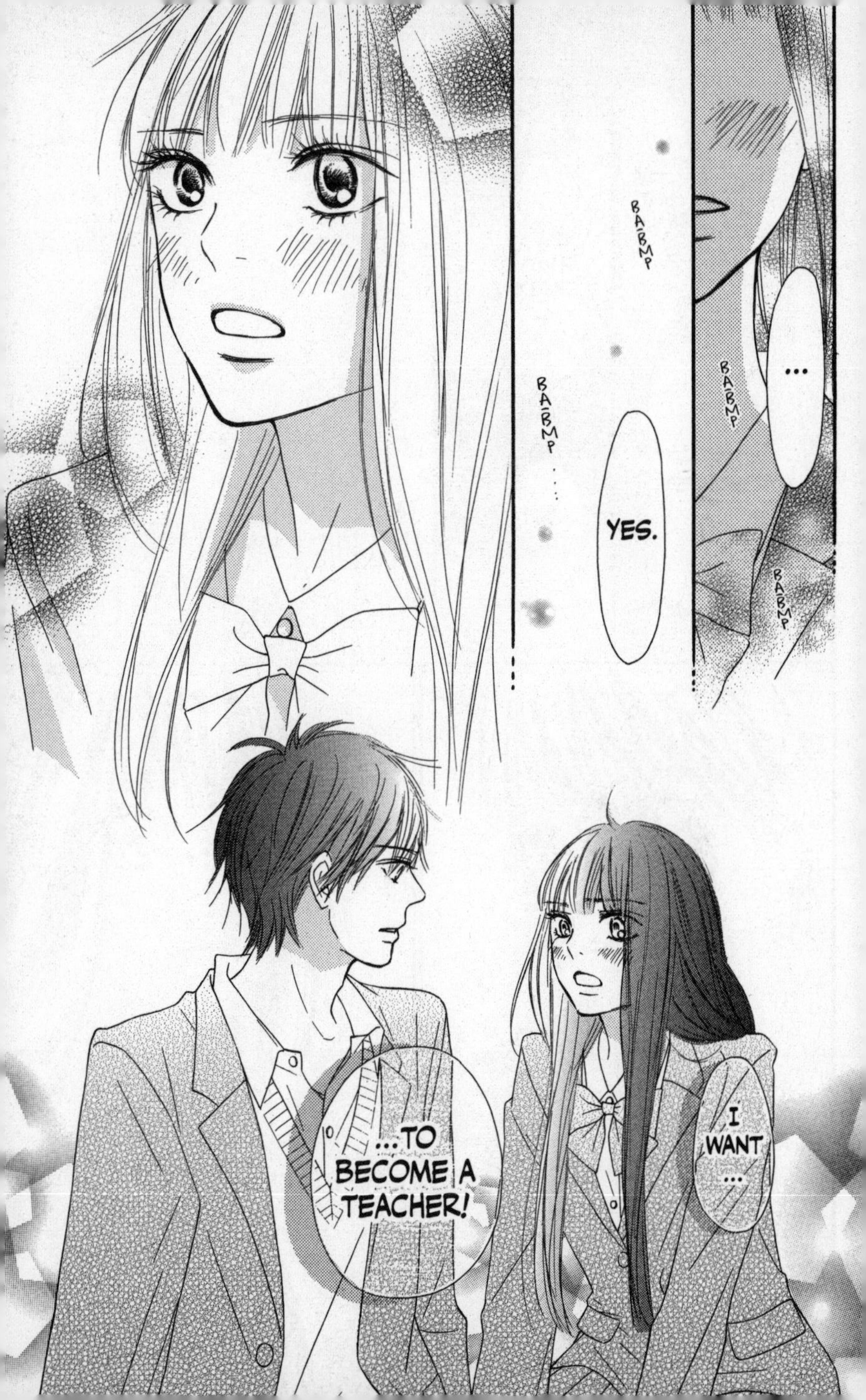

...
BA-BMP
BA-BMP
BA-BMP
BA-BMP ...
YES.
I WANT ...
...TO BECOME A TEACHER!

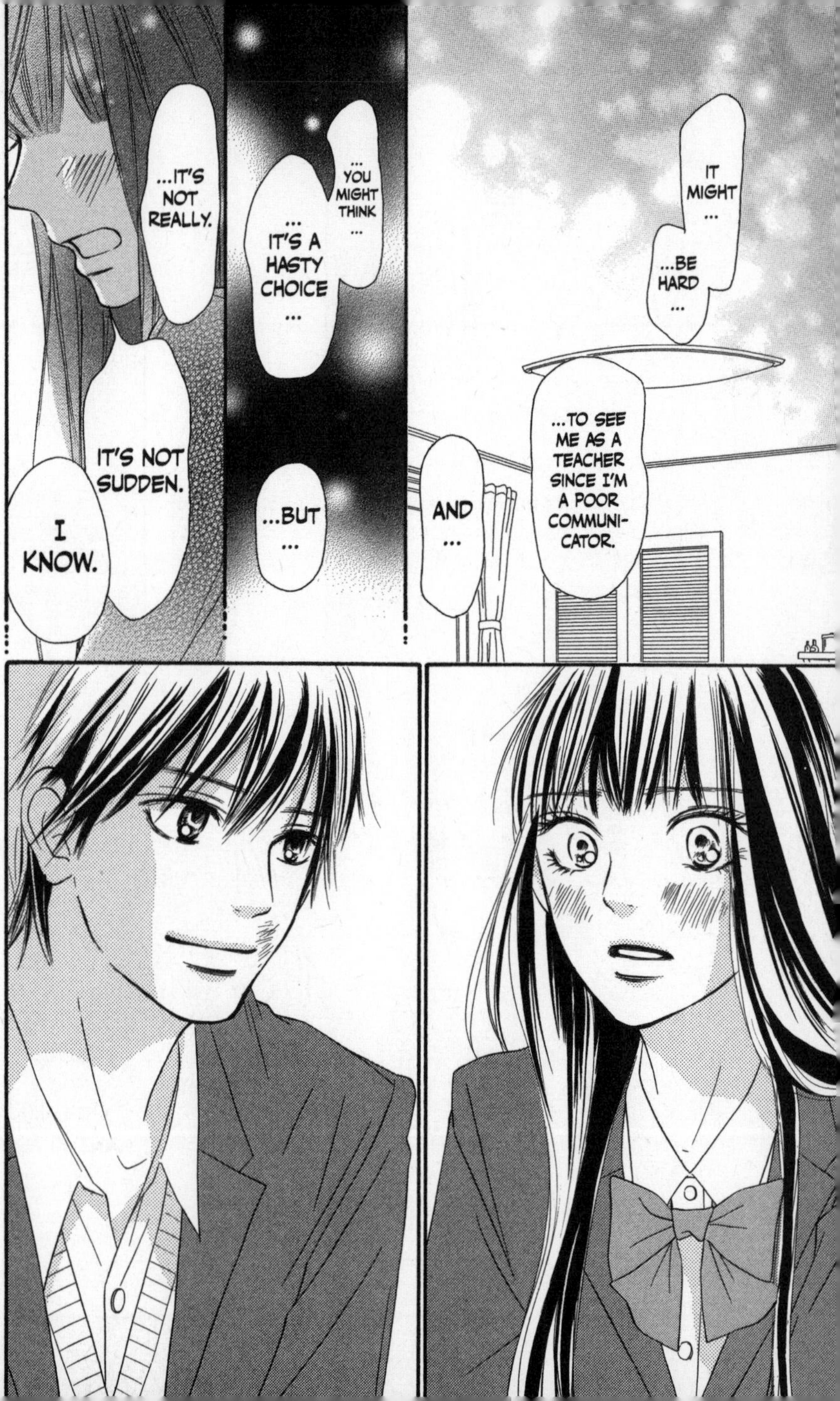
IT MIGHT ...
...BE HARD ...
...TO SEE ME AS A TEACHER SINCE I'M A POOR COMMUNICATOR.
AND ...
... YOU MIGHT THINK ...
... IT'S A HASTY CHOICE ...
...BUT ...
...IT'S NOT REALLY.
IT'S NOT SUDDEN.
I KNOW.

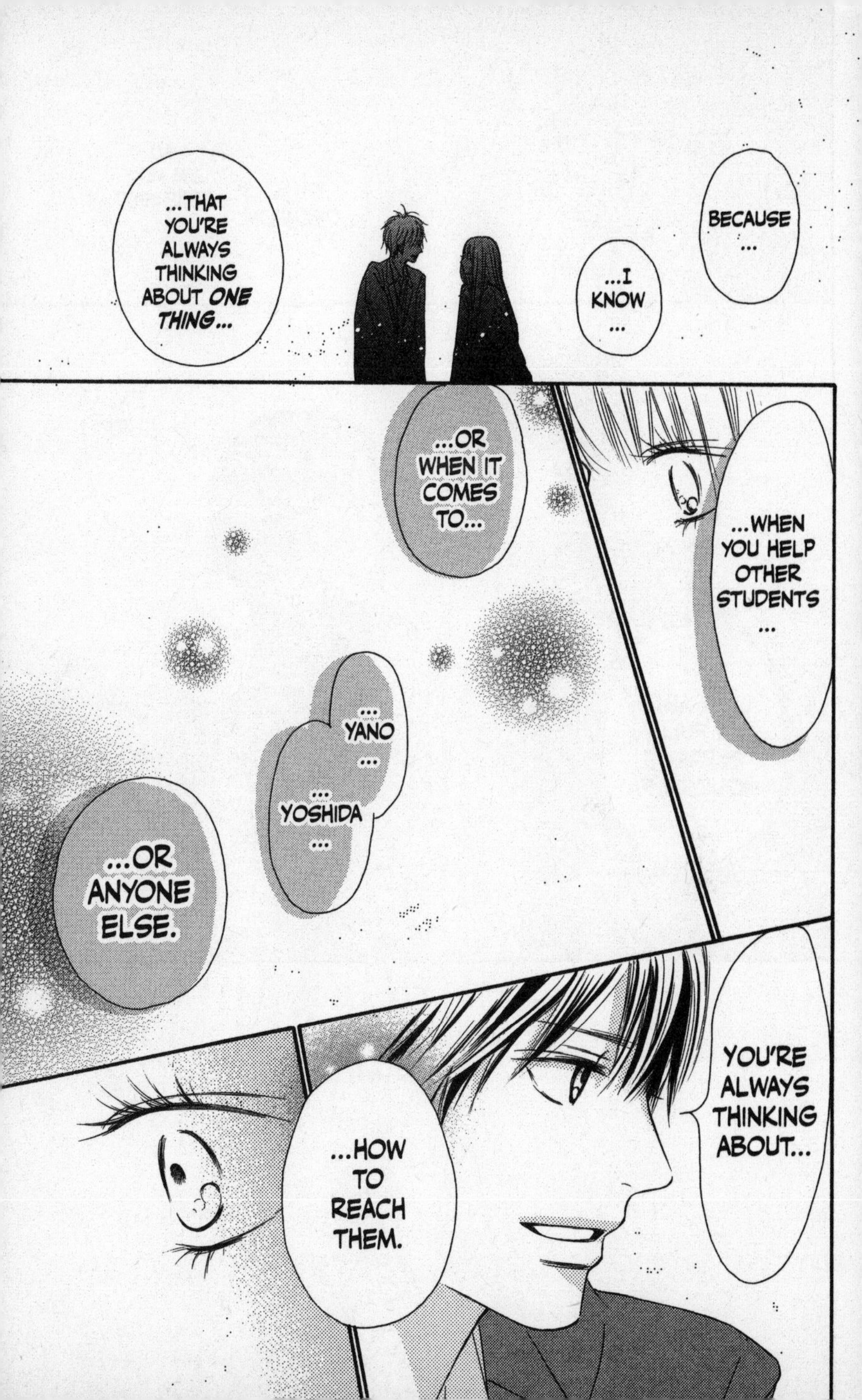

BECAUSE ...
...I KNOW ...
...THAT YOU'RE ALWAYS THINKING ABOUT *ONE THING*...
...WHEN YOU HELP OTHER STUDENTS ...
...OR WHEN IT COMES TO...
... YANO ...
... YOSHIDA ...
...OR ANYONE ELSE.
YOU'RE ALWAYS THINKING ABOUT...
...HOW TO REACH THEM.

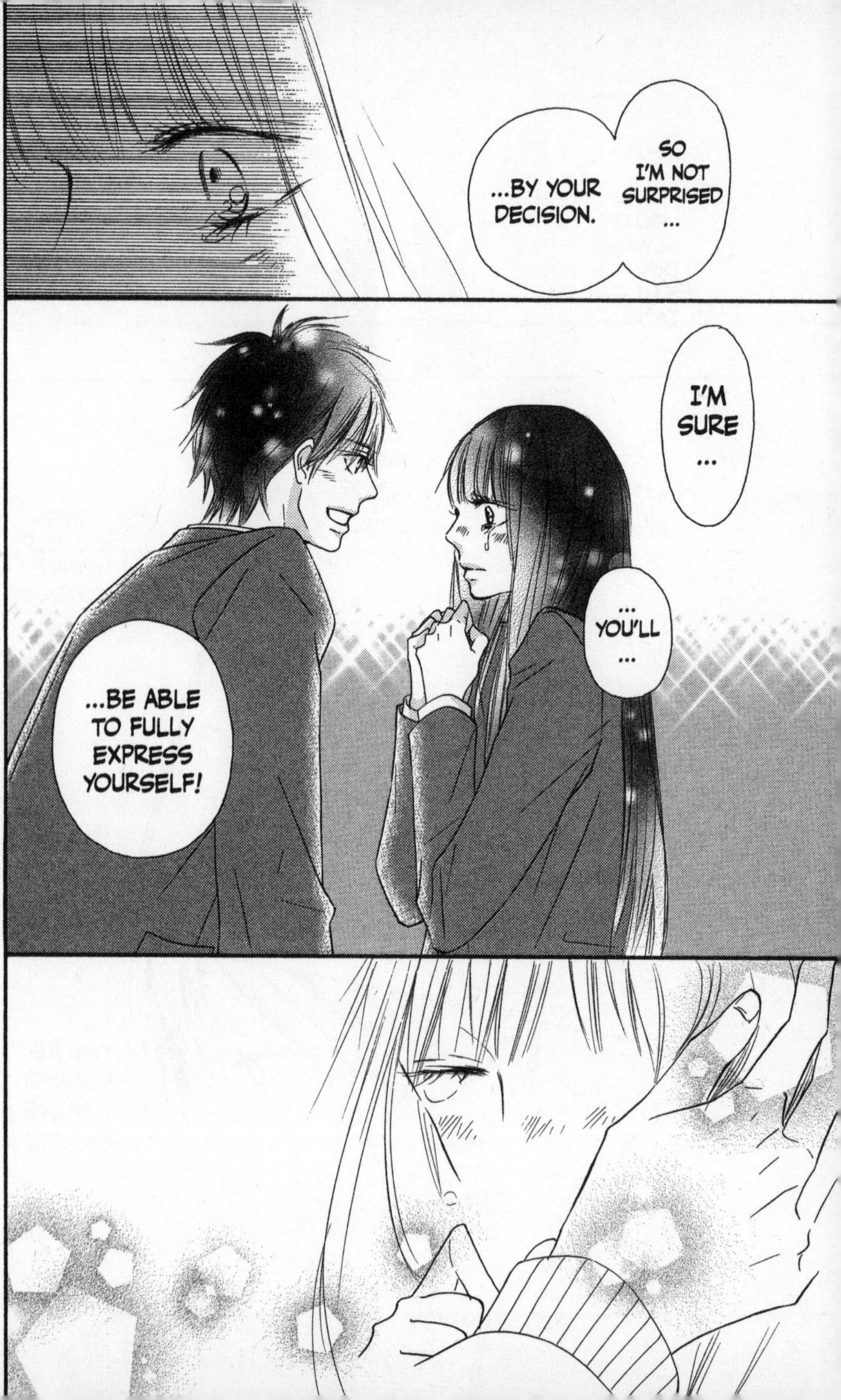
SO I'M NOT SURPRISED ...
...BY YOUR DECISION.
I'M SURE ...
... YOU'LL ...
...BE ABLE TO FULLY EXPRESS YOURSELF!

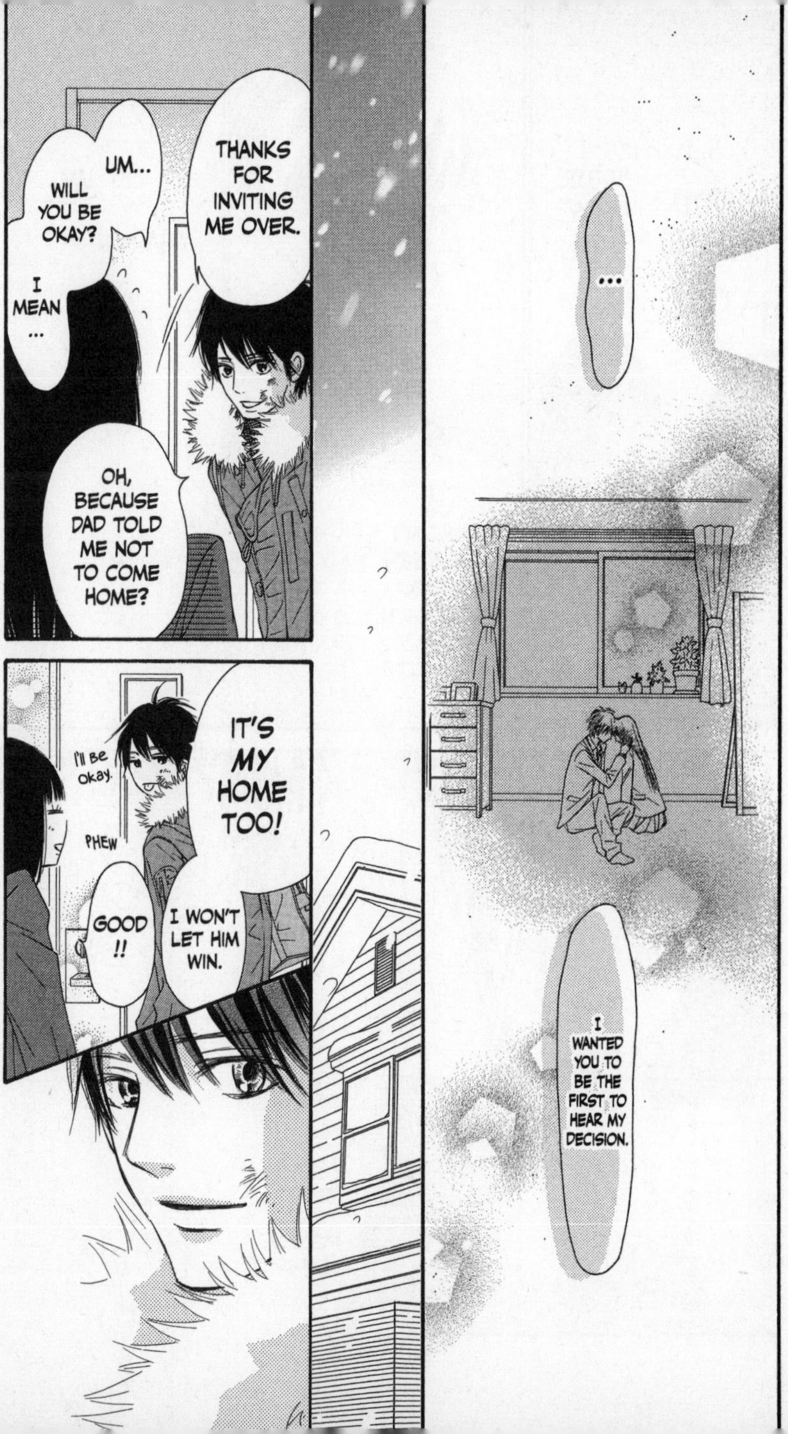
...
I WANTED YOU TO BE THE FIRST TO HEAR MY DECISION.
THANKS FOR INVITING ME OVER.
UM...
WILL YOU BE OKAY?
I MEAN ...
OH, BECAUSE DAD TOLD ME NOT TO COME HOME?
IT'S *MY* HOME TOO!
I'll be okay.
I WON'T LET HIM WIN.
GOOD !!
PHEW

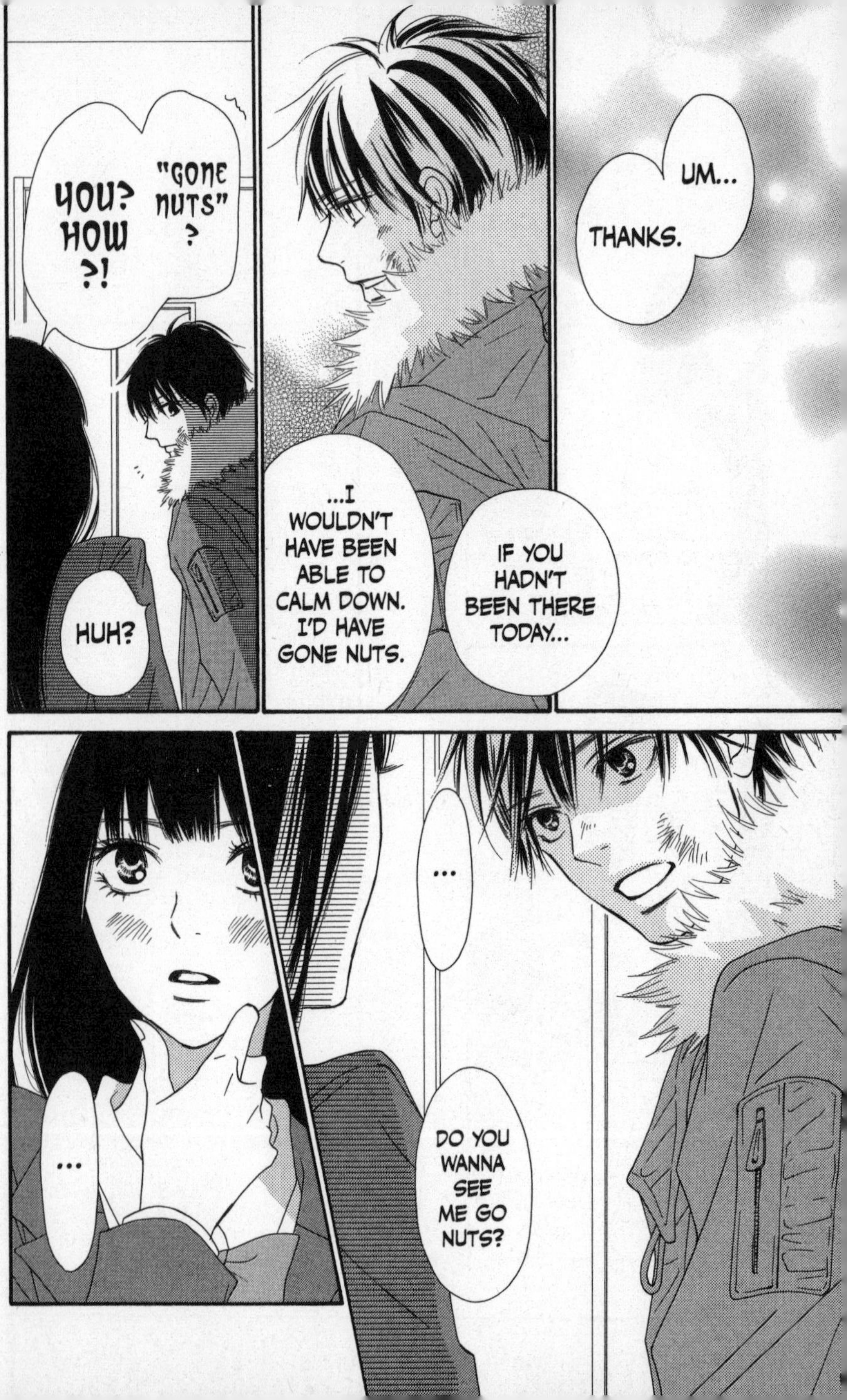
UM... THANKS.
IF YOU HADN'T BEEN THERE TODAY...
...I WOULDN'T HAVE BEEN ABLE TO CALM DOWN. I'D HAVE GONE NUTS.
"GONE NUTS"?
YOU? HOW?!
HUH?
...
DO YOU WANNA SEE ME GO NUTS?
...

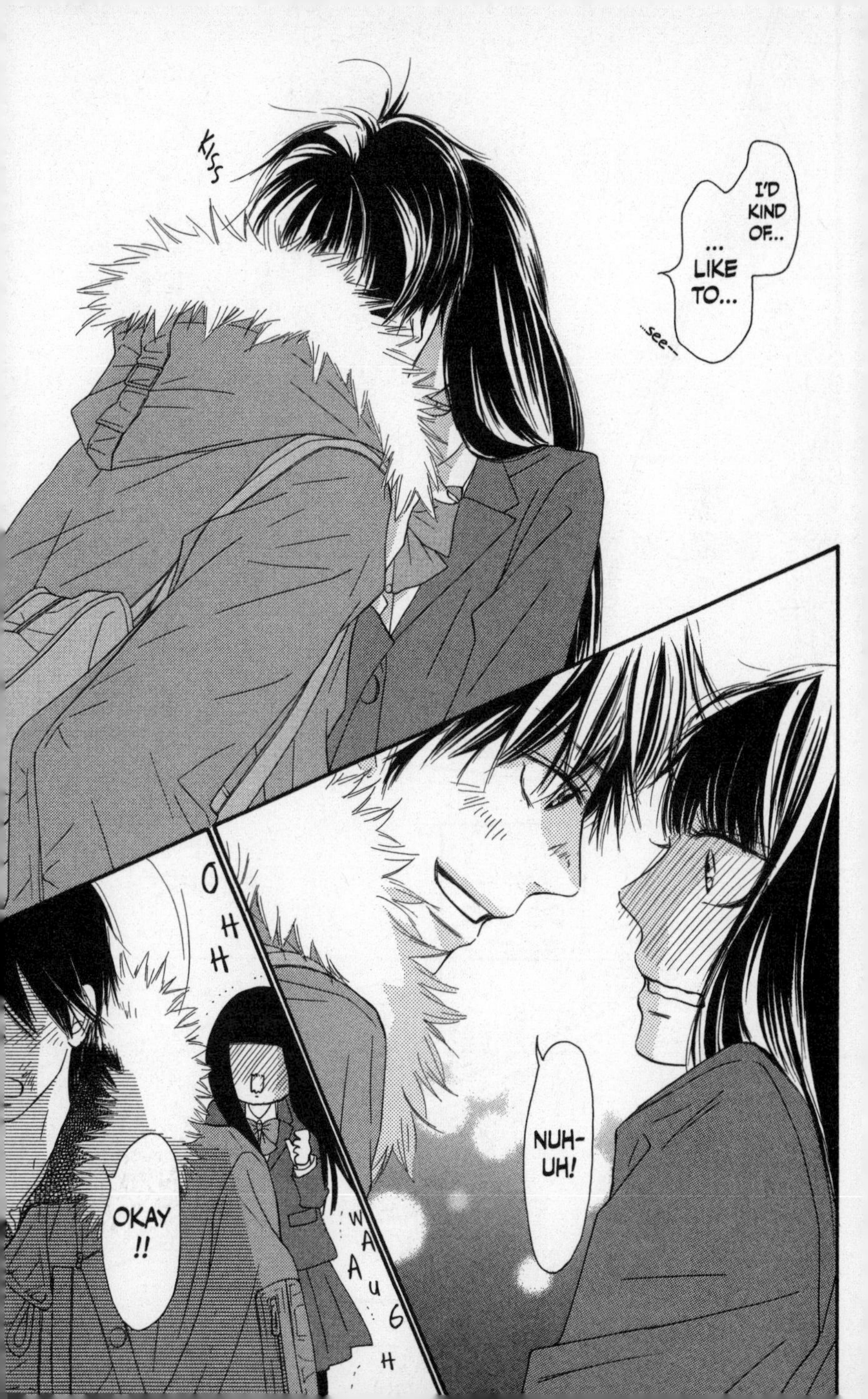
I'D KIND OF... ...LIKE TO...
...see...
KISS
NUH-UH!
WAAUGH
OHH
OKAY !!

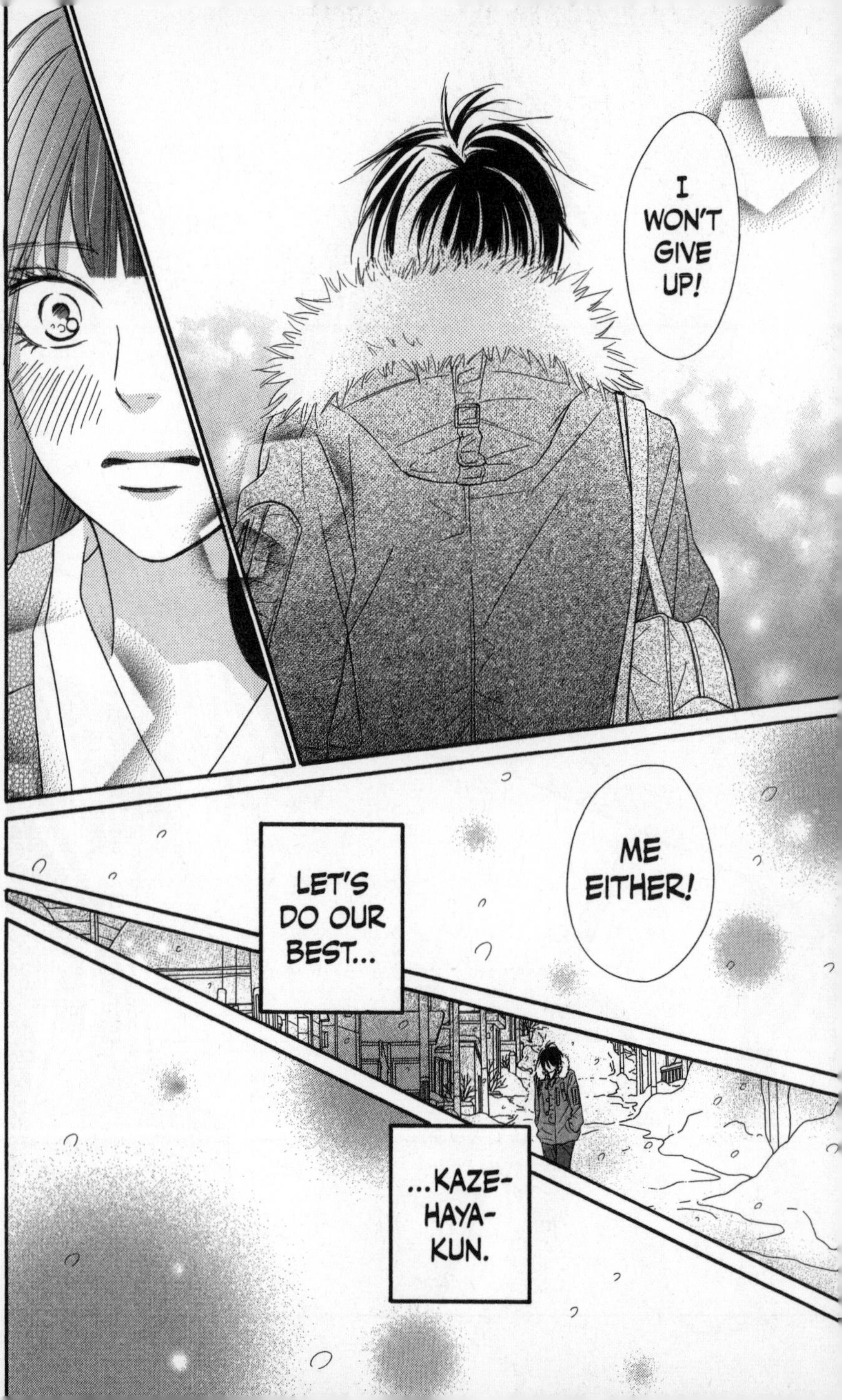
I WON'T GIVE UP!
ME EITHER!
LET'S DO OUR BEST...
...KAZE-HAYA-KUN.

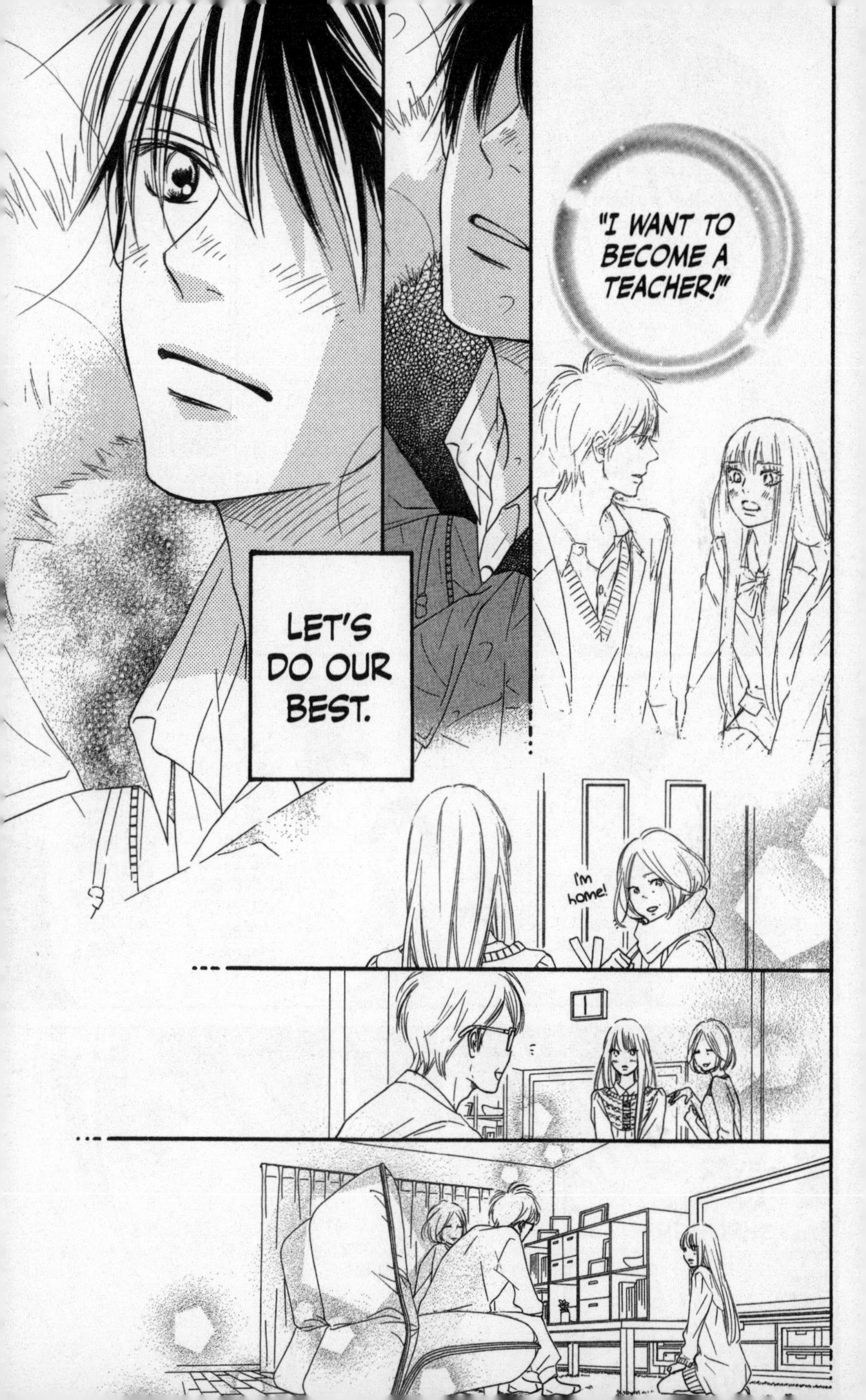
"I WANT TO BECOME A TEACHER!"
LET'S DO OUR BEST.
I'm home!

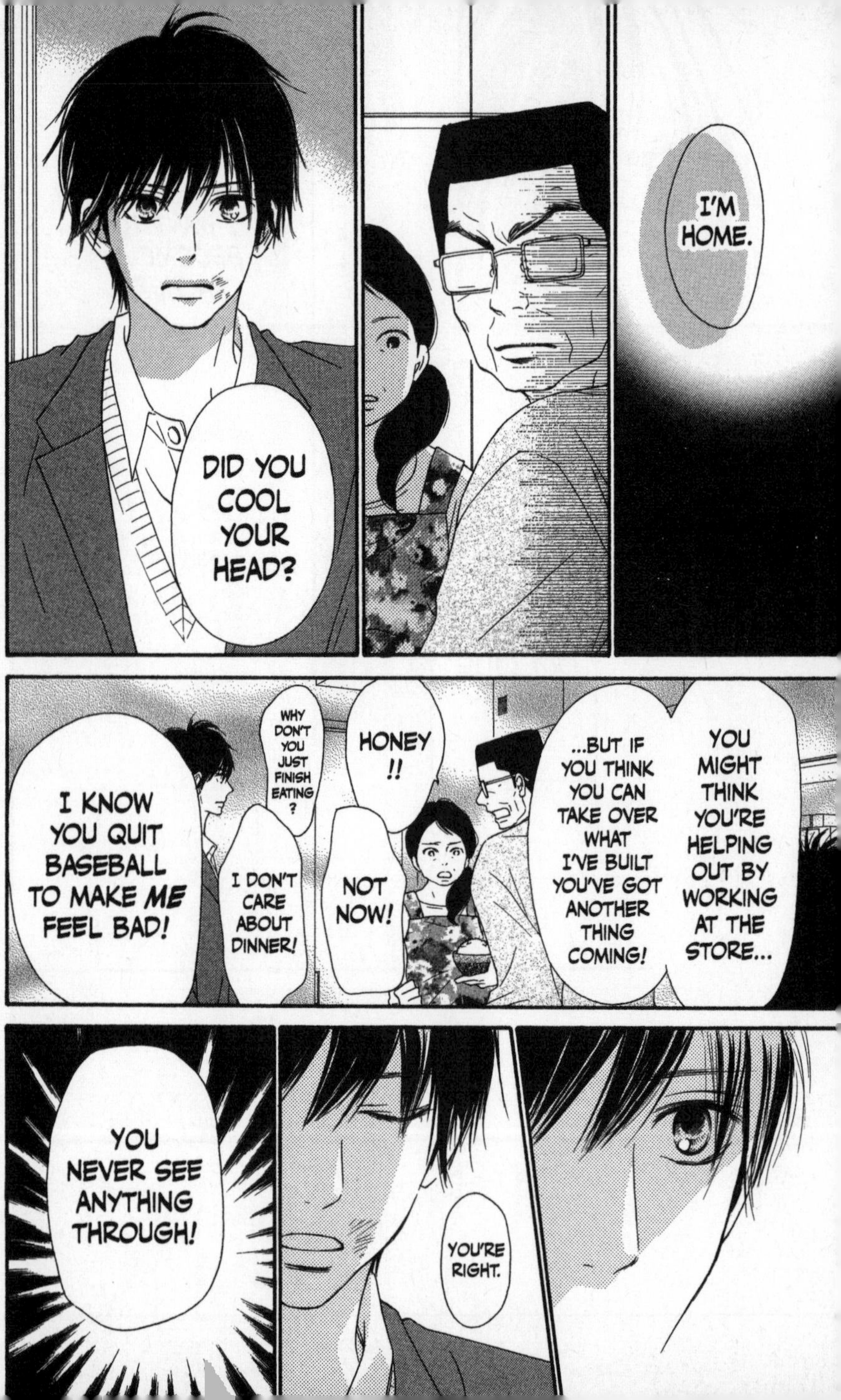
I'M HOME.
DID YOU COOL YOUR HEAD?
YOU MIGHT THINK YOU'RE HELPING OUT BY WORKING AT THE STORE...
...BUT IF YOU THINK YOU CAN TAKE OVER WHAT I'VE BUILT YOU'VE GOT ANOTHER THING COMING!
HONEY !!
NOT NOW!
WHY DON'T YOU JUST FINISH EATING?
I DON'T CARE ABOUT DINNER!
I KNOW YOU QUIT BASEBALL TO MAKE *ME* FEEL BAD!
YOU'RE RIGHT.
YOU NEVER SEE ANYTHING THROUGH!

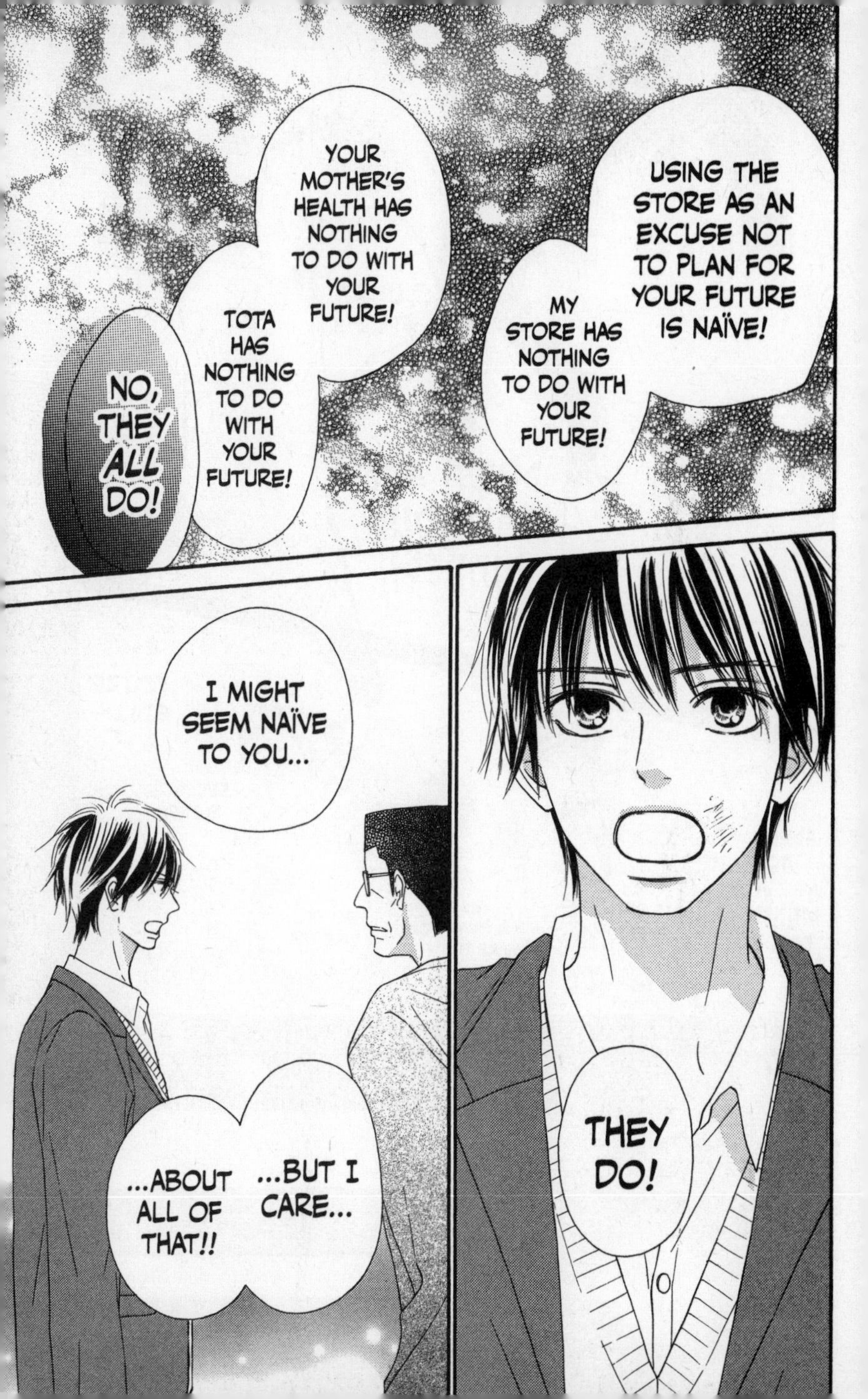
USING THE STORE AS AN EXCUSE NOT TO PLAN FOR YOUR FUTURE IS NAÏVE!
MY STORE HAS NOTHING TO DO WITH YOUR FUTURE!
YOUR MOTHER'S HEALTH HAS NOTHING TO DO WITH YOUR FUTURE!
TOTA HAS NOTHING TO DO WITH YOUR FUTURE!
NO, THEY *ALL* DO!
THEY DO!
I MIGHT SEEM NAÏVE TO YOU...
...BUT I CARE...
...ABOUT ALL OF THAT!!

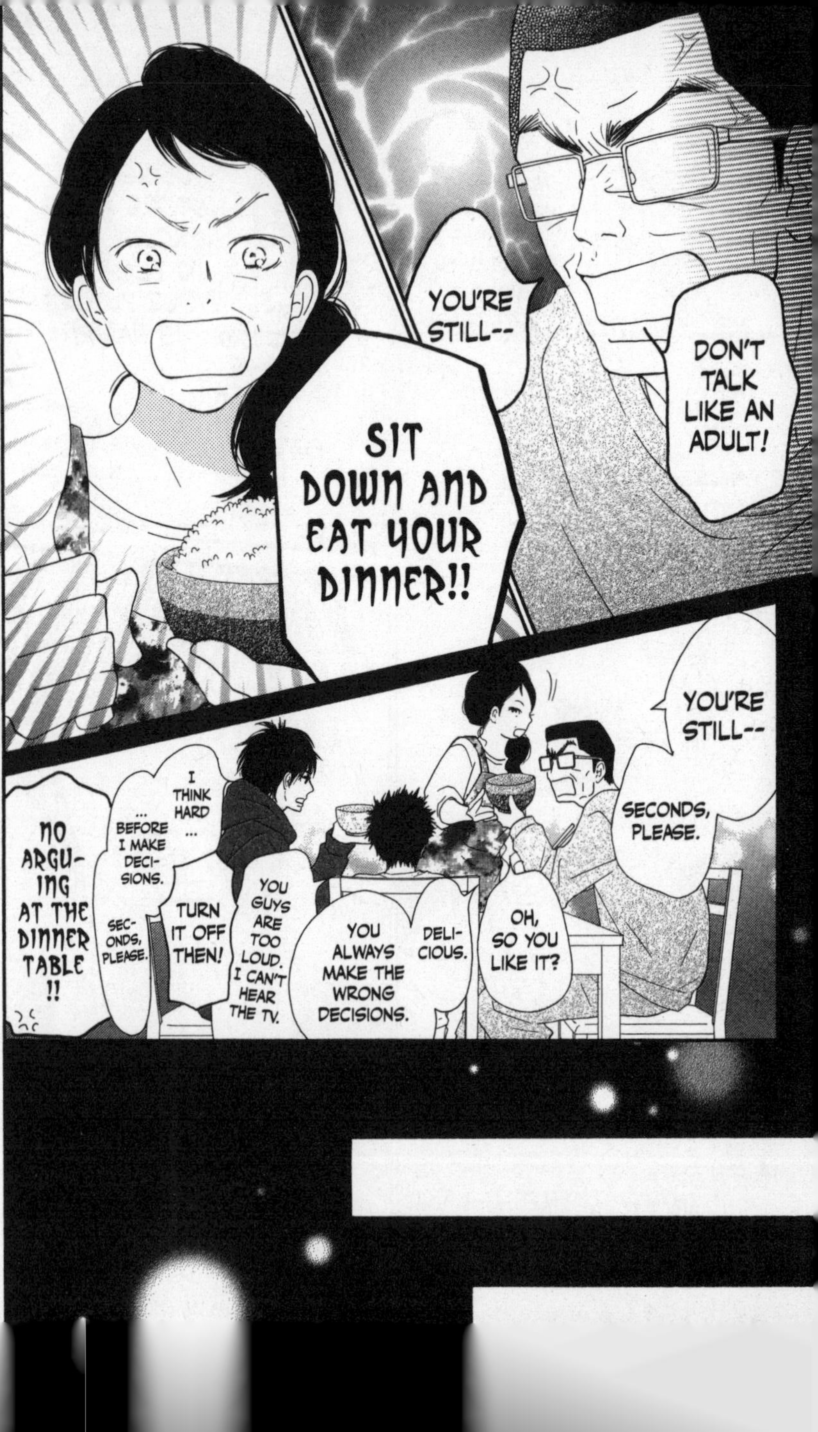
DON'T TALK LIKE AN ADULT!
YOU'RE STILL--
SIT DOWN AND EAT YOUR DINNER!!
YOU'RE STILL--
SECONDS, PLEASE.
OH, SO YOU LIKE IT?
DELICIOUS.
YOU ALWAYS MAKE THE WRONG DECISIONS.
YOU GUYS ARE TOO LOUD. I CAN'T HEAR THE TV.
I THINK HARD ...
... BEFORE I MAKE DECISIONS.
TURN IT OFF THEN!
SECONDS, PLEASE.
NO ARGUING AT THE DINNER TABLE!!

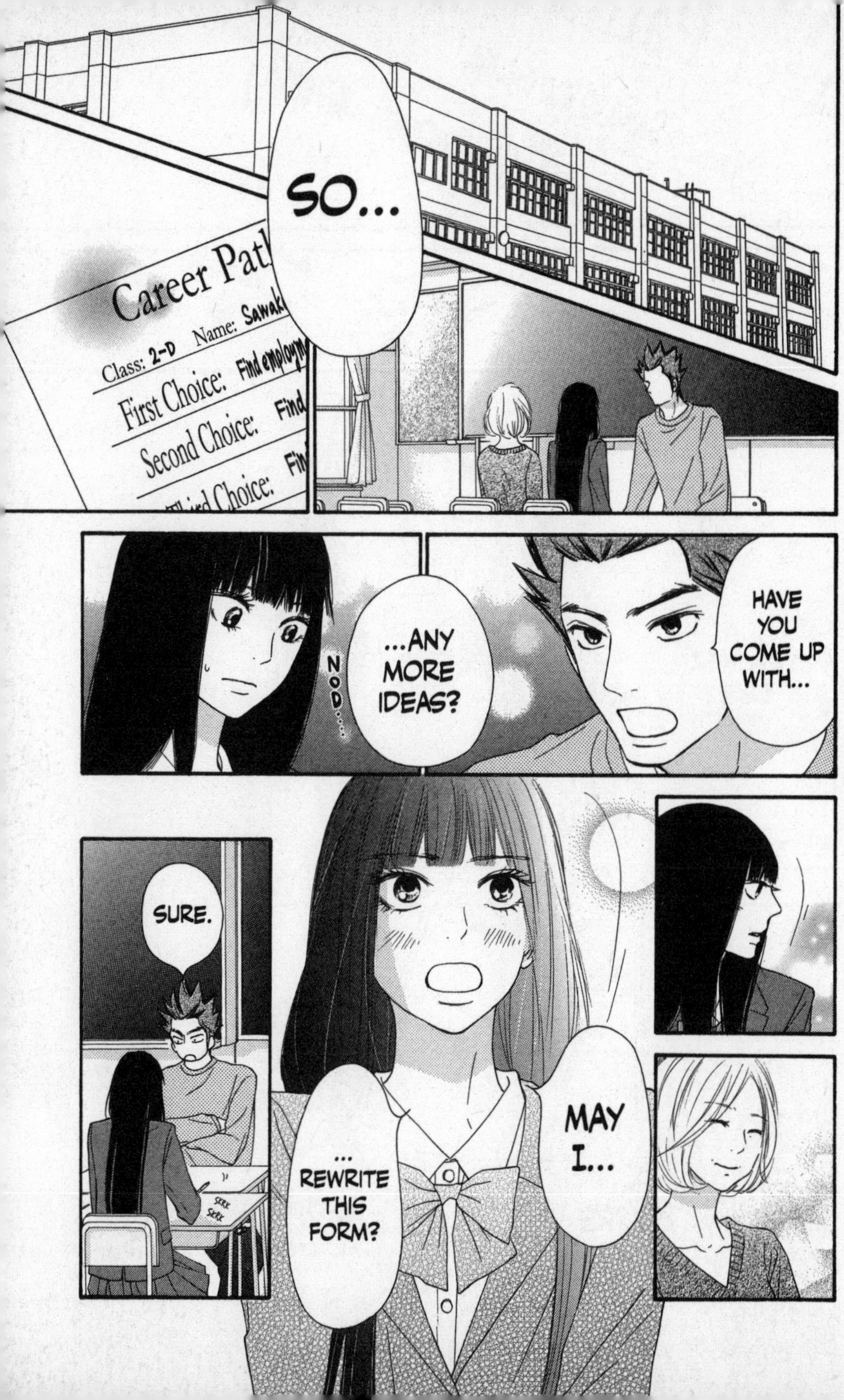
SO...
Career Pat
Class: 2-D Name: Sawak
First Choice: Find employm
Second Choice: Find
Third Choice:
HAVE YOU COME UP WITH...
...ANY MORE IDEAS?
NOD...
MAY I...
...REWRITE THIS FORM?
SURE.
SKRK SKRK

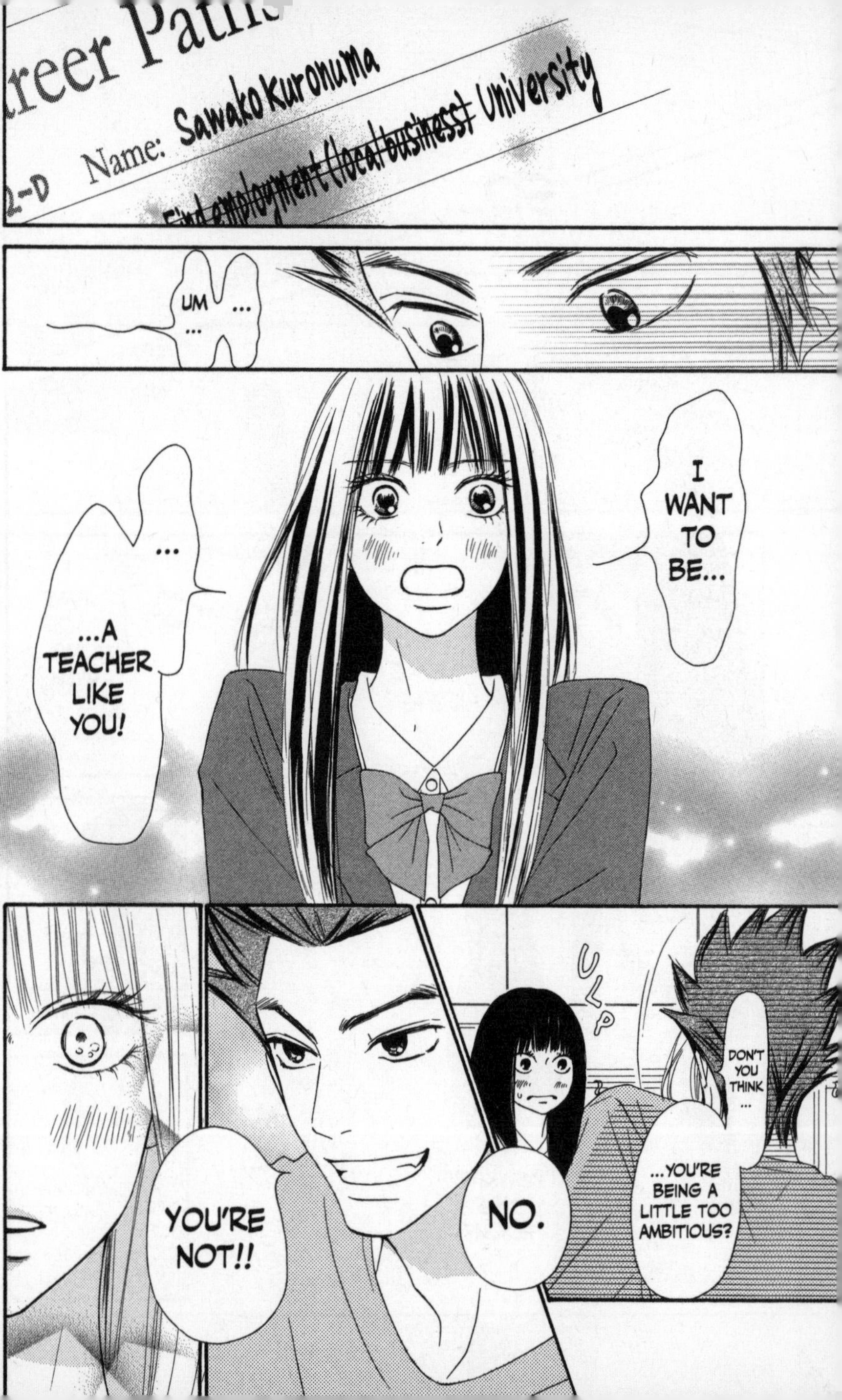
reer Paths
2-D Name: Sawako Kuronuma
~~Find employment (local business)~~ University
UM ... ...
I WANT TO BE...
... ...A TEACHER LIKE YOU!
DON'T YOU THINK ...
...YOU'RE BEING A LITTLE TOO AMBITIOUS?
ULP
NO.
YOU'RE NOT!!

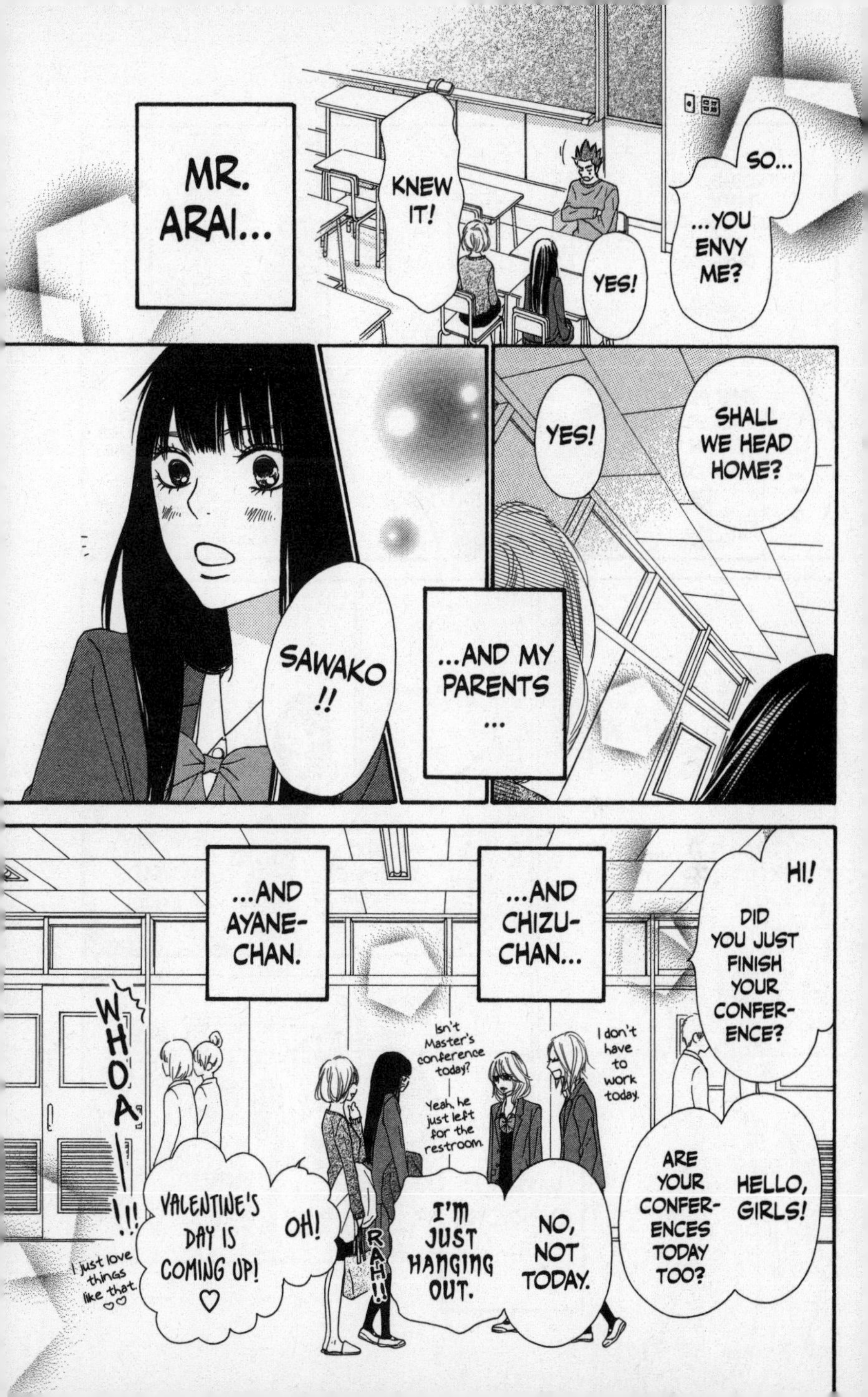
SO... ...YOU ENVY ME?
YES!
KNEW IT!
MR. ARAI...
SHALL WE HEAD HOME?
YES!
...AND MY PARENTS ...
SAWAKO !!
HI! DID YOU JUST FINISH YOUR CONFERENCE?
HELLO, GIRLS!
ARE YOUR CONFERENCES TODAY TOO?
I don't have to work today.
...AND CHIZU-CHAN...
NO, NOT TODAY.
Isn't Master's conference today?
Yeah, he just left for the restroom.
I'M JUST HANGING OUT.
RAH!!
...AND AYANE-CHAN.
OH!
VALENTINE'S DAY IS COMING UP! ♡
WHOA!!!
I just love things like that. ♡♡

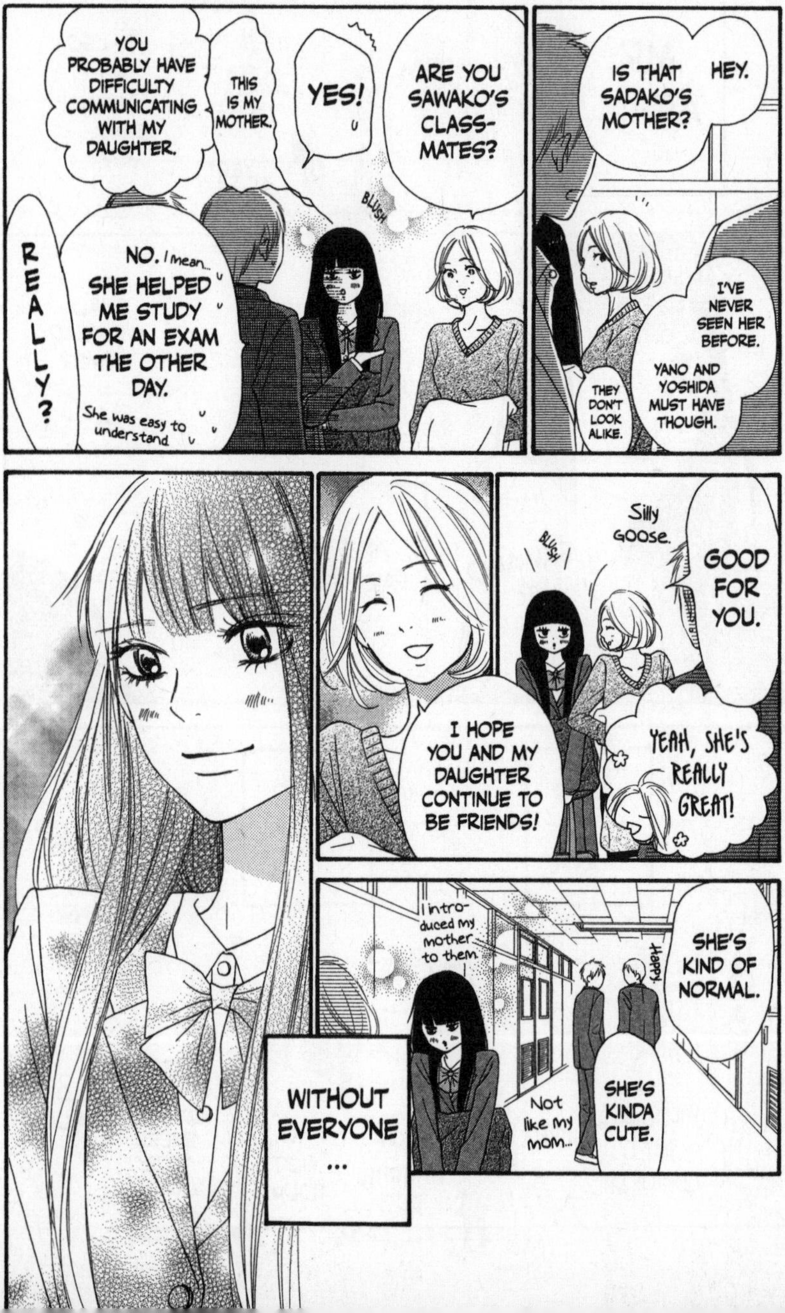
HEY.
IS THAT SADAKO'S MOTHER?
I'VE NEVER SEEN HER BEFORE.
YANO AND YOSHIDA MUST HAVE THOUGH.
THEY DON'T LOOK ALIKE.
ARE YOU SAWAKO'S CLASS-MATES?
BLUSH
YES!
THIS IS MY MOTHER.
YOU PROBABLY HAVE DIFFICULTY COMMUNICATING WITH MY DAUGHTER.
NO. I mean... SHE HELPED ME STUDY FOR AN EXAM THE OTHER DAY.
She was easy to understand
REALLY?
GOOD FOR YOU.
Silly goose.
BLUSH
YEAH, SHE'S REALLY GREAT!
I HOPE YOU AND MY DAUGHTER CONTINUE TO BE FRIENDS!
SHE'S KIND OF NORMAL.
Happy.
I introduced my mother to them.
SHE'S KINDA CUTE.
Not like my mom...
WITHOUT EVERYONE ...

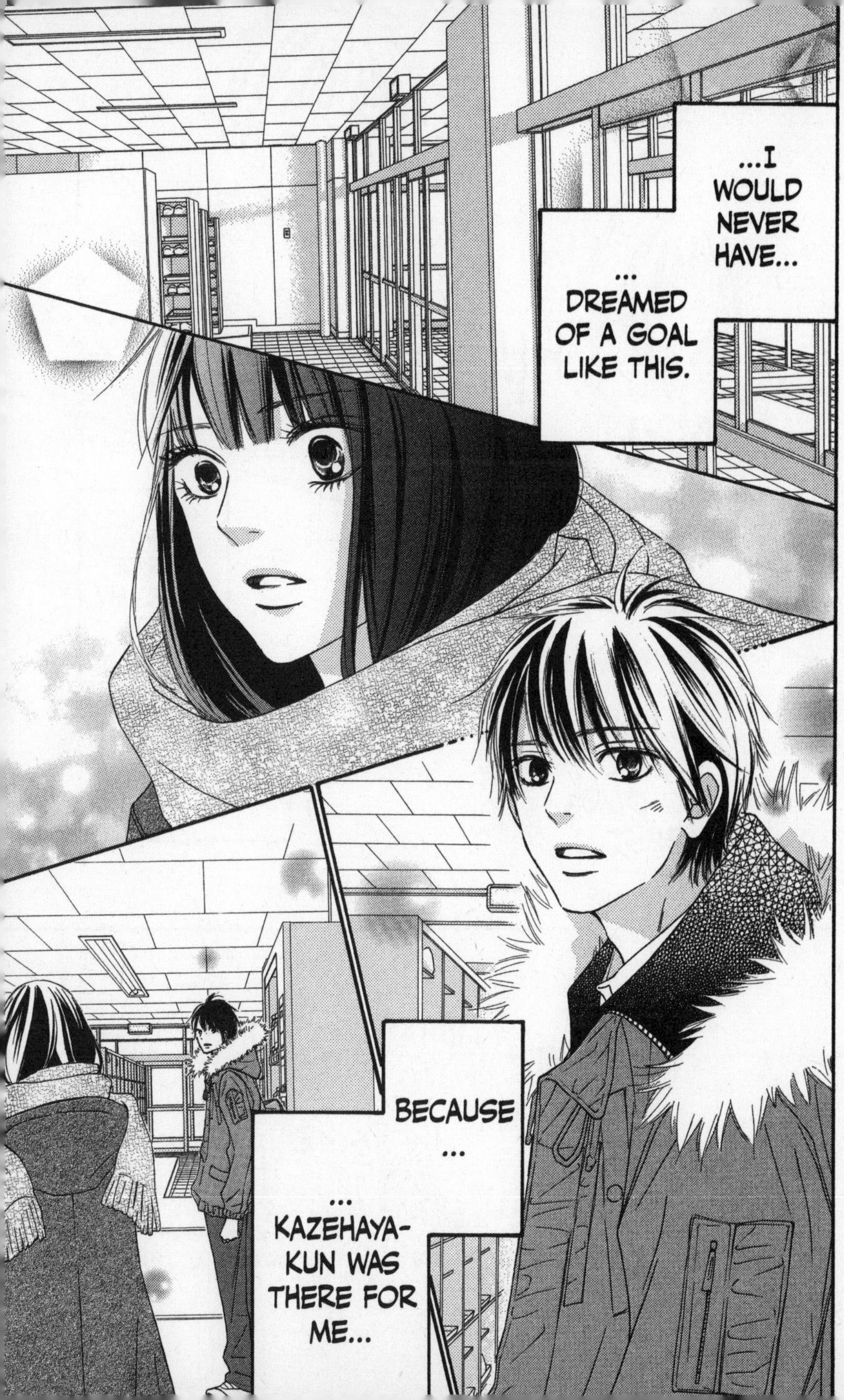
...I WOULD NEVER HAVE...
... DREAMED OF A GOAL LIKE THIS.
BECAUSE ...
... KAZEHAYA-KUN WAS THERE FOR ME...

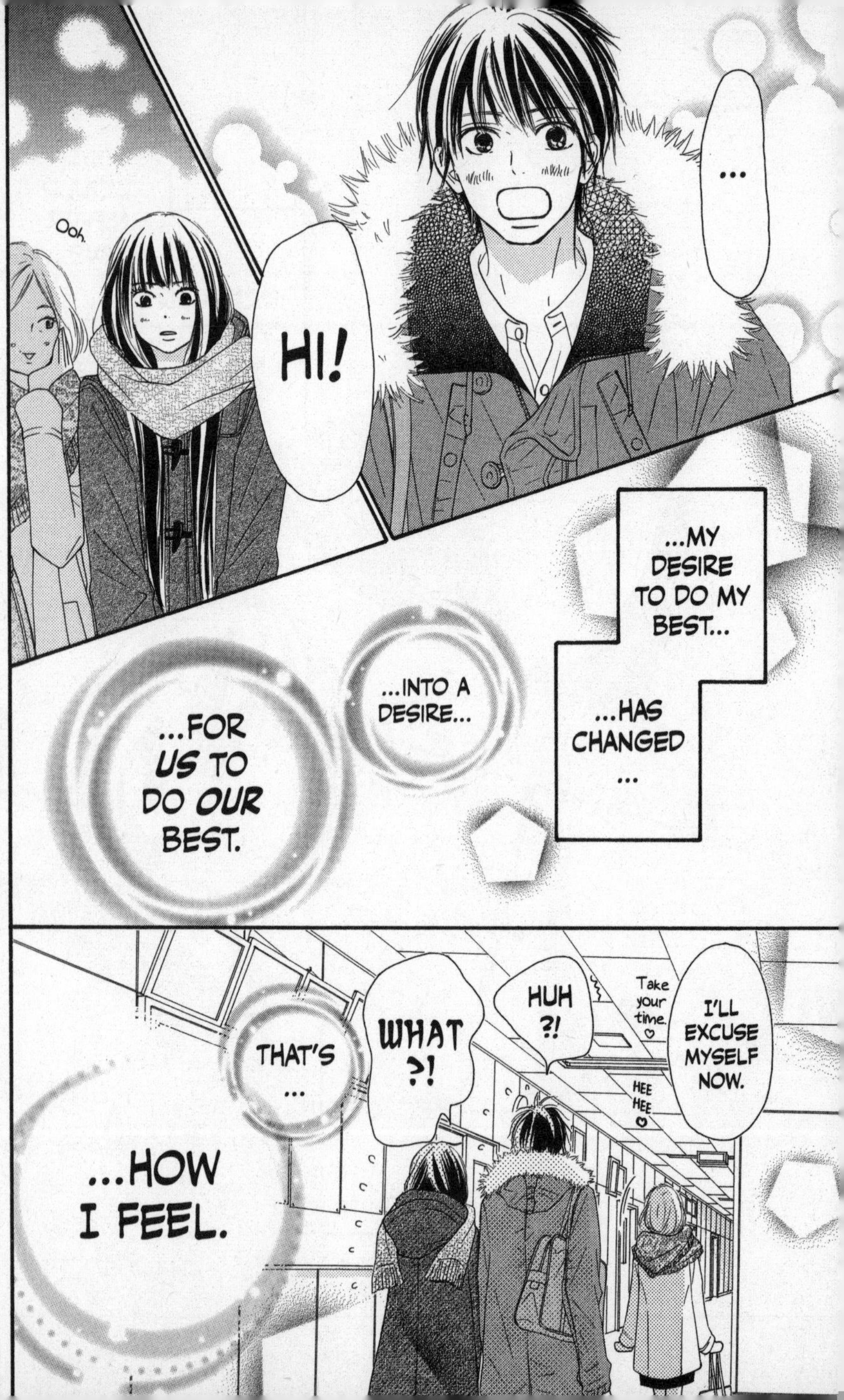
...
HI!
Ooh.
...MY DESIRE TO DO MY BEST...
...HAS CHANGED ...
...INTO A DESIRE...
...FOR *US* TO DO *OUR* BEST.
I'LL EXCUSE MYSELF NOW.
Take your time. ♡
HEE HEE ♡
HUH ?!
WHAT ?!
THAT'S ...
...HOW I FEEL.

Episode 81: Just a Thought

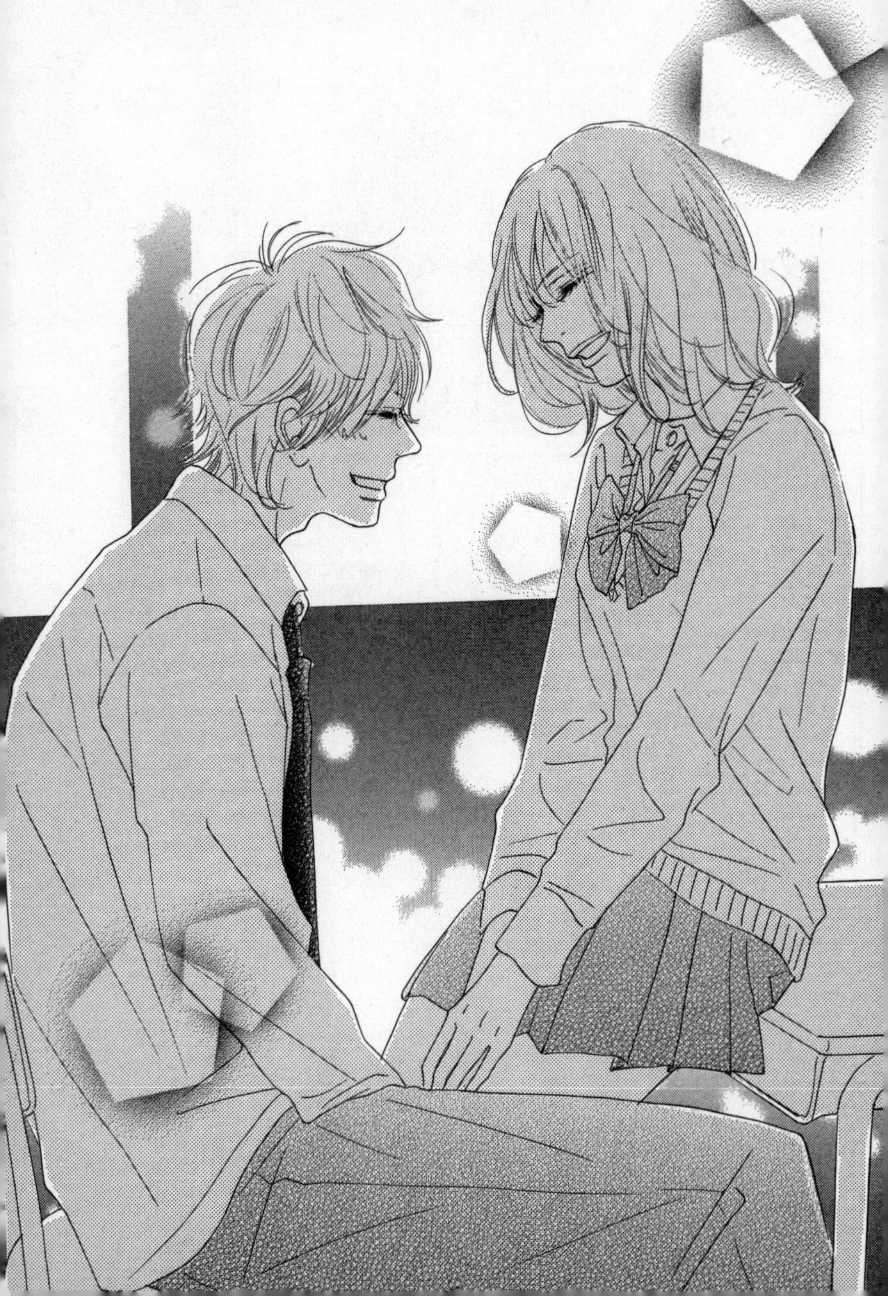

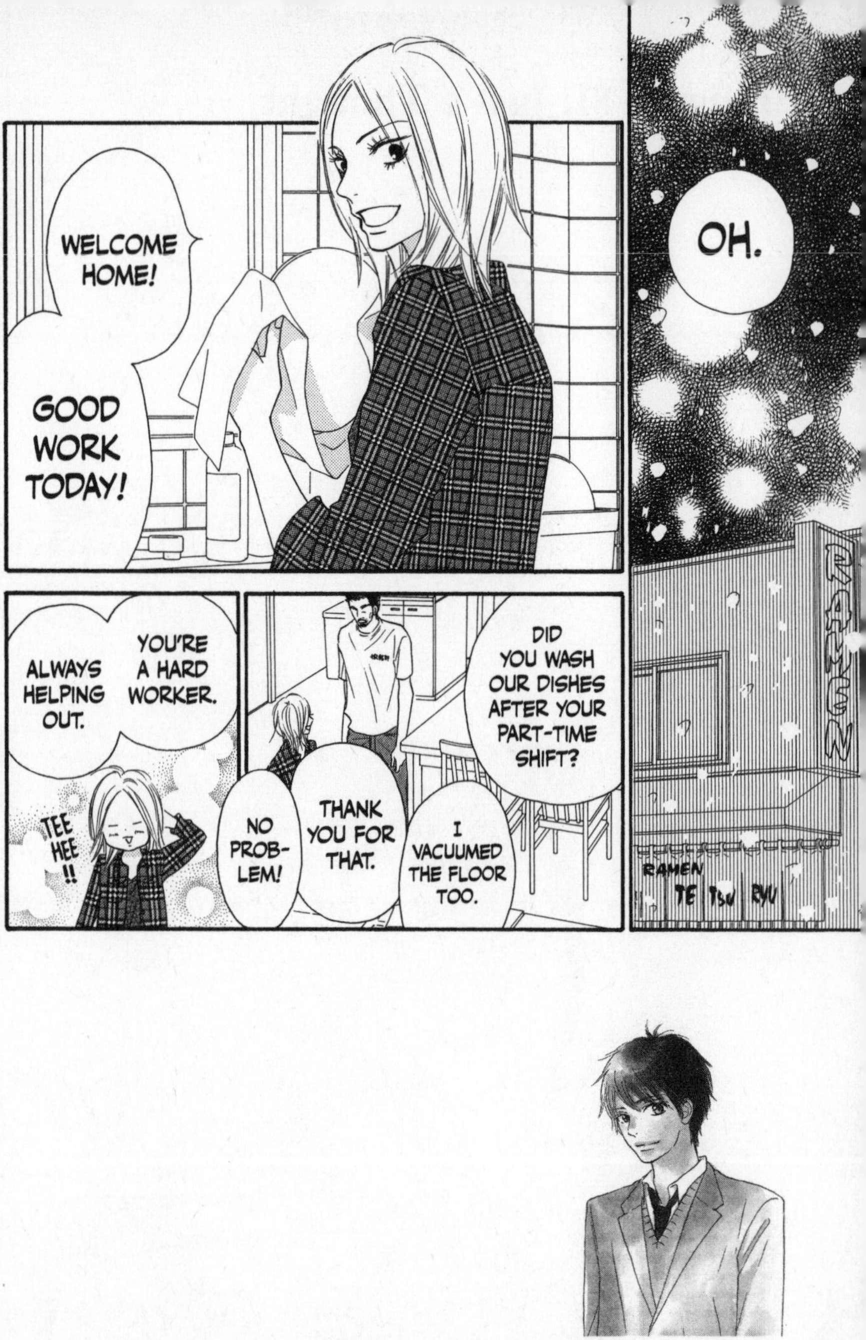
OH.
RAMEN
RAMEN TE TSU RYU
WELCOME HOME!
GOOD WORK TODAY!
DID YOU WASH OUR DISHES AFTER YOUR PART-TIME SHIFT?
I VACUUMED THE FLOOR TOO.
THANK YOU FOR THAT.
NO PROB-LEM!
YOU'RE A HARD WORKER.
ALWAYS HELPING OUT.
TEE HEE!!

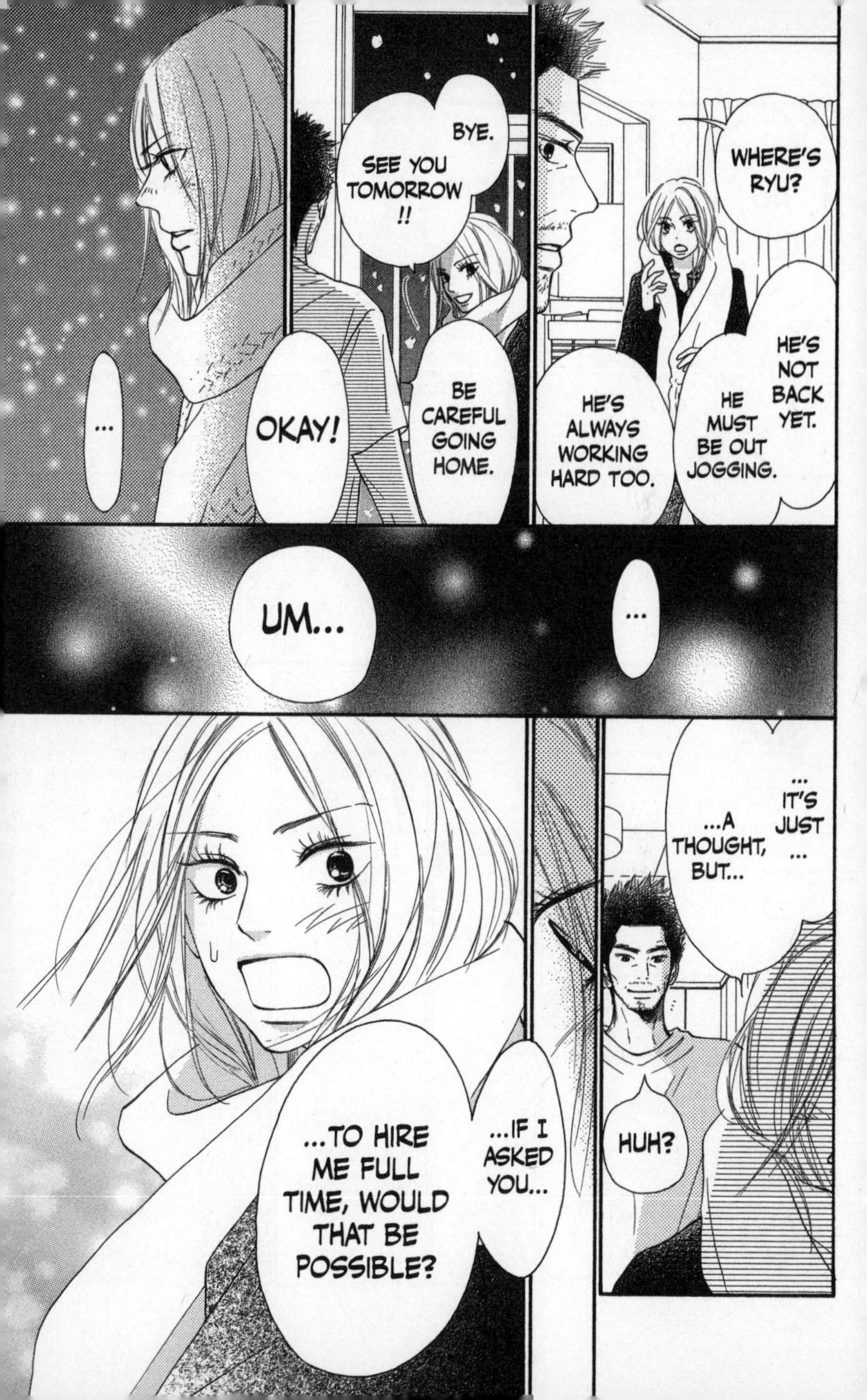
WHERE'S RYU?
HE'S NOT BACK YET.
HE MUST BE OUT JOGGING.
HE'S ALWAYS WORKING HARD TOO.
BYE. SEE YOU TOMORROW !!
BE CAREFUL GOING HOME.
OKAY!
...
...
UM...
... IT'S JUST ...
...A THOUGHT, BUT...
HUH?
...IF I ASKED YOU...
...TO HIRE ME FULL TIME, WOULD THAT BE POSSIBLE?

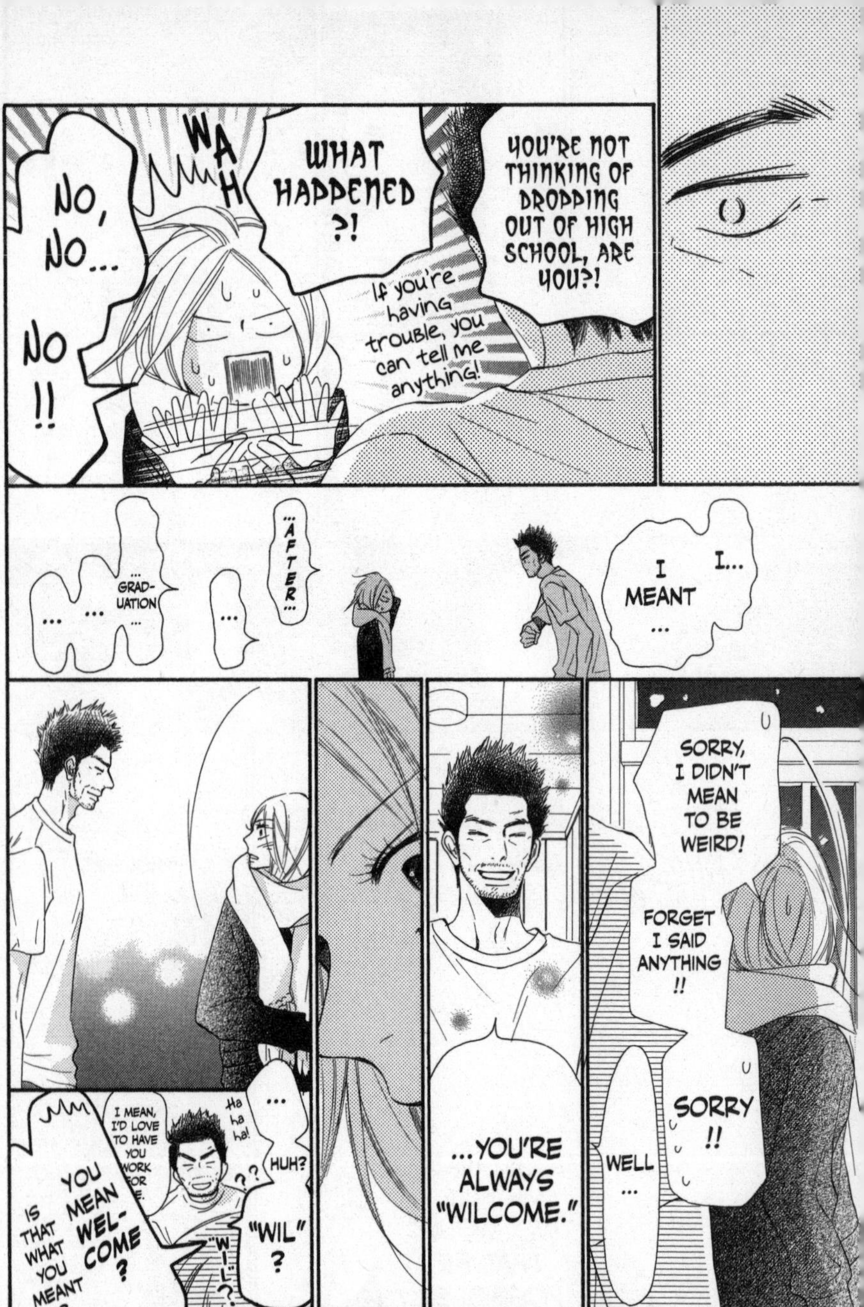
YOU'RE NOT THINKING OF DROPPING OUT OF HIGH SCHOOL, ARE YOU?!
WHAT HAPPENED ?!
If you're having trouble, you can tell me anything!
WAH
NO, NO...
NO !!
I...
I MEANT ...
...AFTER...
...
... ... GRAD-UATION ...
SORRY, I DIDN'T MEAN TO BE WEIRD!
FORGET I SAID ANYTHING !!
SORRY !!
WELL ...
...YOU'RE ALWAYS "WILCOME."
...
HUH?
Ha ha ha!
"WIL" ?
??
"WIL"?
I MEAN, I'D LOVE TO HAVE YOU
YOU MEAN WEL-COME ?
IS THAT WHAT YOU MEANT ?

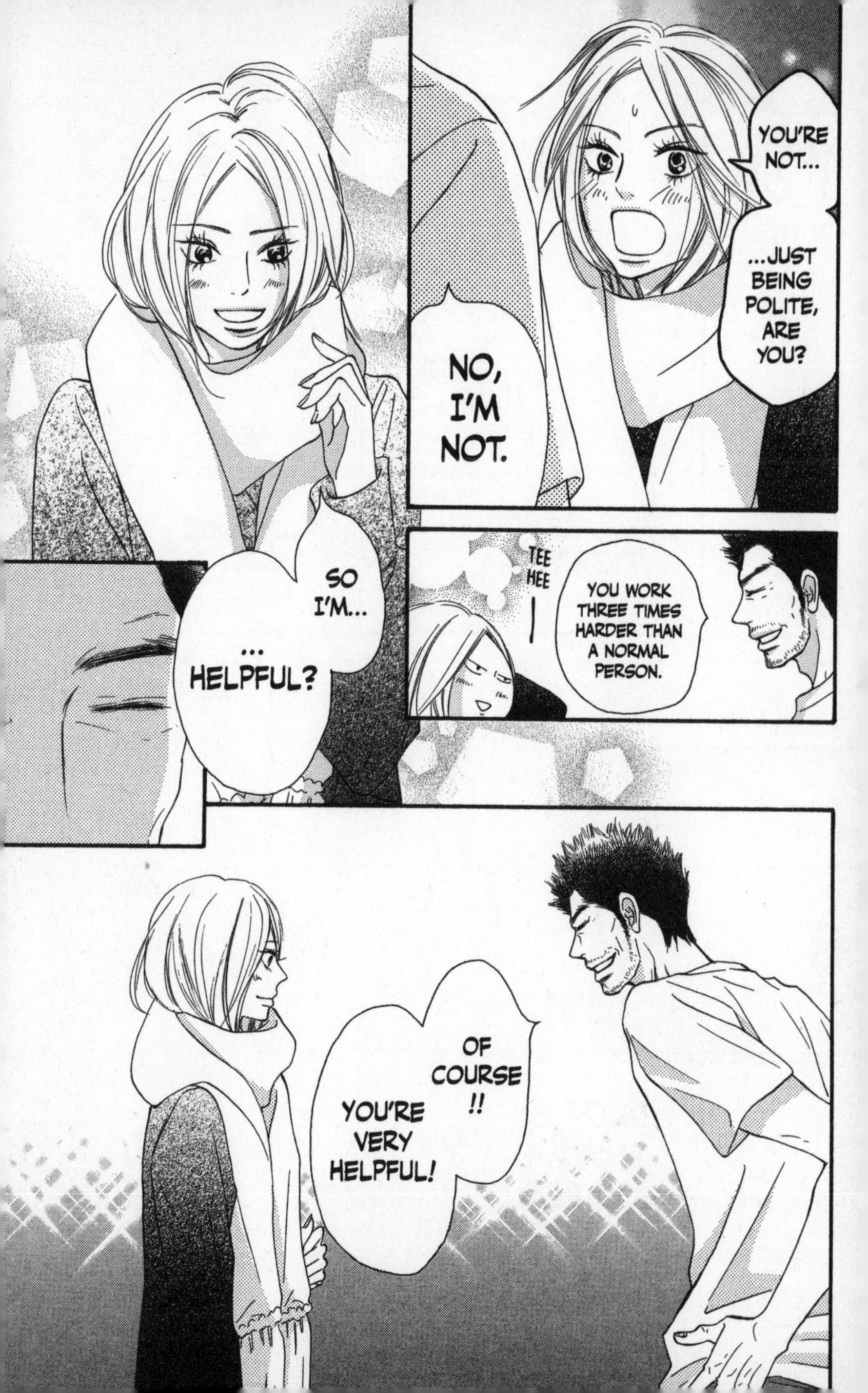
YOU'RE NOT...
...JUST BEING POLITE, ARE YOU?
NO, I'M NOT.
TEE HEE
YOU WORK THREE TIMES HARDER THAN A NORMAL PERSON.
SO I'M... ...HELPFUL?
OF COURSE!!
YOU'RE VERY HELPFUL!

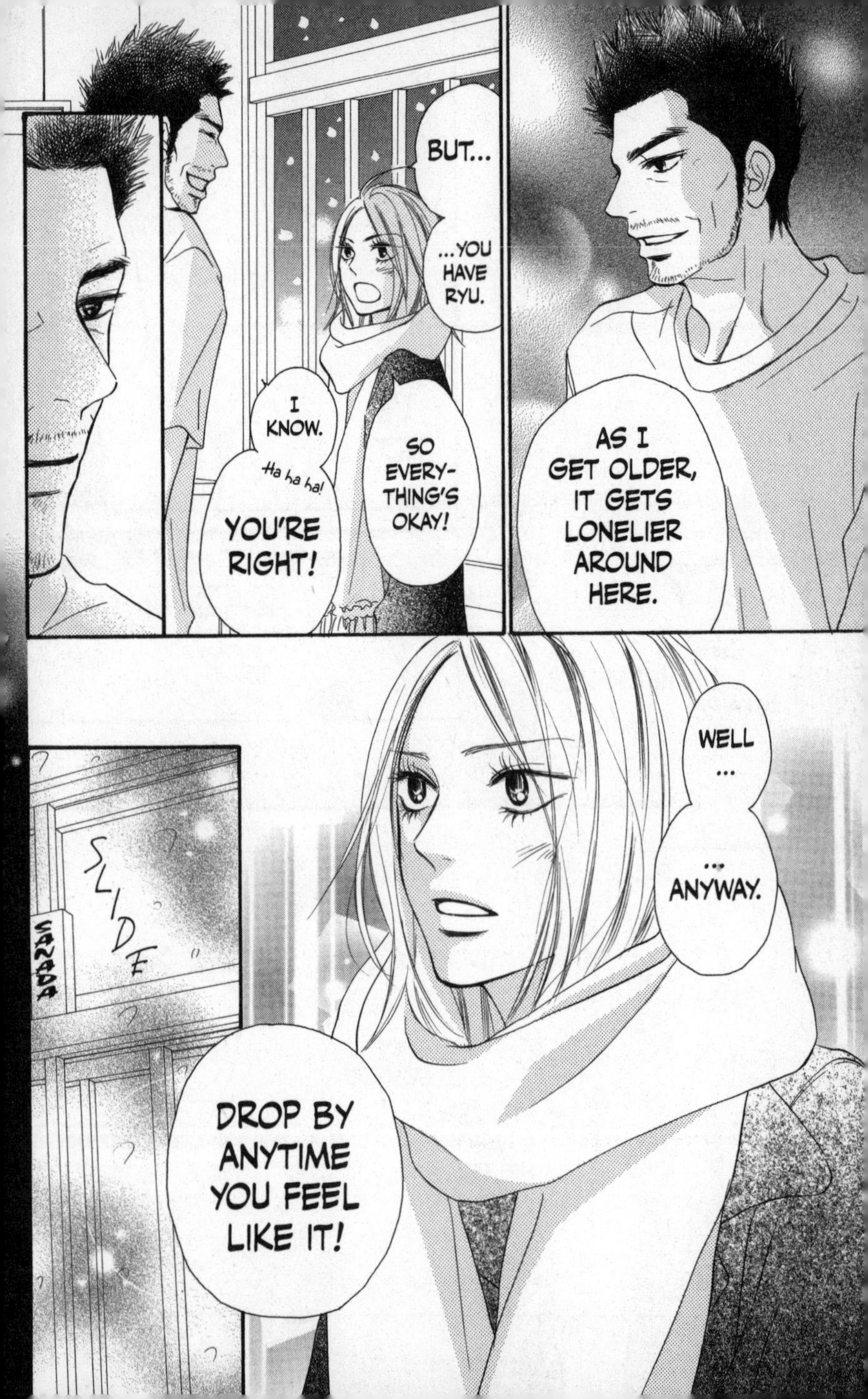
AS I GET OLDER, IT GETS LONELIER AROUND HERE.
BUT...
...YOU HAVE RYU.
SO EVERY-THING'S OKAY!
I KNOW.
Ha ha ha!
YOU'RE RIGHT!
WELL...
...ANYWAY.
DROP BY ANYTIME YOU FEEL LIKE IT!
SLIDE
SANADA

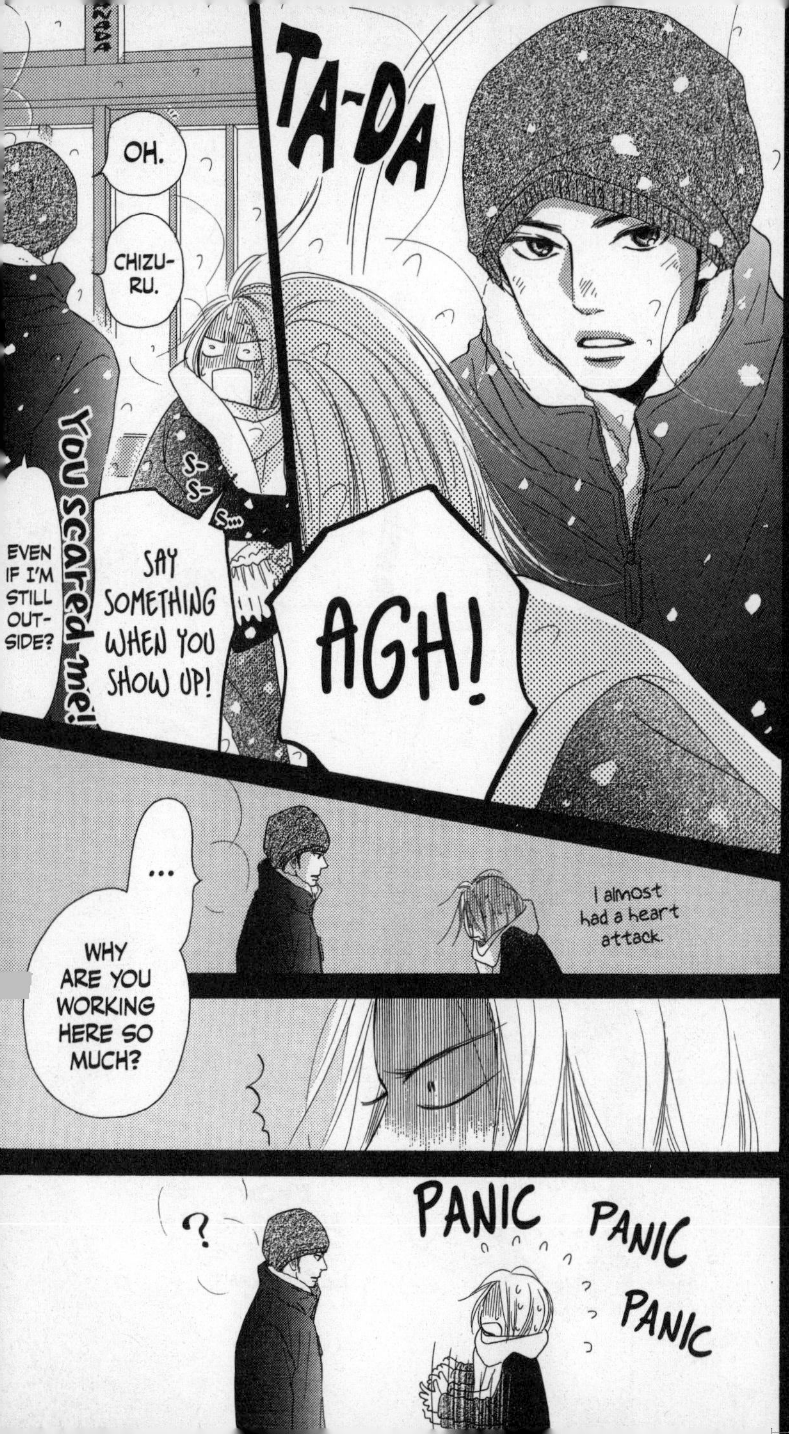
TA-DA
AGH!
OH.
CHIZU-RU.
S- S- S...
You scared me!
SAY SOMETHING WHEN YOU SHOW UP!
EVEN IF I'M STILL OUT-SIDE?
I almost had a heart attack.
...
WHY ARE YOU WORKING HERE SO MUCH?
PANIC PANIC PANIC
?

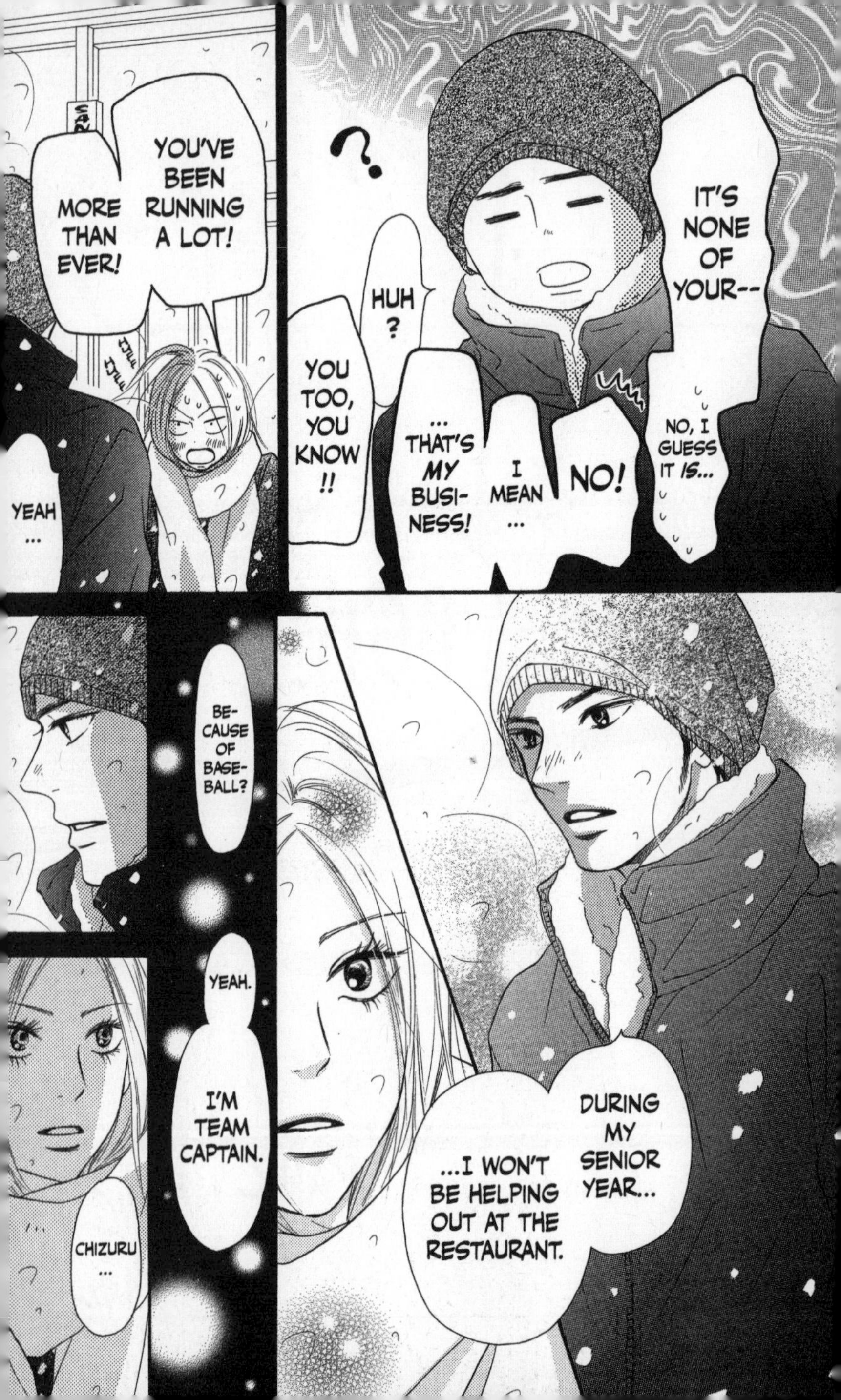
IT'S NONE OF YOUR--
HUH?
NO, I GUESS IT *IS*...
NO!
I MEAN...
...THAT'S *MY* BUSINESS!
YOU TOO, YOU KNOW!!
YOU'VE BEEN RUNNING A LOT!
MORE THAN EVER!
YEAH...
DURING MY SENIOR YEAR...
...I WON'T BE HELPING OUT AT THE RESTAURANT.
BECAUSE OF BASEBALL?
YEAH.
I'M TEAM CAPTAIN.
CHIZURU...

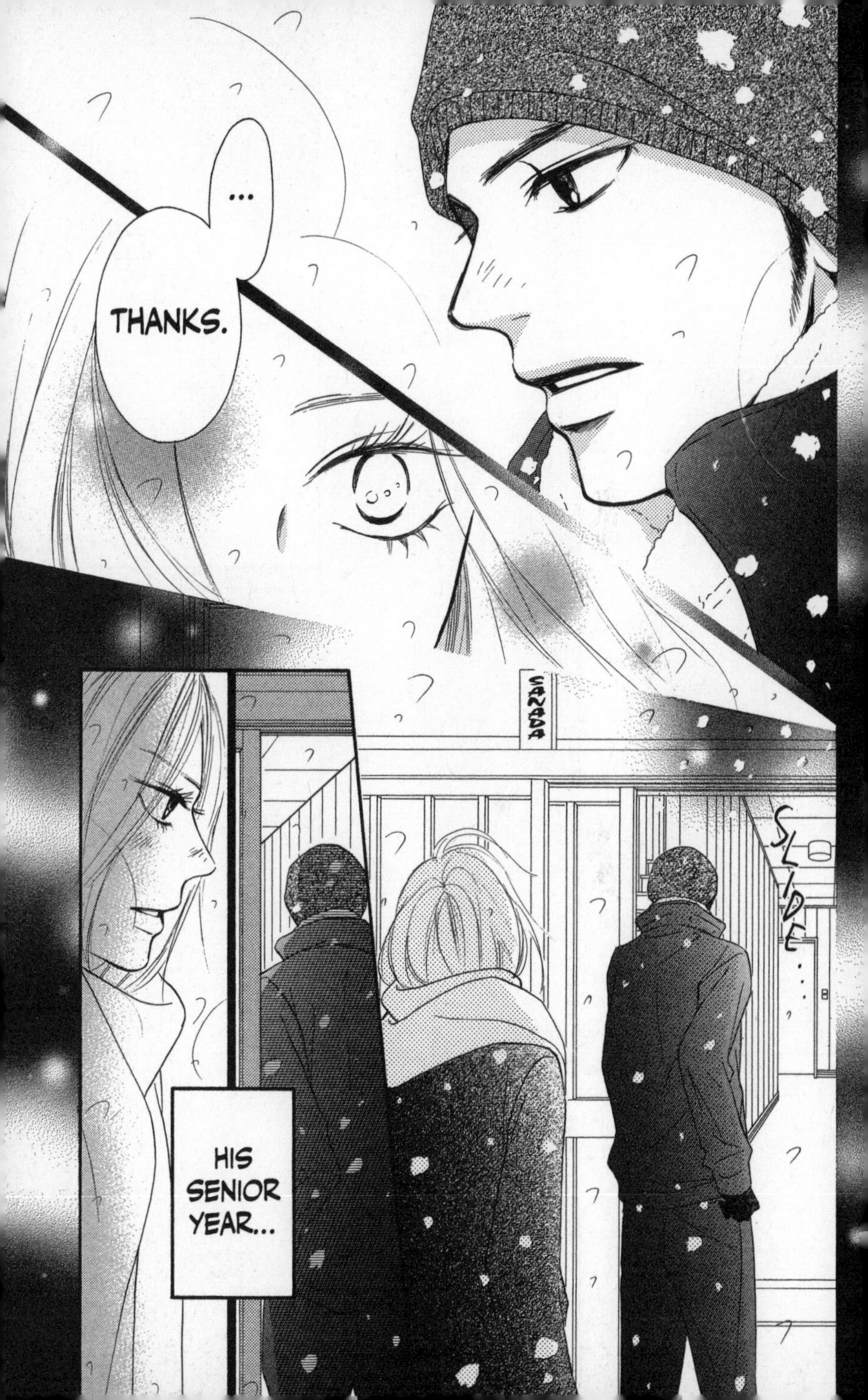
...
THANKS.
SANADA
SLIDE...
HIS SENIOR YEAR...

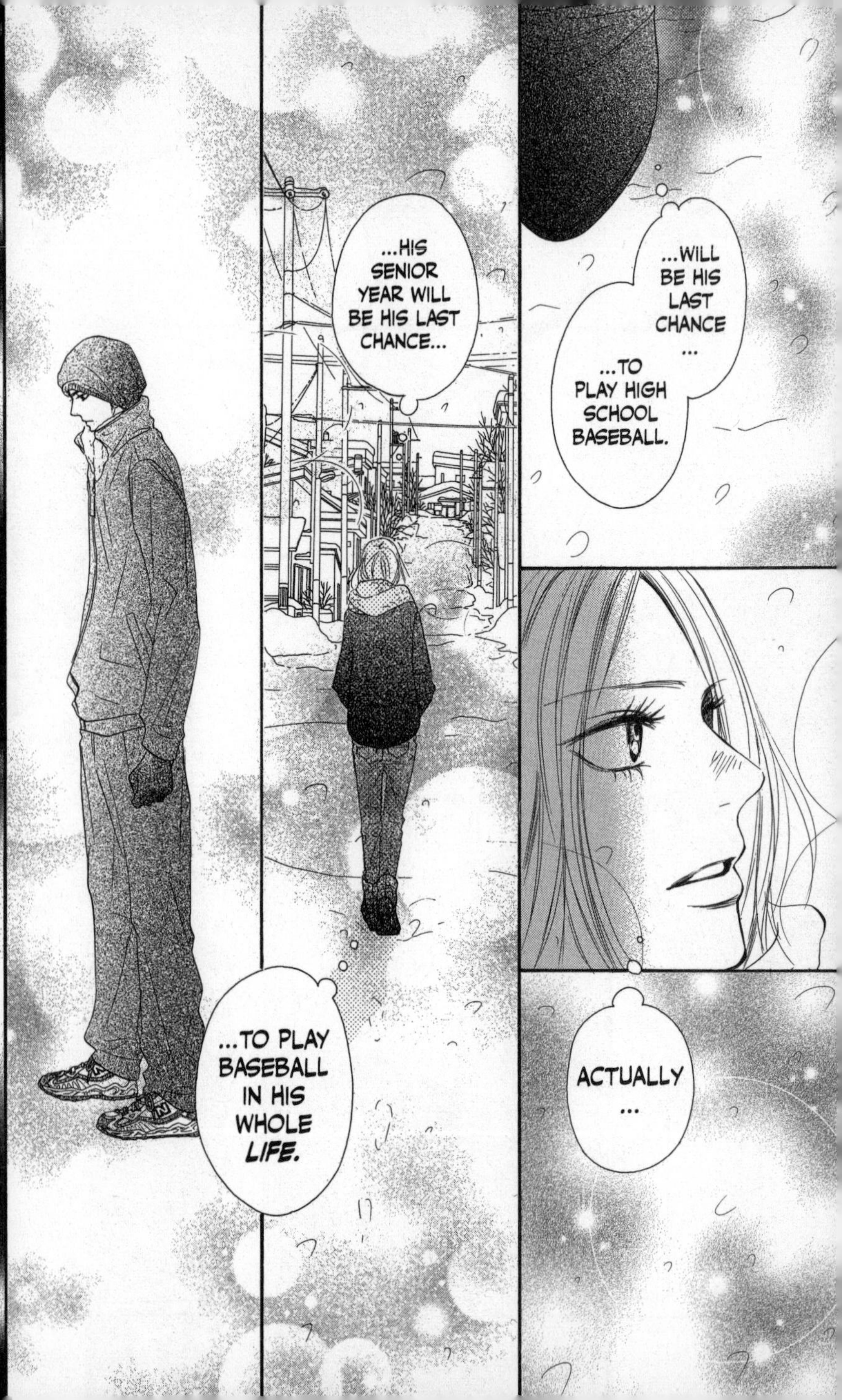
...WILL BE HIS LAST CHANCE ...
...TO PLAY HIGH SCHOOL BASEBALL.
ACTUALLY ...
...HIS SENIOR YEAR WILL BE HIS LAST CHANCE...
...TO PLAY BASEBALL IN HIS WHOLE *LIFE.*

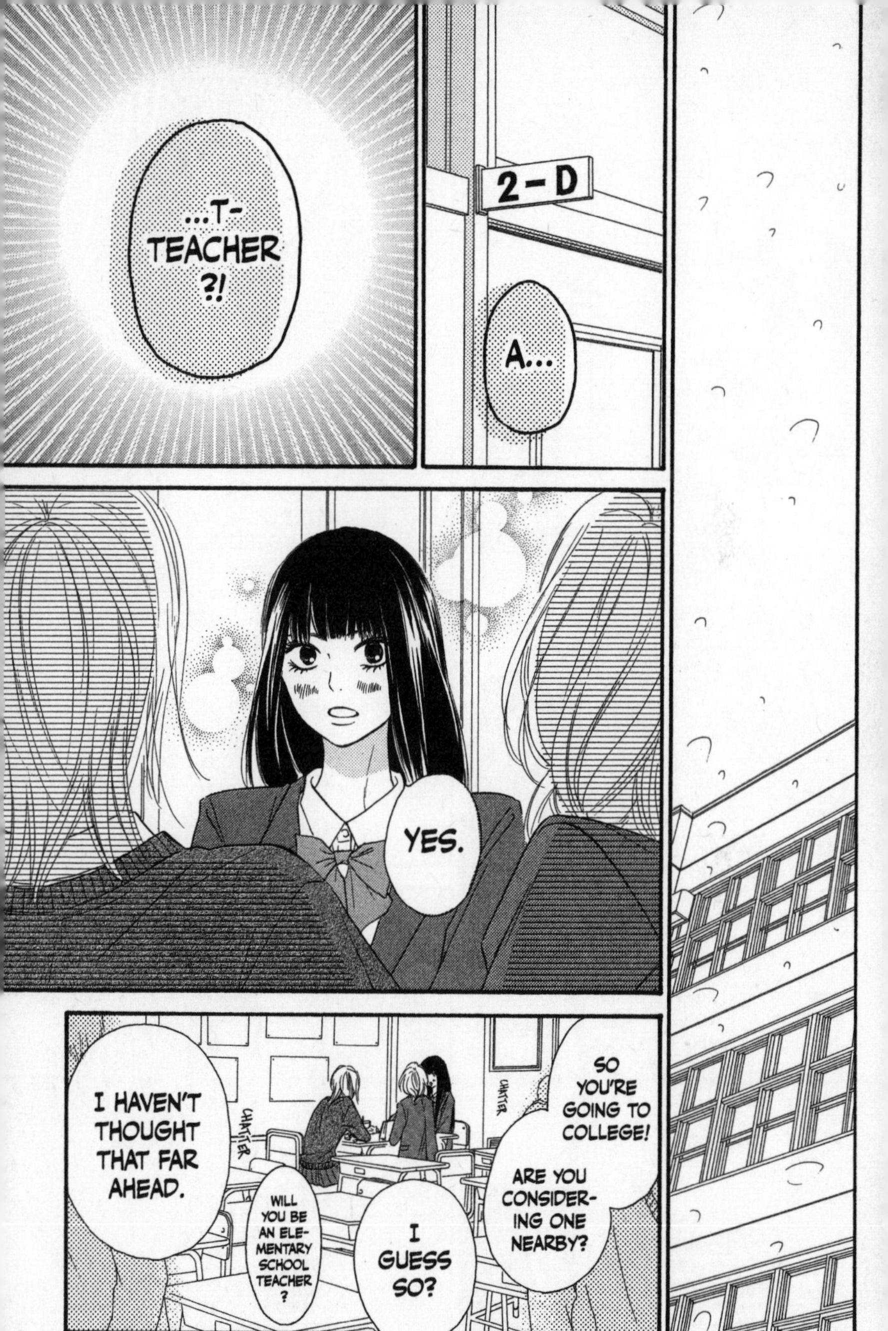
2-D
A...
...T-TEACHER?!
YES.
SO YOU'RE GOING TO COLLEGE!
ARE YOU CONSIDERING ONE NEARBY?
CHATTER
I GUESS SO?
WILL YOU BE AN ELEMENTARY SCHOOL TEACHER?
CHATTER
I HAVEN'T THOUGHT THAT FAR AHEAD.

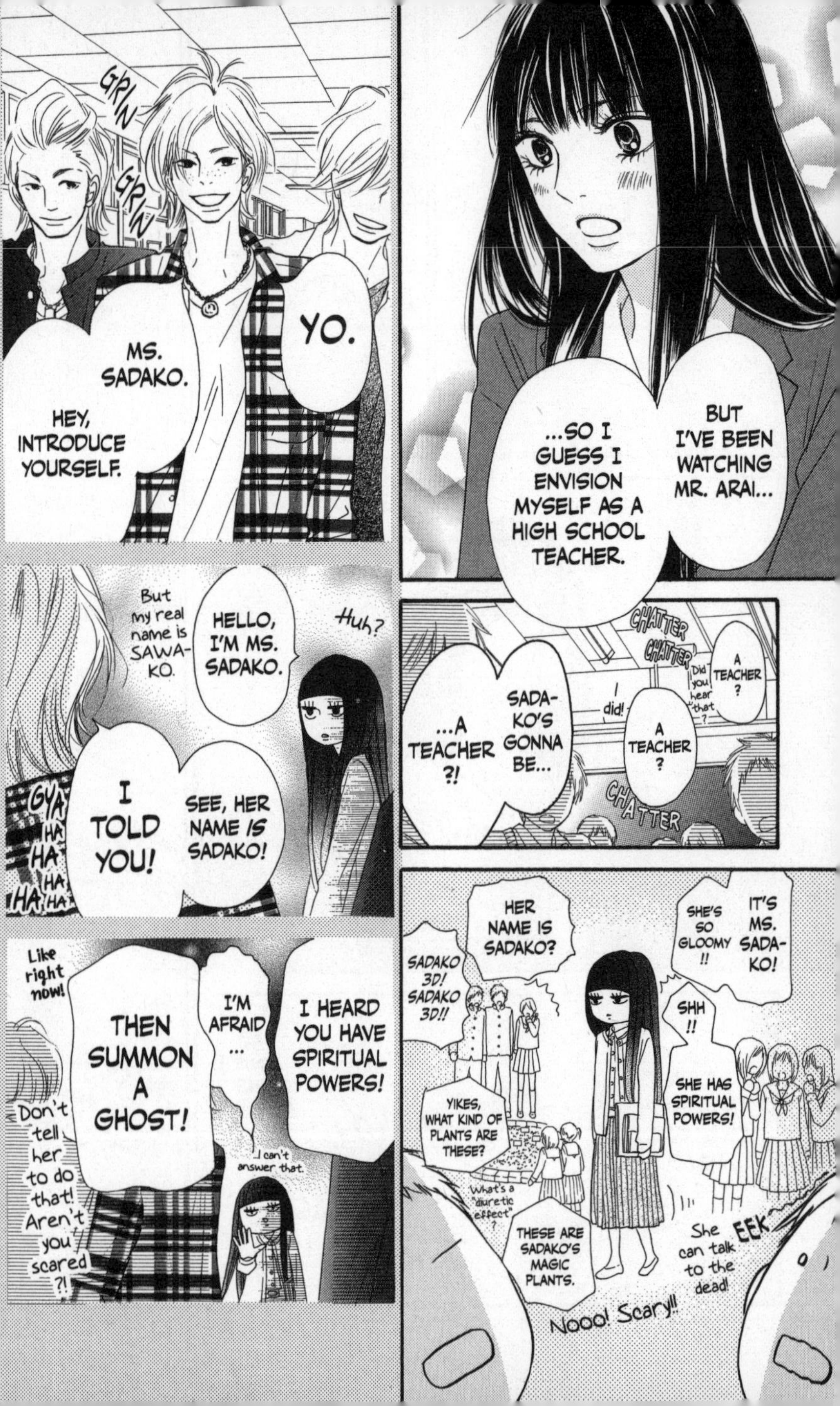
BUT I'VE BEEN WATCHING MR. ARAI...
...SO I GUESS I ENVISION MYSELF AS A HIGH SCHOOL TEACHER.
CHATTER
CHATTER
A TEACHER?
Did you hear that?
I did!
A TEACHER?
SADAKO'S GONNA BE...
...A TEACHER?!
CHATTER
IT'S MS. SADAKO!
SHE'S SO GLOOMY!!
HER NAME IS SADAKO?
SADAKO 3D! SADAKO 3D!!
SHH!!
SHE HAS SPIRITUAL POWERS!
YIKES, WHAT KIND OF PLANTS ARE THESE?
What's a "diuretic effect"?
THESE ARE SADAKO'S MAGIC PLANTS.
EEK
She can talk to the dead!
Nooo! Scary!!
GRIN
GRIN
YO.
MS. SADAKO.
HEY, INTRODUCE YOURSELF.
Huh?
HELLO, I'M MS. SADAKO.
But my real name is SAWAKO.
SEE, HER NAME IS SADAKO!
I TOLD YOU!
GYAHAHAHAHAHA
I HEARD YOU HAVE SPIRITUAL POWERS!
I'M AFRAID...
I can't answer that.
THEN SUMMON A GHOST!
Like right now!
Don't tell her to do that! Aren't you scared?!

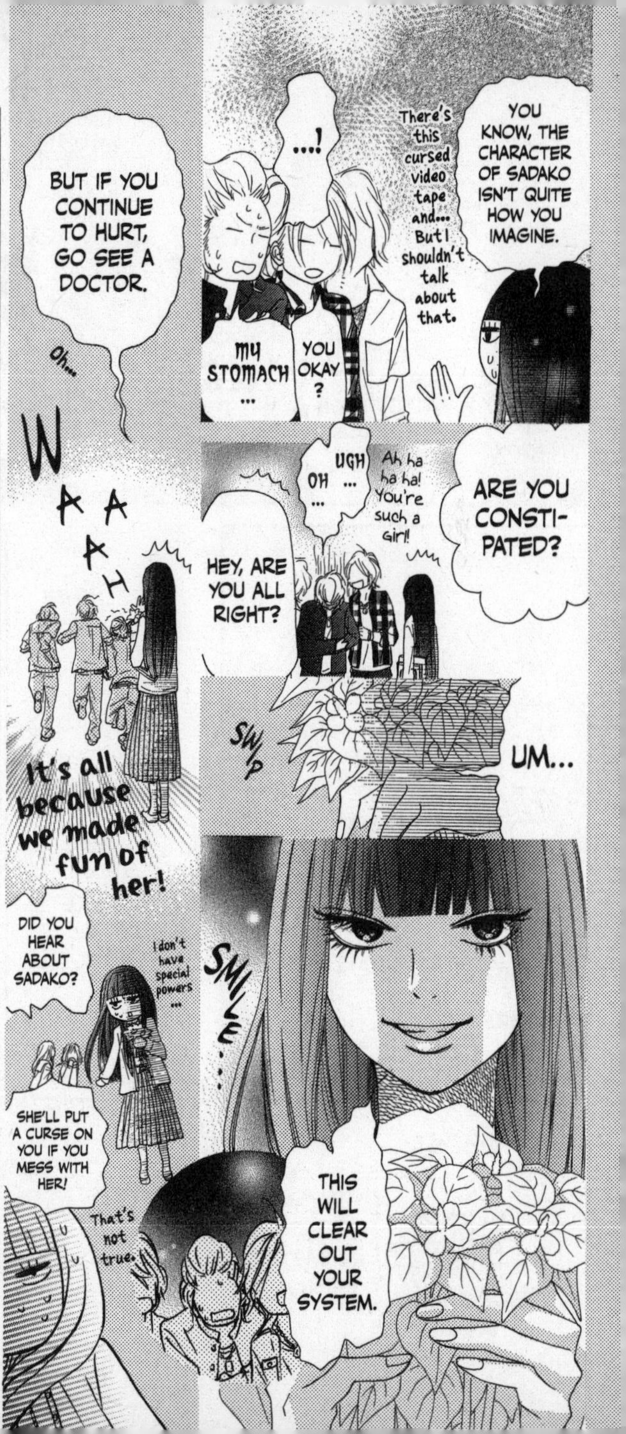
YOU KNOW, THE CHARACTER OF SADAKO ISN'T QUITE HOW YOU IMAGINE.
There's this cursed video tape and... But I shouldn't talk about that.
...!
YOU OKAY?
my STOMACH...
ARE YOU CONSTI-PATED?
Ah ha ha! You're such a Girl!
UGH ...
OH ...
HEY, ARE YOU ALL RIGHT?
UM...
SWIP
SMILE...
THIS WILL CLEAR OUT YOUR SYSTEM.
BUT IF YOU CONTINUE TO HURT, GO SEE A DOCTOR.
Oh...
WAAAH
It's all because we made fun of her!
DID YOU HEAR ABOUT SADAKO?
I don't have special powers...
SHE'LL PUT A CURSE ON YOU IF YOU MESS WITH HER!
That's not true.

KARUPIN on JAPAN 1

Hello! How are you? This is Shiina.

There are only two sidebars this time! What should I write?

Anyway, here's volume 20! What a surprise...for me! I don't remember what was going on (in my life) when I started writing this story. But readers who were only elementary school students back then must have grown up into young women by now!

I didn't have a child when I started this manga, so I spent all day working on it. Now I get up in the morning and sometimes make lunch for my daughter and see her off to school before starting to work. Later, I pick her up, and I go to bed with her at night. Although, when the deadline crunch comes there's little distinction between morning, noon and night. I put makeup on at least once a month... when I go out for a meeting! But the rest of the month? Nope!

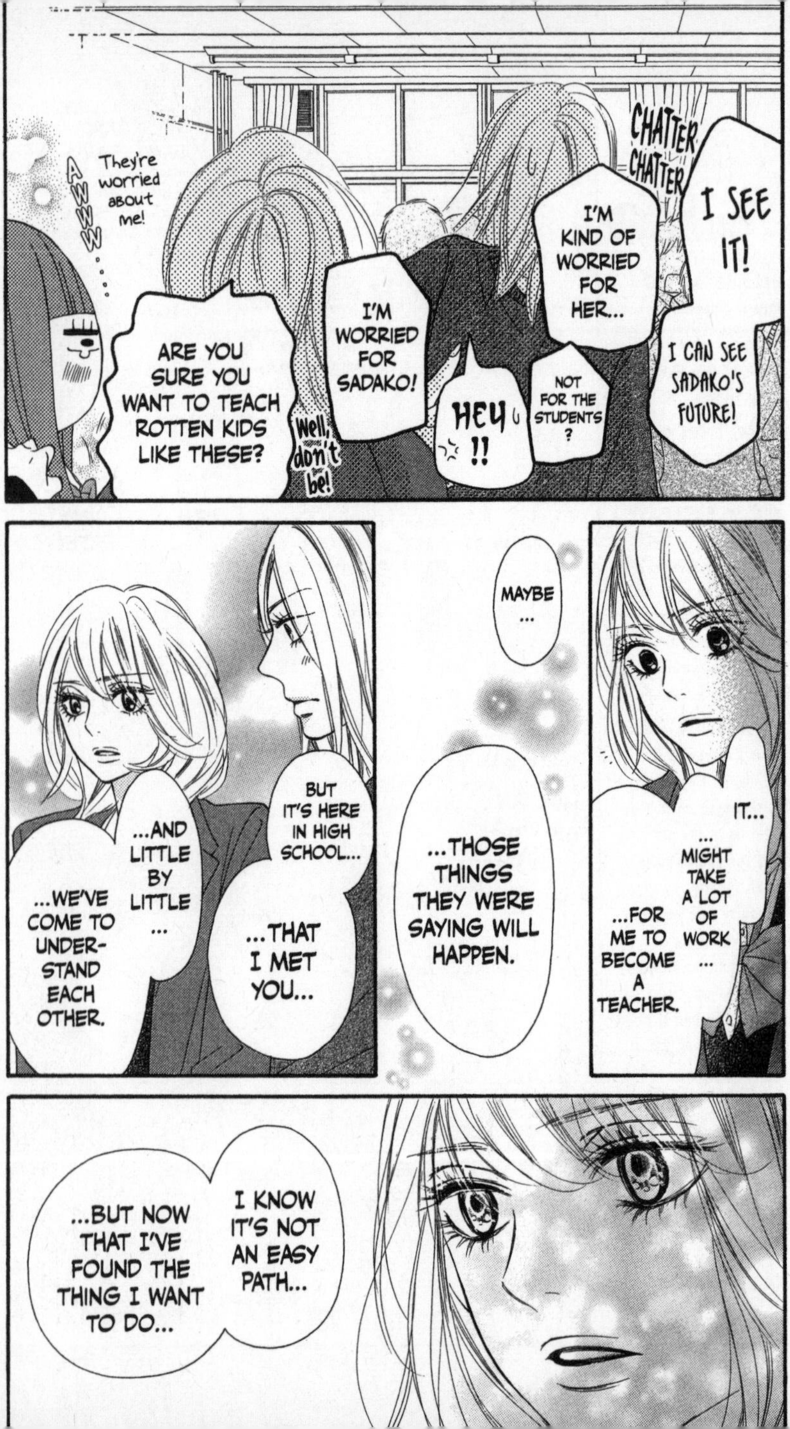
CHATTER CHATTER
I SEE IT!
I CAN SEE SADAKO'S FUTURE!
I'M KIND OF WORRIED FOR HER...
NOT FOR THE STUDENTS?
HEY!!
I'M WORRIED FOR SADAKO!
Well, don't be!
ARE YOU SURE YOU WANT TO TEACH ROTTEN KIDS LIKE THESE?
AWWWW...
They're worried about me!
IT...
...MIGHT TAKE A LOT OF WORK...
...FOR ME TO BECOME A TEACHER.
MAYBE...
...THOSE THINGS THEY WERE SAYING WILL HAPPEN.
BUT IT'S HERE IN HIGH SCHOOL...
...THAT I MET YOU...
...AND LITTLE BY LITTLE...
...WE'VE COME TO UNDER-STAND EACH OTHER.
I KNOW IT'S NOT AN EASY PATH...
...BUT NOW THAT I'VE FOUND THE THING I WANT TO DO...

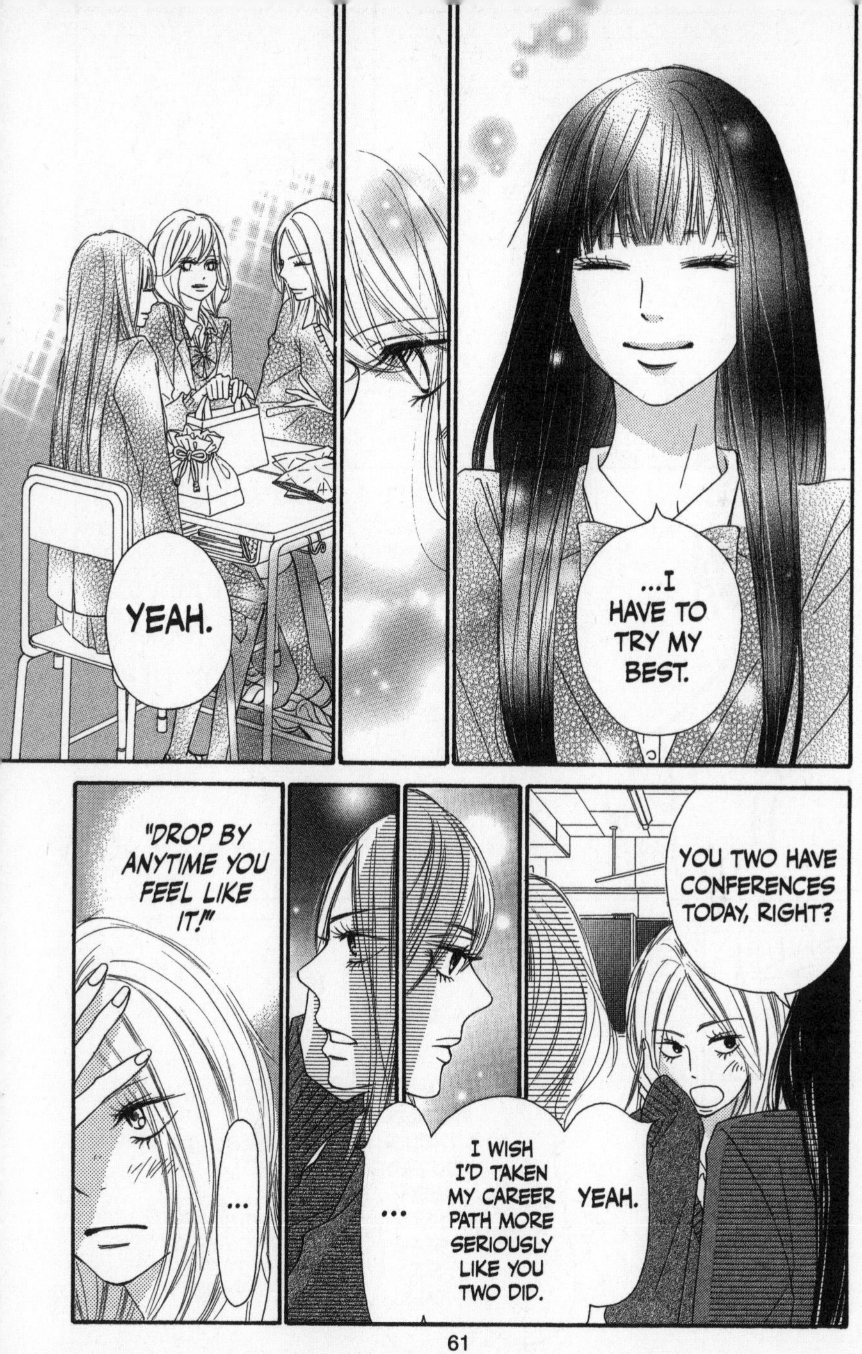

...I HAVE TO TRY MY BEST.
YEAH.
YOU TWO HAVE CONFERENCES TODAY, RIGHT?
YEAH.
I WISH I'D TAKEN MY CAREER PATH MORE SERIOUSLY LIKE YOU TWO DID.
...
"DROP BY ANYTIME YOU FEEL LIKE IT!"
...

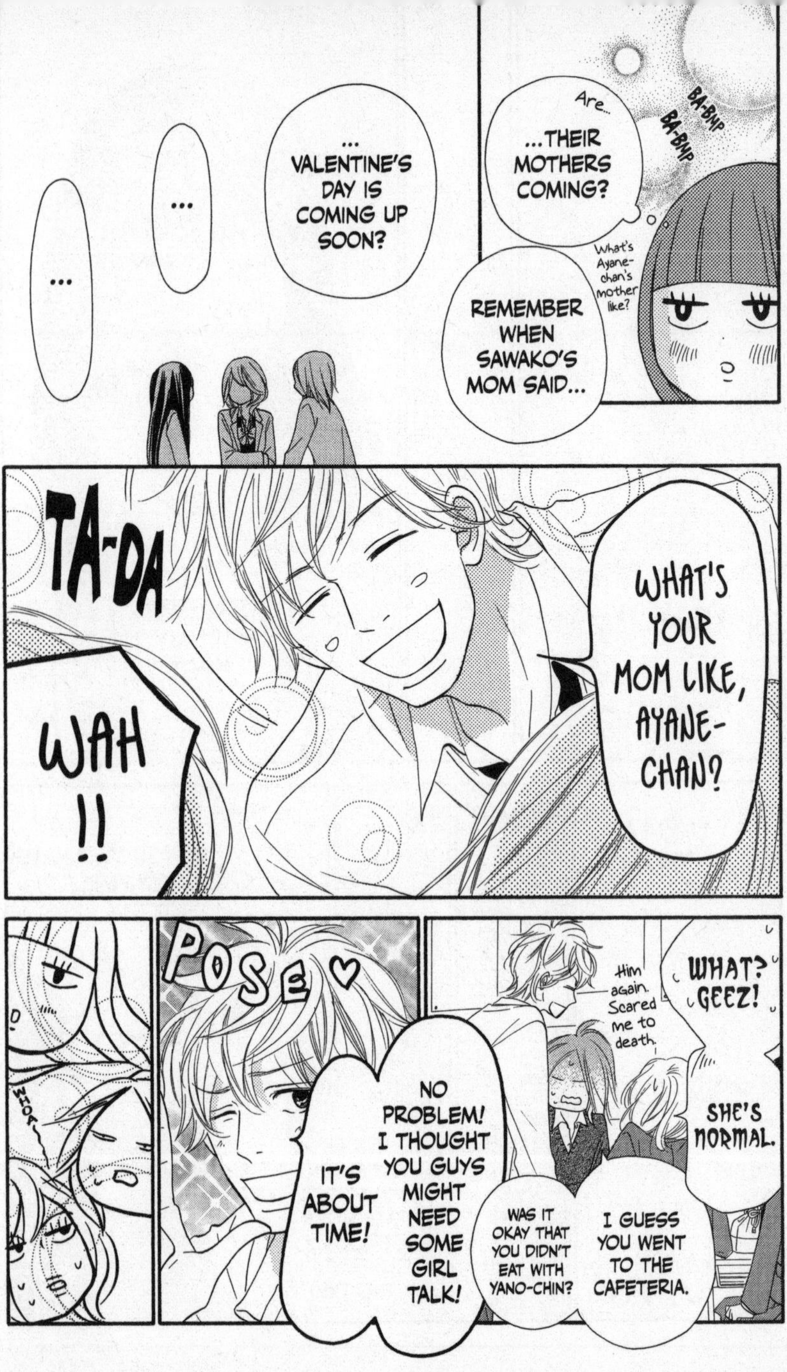
BA-BMP
BA-BMP
Are...
...THEIR MOTHERS COMING?
What's Ayane-chan's mother like?
REMEMBER WHEN SAWAKO'S MOM SAID...
... VALENTINE'S DAY IS COMING UP SOON?
...
...
WHAT'S YOUR MOM LIKE, AYANE-CHAN?
TA-DA
WAH !!
WHAT? GEEZ!
Him again. Scared me to death.
SHE'S NORMAL.
I GUESS YOU WENT TO THE CAFETERIA.
WAS IT OKAY THAT YOU DIDN'T EAT WITH YANO-CHIN?
POSE ♥
NO PROBLEM! I THOUGHT YOU GUYS MIGHT NEED SOME GIRL TALK!
IT'S ABOUT TIME!
WHOA...

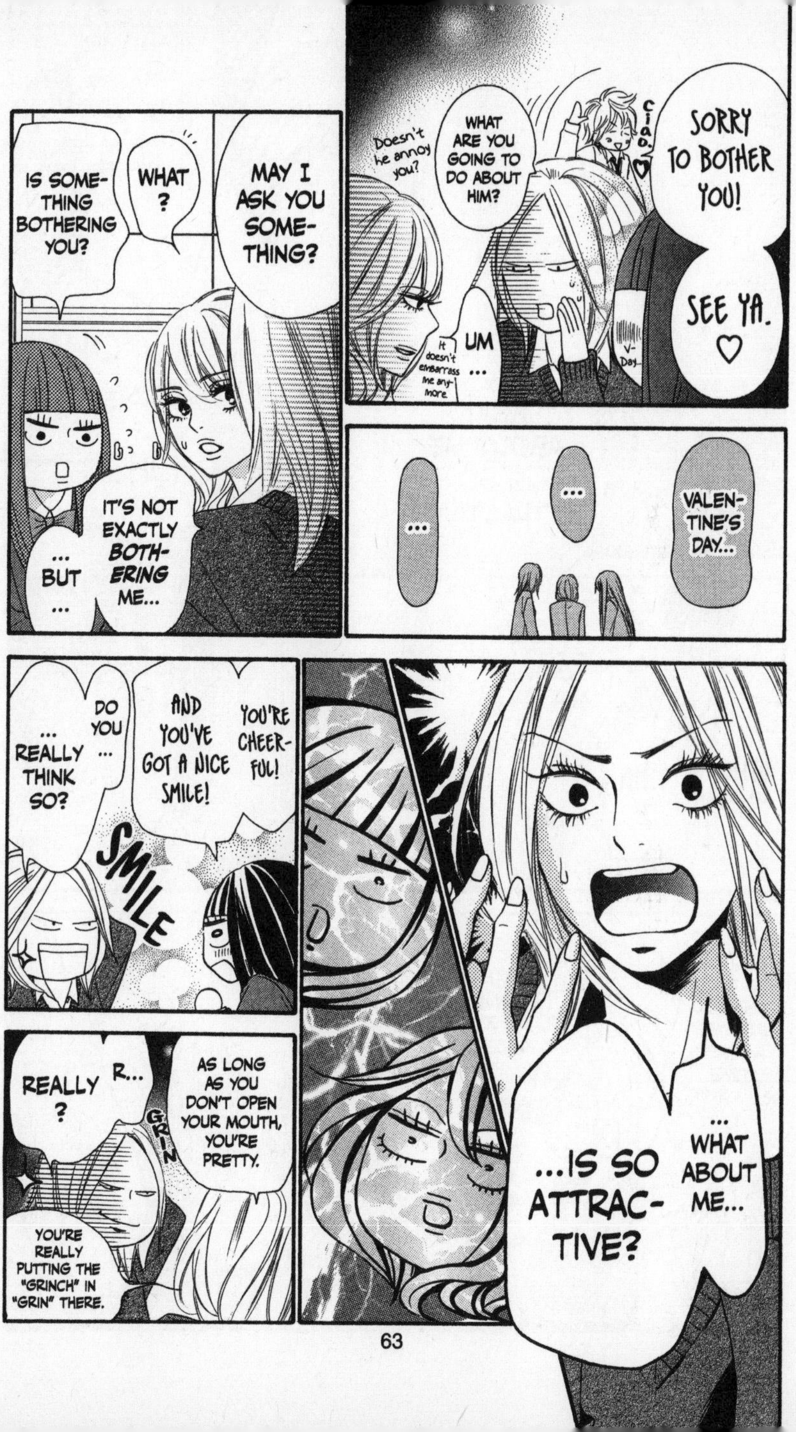
SORRY TO BOTHER YOU!
SEE YA. ♡
CIAO. ♡
V-Day...
WHAT ARE YOU GOING TO DO ABOUT HIM?
Doesn't he annoy you?
UM ...
It doesn't embarrass me anymore
VALENTINE'S DAY...
...
...
MAY I ASK YOU SOMETHING?
WHAT ?
IS SOMETHING BOTHERING YOU?
IT'S NOT EXACTLY BOTHERING ME...
... BUT ...
... WHAT ABOUT ME...
...IS SO ATTRACTIVE?
YOU'RE CHEERFUL!
AND YOU'VE GOT A NICE SMILE!
DO YOU ...
... REALLY THINK SO?
SMILE
AS LONG AS YOU DON'T OPEN YOUR MOUTH, YOU'RE PRETTY.
R...
REALLY ?
GRIN
YOU'RE REALLY PUTTING THE "GRINCH" IN "GRIN" THERE.

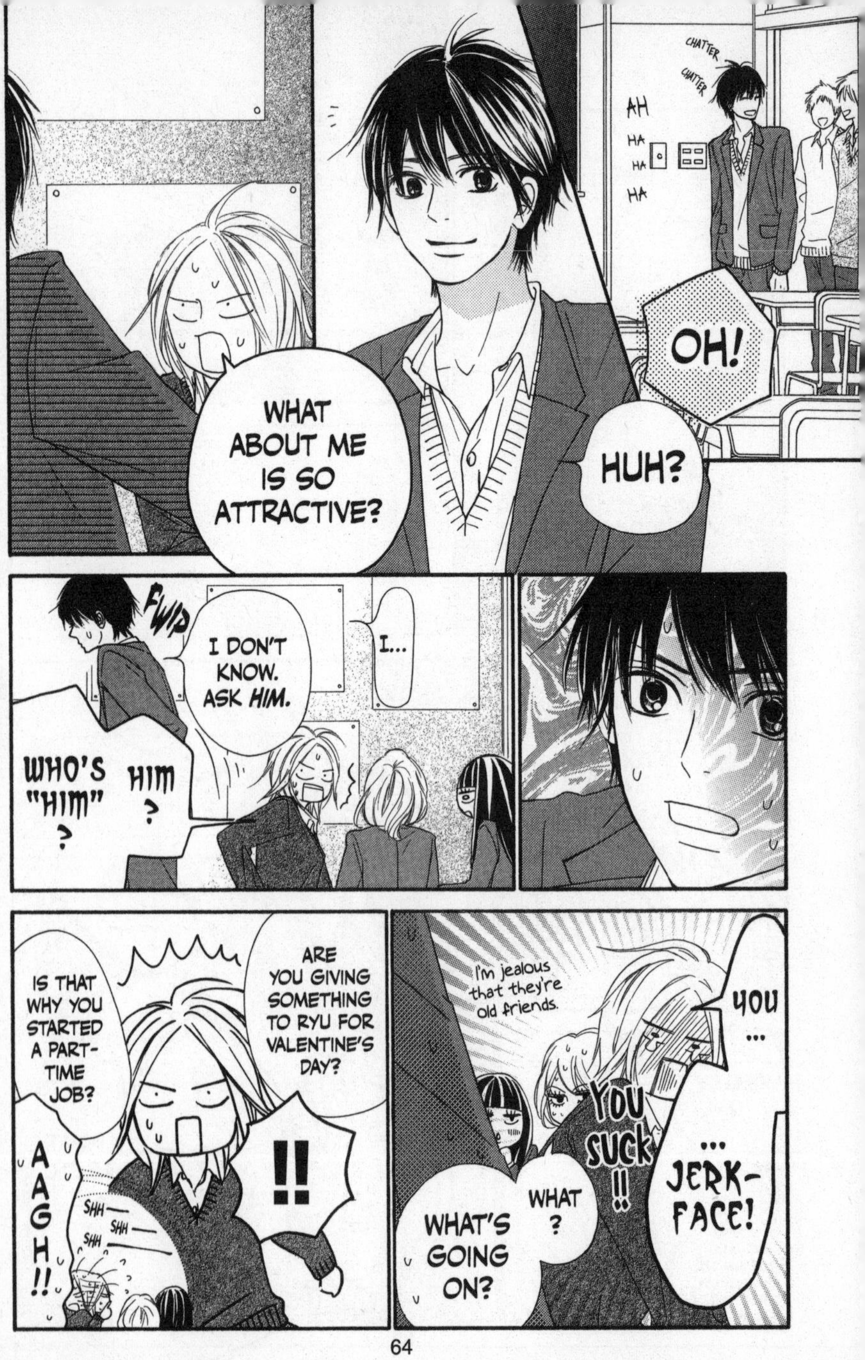
CHATTER
CHATTER
AH HA HA HA
OH!
HUH?
WHAT ABOUT ME IS SO ATTRACTIVE?
I...
I DON'T KNOW. ASK HIM.
FWIP
HIM?
WHO'S "HIM"?
YOU...
...JERK-FACE!
YOU SUCK!!
I'm jealous that they're old friends.
WHAT?
WHAT'S GOING ON?
ARE YOU GIVING SOMETHING TO RYU FOR VALENTINE'S DAY?
!!
IS THAT WHY YOU STARTED A PART-TIME JOB?
AAGH!!
SHH— SHH— SHH—

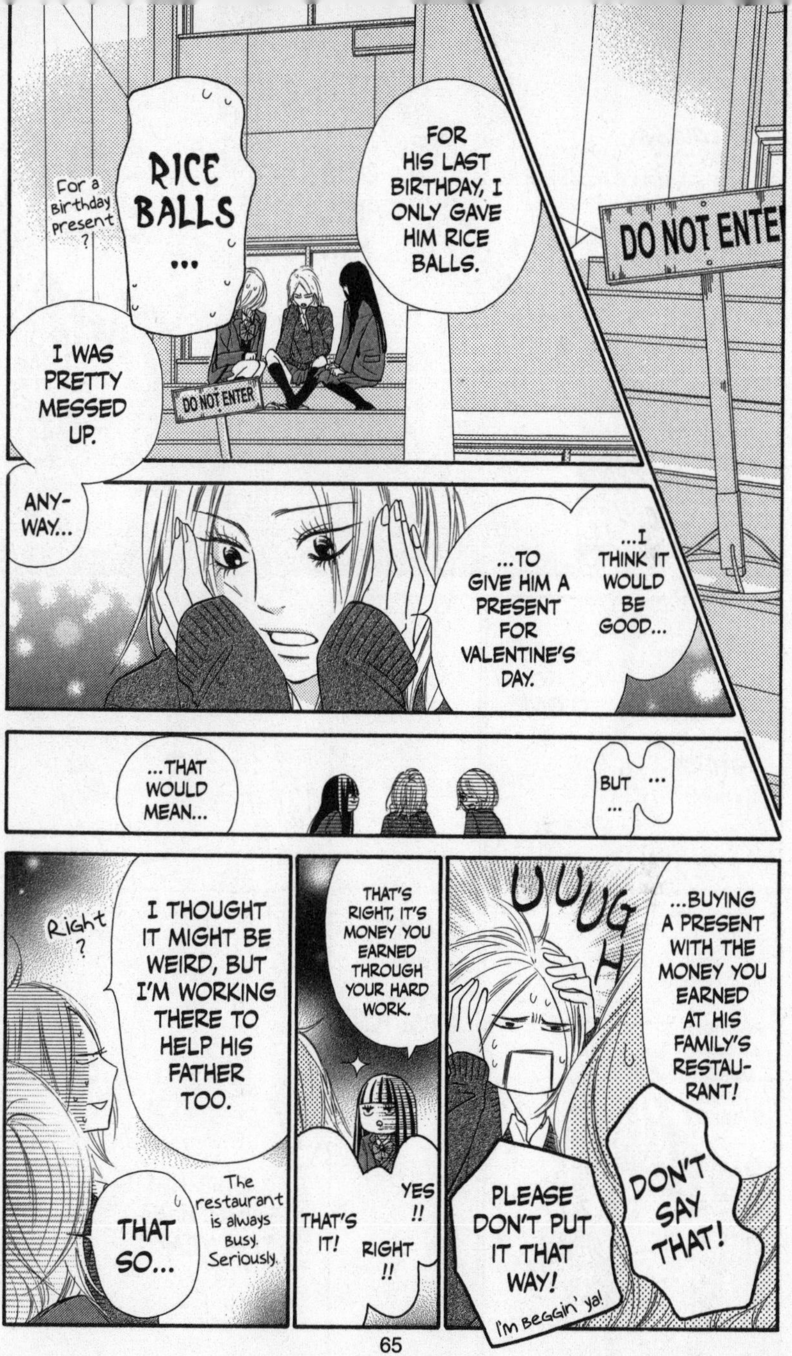
DO NOT ENTE
FOR HIS LAST BIRTHDAY, I ONLY GAVE HIM RICE BALLS.
RICE BALLS...
For a birthday present?
I WAS PRETTY MESSED UP.
DO NOT ENTER
ANY-WAY...
...I THINK IT WOULD BE GOOD...
...TO GIVE HIM A PRESENT FOR VALENTINE'S DAY.
BUT...
...
...THAT WOULD MEAN...
...BUYING A PRESENT WITH THE MONEY YOU EARNED AT HIS FAMILY'S RESTAU-RANT!
UUUGH
DON'T SAY THAT!
PLEASE DON'T PUT IT THAT WAY!
I'm beggin' ya!
THAT'S RIGHT, IT'S MONEY YOU EARNED THROUGH YOUR HARD WORK.
YES!!
RIGHT!!
THAT'S IT!
I THOUGHT IT MIGHT BE WEIRD, BUT I'M WORKING THERE TO HELP HIS FATHER TOO.
Right?
The restaurant is always busy. Seriously.
THAT SO...

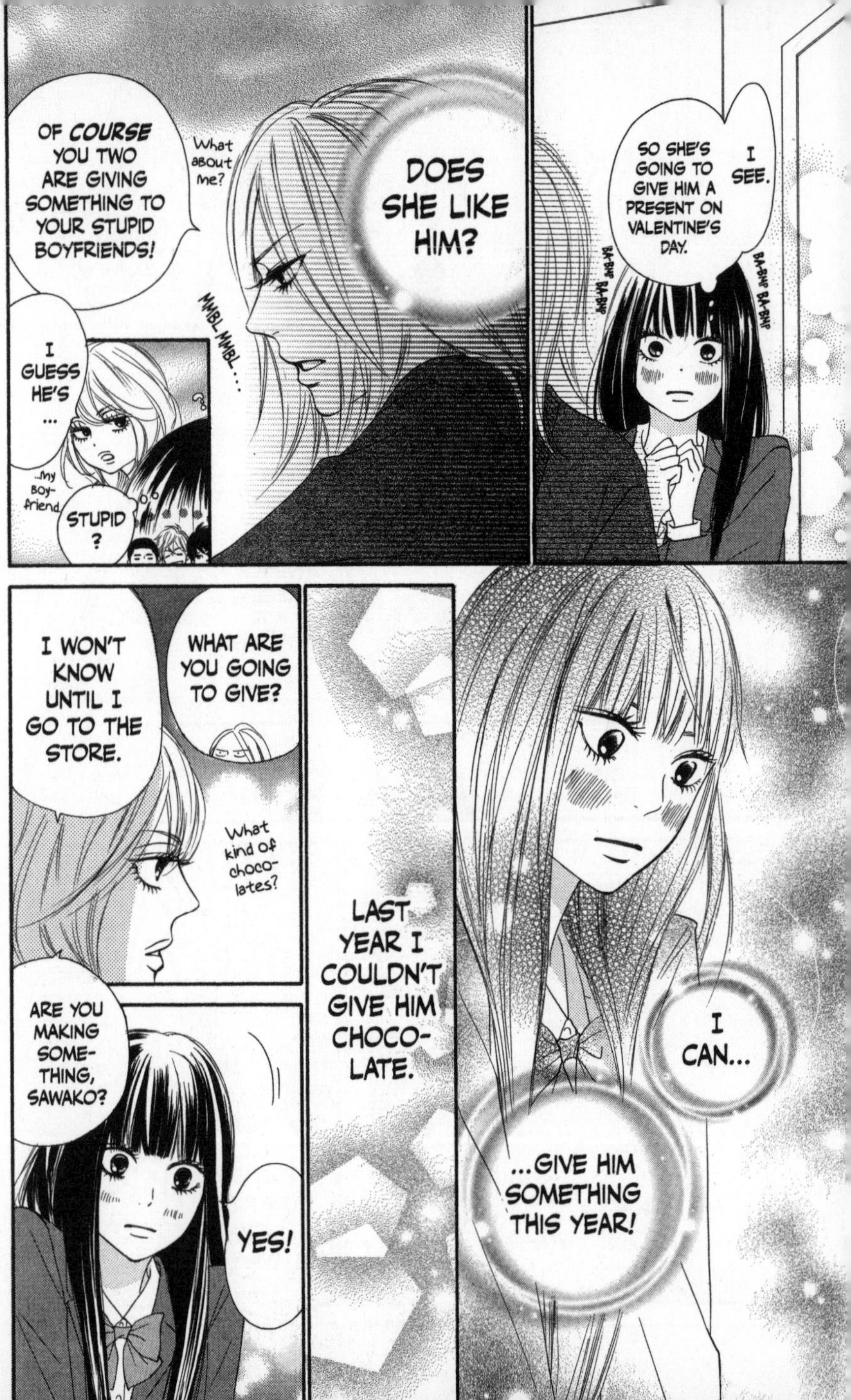
SO SHE'S GOING TO GIVE HIM A PRESENT ON VALENTINE'S DAY.
I SEE.
BA-BMP BA-BMP
BA-BMP BA-BMP
DOES SHE LIKE HIM?
MMBL MMBL...
What about me?
OF COURSE YOU TWO ARE GIVING SOMETHING TO YOUR STUPID BOYFRIENDS!
I GUESS HE'S ...
...My Boy-friend
STUPID?
I CAN...
...GIVE HIM SOMETHING THIS YEAR!
LAST YEAR I COULDN'T GIVE HIM CHOCO-LATE.
WHAT ARE YOU GOING TO GIVE?
I WON'T KNOW UNTIL I GO TO THE STORE.
What kind of choco-lates?
ARE YOU MAKING SOME-THING, SAWAKO?
YES!

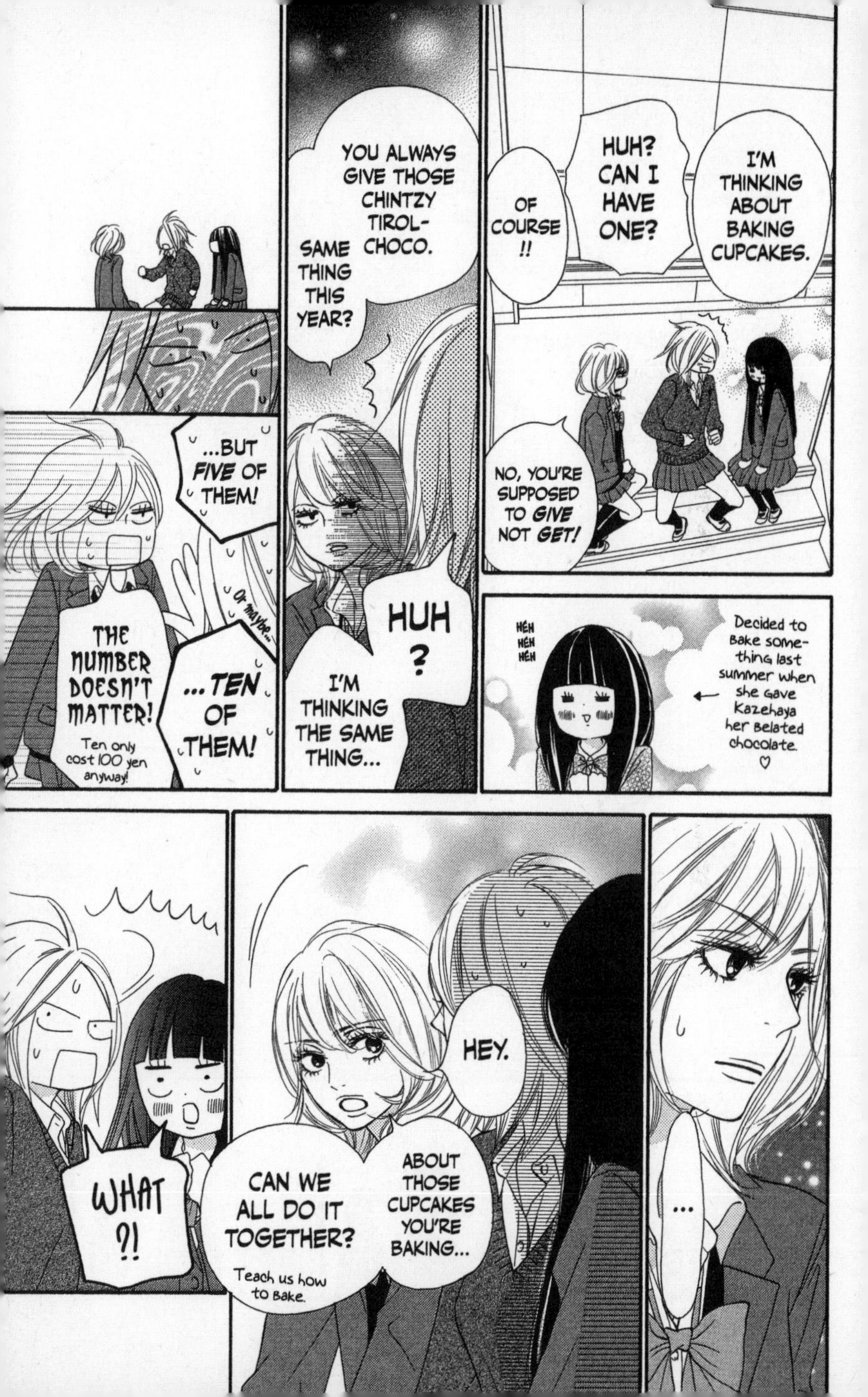
I'M THINKING ABOUT BAKING CUPCAKES.
HUH? CAN I HAVE ONE?
OF COURSE !!
NO, YOU'RE SUPPOSED TO GIVE NOT GET!
HEH HEH HEH
Decided to bake something last summer when she gave Kazehaya her belated chocolate. ♡
YOU ALWAYS GIVE THOSE CHINTZY TIROL-CHOCO.
SAME THING THIS YEAR?
HUH ?
I'M THINKING THE SAME THING...
...BUT FIVE OF THEM!
Or maybe...
...TEN OF THEM!
THE NUMBER DOESN'T MATTER!
Ten only cost 100 yen anyway!
...
HEY.
ABOUT THOSE CUPCAKES YOU'RE BAKING...
CAN WE ALL DO IT TOGETHER?
Teach us how to bake.
WHAT ?!

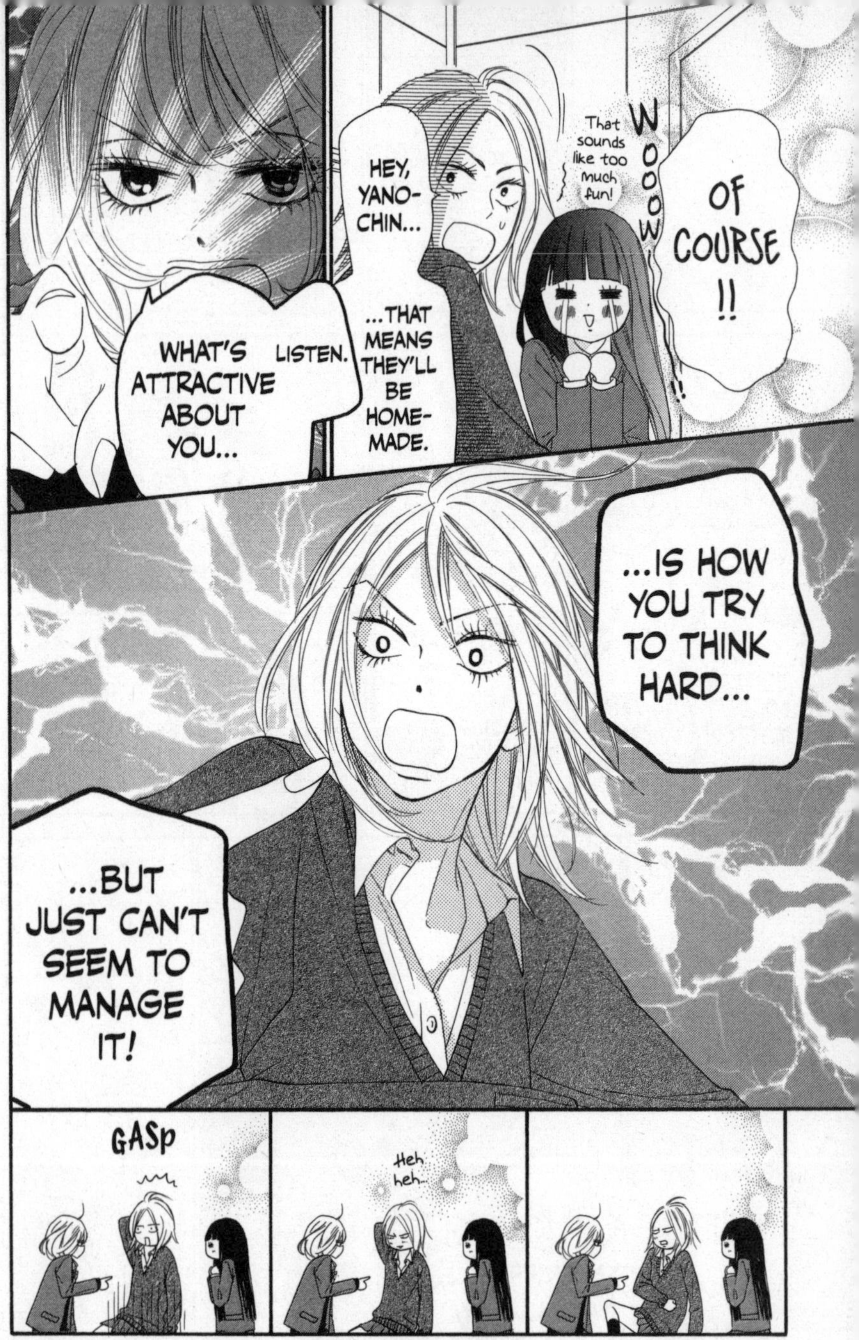
OF COURSE!!
WOOOW!!
That sounds like too much fun!
HEY, YANO-CHIN...
...THAT MEANS THEY'LL BE HOMEMADE.
LISTEN.
WHAT'S ATTRACTIVE ABOUT YOU...
...IS HOW YOU TRY TO THINK HARD...
...BUT JUST CAN'T SEEM TO MANAGE IT!
Heh heh..
GASp

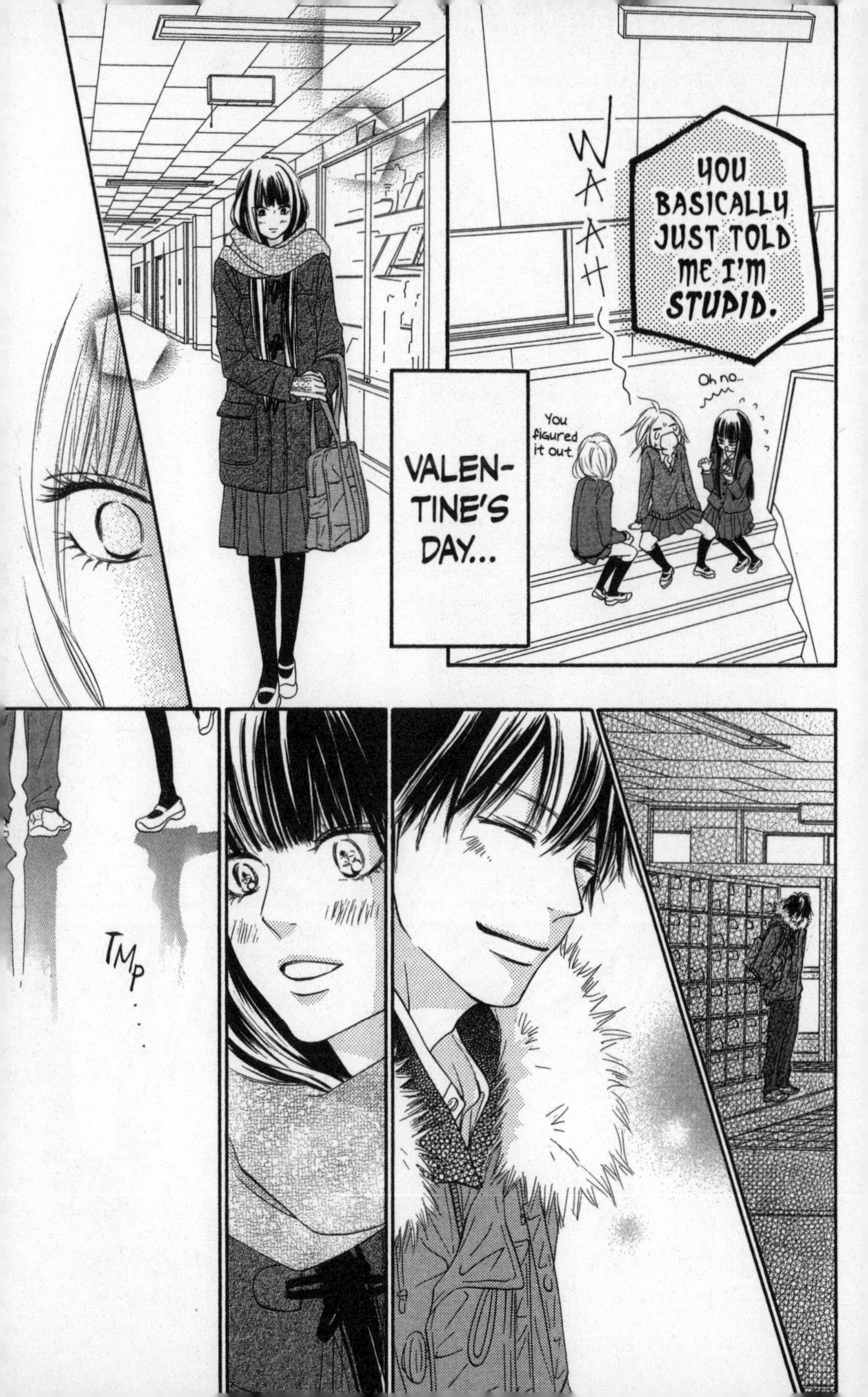
YOU BASICALLY JUST TOLD ME I'M STUPID.
WAAH
Oh no...
You figured it out.
VALEN-TINE'S DAY...
TMP

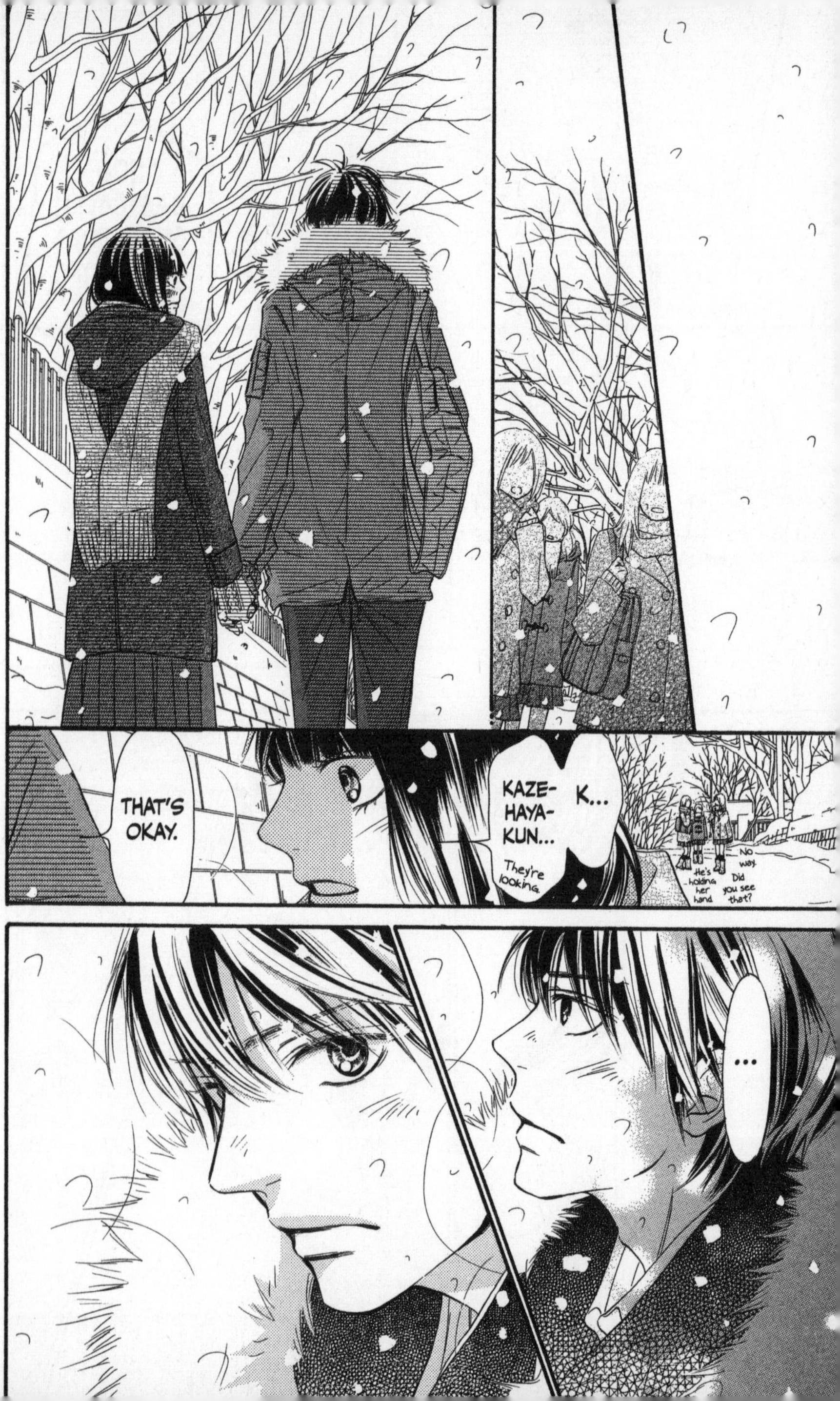
No way.
Did you see that?
He's holding her hand
K...
KAZE-HAYA-KUN...
They're looking.
THAT'S OKAY.
...

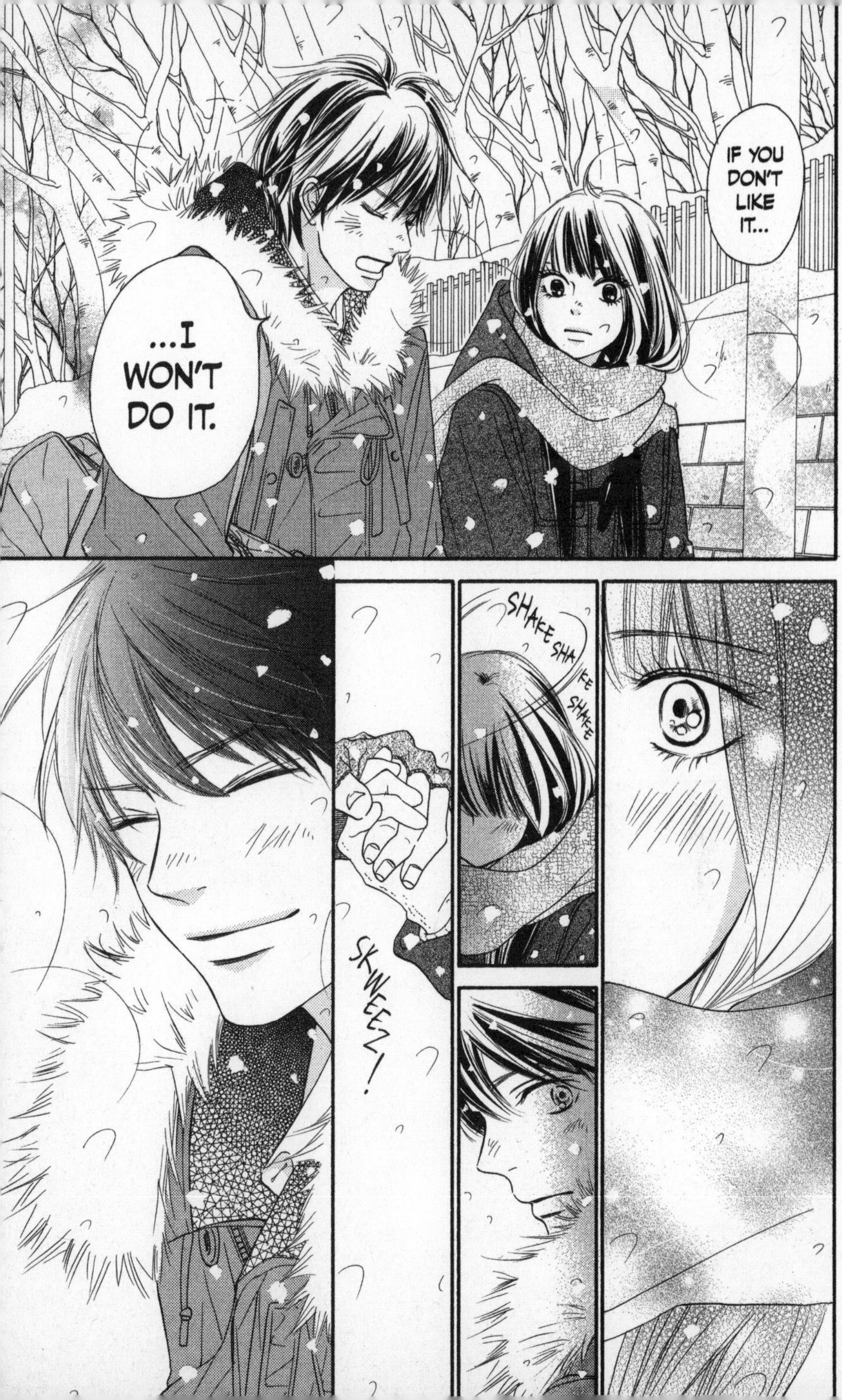
IF YOU DON'T LIKE IT...
...I WON'T DO IT.
SHAKE SHAKE SHAKE
SKWEEZ!

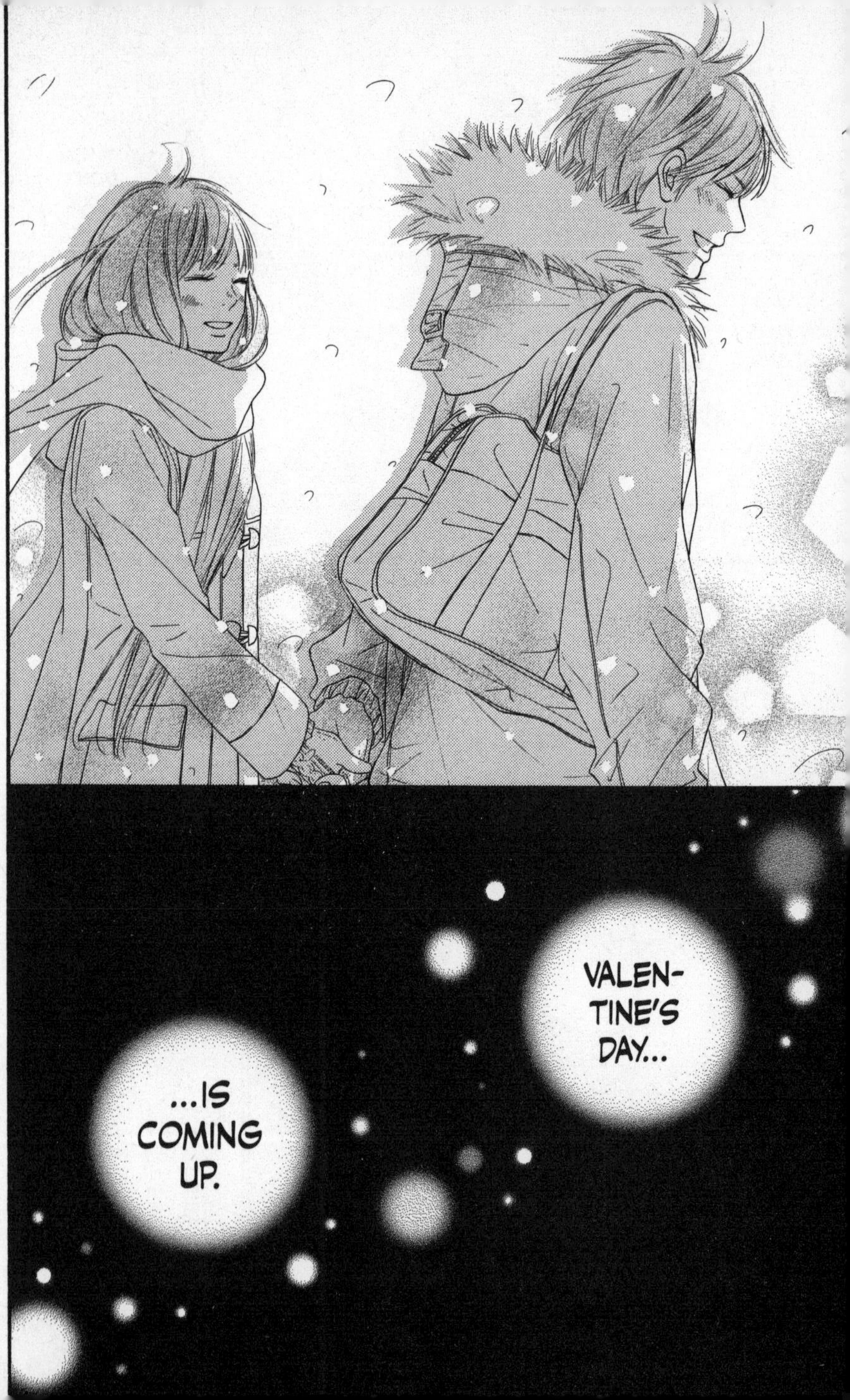
VALEN-TINE'S DAY...
...IS COMING UP.

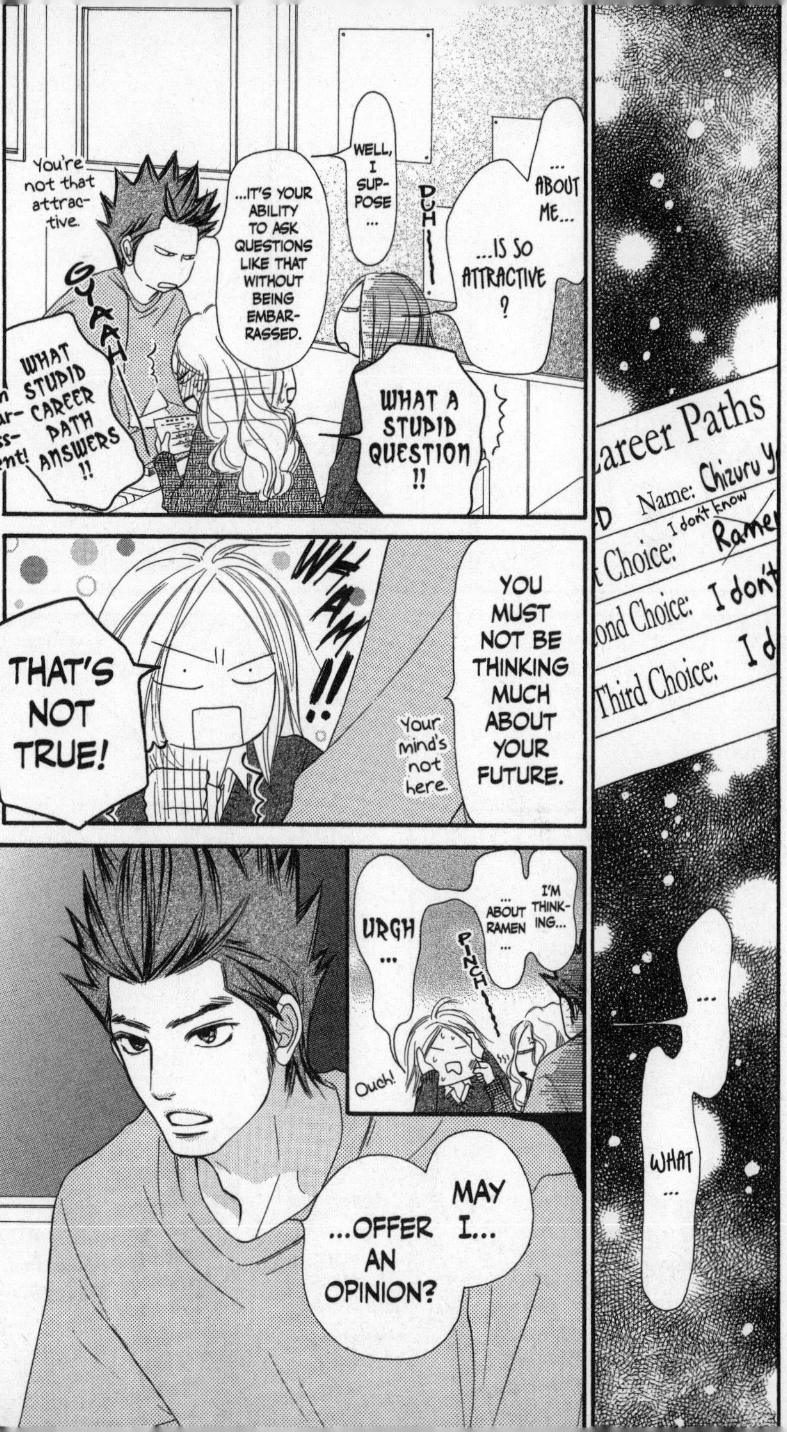
areer Paths
Name: Chizuru Y
Choice: I don't know Ramen
ond Choice: I don't
Third Choice: I d
...
WHAT...
...ABOUT ME...
...IS SO ATTRACTIVE?
DUH—
WELL, I SUPPOSE...
...IT'S YOUR ABILITY TO ASK QUESTIONS LIKE THAT WITHOUT BEING EMBARRASSED.
You're not that attractive.
WHAT A STUPID QUESTION!!
GYAAH
WHAT STUPID CAREER PATH ANSWERS!!
This is an embarrassment!
YOU MUST NOT BE THINKING MUCH ABOUT YOUR FUTURE.
Your mind's not here.
WHAM!!
THAT'S NOT TRUE!
I'M THINKING...
...ABOUT RAMEN...
PINCH—
URGH...
Ouch!
MAY I...
...OFFER AN OPINION?

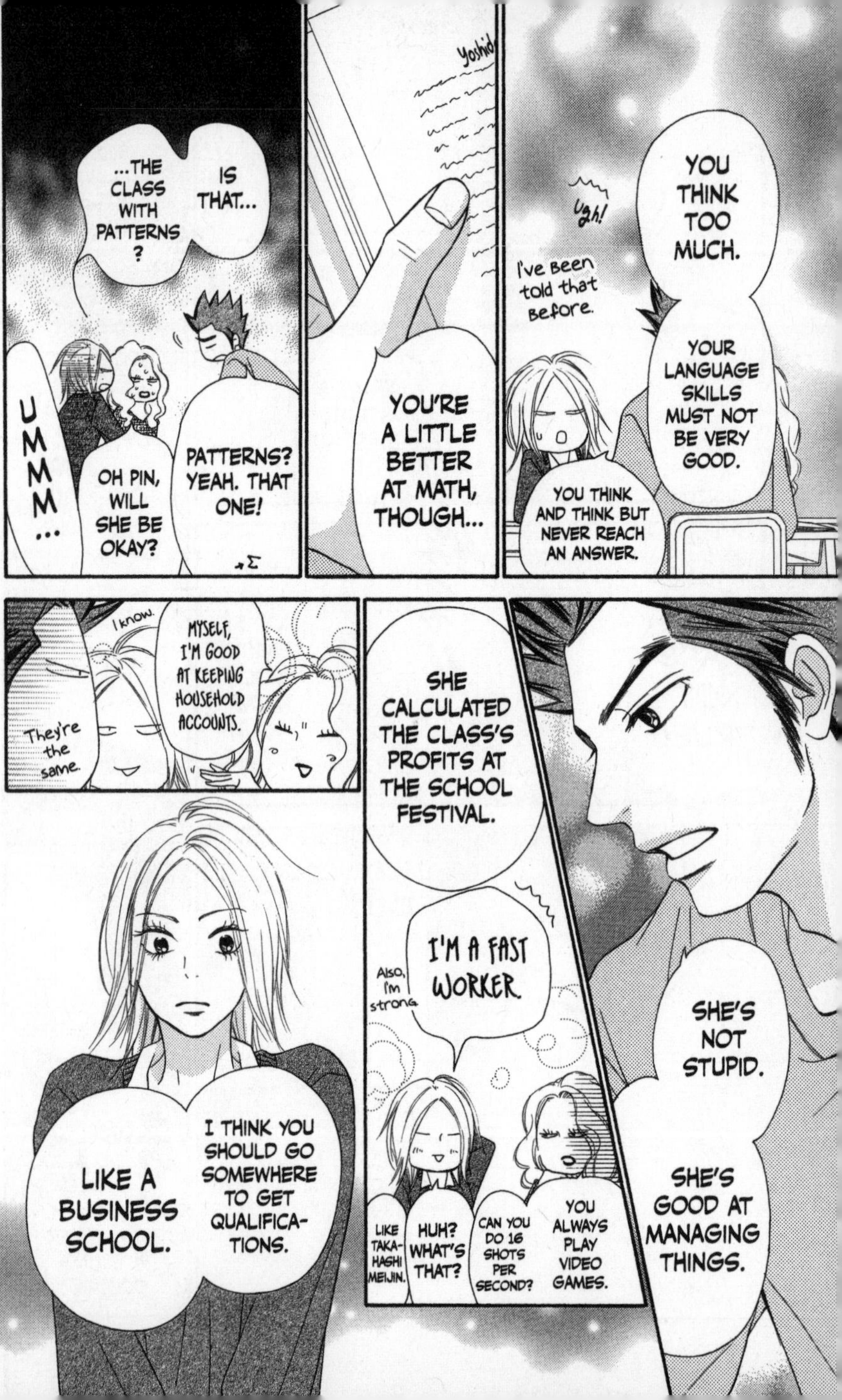
YOU THINK TOO MUCH.
YOUR LANGUAGE SKILLS MUST NOT BE VERY GOOD.
Ugh!
I've been told that before.
YOU THINK AND THINK BUT NEVER REACH AN ANSWER.
Yoshid
YOU'RE A LITTLE BETTER AT MATH, THOUGH...
IS THAT...
...THE CLASS WITH PATTERNS?
PATTERNS? YEAH. THAT ONE!
OH PIN, WILL SHE BE OKAY?
UMMM...
SHE'S NOT STUPID.
SHE'S GOOD AT MANAGING THINGS.
SHE CALCULATED THE CLASS'S PROFITS AT THE SCHOOL FESTIVAL.
I'M A FAST WORKER.
Also, I'm strong.
YOU ALWAYS PLAY VIDEO GAMES.
CAN YOU DO 16 SHOTS PER SECOND?
HUH? WHAT'S THAT?
LIKE TAKAHASHI MEIJIN.
I know.
MYSELF, I'M GOOD AT KEEPING HOUSEHOLD ACCOUNTS.
They're the same.
I THINK YOU SHOULD GO SOMEWHERE TO GET QUALIFICATIONS.
LIKE A BUSINESS SCHOOL.

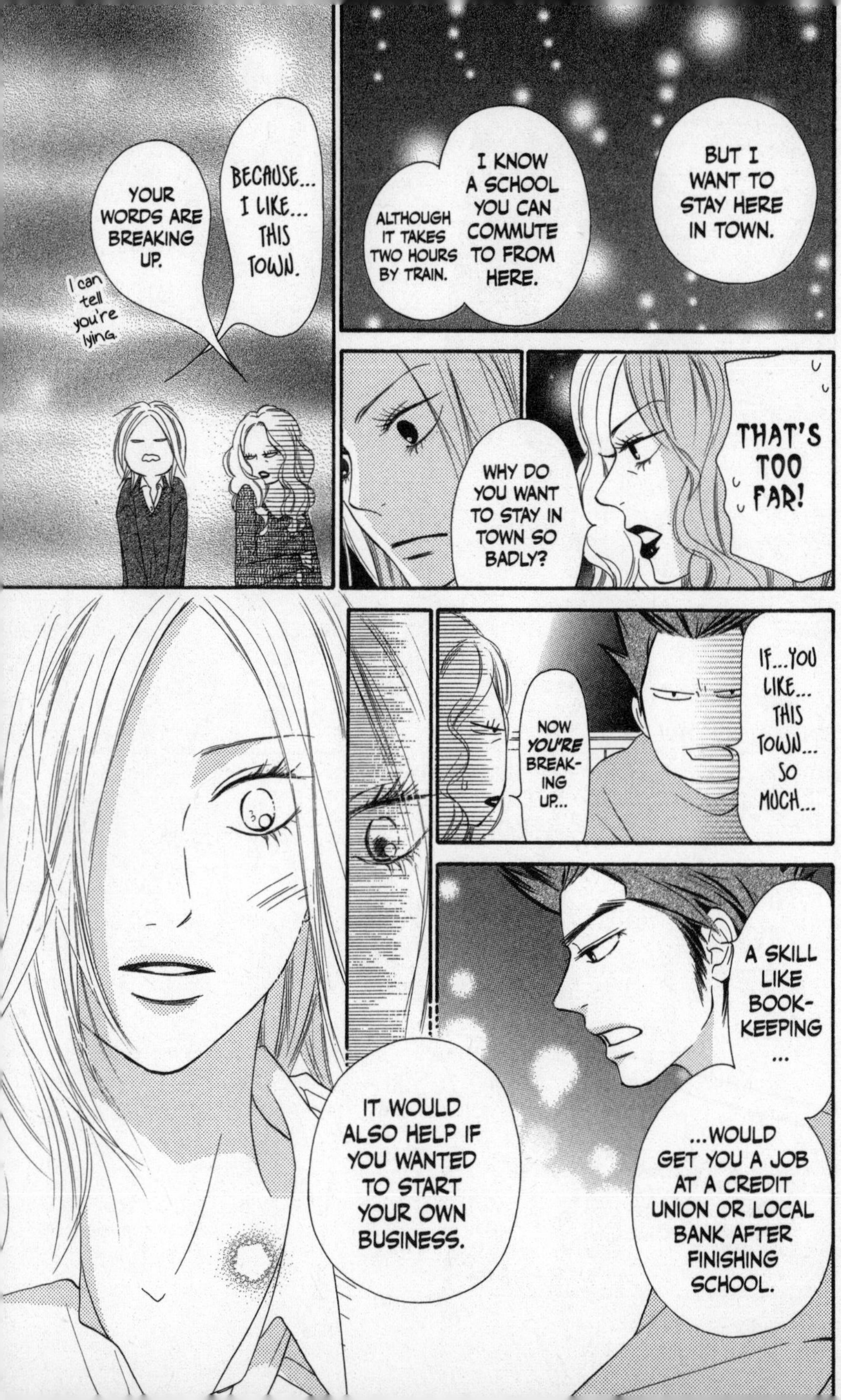
BUT I WANT TO STAY HERE IN TOWN.
I KNOW A SCHOOL YOU CAN COMMUTE TO FROM HERE.
ALTHOUGH IT TAKES TWO HOURS BY TRAIN.
THAT'S TOO FAR!
WHY DO YOU WANT TO STAY IN TOWN SO BADLY?
BECAUSE... I LIKE... THIS TOWN.
YOUR WORDS ARE BREAKING UP.
I can tell you're lying.
IF...YOU LIKE... THIS TOWN... SO MUCH...
NOW *YOU'RE* BREAKING UP...
A SKILL LIKE BOOK-KEEPING ...
...WOULD GET YOU A JOB AT A CREDIT UNION OR LOCAL BANK AFTER FINISHING SCHOOL.
IT WOULD ALSO HELP IF YOU WANTED TO START YOUR OWN BUSINESS.

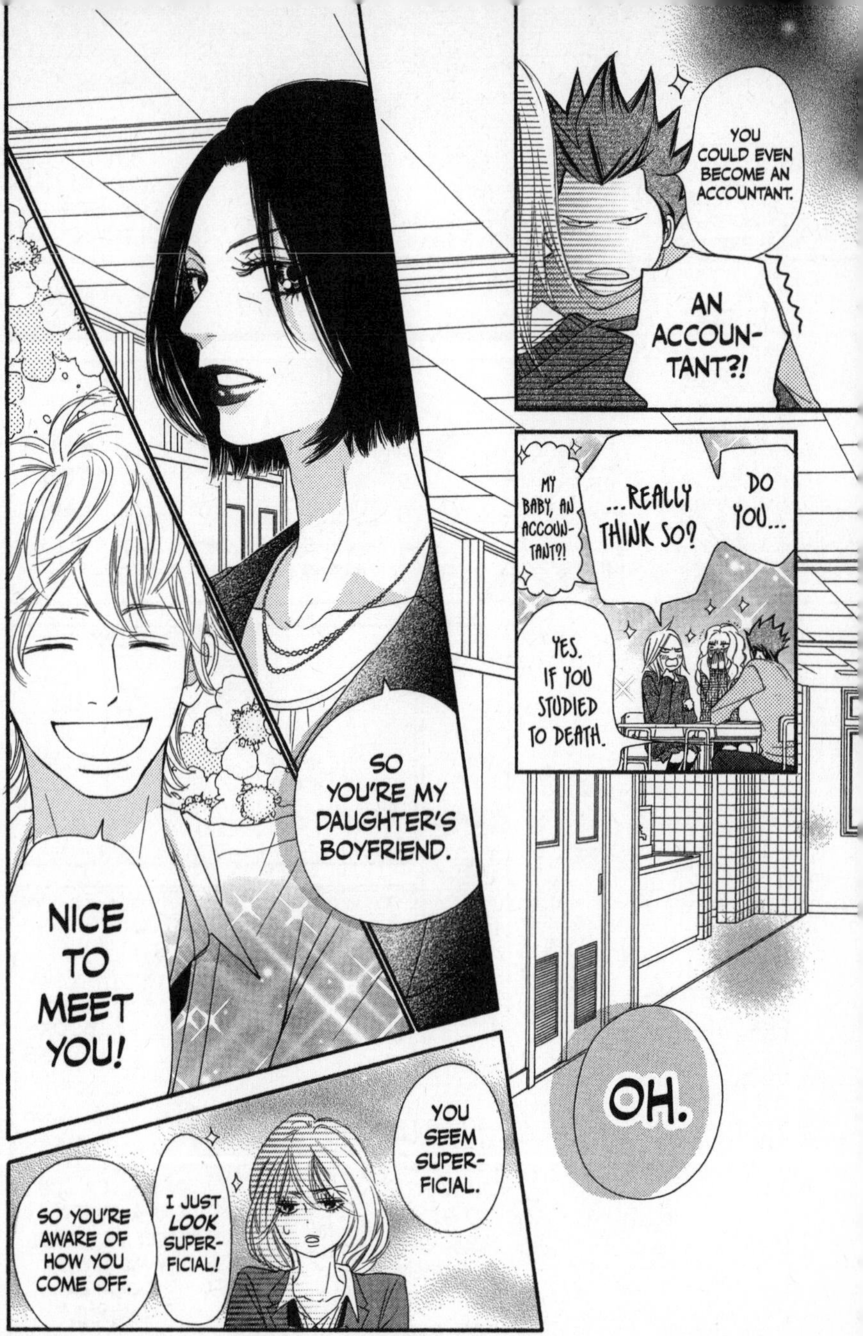
YOU COULD EVEN BECOME AN ACCOUNTANT.
AN ACCOUN-TANT?!
DO YOU...
...REALLY THINK SO?
MY BABY, AN ACCOUN-TANT?!
YES. IF YOU STUDIED TO DEATH.
OH.
SO YOU'RE MY DAUGHTER'S BOYFRIEND.
NICE TO MEET YOU!
YOU SEEM SUPER-FICIAL.
I JUST *LOOK* SUPER-FICIAL!
SO YOU'RE AWARE OF HOW YOU COME OFF.

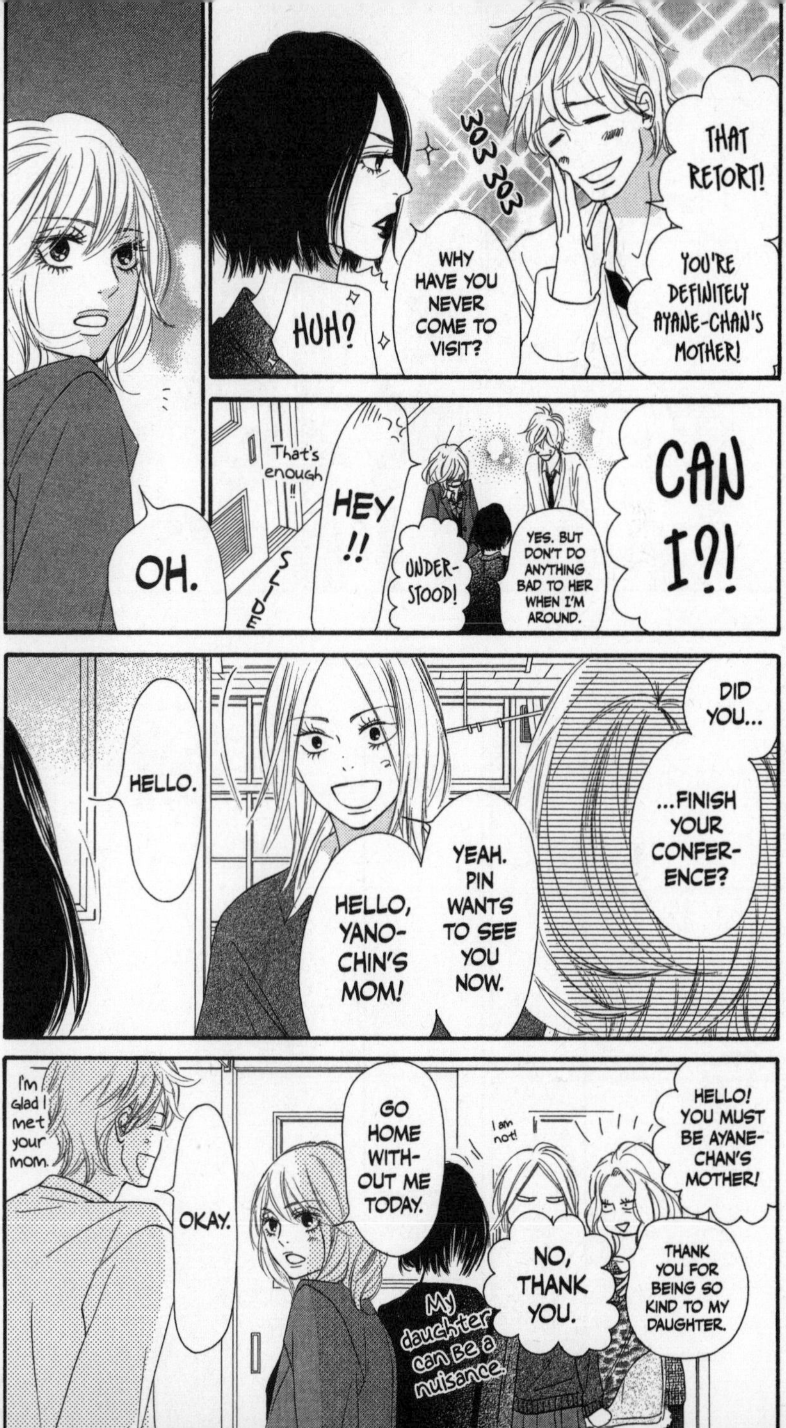
THAT RETORT!
YOU'RE DEFINITELY AYANE-CHAN'S MOTHER!
303 303
WHY HAVE YOU NEVER COME TO VISIT?
HUH?
CAN I?!
YES. BUT DON'T DO ANYTHING BAD TO HER WHEN I'M AROUND.
UNDER-STOOD!
HEY!!
That's enough!!
SLIDE
OH.
DID YOU...
...FINISH YOUR CONFER-ENCE?
YEAH. PIN WANTS TO SEE YOU NOW.
HELLO, YANO-CHIN'S MOM!
HELLO.
HELLO! YOU MUST BE AYANE-CHAN'S MOTHER!
THANK YOU FOR BEING SO KIND TO MY DAUGHTER.
I am not!
NO, THANK YOU.
My daughter can be a nuisance.
GO HOME WITH-OUT ME TODAY.
OKAY.
I'm glad I met your mom.

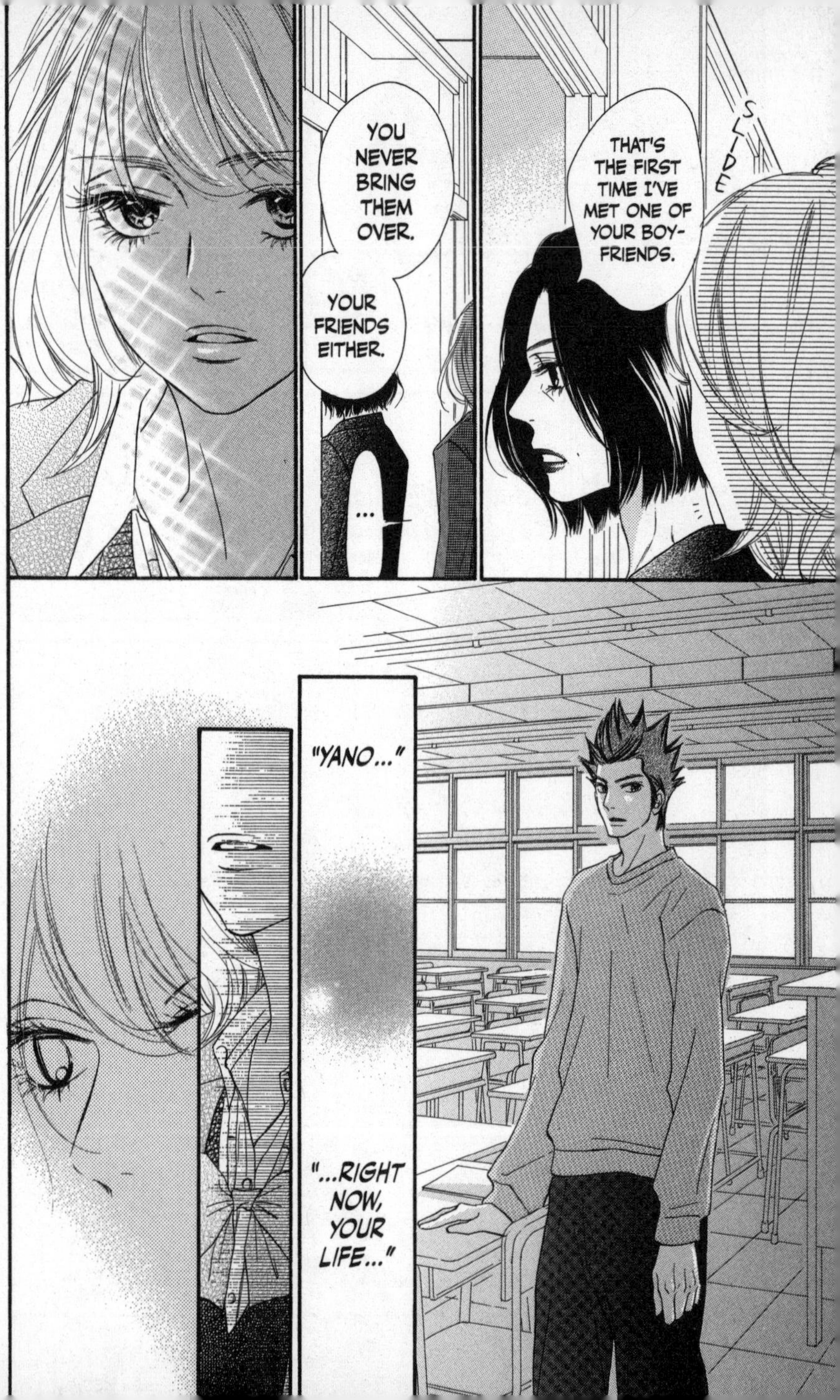
SLIDE
THAT'S THE FIRST TIME I'VE MET ONE OF YOUR BOY-FRIENDS.
YOU NEVER BRING THEM OVER.
YOUR FRIENDS EITHER.
...
"YANO..."
"...RIGHT NOW, YOUR LIFE..."

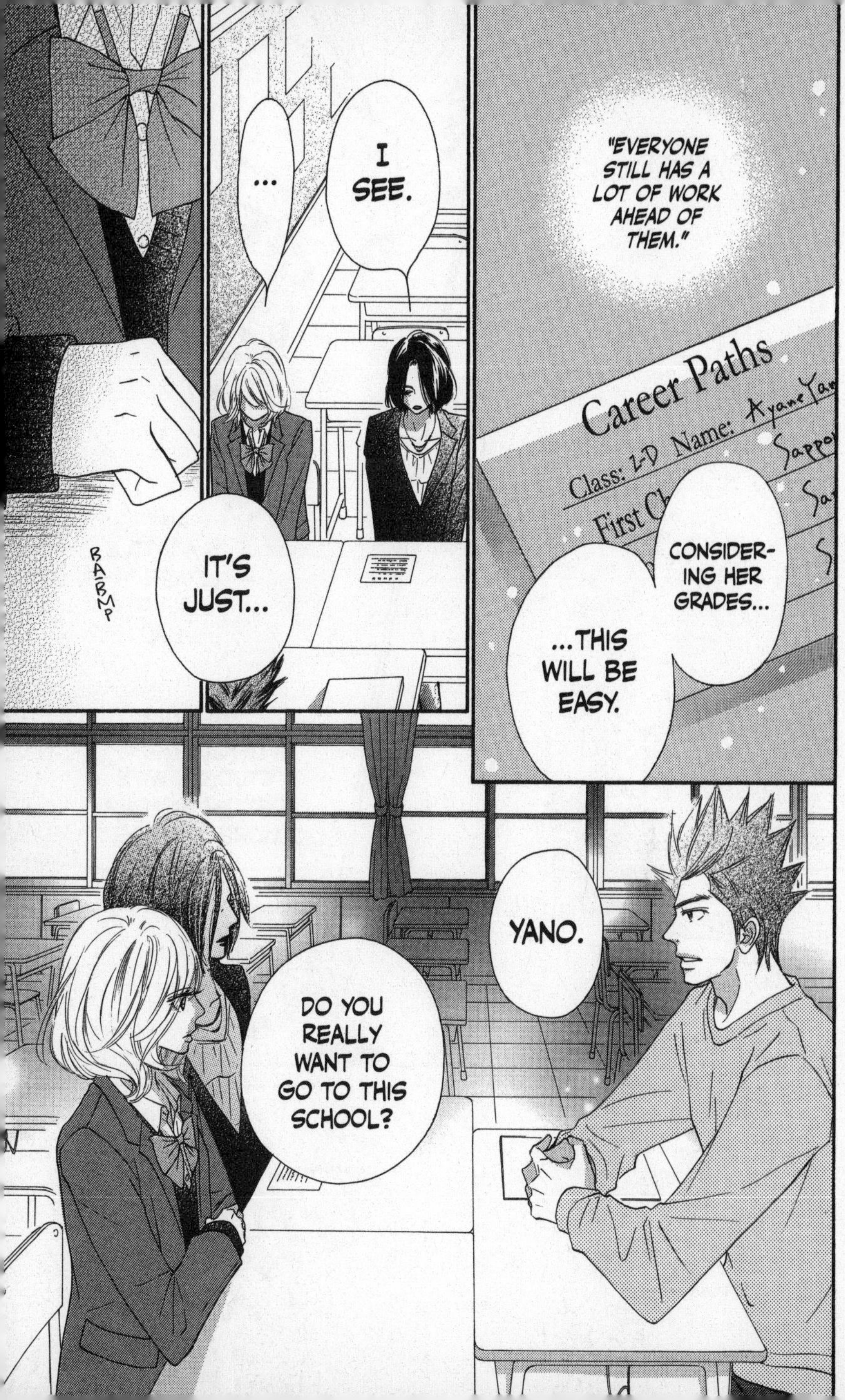
"EVERYONE STILL HAS A LOT OF WORK AHEAD OF THEM."
Career Paths
Class: 2-D Name:
CONSIDER-ING HER GRADES...
...THIS WILL BE EASY.
I SEE.
...
IT'S JUST...
BABMP
YANO.
DO YOU REALLY WANT TO GO TO THIS SCHOOL?

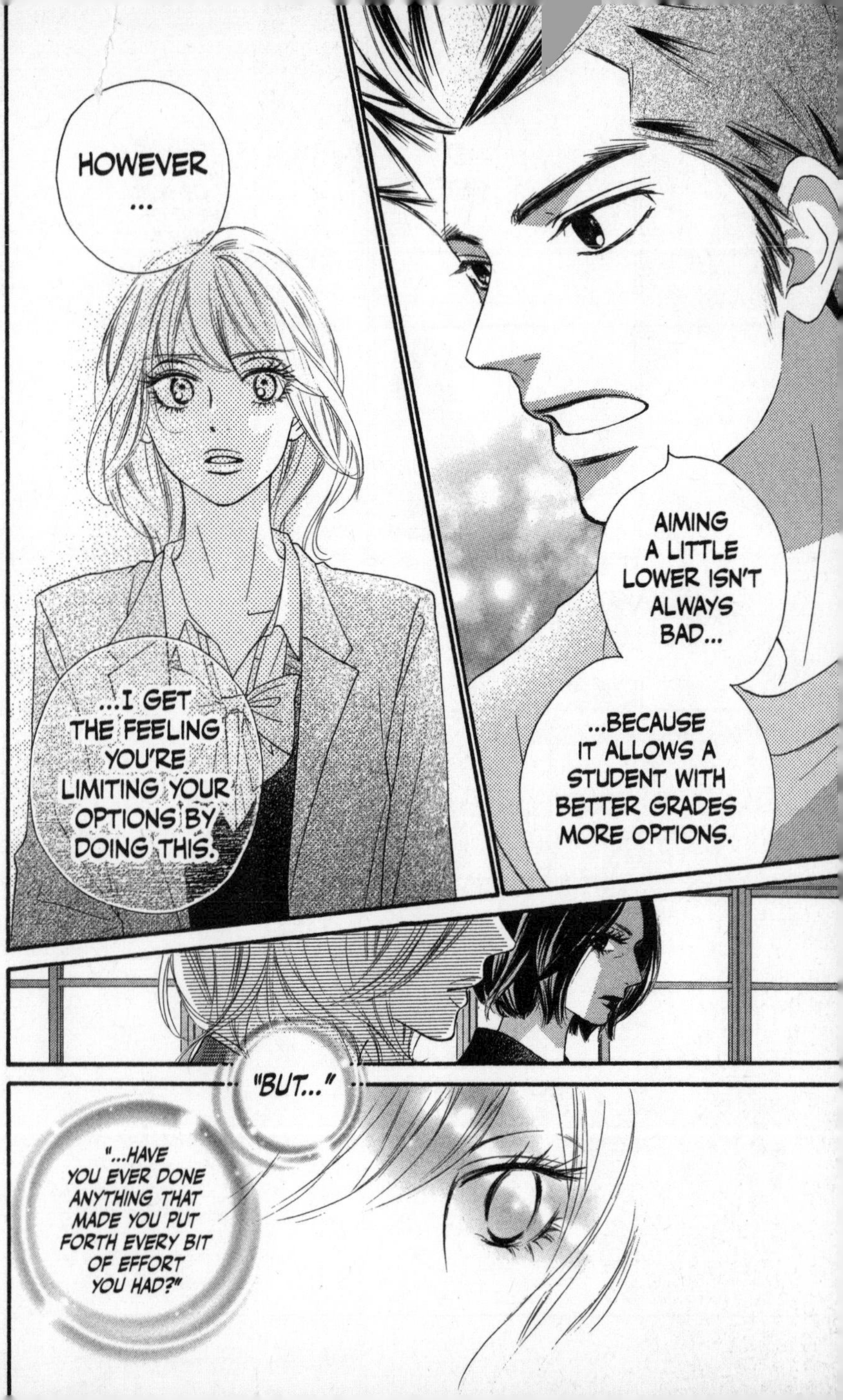
AIMING A LITTLE LOWER ISN'T ALWAYS BAD...
...BECAUSE IT ALLOWS A STUDENT WITH BETTER GRADES MORE OPTIONS.
HOWEVER...
...I GET THE FEELING YOU'RE LIMITING YOUR OPTIONS BY DOING THIS.
"BUT..."
"...HAVE YOU EVER DONE ANYTHING THAT MADE YOU PUT FORTH EVERY BIT OF EFFORT YOU HAD?"

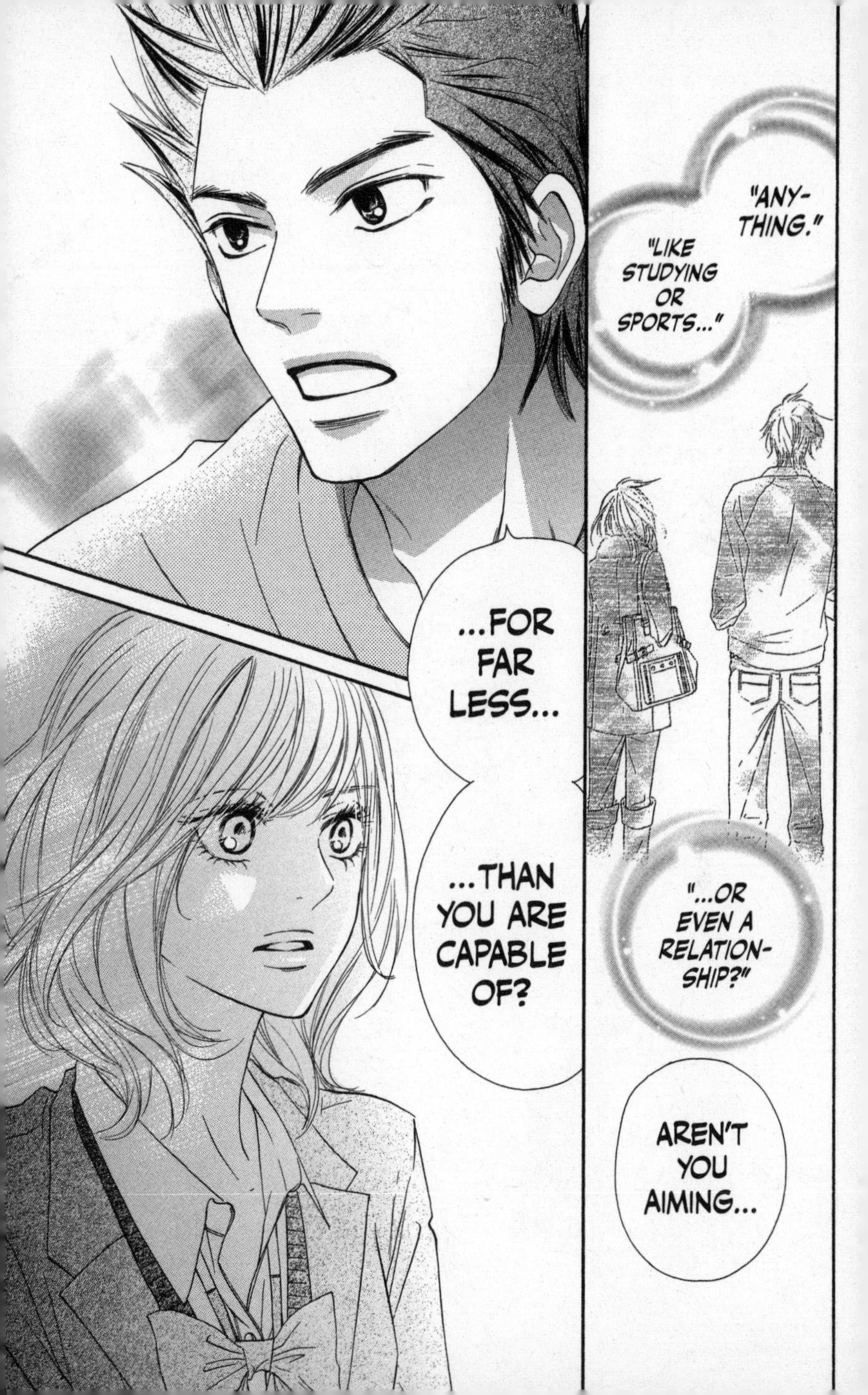
"ANY-THING."
"LIKE STUDYING OR SPORTS..."
"...OR EVEN A RELATION-SHIP?"
AREN'T YOU AIMING...
...FOR FAR LESS...
...THAN YOU ARE CAPABLE OF?

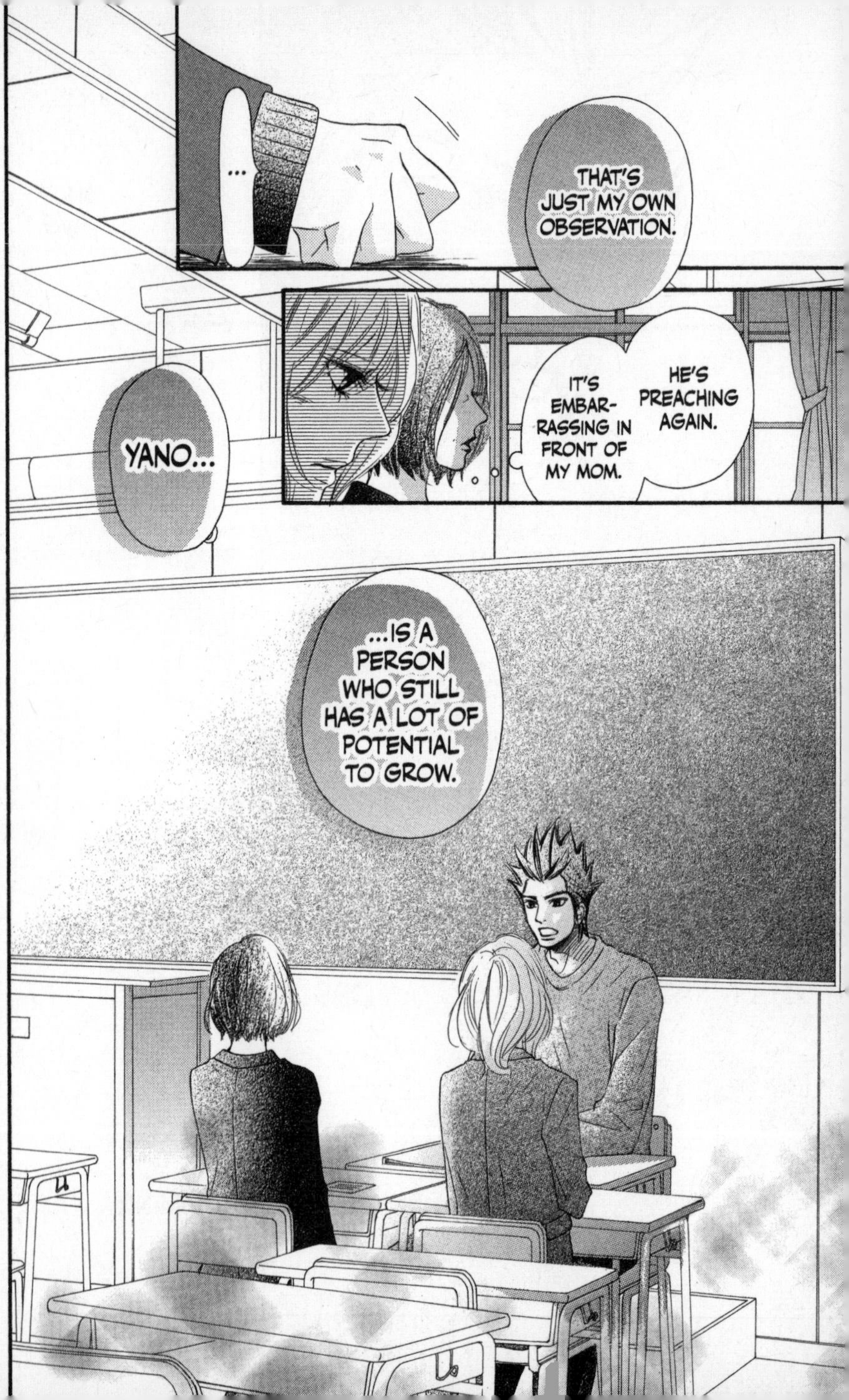
THAT'S JUST MY OWN OBSERVATION.
...
HE'S PREACHING AGAIN.
IT'S EMBAR-RASSING IN FRONT OF MY MOM.
YANO...
...IS A PERSON WHO STILL HAS A LOT OF POTENTIAL TO GROW.

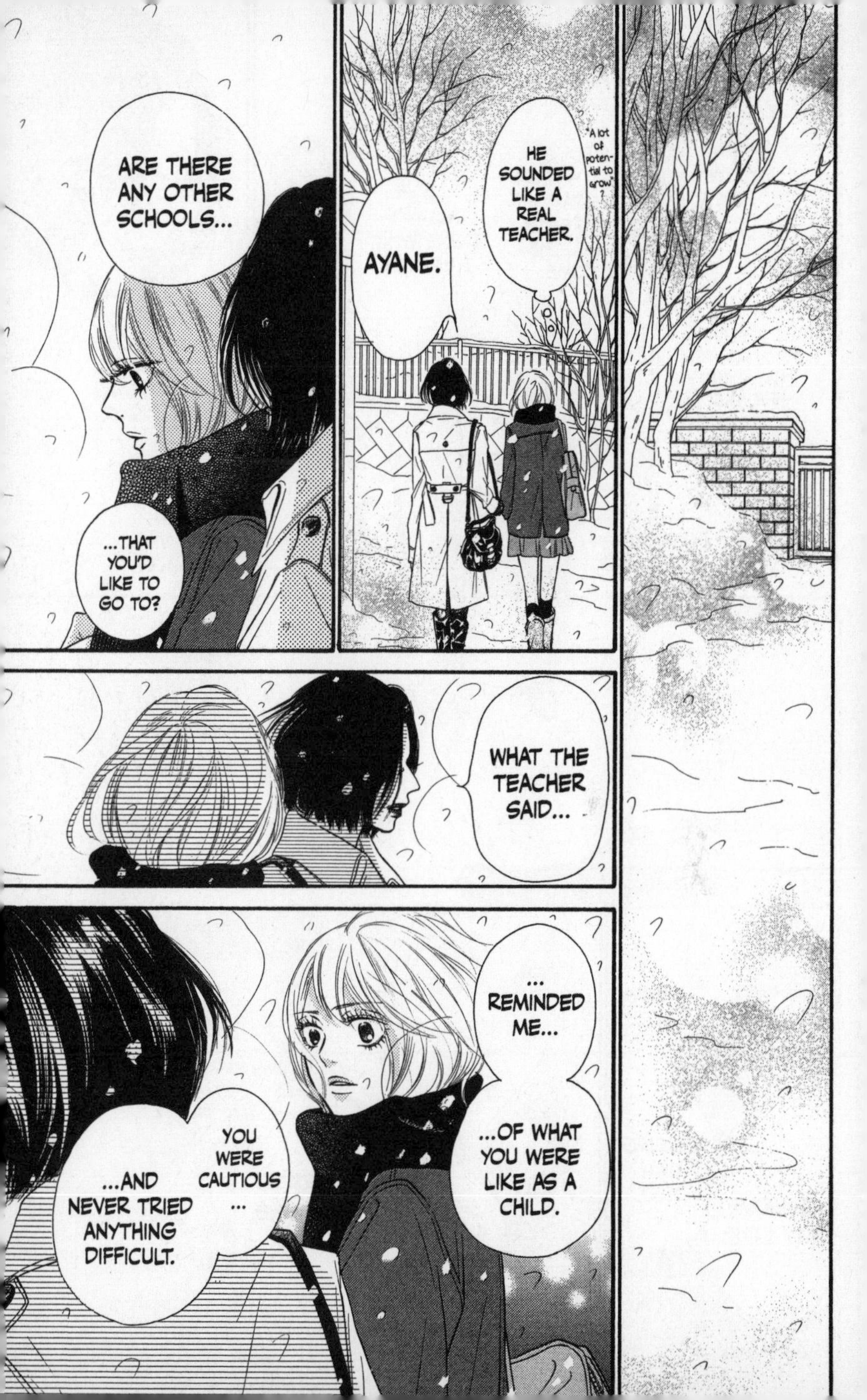
"A lot of potential to grow"?
HE SOUNDED LIKE A REAL TEACHER.
AYANE.
ARE THERE ANY OTHER SCHOOLS...
...THAT YOU'D LIKE TO GO TO?
WHAT THE TEACHER SAID...
...REMINDED ME...
...OF WHAT YOU WERE LIKE AS A CHILD.
YOU WERE CAUTIOUS...
...AND NEVER TRIED ANYTHING DIFFICULT.

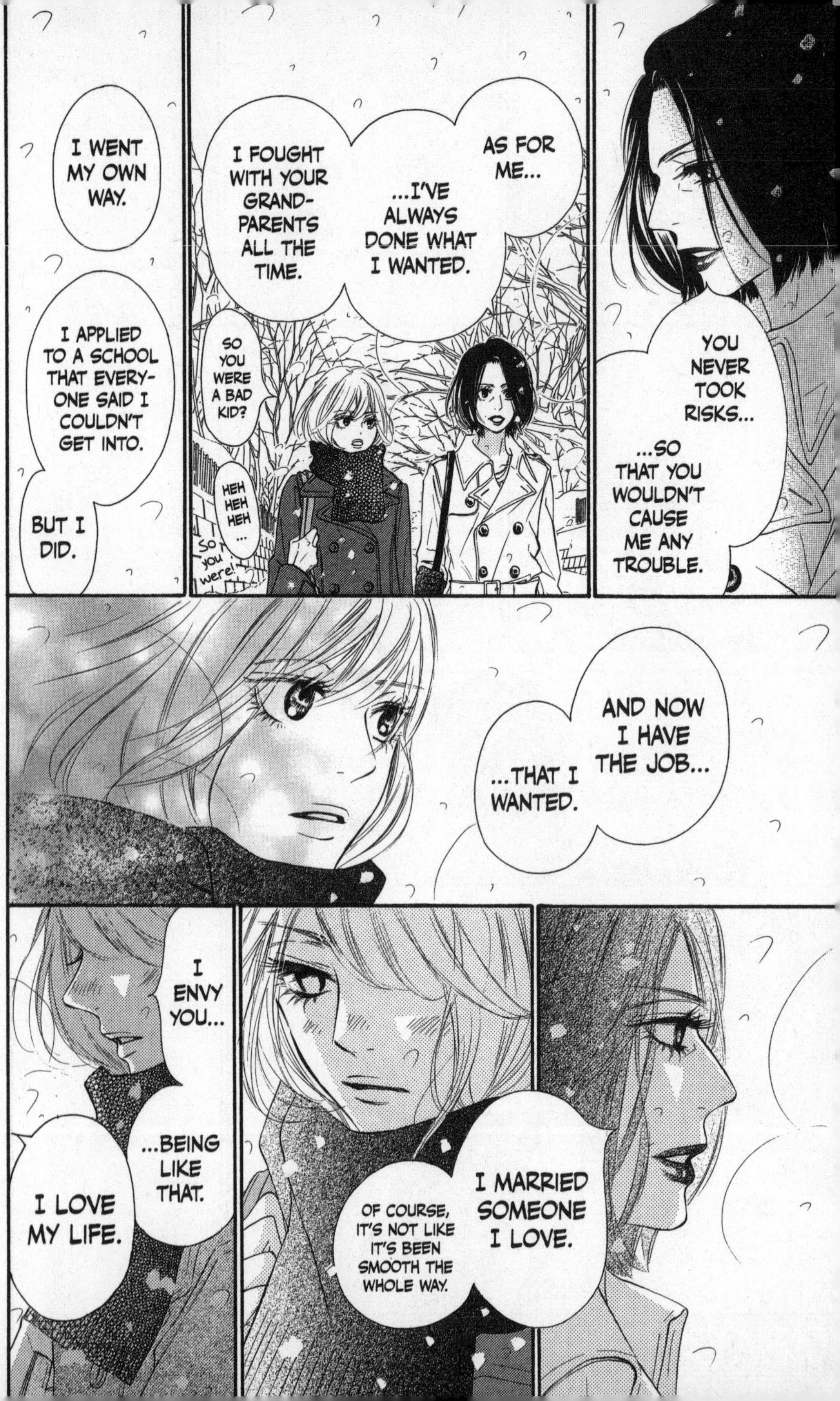
YOU NEVER TOOK RISKS...
...SO THAT YOU WOULDN'T CAUSE ME ANY TROUBLE.
AS FOR ME...
...I'VE ALWAYS DONE WHAT I WANTED.
I FOUGHT WITH YOUR GRAND-PARENTS ALL THE TIME.
SO YOU WERE A BAD KID?
HEH HEH HEH...
So you were!
I WENT MY OWN WAY.
I APPLIED TO A SCHOOL THAT EVERY-ONE SAID I COULDN'T GET INTO.
BUT I DID.
AND NOW I HAVE THE JOB...
...THAT I WANTED.
I MARRIED SOMEONE I LOVE.
OF COURSE, IT'S NOT LIKE IT'S BEEN SMOOTH THE WHOLE WAY.
I ENVY YOU...
...BEING LIKE THAT.
I LOVE MY LIFE.

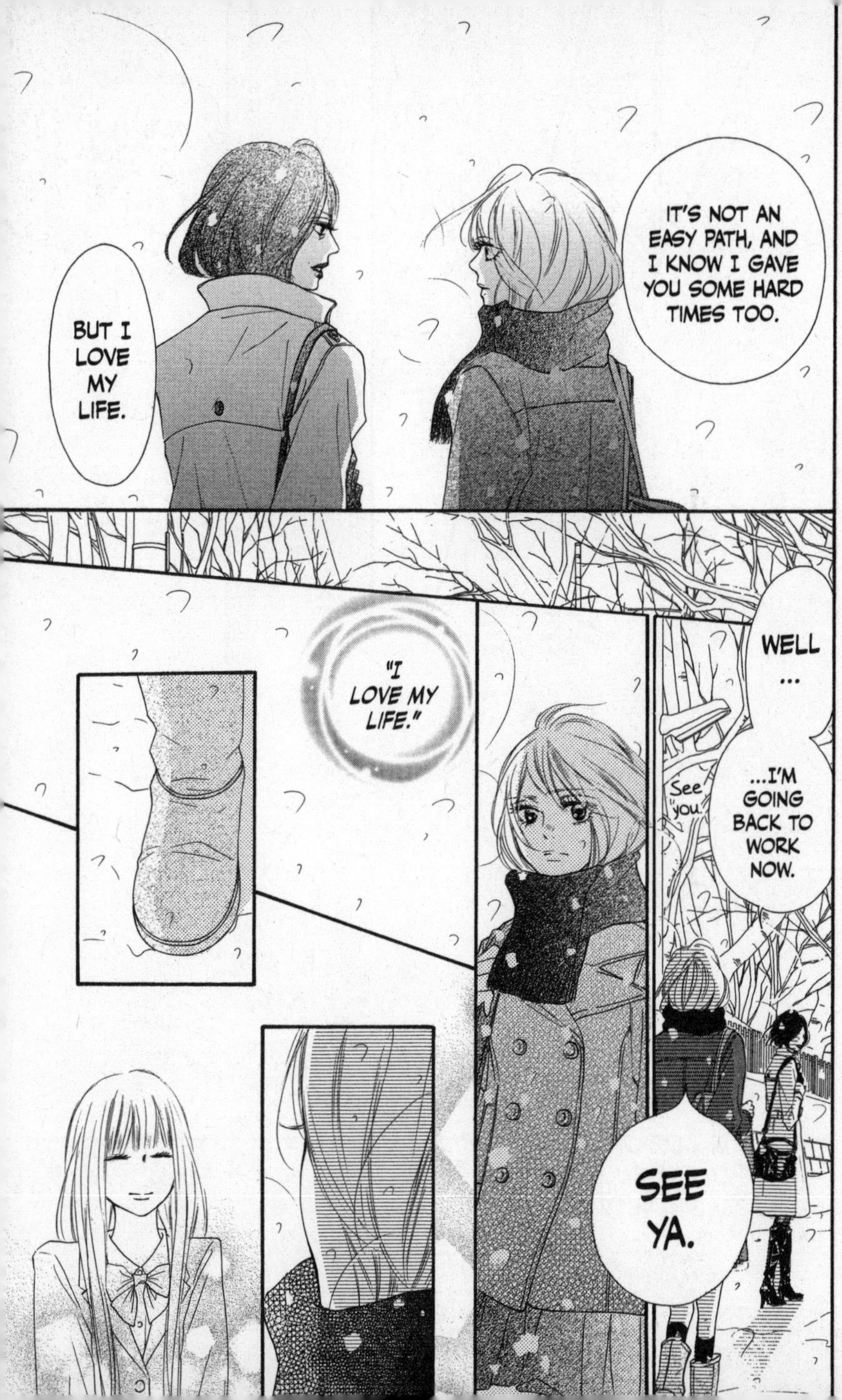
IT'S NOT AN EASY PATH, AND I KNOW I GAVE YOU SOME HARD TIMES TOO.
BUT I LOVE MY LIFE.
WELL ...
...I'M GOING BACK TO WORK NOW.
See you.
SEE YA.
"I LOVE MY LIFE."

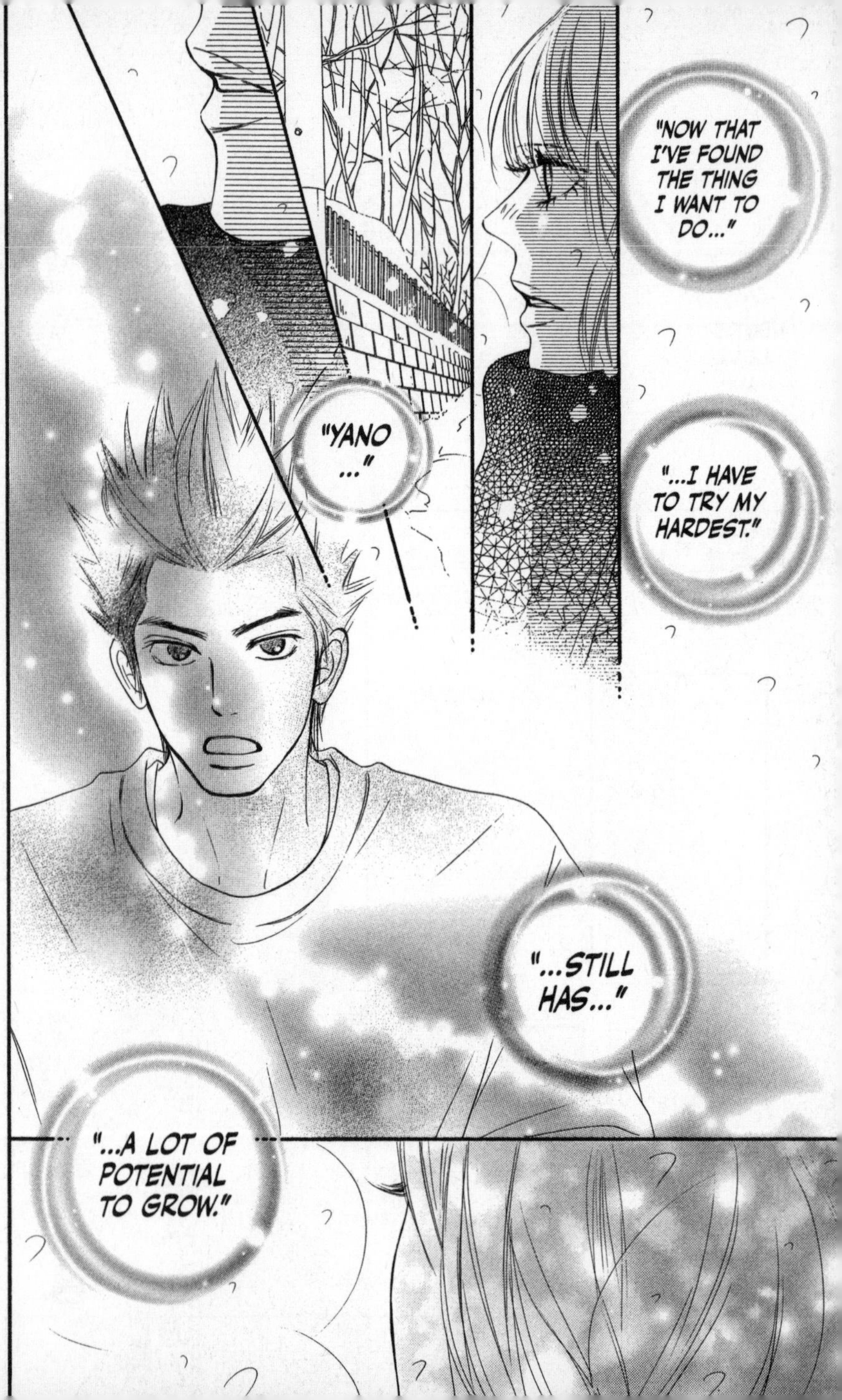
"NOW THAT I'VE FOUND THE THING I WANT TO DO..."
"...I HAVE TO TRY MY HARDEST."
"YANO ..."
"...STILL HAS..."
"...A LOT OF POTENTIAL TO GROW."

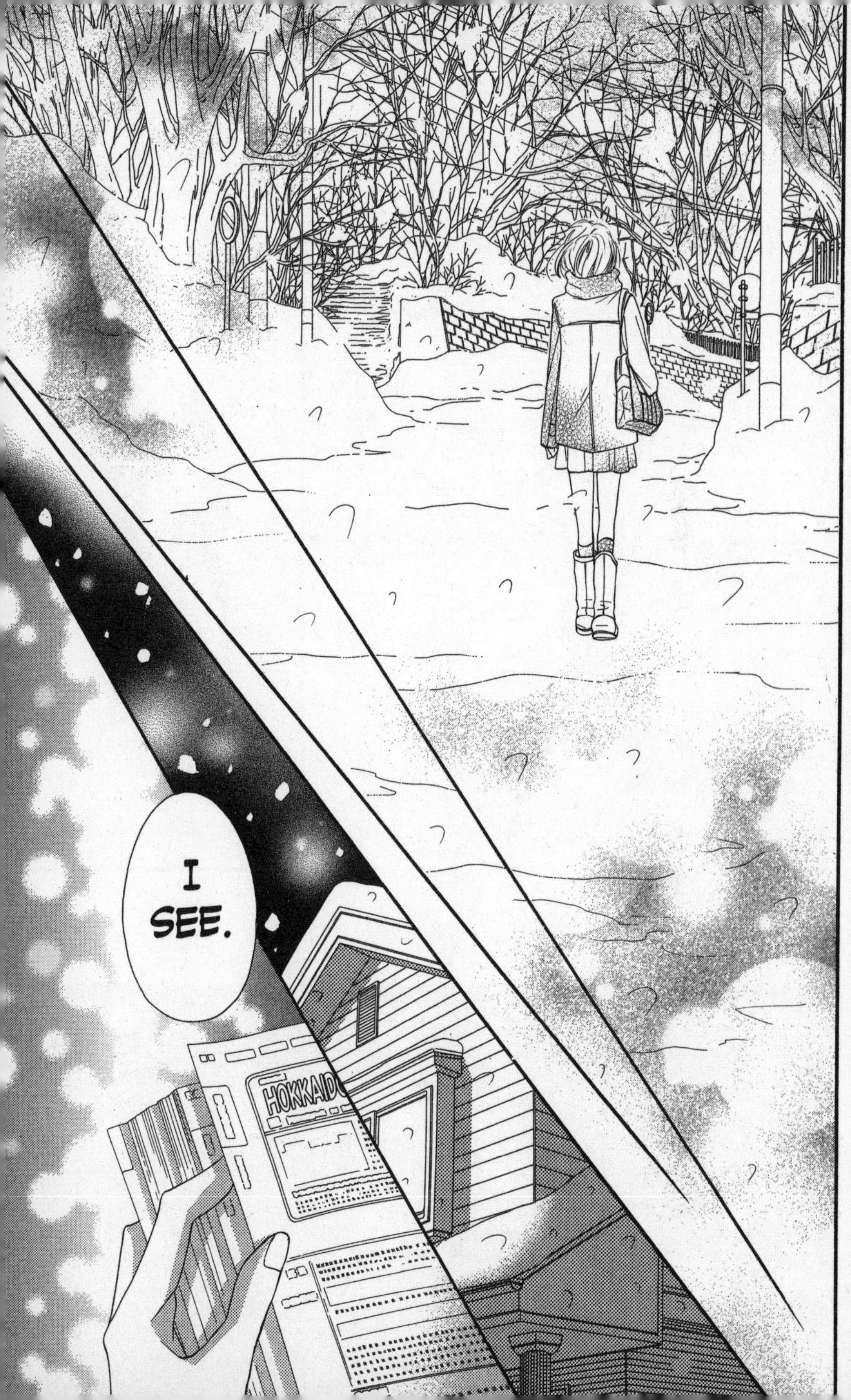
I SEE.
HOKKAIDO

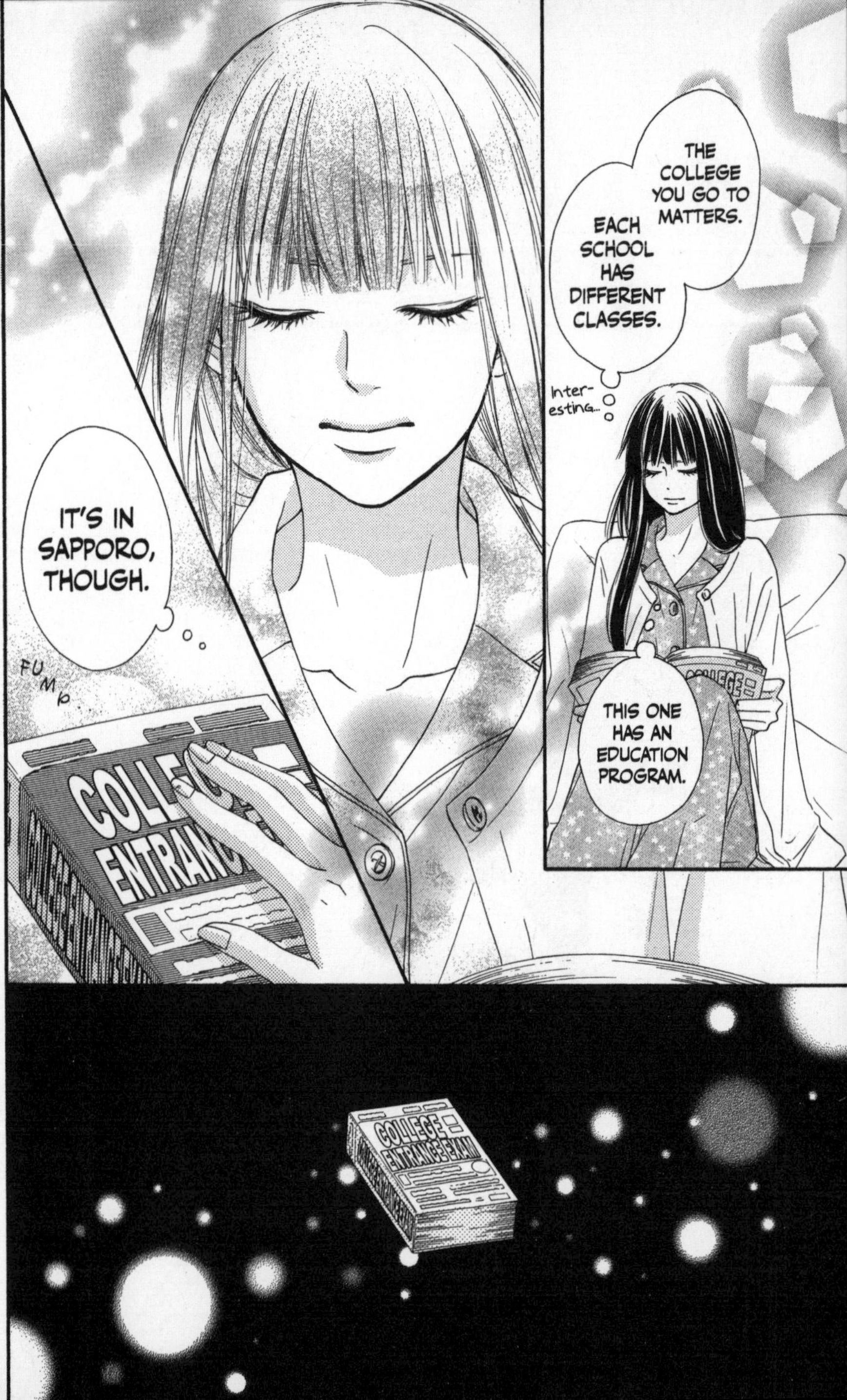
THE COLLEGE YOU GO TO MATTERS.
EACH SCHOOL HAS DIFFERENT CLASSES.
Inter-esting...
THIS ONE HAS AN EDUCATION PROGRAM.
IT'S IN SAPPORO, THOUGH.
FUMP
COLLEGE ENTRANCE EXAM

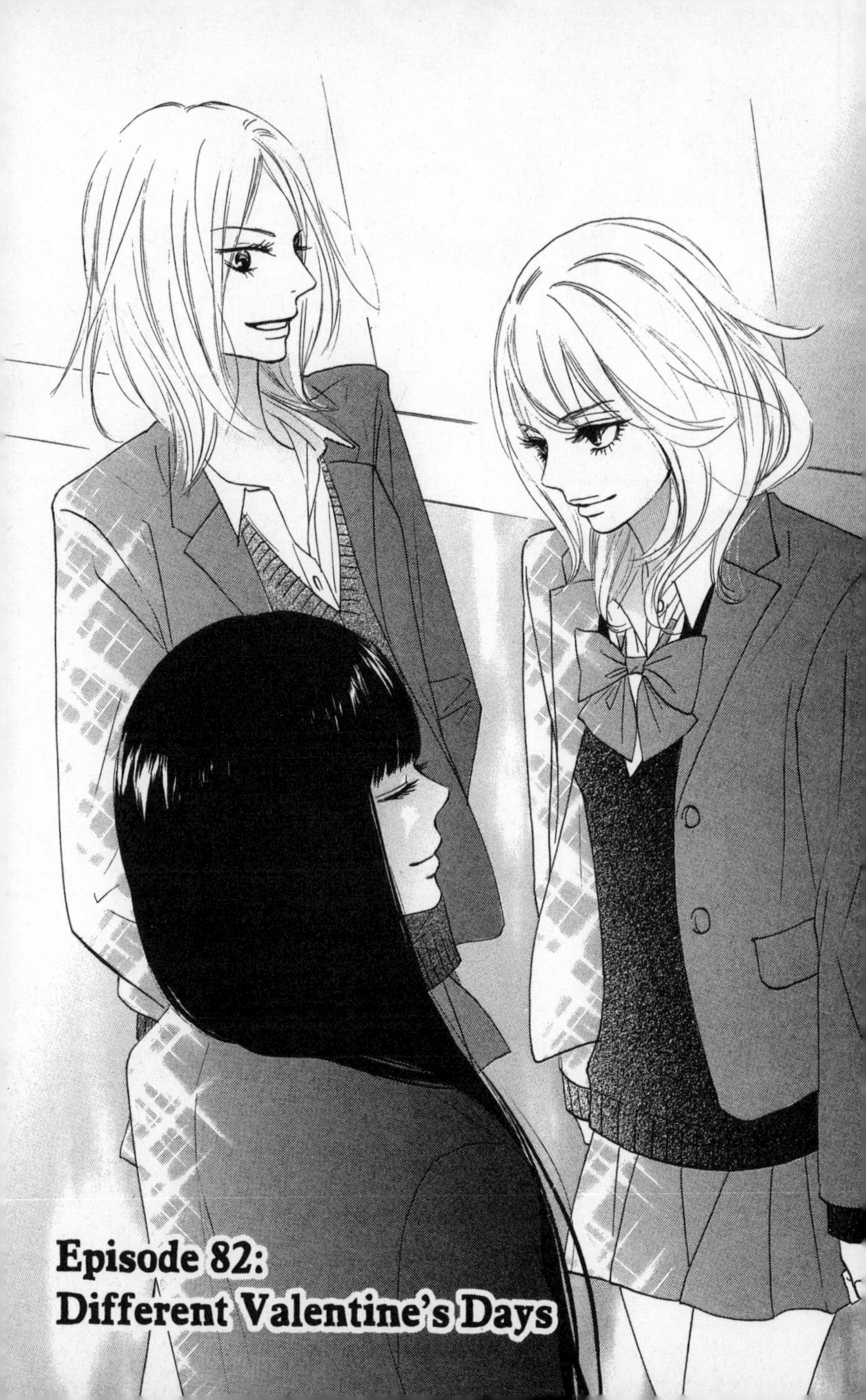

Episode 82: Different Valentine's Days

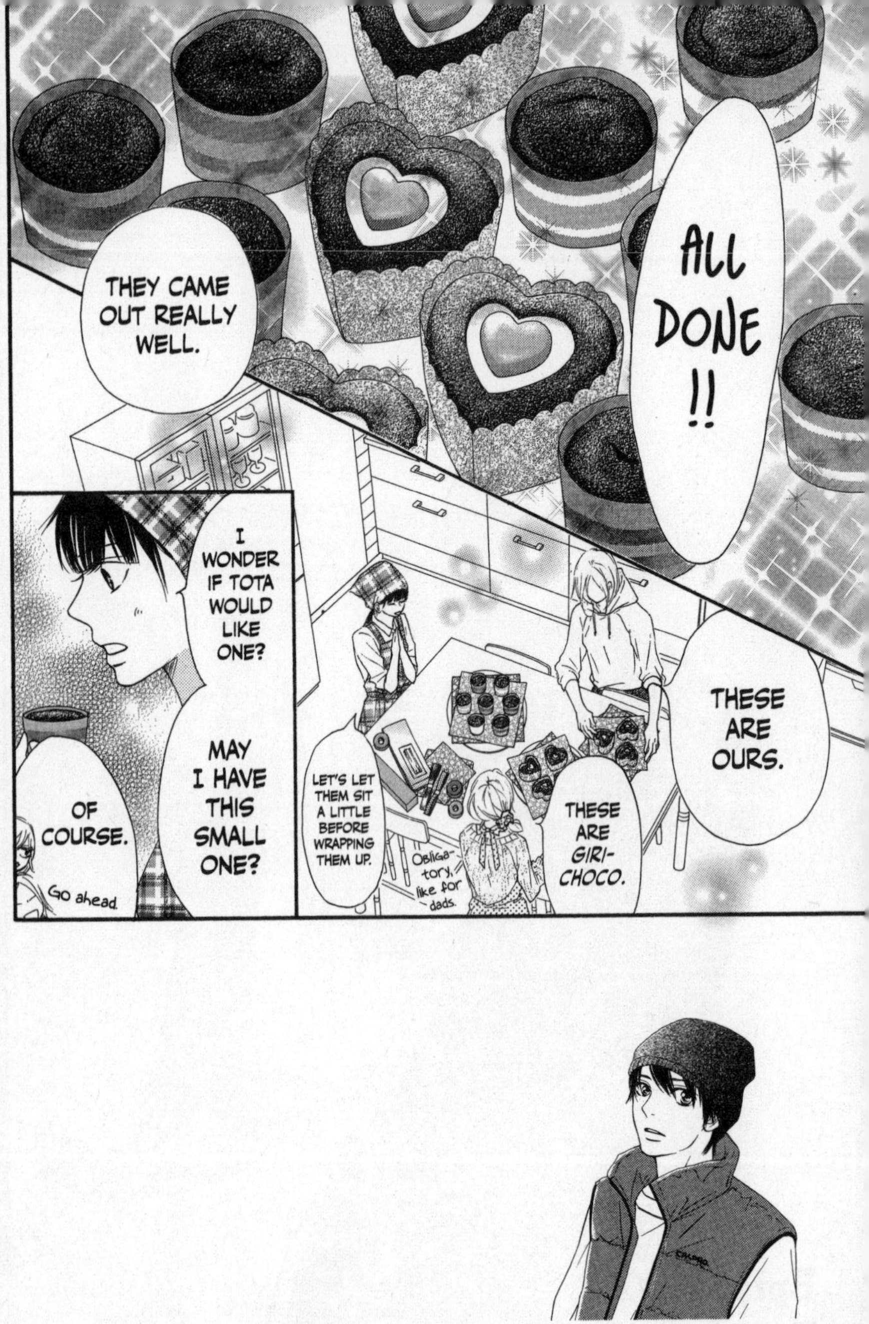
ALL DONE!!
THEY CAME OUT REALLY WELL.
THESE ARE OURS.
THESE ARE GIRI-CHOCO.
Obligatory, like for dads.
LET'S LET THEM SIT A LITTLE BEFORE WRAPPING THEM UP.
I WONDER IF TOTA WOULD LIKE ONE?
MAY I HAVE THIS SMALL ONE?
OF COURSE.
Go ahead.

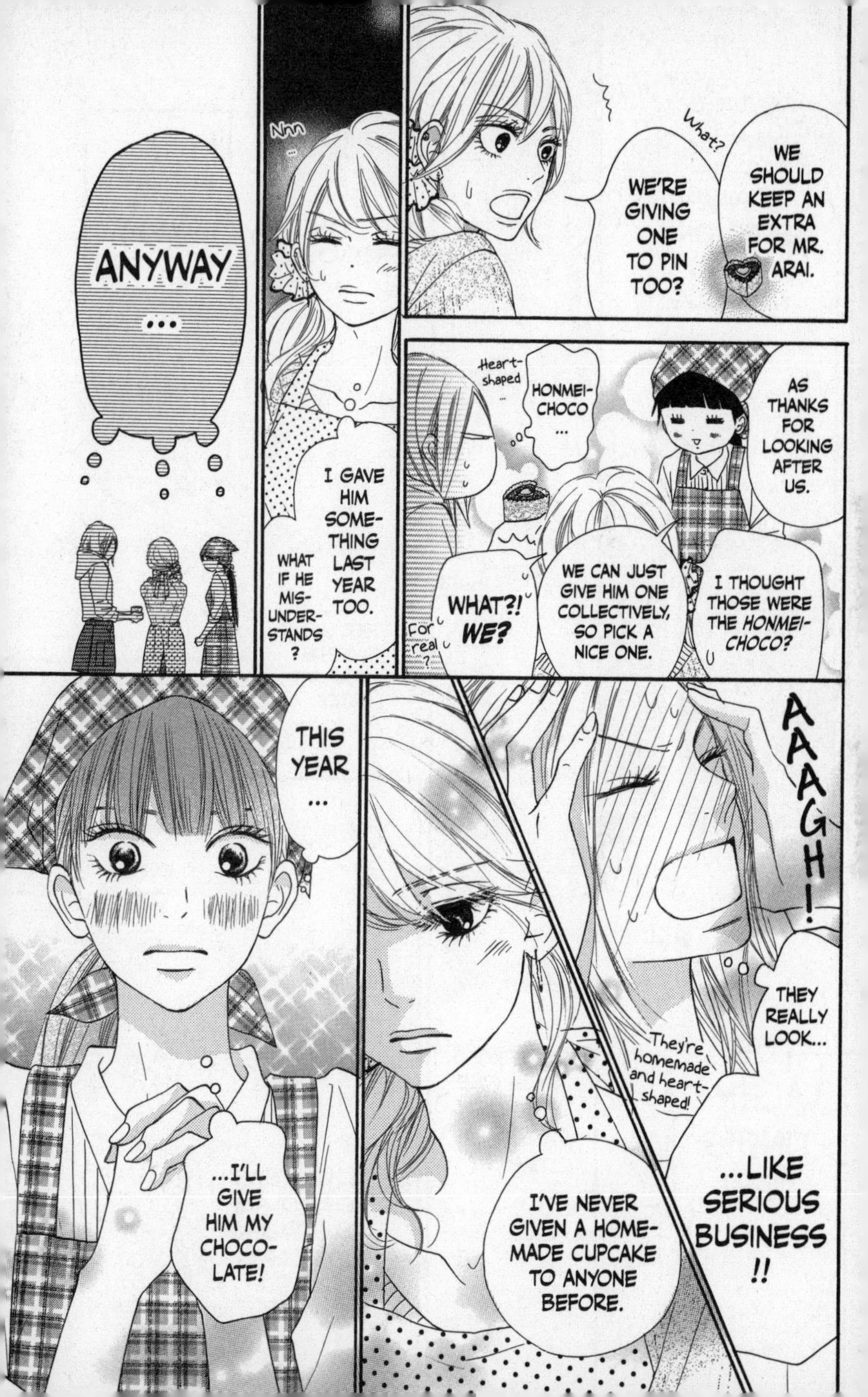
WE SHOULD KEEP AN EXTRA FOR MR. ARAI.
What?
WE'RE GIVING ONE TO PIN TOO?
AS THANKS FOR LOOKING AFTER US.
I THOUGHT THOSE WERE THE *HONMEI-CHOCO?*
HONMEI-CHOCO...
Heart-shaped...
WE CAN JUST GIVE HIM ONE COLLECTIVELY, SO PICK A NICE ONE.
WHAT?! *WE?*
For real?
Nnn...
I GAVE HIM SOMETHING LAST YEAR TOO.
WHAT IF HE MISUNDERSTANDS?
ANYWAY...
AAAGH!
THEY REALLY LOOK...
They're homemade and heart-shaped!
...LIKE SERIOUS BUSINESS!!
I'VE NEVER GIVEN A HOMEMADE CUPCAKE TO ANYONE BEFORE.
THIS YEAR...
...I'LL GIVE HIM MY CHOCOLATE!

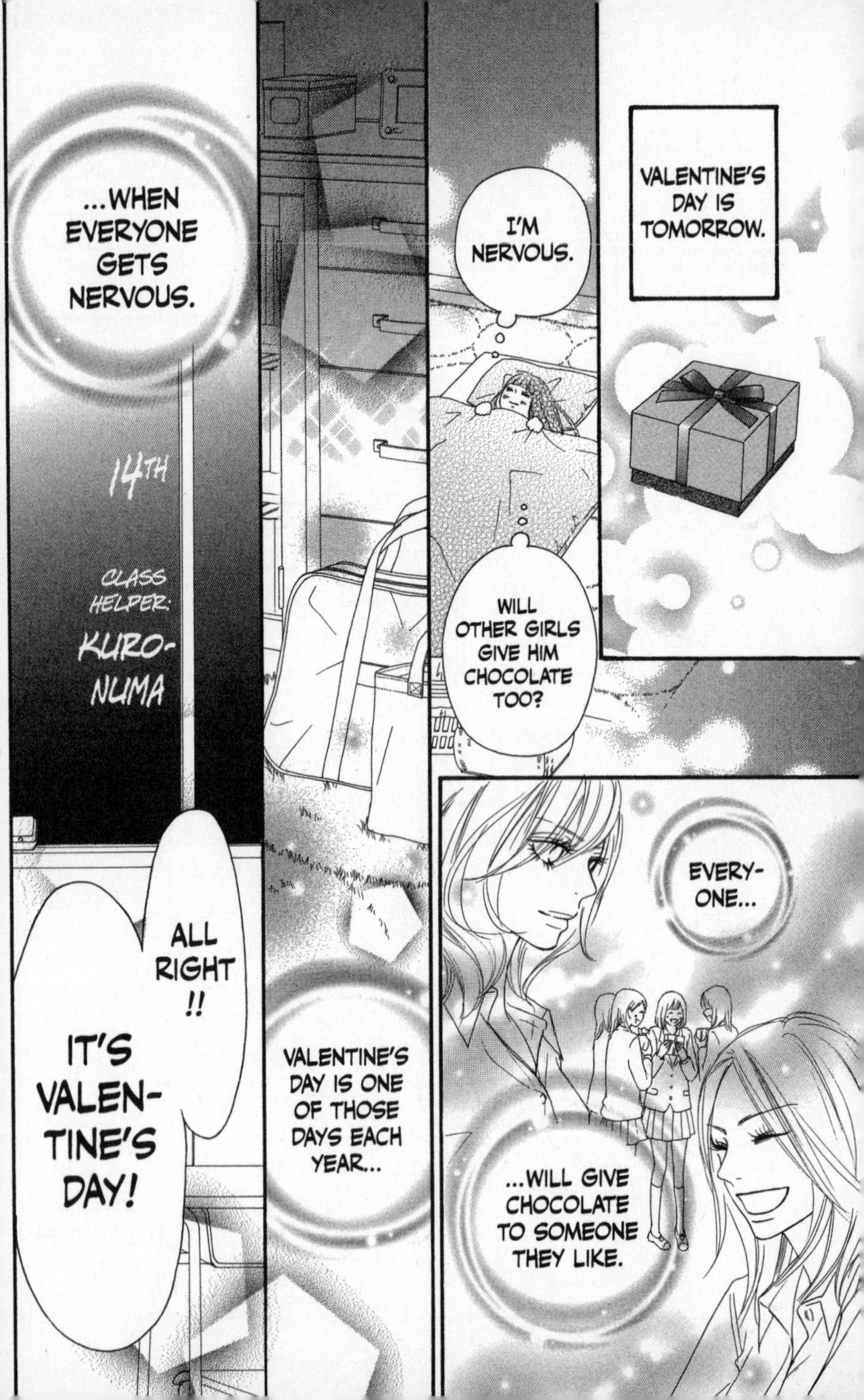
VALENTINE'S DAY IS TOMORROW.
I'M NERVOUS.
WILL OTHER GIRLS GIVE HIM CHOCOLATE TOO?
EVERY-ONE...
...WILL GIVE CHOCOLATE TO SOMEONE THEY LIKE.
VALENTINE'S DAY IS ONE OF THOSE DAYS EACH YEAR...
...WHEN EVERYONE GETS NERVOUS.
14TH
CLASS HELPER:
KURO-NUMA
ALL RIGHT!!
IT'S VALEN-TINE'S DAY!

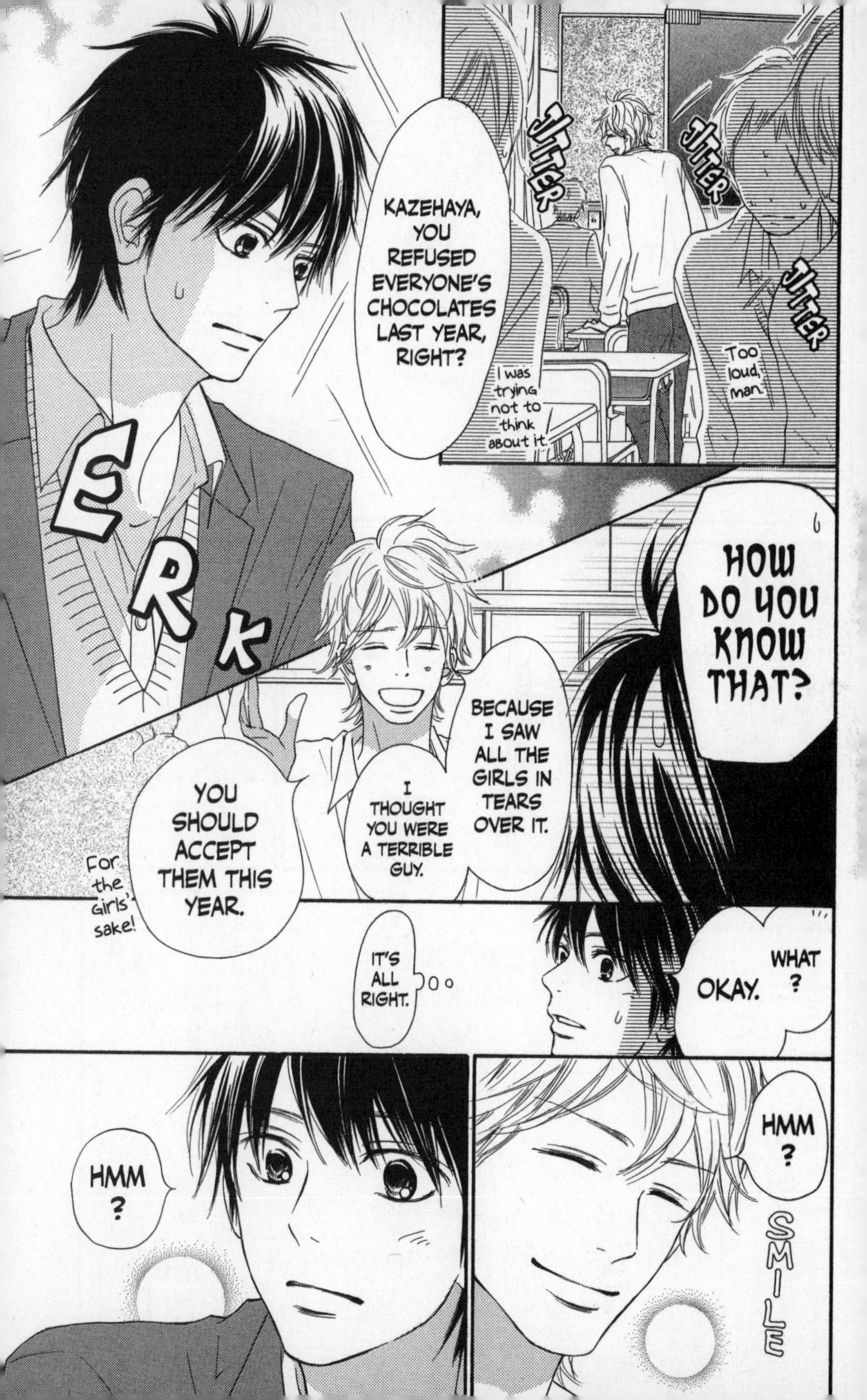
JITTER
JITTER
JITTER
Too loud, man.
I was trying not to think about it.
KAZEHAYA, YOU REFUSED EVERYONE'S CHOCOLATES LAST YEAR, RIGHT?
ERK
HOW DO YOU KNOW THAT?
BECAUSE I SAW ALL THE GIRLS IN TEARS OVER IT.
I THOUGHT YOU WERE A TERRIBLE GUY.
YOU SHOULD ACCEPT THEM THIS YEAR.
For the girls' sake!
WHAT?
OKAY.
IT'S ALL RIGHT.
HMM?
SMILE
HMM?

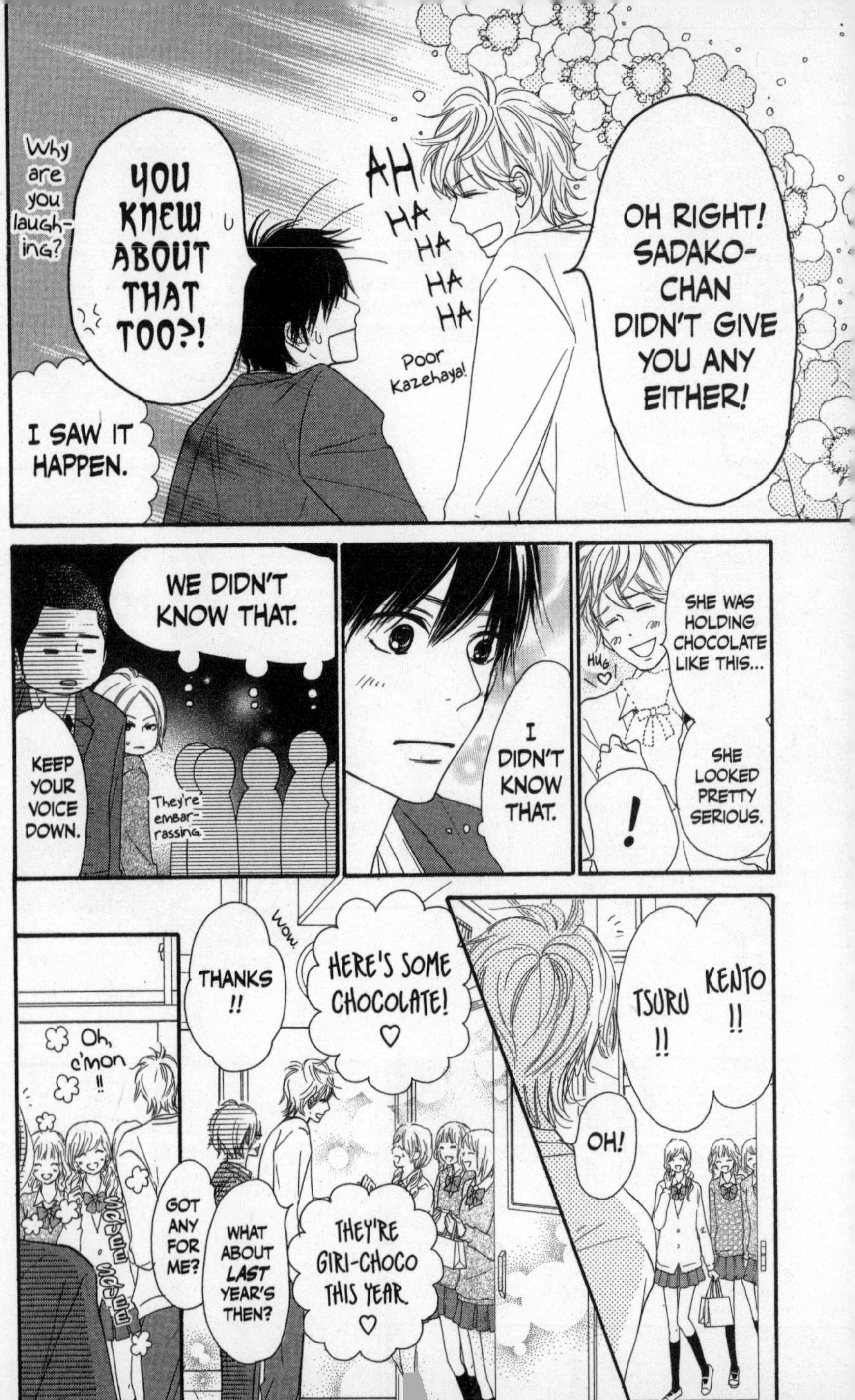
OH RIGHT! SADAKO-CHAN DIDN'T GIVE YOU ANY EITHER!
AH HA HA HA HA
Poor Kazehaya!
YOU KNEW ABOUT THAT TOO?!
Why are you laugh-ing?
I SAW IT HAPPEN.
SHE WAS HOLDING CHOCOLATE LIKE THIS...
HUG ♡
SHE LOOKED PRETTY SERIOUS.
!
I DIDN'T KNOW THAT.
WE DIDN'T KNOW THAT.
KEEP YOUR VOICE DOWN.
They're embar-rassing.
KENTO !!
TSURU !!
OH!
HERE'S SOME CHOCOLATE! ♡
Wow
THANKS !!
Oh, c'mon !!
THEY'RE GIRI-CHOCO THIS YEAR. ♡
WHAT ABOUT LAST YEAR'S THEN?
GOT ANY FOR ME?

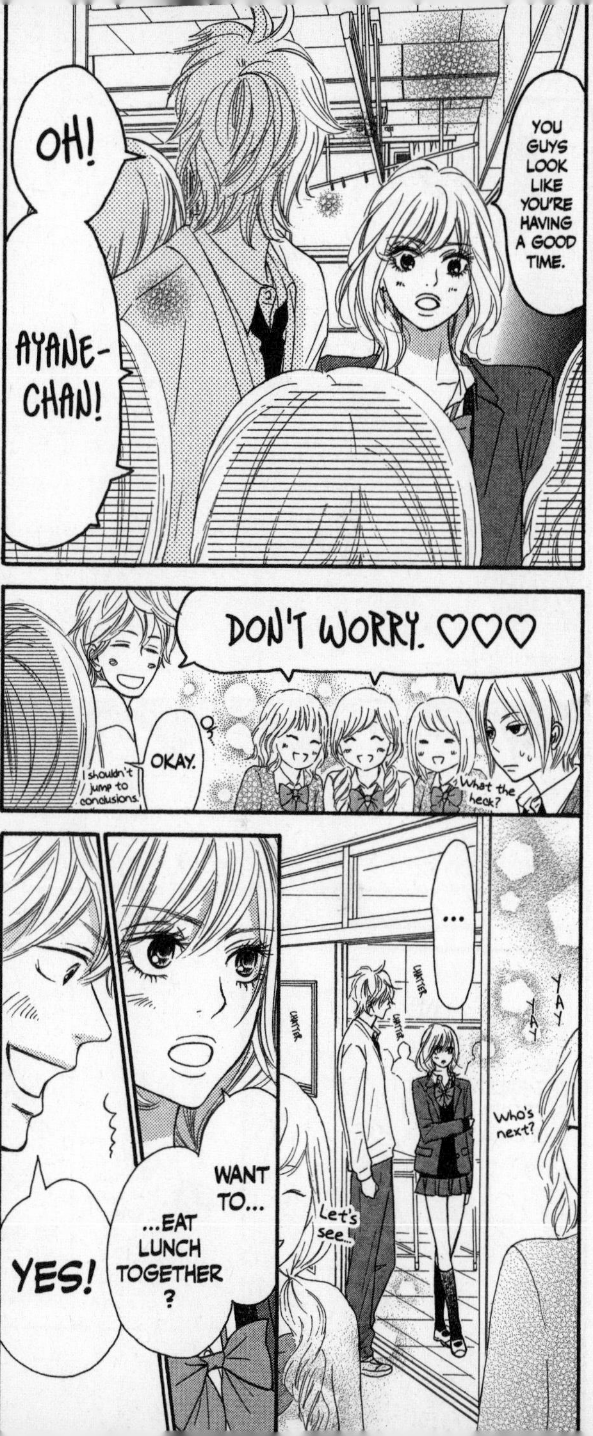
YOU GUYS LOOK LIKE YOU'RE HAVING A GOOD TIME.
OH!
AYANE-CHAN!
DON'T WORRY. ♡♡♡
What the heck?
OKAY.
I shouldn't jump to conclusions.
YAY
YAY
Who's next?
...
CHATTER
CHATTER
CHATTER
Let's see...
WANT TO...
...EAT LUNCH TOGETHER?
YES!

KARUPIN on JAPAN 2

I usually do cuts early in the month. Then after the meeting, I do storyboards, which come before the pencils. I only go out to pick up my daughter from school and to do grocery shopping. But when I do storyboards, I sometimes go to coffee shops. If I stay home, I start doing housework and make no progress on the manga. I'd like to start getting health checkups, but it's difficult to make time.

Oh no...

I wish I could draw faster--I mean, work faster in general! I'm a slowpoke!

This isn't related, but I switched from India ink to regular ink. Can you tell the difference? I can't!

The next volume will be the first one in the twenties, but I won't forget how I felt in the beginning and I'll do my best!

Karuho Shiina

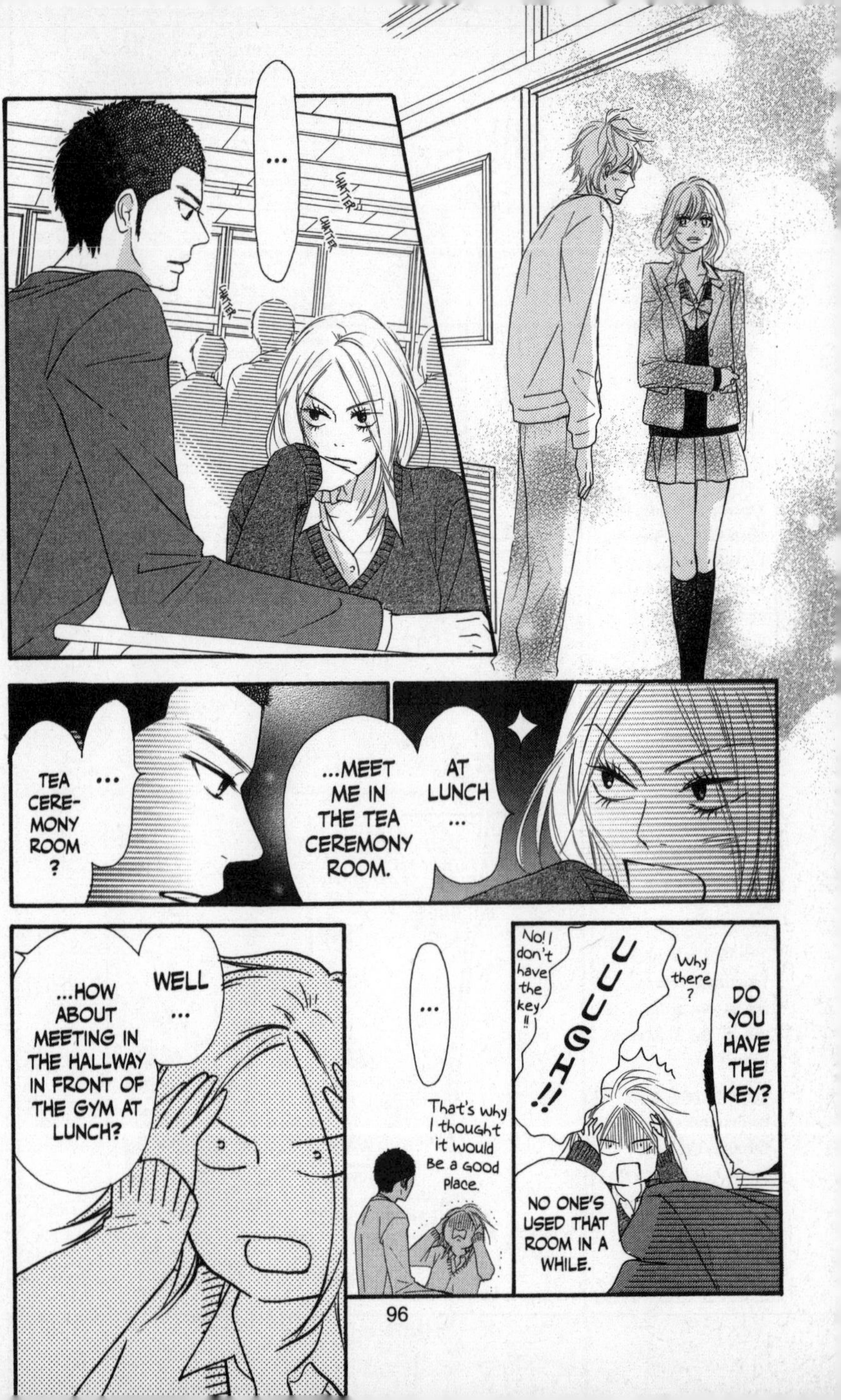
...
CHATTER
CHATTER
CHATTER
AT LUNCH...
...MEET ME IN THE TEA CEREMONY ROOM.
...
TEA CERE-MONY ROOM?
DO YOU HAVE THE KEY?
Why there?
UUUGH!!
No! I don't have the key!!
NO ONE'S USED THAT ROOM IN A WHILE.
...
That's why I thought it would be a good place.
WELL...
...HOW ABOUT MEETING IN THE HALLWAY IN FRONT OF THE GYM AT LUNCH?

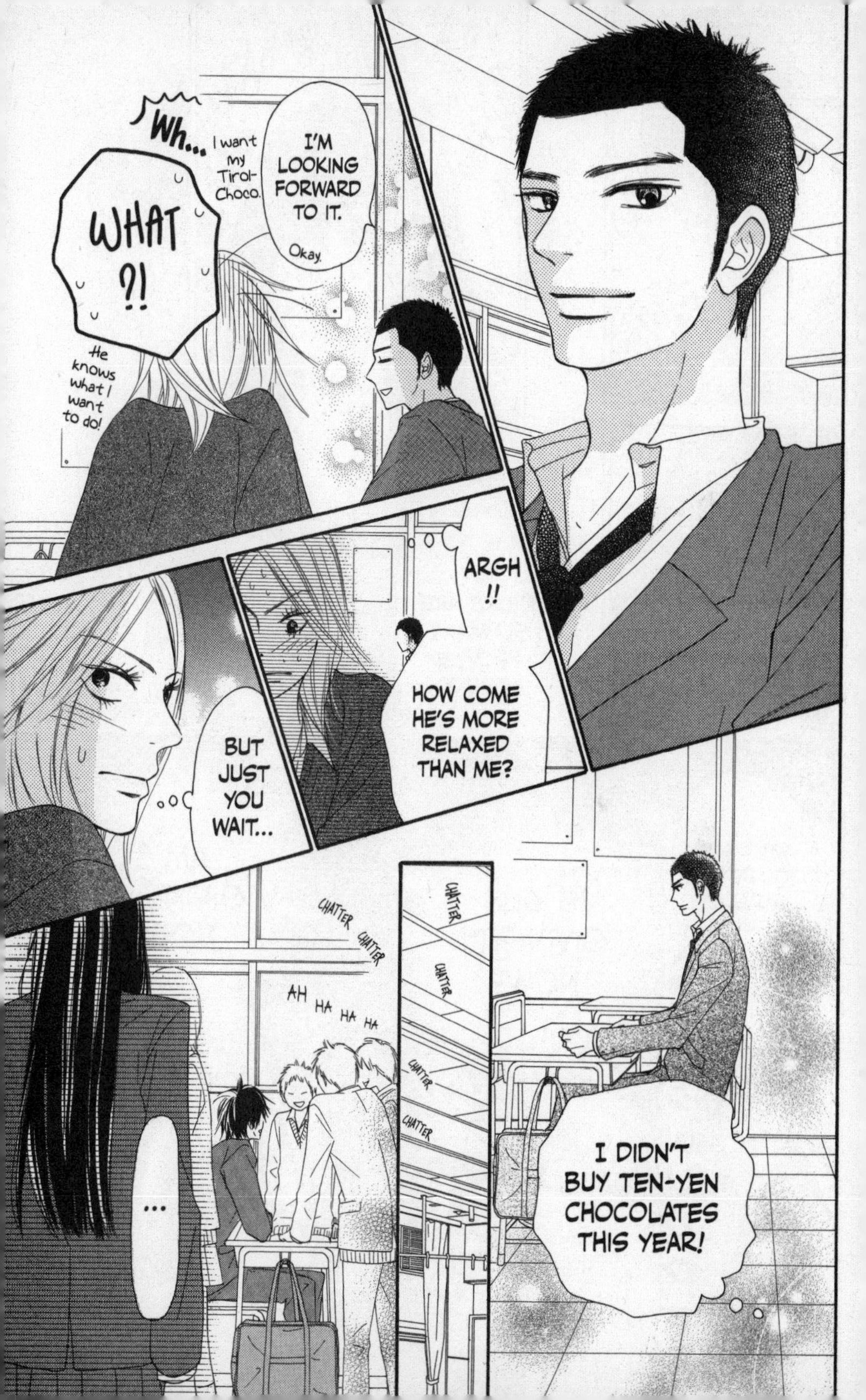
I'M LOOKING FORWARD TO IT.
I want my Tirol-Choco.
Okay.
Wh...
WHAT ?!
He knows what I want to do!
ARGH !!
HOW COME HE'S MORE RELAXED THAN ME?
BUT JUST YOU WAIT...
I DIDN'T BUY TEN-YEN CHOCOLATES THIS YEAR!
CHATTER
CHATTER
CHATTER
CHATTER
CHATTER
CHATTER
AH HA HA HA
...

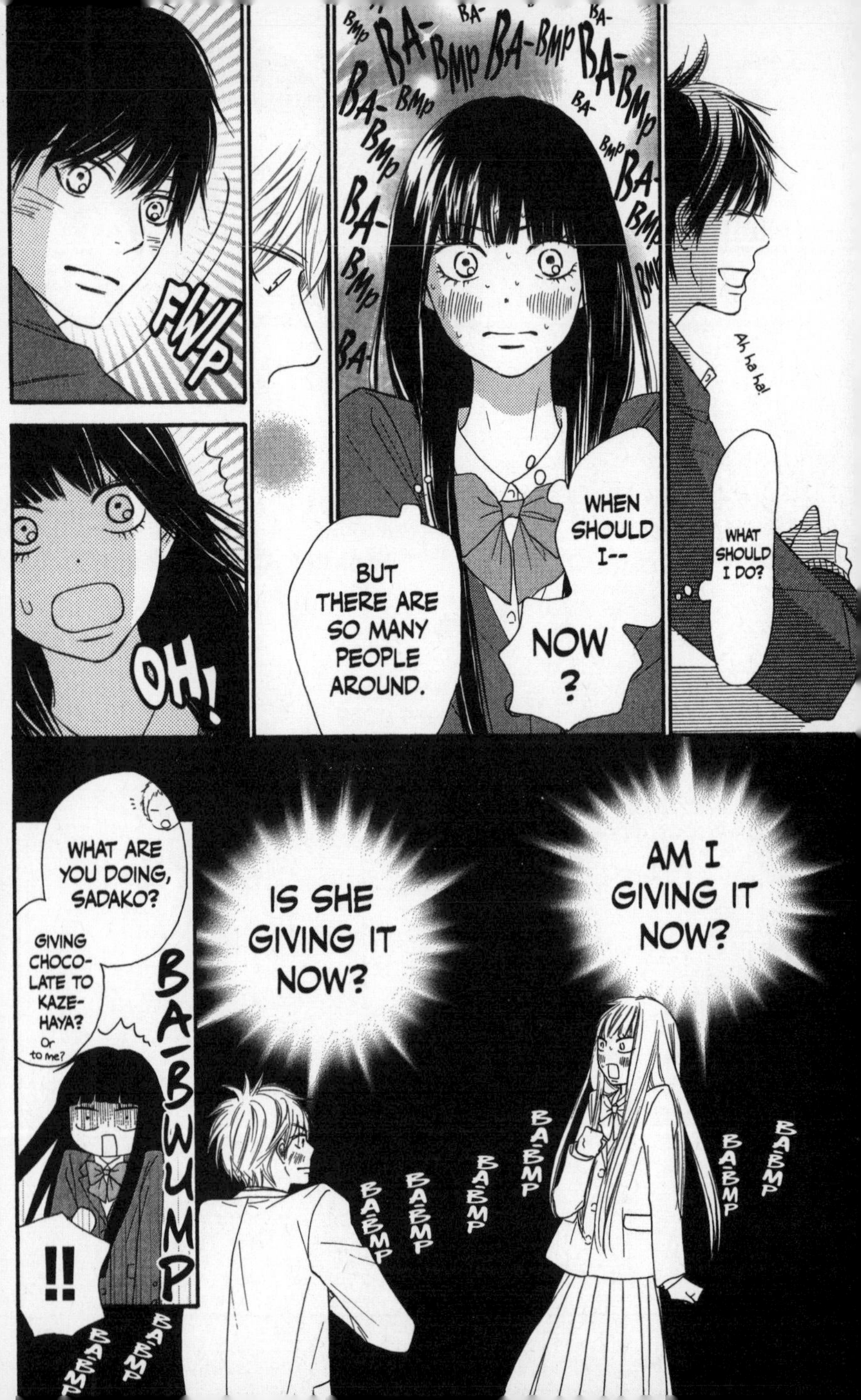

Ah ha ha!
WHAT SHOULD I DO?
BA-BMP BA-BMP BA-BMP BA-BMP BA-BMP BA-BMP BA-BMP BA-
WHEN SHOULD I--
NOW?
BUT THERE ARE SO MANY PEOPLE AROUND.
FWIP
OH!
AM I GIVING IT NOW?
BA-BMP BA-BMP
BA-BMP
IS SHE GIVING IT NOW?
BA-BMP BA-BMP BA-BMP
WHAT ARE YOU DOING, SADAKO?
GIVING CHOCOLATE TO KAZEHAYA?
Or to me?
BA-BWUMP
!!
BA-BMP BA-BMP

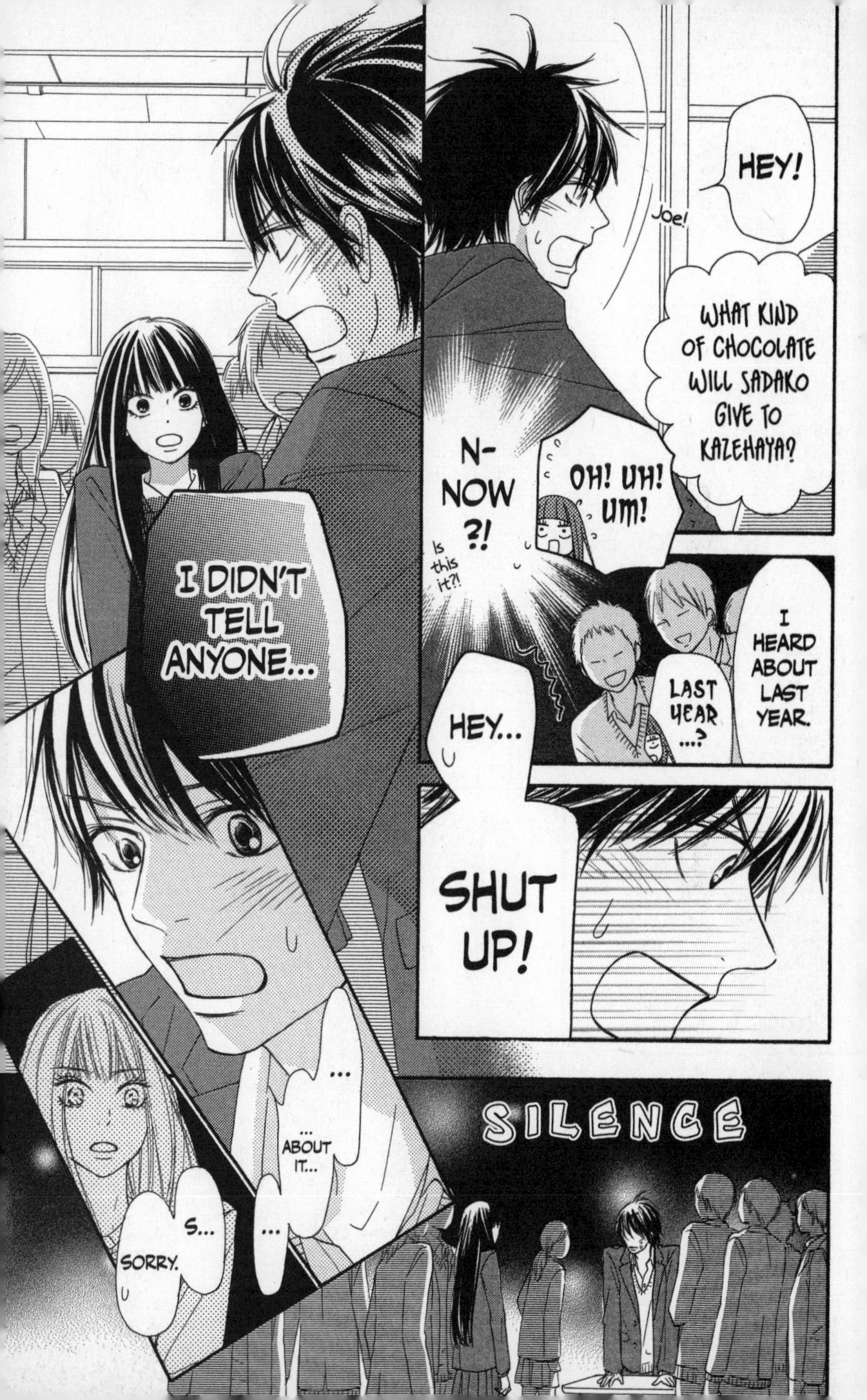
HEY!
Joe!
WHAT KIND OF CHOCOLATE WILL SADAKO GIVE TO KAZEHAYA?
OH! UH! UM!
N-NOW?!
Is this it?!
I HEARD ABOUT LAST YEAR.
LAST YEAR...?
HEY...
SHUT UP!
I DIDN'T TELL ANYONE...
...
...ABOUT IT...
...
S...
SORRY.
SILENCE

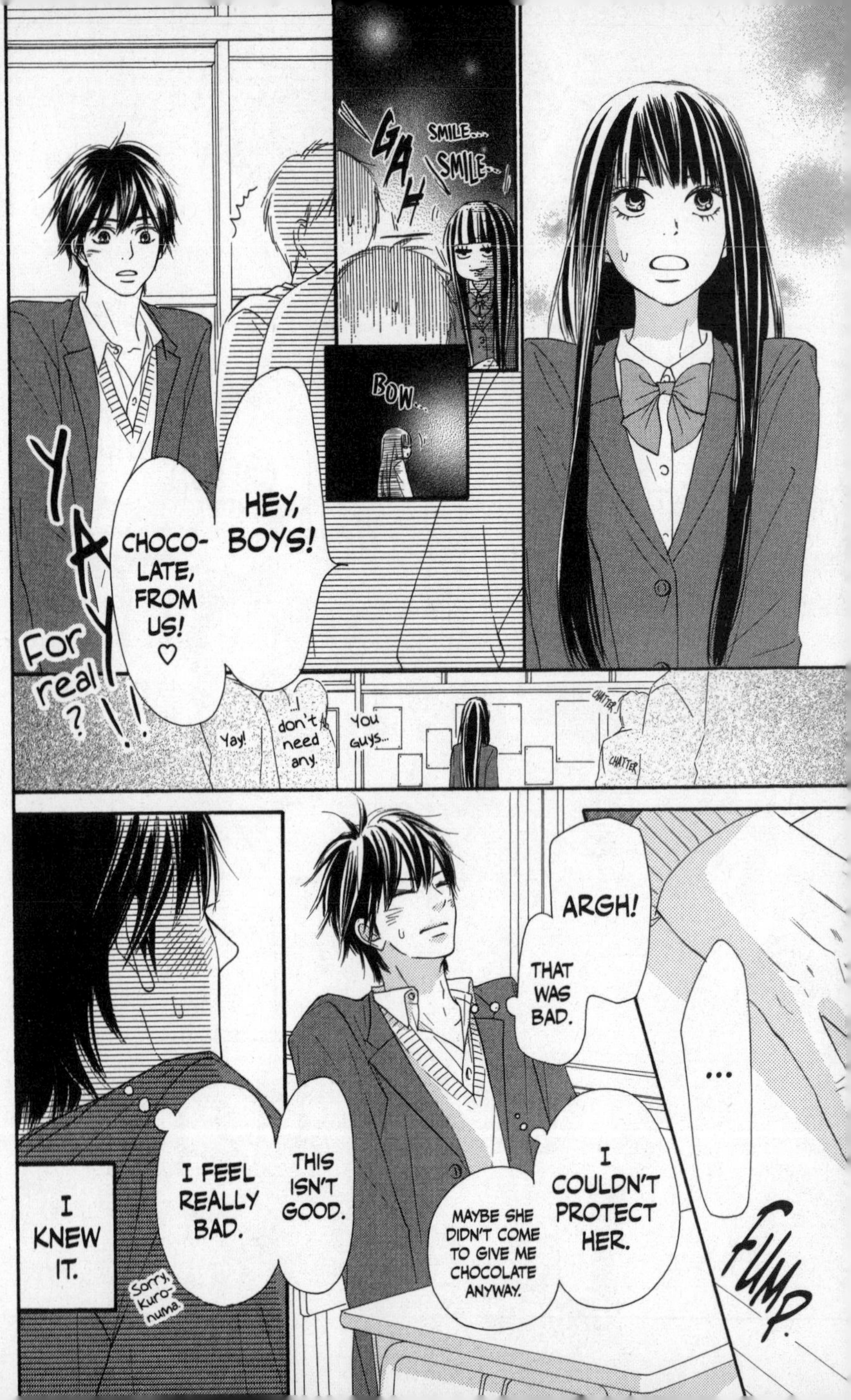
GAH
SMILE...
SMILE...
BOW...
HEY, BOYS!
CHOCO-LATE, FROM US! ♡
YAY!!
For real?
CHATTER
CHATTER
You guys...
...I don't need any.
Yay!
...
FUMP
ARGH!
THAT WAS BAD.
I COULDN'T PROTECT HER.
MAYBE SHE DIDN'T COME TO GIVE ME CHOCOLATE ANYWAY.
THIS ISN'T GOOD.
I FEEL REALLY BAD.
Sorry, Kuro-numa.
I KNEW IT.

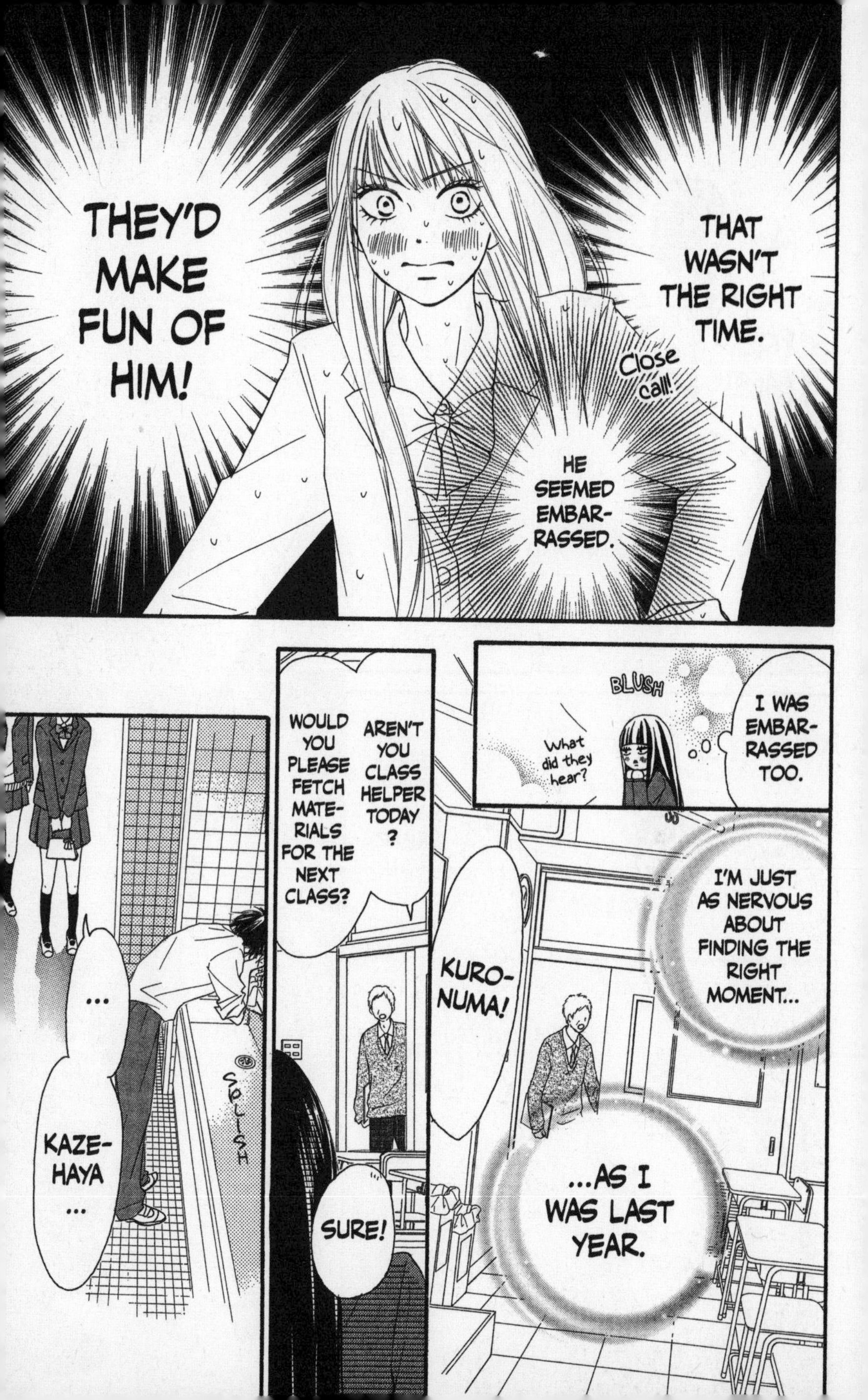
THAT WASN'T THE RIGHT TIME.
Close call!
THEY'D MAKE FUN OF HIM!
HE SEEMED EMBAR-RASSED.
I WAS EMBAR-RASSED TOO.
BLUSH
What did they hear?
I'M JUST AS NERVOUS ABOUT FINDING THE RIGHT MOMENT...
...AS I WAS LAST YEAR.
AREN'T YOU CLASS HELPER TODAY?
WOULD YOU PLEASE FETCH MATE-RIALS FOR THE NEXT CLASS?
KURO-NUMA!
SURE!
SPLISH
...
KAZE-HAYA
...

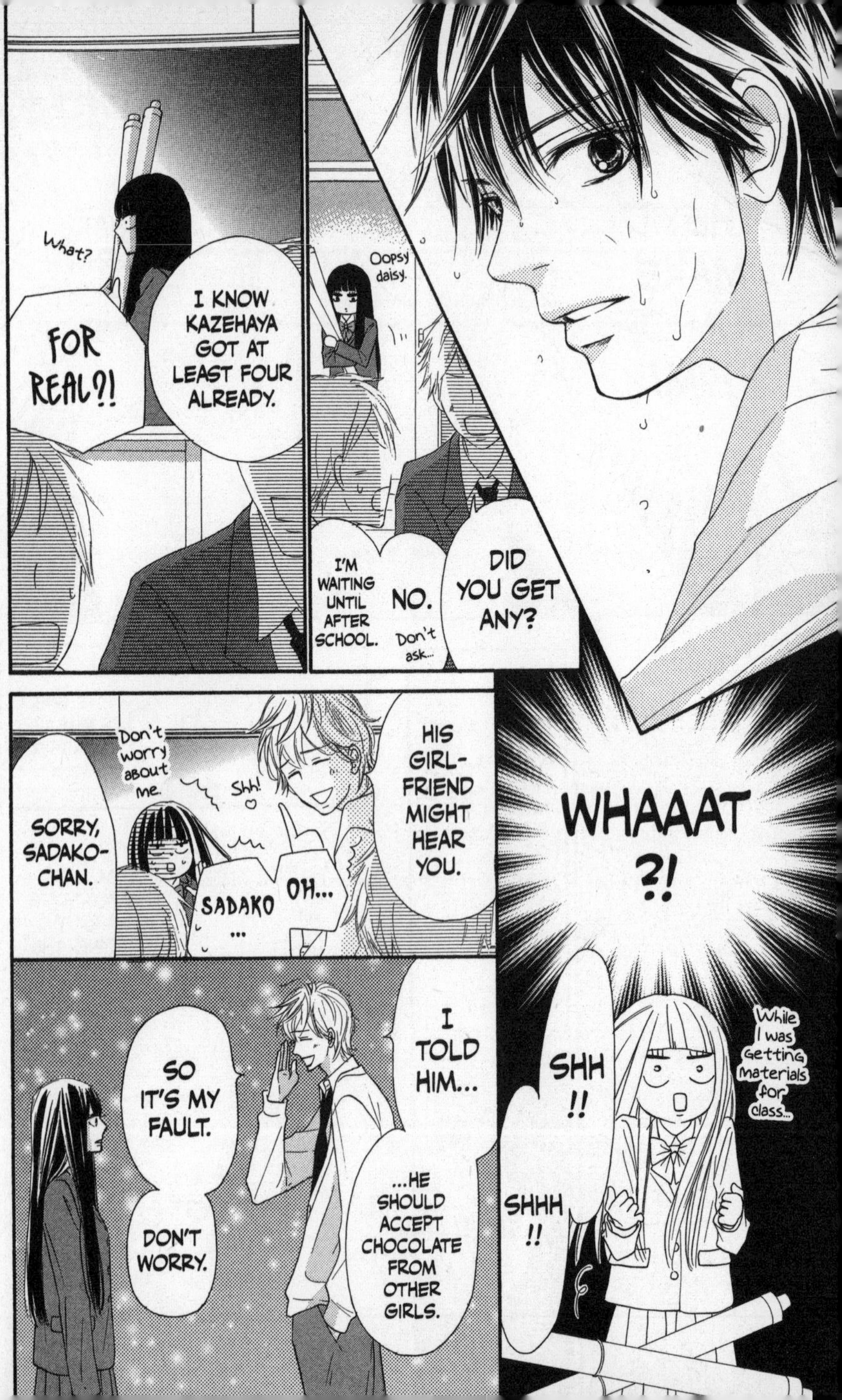
DID YOU GET ANY?
NO.
Don't ask...
I'M WAITING UNTIL AFTER SCHOOL.
Oopsy daisy.
I KNOW KAZEHAYA GOT AT LEAST FOUR ALREADY.
FOR REAL?!
What?
WHAAAT ?!
While I was getting materials for class...
SHH !!
SHHH !!
HIS GIRL-FRIEND MIGHT HEAR YOU.
Shh!
OH...
SADAKO ...
Don't worry about me.
SORRY, SADAKO-CHAN.
I TOLD HIM...
...HE SHOULD ACCEPT CHOCOLATE FROM OTHER GIRLS.
SO IT'S MY FAULT.
DON'T WORRY.

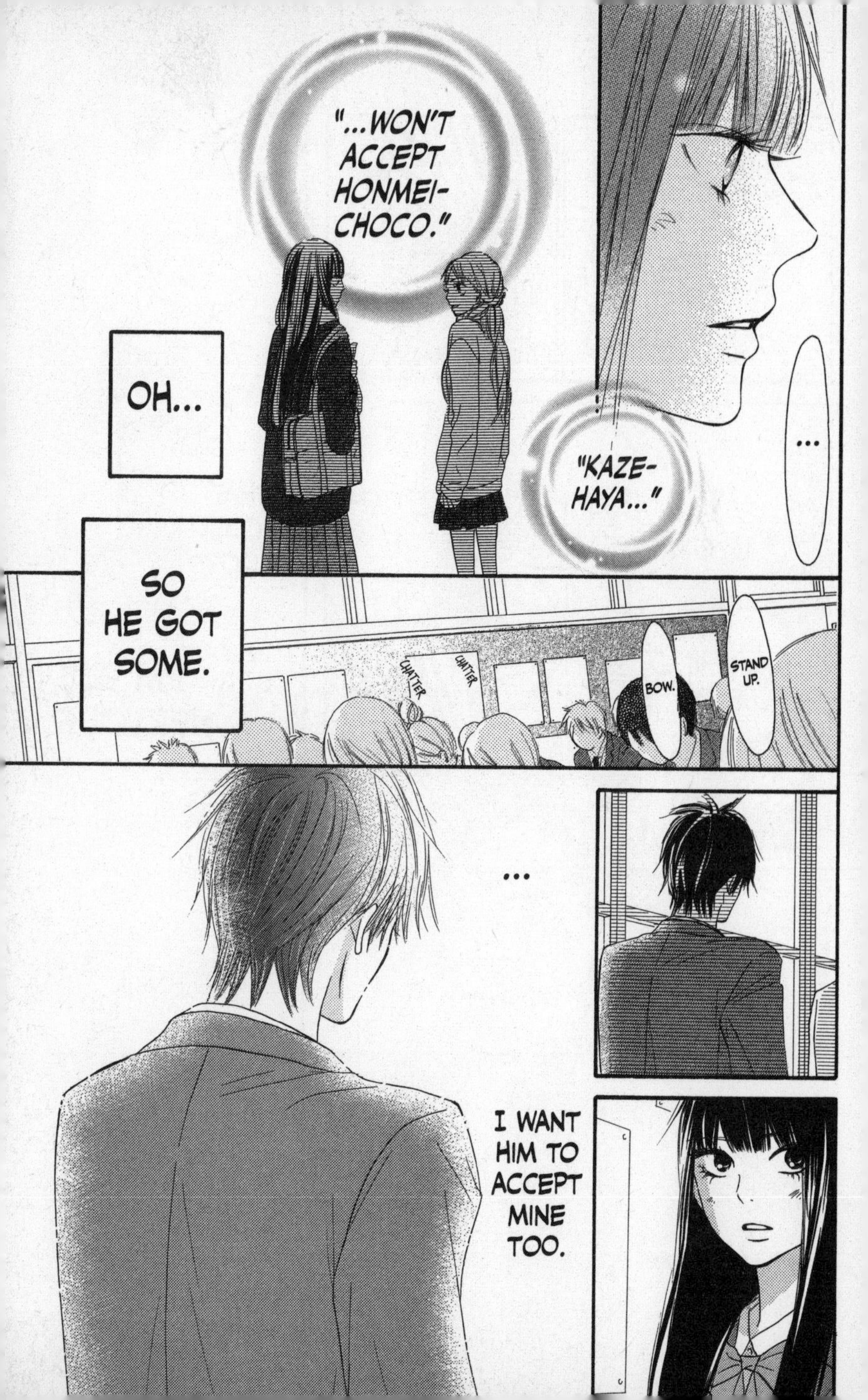
...
"KAZE-HAYA..."
"...WON'T ACCEPT HONMEI-CHOCO."
OH...
SO HE GOT SOME.
STAND UP.
BOW.
CHATTER
CHATTER
I WANT HIM TO ACCEPT MINE TOO.
...

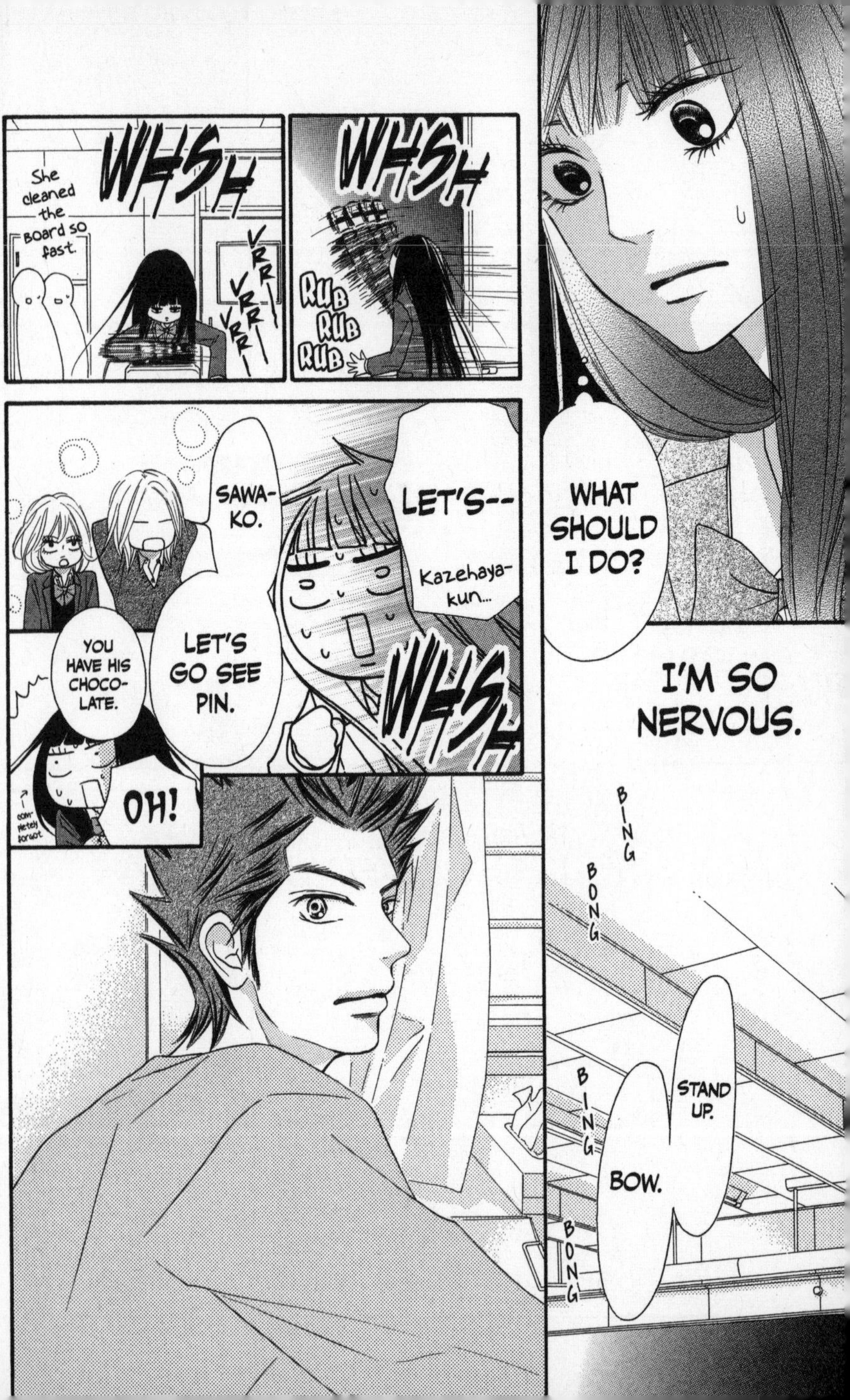
WHAT SHOULD I DO?
I'M SO NERVOUS.
BING BONG
BING BONG
STAND UP.
BOW.
WHSH
RUB RUB RUB
WHSH
She cleaned the board so fast.
VRR VRR VRR
LET'S--
Kazehaya-kun...
SAWAKO.
WHSH
LET'S GO SEE PIN.
YOU HAVE HIS CHOCOLATE.
OH!
completely forgot

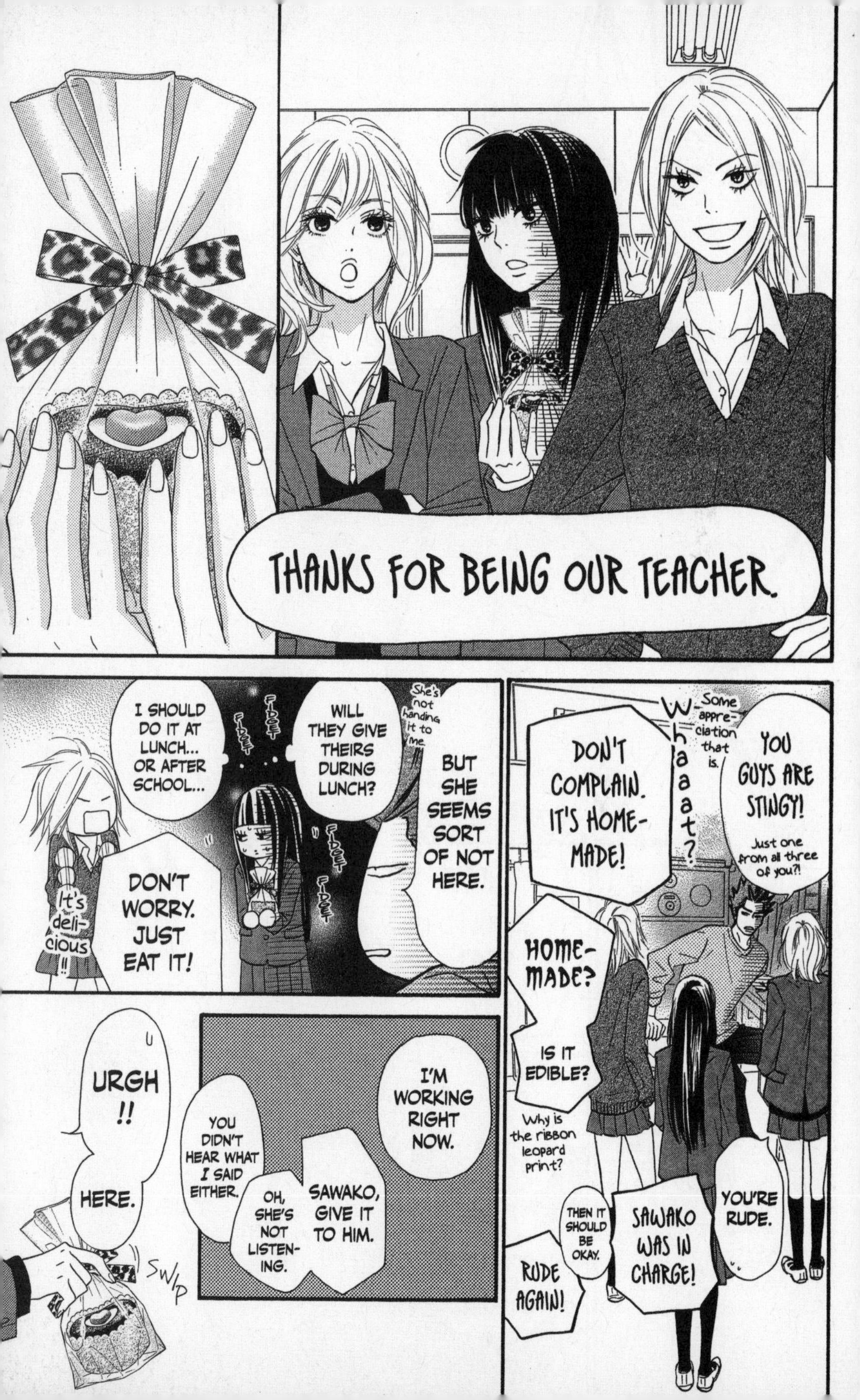
THANKS FOR BEING OUR TEACHER.
YOU GUYS ARE STINGY!
Just one from all three of you?!
Some appreciation that is.
Whaaat?
DON'T COMPLAIN. IT'S HOMEMADE!
HOMEMADE?
IS IT EDIBLE?
Why is the ribbon leopard print?
YOU'RE RUDE.
SAWAKO WAS IN CHARGE!
THEN IT SHOULD BE OKAY.
RUDE AGAIN!
BUT SHE SEEMS SORT OF NOT HERE.
She's not handing it to me.
WILL THEY GIVE THEIRS DURING LUNCH?
FIDGET FIDGET
FIDGET FIDGET
I SHOULD DO IT AT LUNCH... OR AFTER SCHOOL...
DON'T WORRY. JUST EAT IT!
It's delicious!!
I'M WORKING RIGHT NOW.
SAWAKO, GIVE IT TO HIM.
YOU DIDN'T HEAR WHAT I SAID EITHER.
OH, SHE'S NOT LISTENING.
URGH!!
HERE.
SWIP

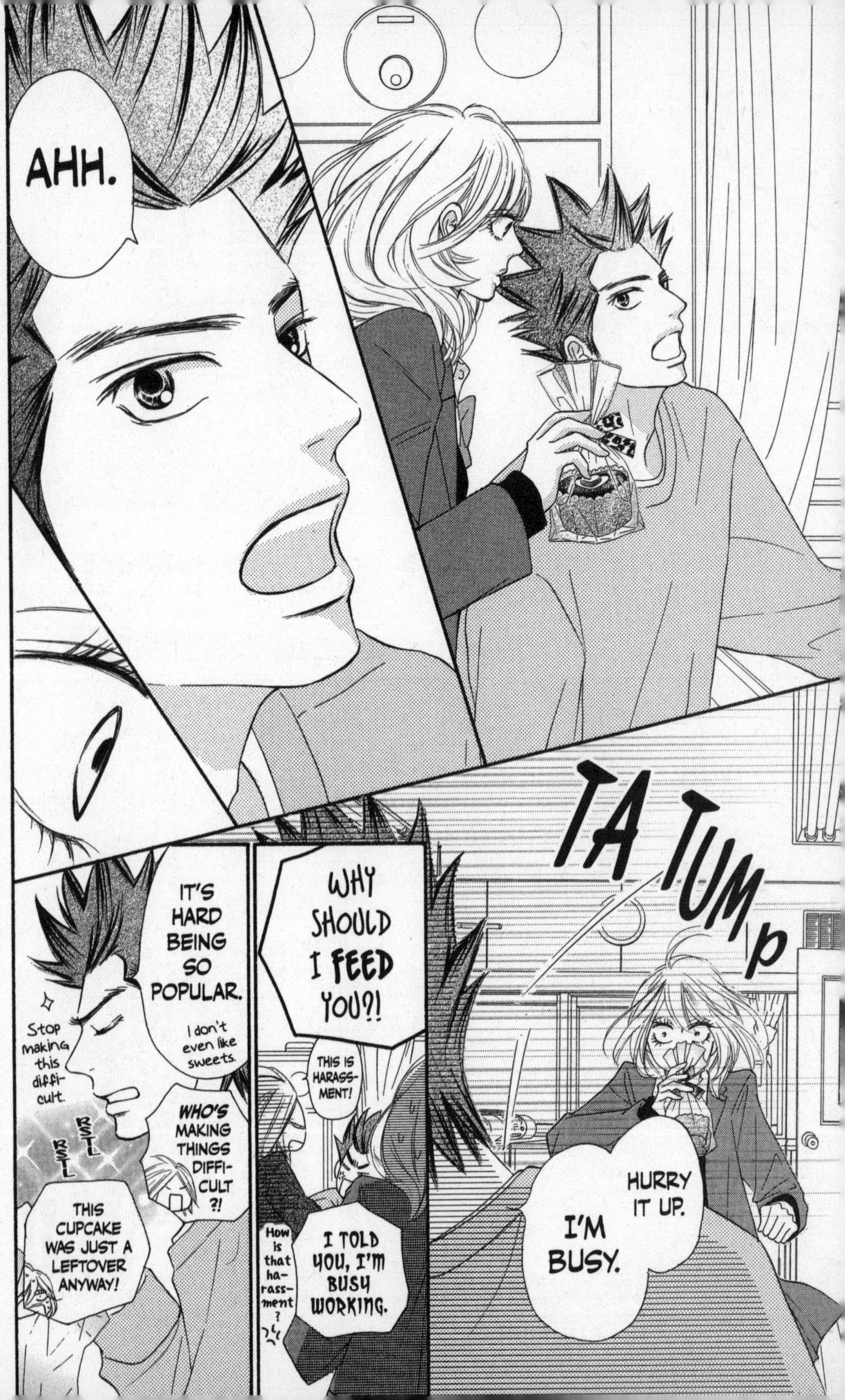
AHH.
TA TUMP
HURRY IT UP.
I'M BUSY.
WHY SHOULD I FEED YOU?!
THIS IS HARASSMENT!
I TOLD YOU, I'M BUSY WORKING.
How is that harassment?
IT'S HARD BEING SO POPULAR.
I don't even like sweets.
Stop making this difficult.
WHO'S MAKING THINGS DIFFICULT?!
RSTL
RSTL
THIS CUPCAKE WAS JUST A LEFTOVER ANYWAY!

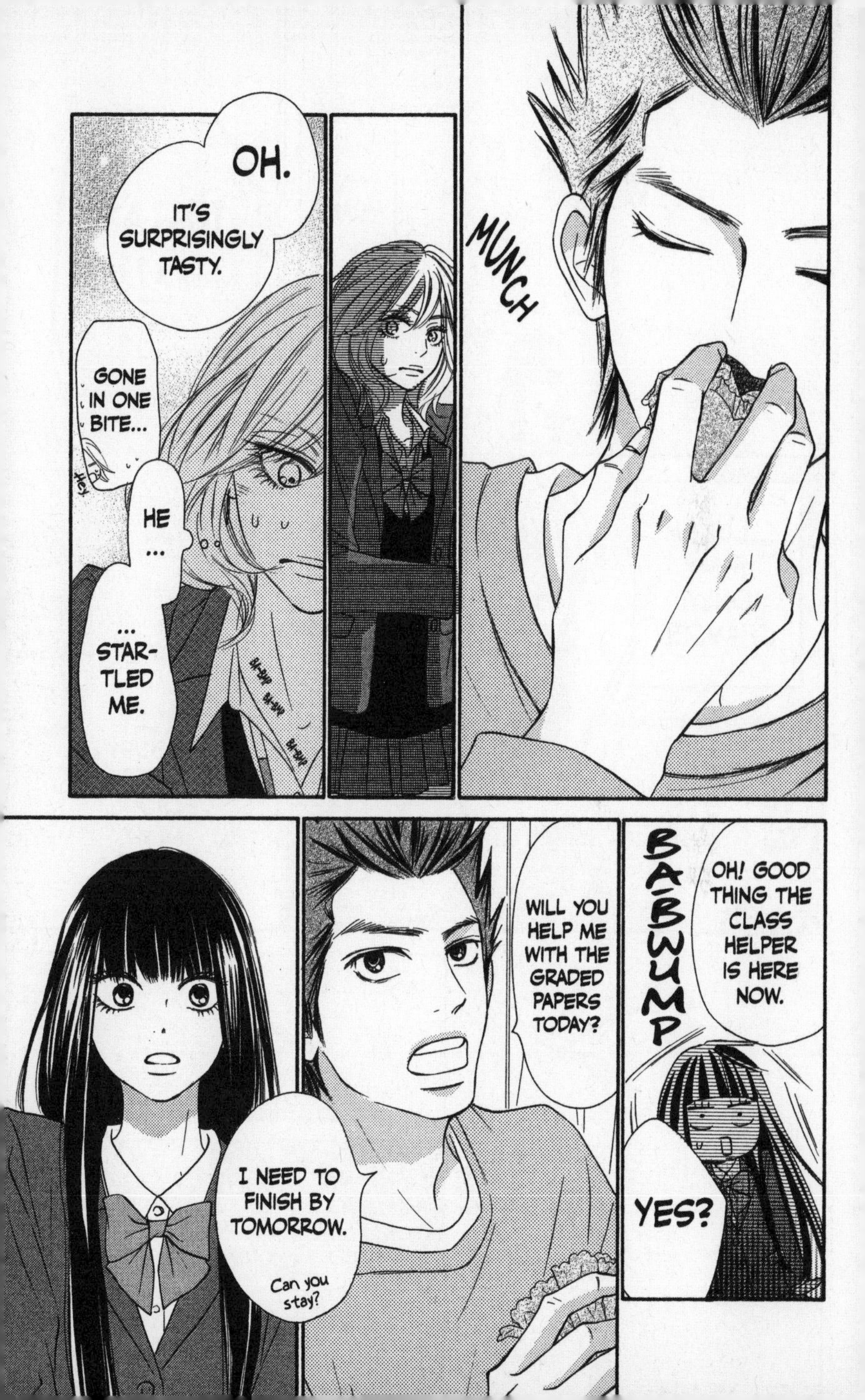
MUNCH
OH.
IT'S SURPRISINGLY TASTY.
GONE IN ONE BITE...
Hey
HE...
...STARTLED ME.
OH! GOOD THING THE CLASS HELPER IS HERE NOW.
BABWUMP
YES?
WILL YOU HELP ME WITH THE GRADED PAPERS TODAY?
I NEED TO FINISH BY TOMORROW.
Can you stay?

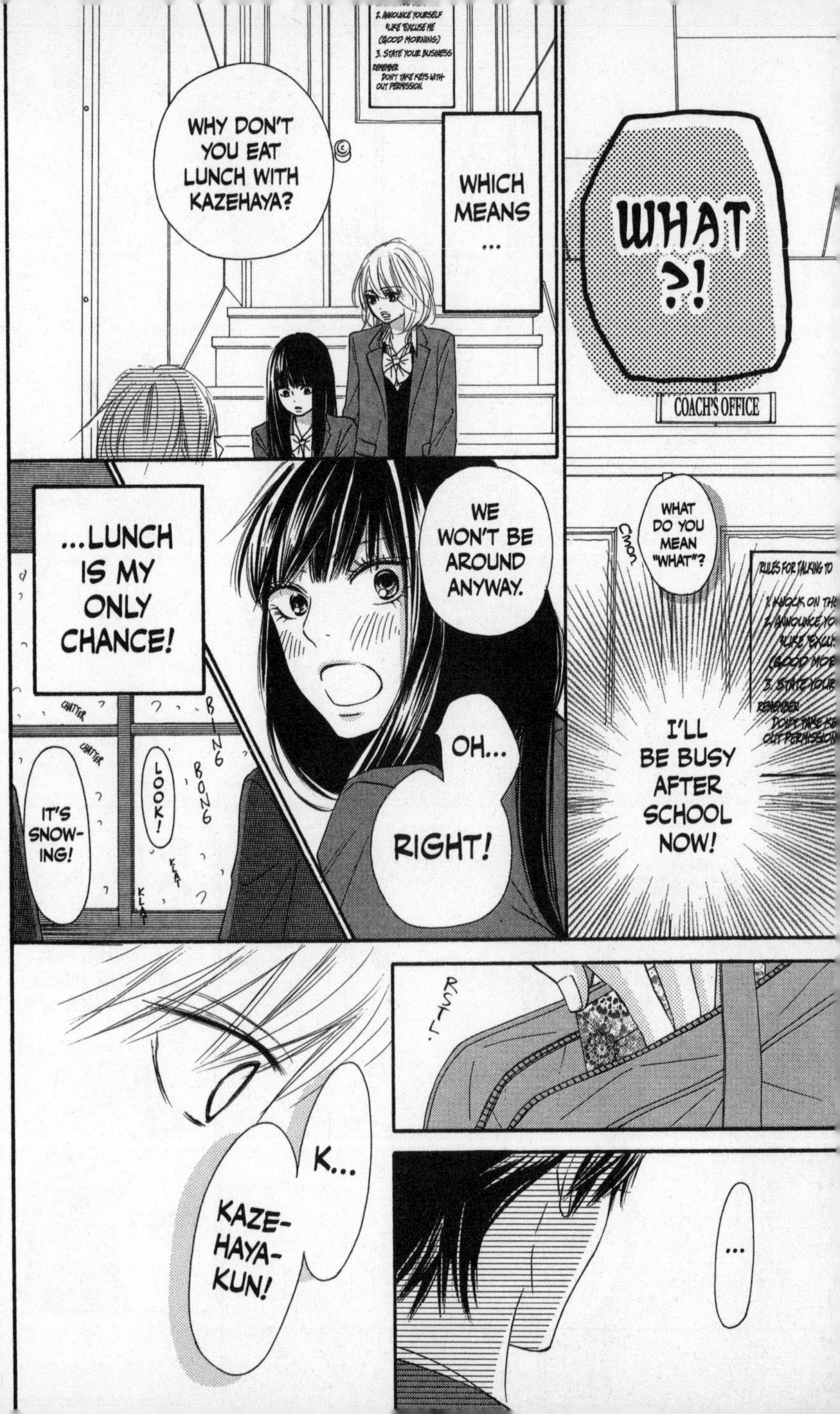
WHAT ?!
COACH'S OFFICE
2. ANNOUNCE YOURSELF LIKE "EXCUSE ME (GOOD MORNING)"
3. STATE YOUR BUSINESS
REMEMBER DON'T TAKE KEYS WITH-OUT PERMISSION.
WHICH MEANS ...
WHY DON'T YOU EAT LUNCH WITH KAZEHAYA?
WHAT DO YOU MEAN "WHAT"?
C'MON.
RULES FOR TALKING TO
I'LL BE BUSY AFTER SCHOOL NOW!
WE WON'T BE AROUND ANYWAY.
OH...
RIGHT!
...LUNCH IS MY ONLY CHANCE!
BING BONG
LOOK!
IT'S SNOWING-ING!
CHATTER
CHATTER
KLAT
KLAT
RSTL.
...
K...
KAZE-HAYA-KUN!

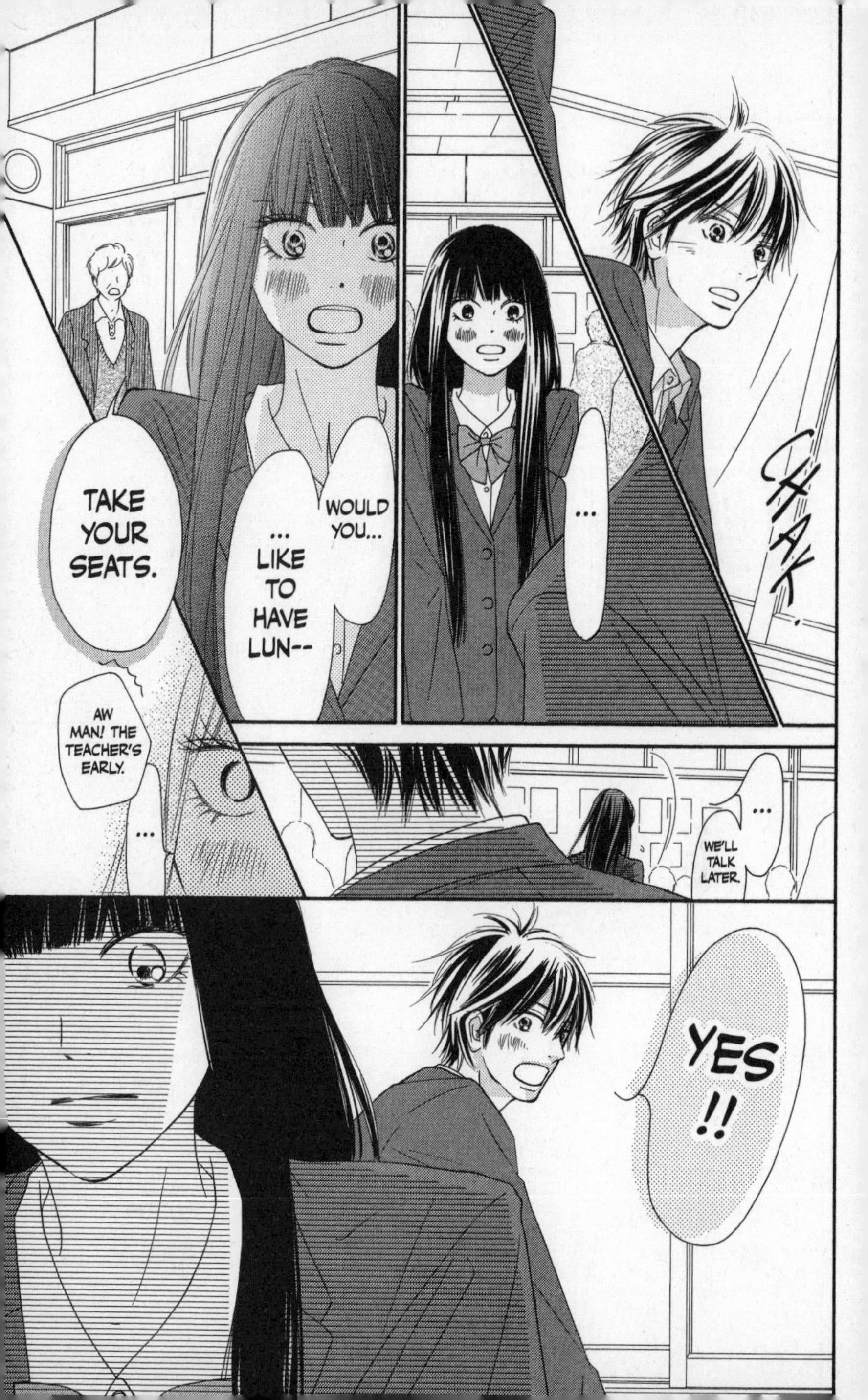

CHAK.
...
WOULD YOU...
... LIKE TO HAVE LUN--
TAKE YOUR SEATS.
...
WE'LL TALK LATER.
AW MAN! THE TEACHER'S EARLY.
...
YES !!

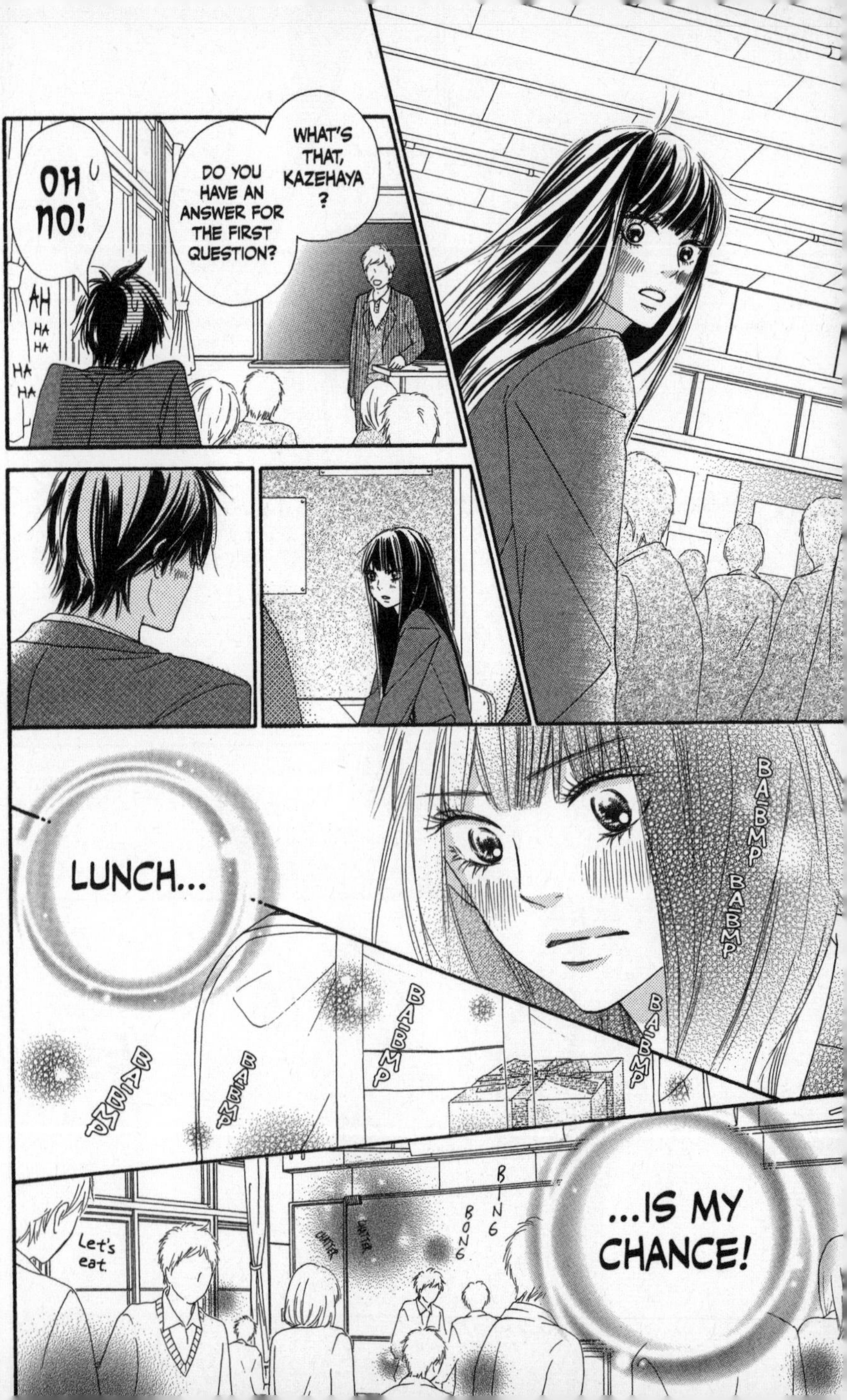

WHAT'S THAT, KAZEHAYA?
DO YOU HAVE AN ANSWER FOR THE FIRST QUESTION?
OH NO!
AH HA HA
HA HA
BA-BUMP BA-BUMP
LUNCH...
BA-BUMP
BA-BUMP
BA-BUMP
BA-BUMP
...IS MY CHANCE!
BING BONG
CHATTER
CHATTER
Let's eat.

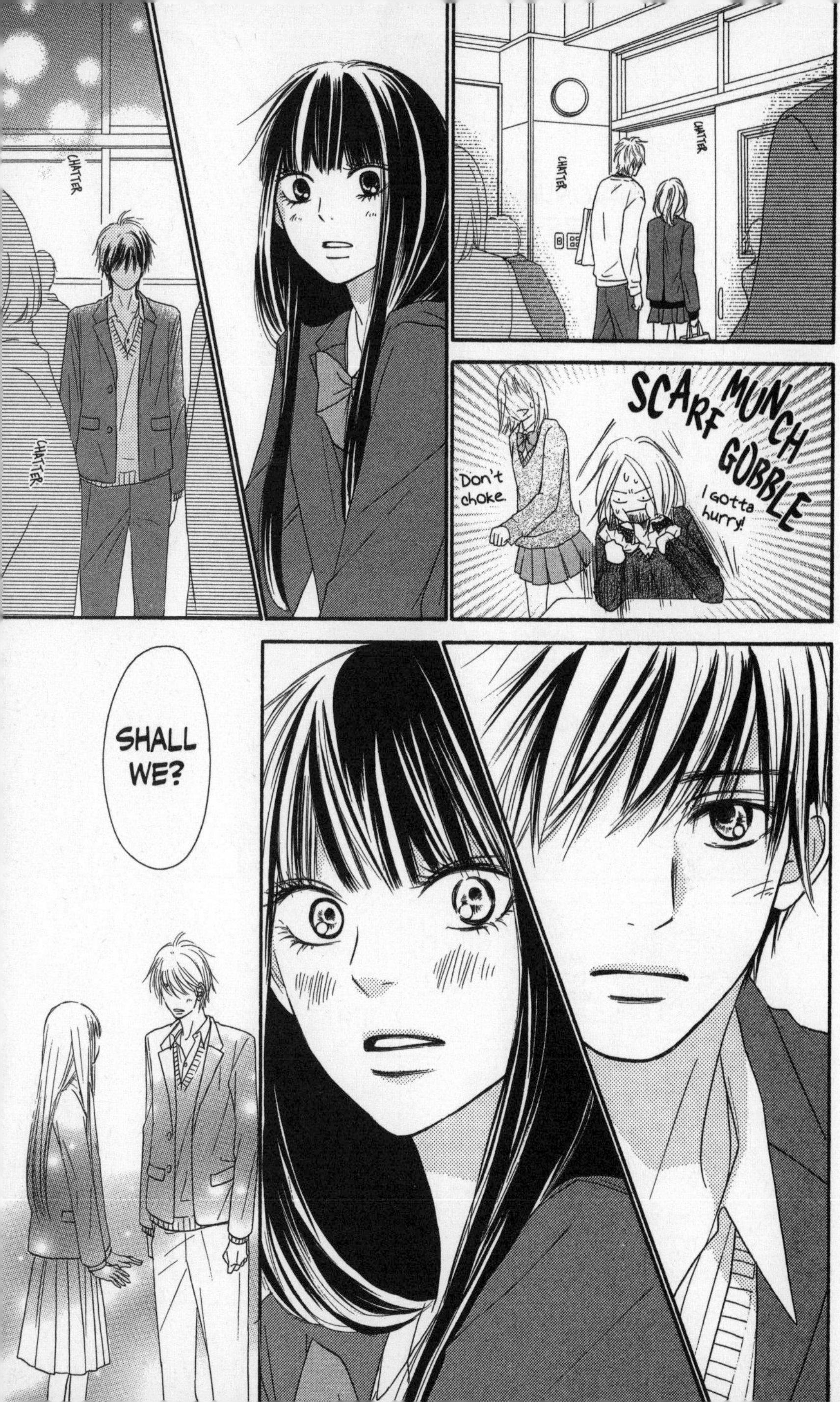
CHATTER
CHATTER
MUNCH
SCARF
GOBBLE
I gotta hurry!
Don't choke.
CHATTER
CHATTER
SHALL WE?

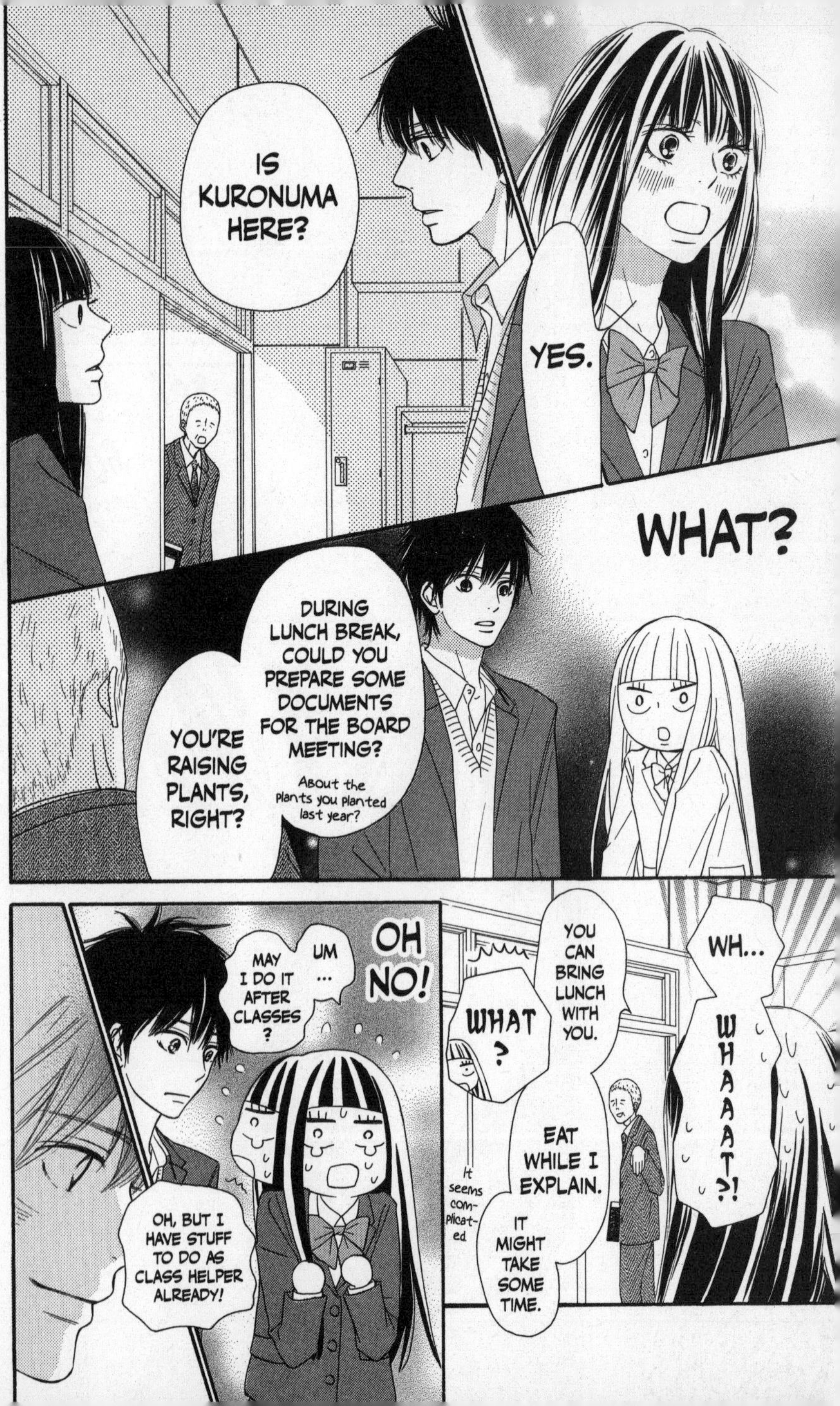
IS KURONUMA HERE?
YES.
WHAT?
DURING LUNCH BREAK, COULD YOU PREPARE SOME DOCUMENTS FOR THE BOARD MEETING?
About the plants you planted last year?
YOU'RE RAISING PLANTS, RIGHT?
WH... WHAAAT?!
YOU CAN BRING LUNCH WITH YOU.
WHAT?
EAT WHILE I EXPLAIN.
IT MIGHT TAKE SOME TIME.
It seems complicated.
OH NO!
UM ...
MAY I DO IT AFTER CLASSES?
OH, BUT I HAVE STUFF TO DO AS CLASS HELPER ALREADY!

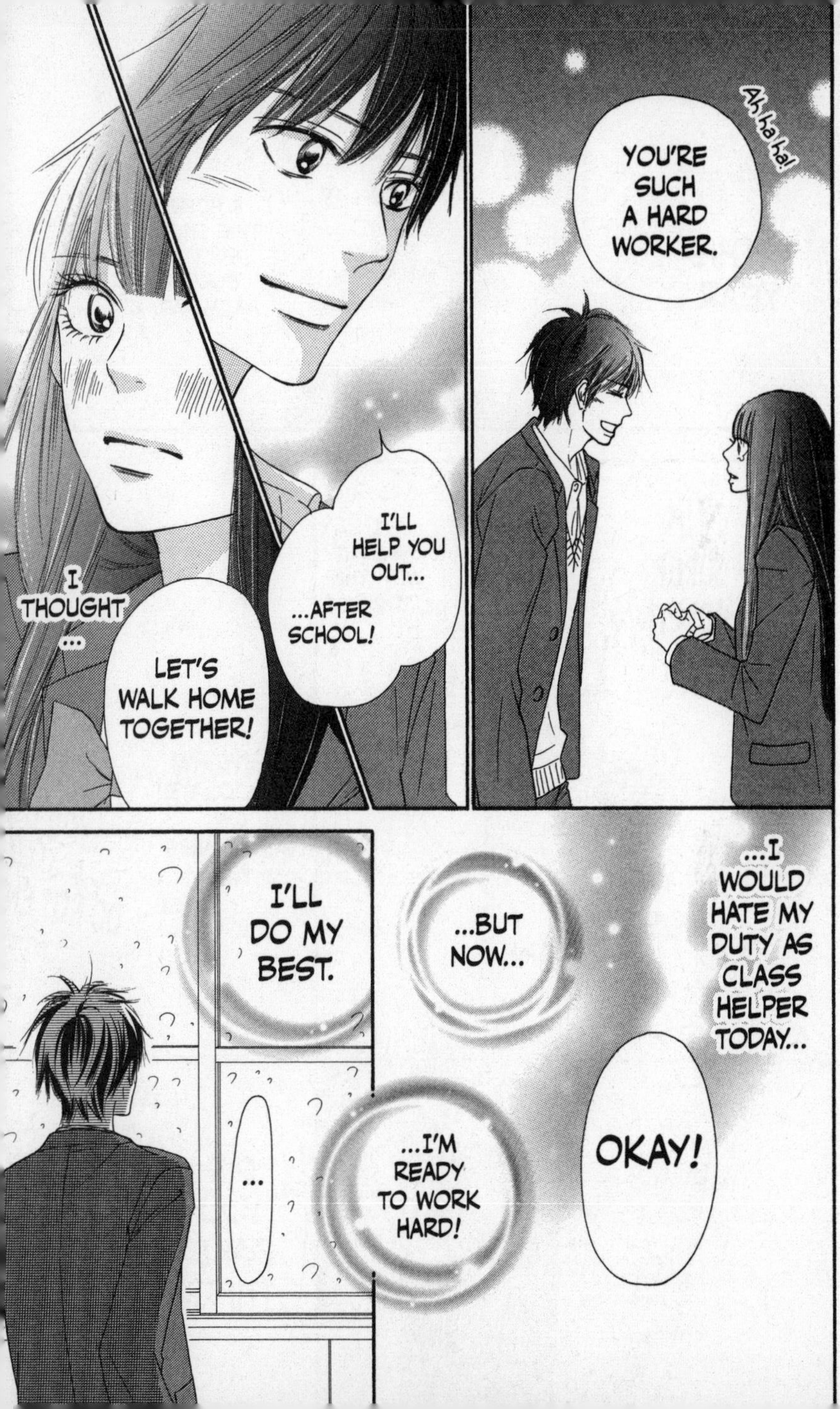
Ah ha ha!
YOU'RE SUCH A HARD WORKER.
I'LL HELP YOU OUT...
...AFTER SCHOOL!
I THOUGHT...
LET'S WALK HOME TOGETHER!
...I WOULD HATE MY DUTY AS CLASS HELPER TODAY...
...BUT NOW...
I'LL DO MY BEST.
OKAY!
...I'M READY TO WORK HARD!
...

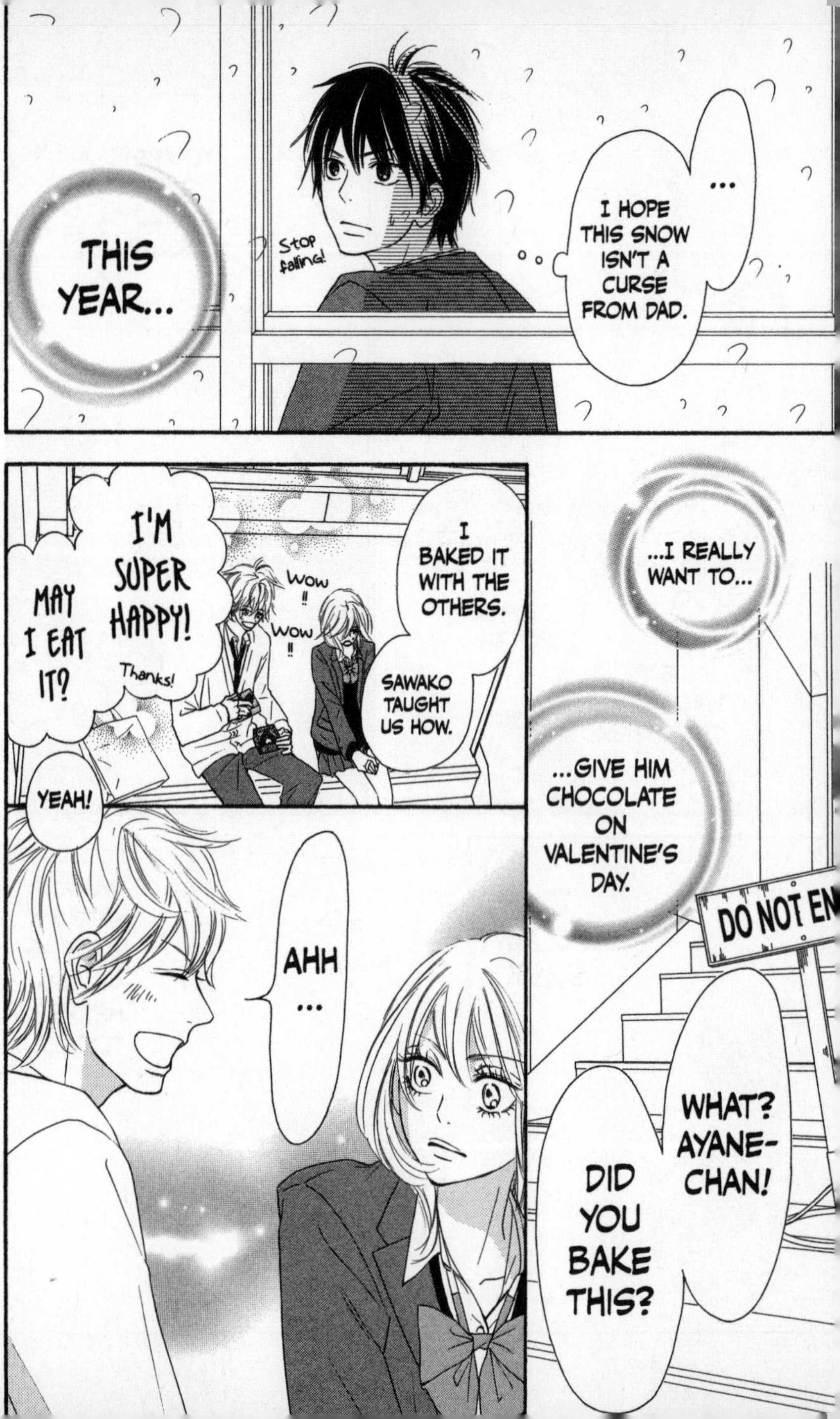
...
I HOPE THIS SNOW ISN'T A CURSE FROM DAD.
Stop falling!
THIS YEAR...
...I REALLY WANT TO...
...GIVE HIM CHOCOLATE ON VALENTINE'S DAY.
I BAKED IT WITH THE OTHERS.
SAWAKO TAUGHT US HOW.
Wow!!
Wow!!
I'M SUPER HAPPY!
Thanks!
MAY I EAT IT?
YEAH!
DO NOT EN
WHAT? AYANE-CHAN!
DID YOU BAKE THIS?
AHH...

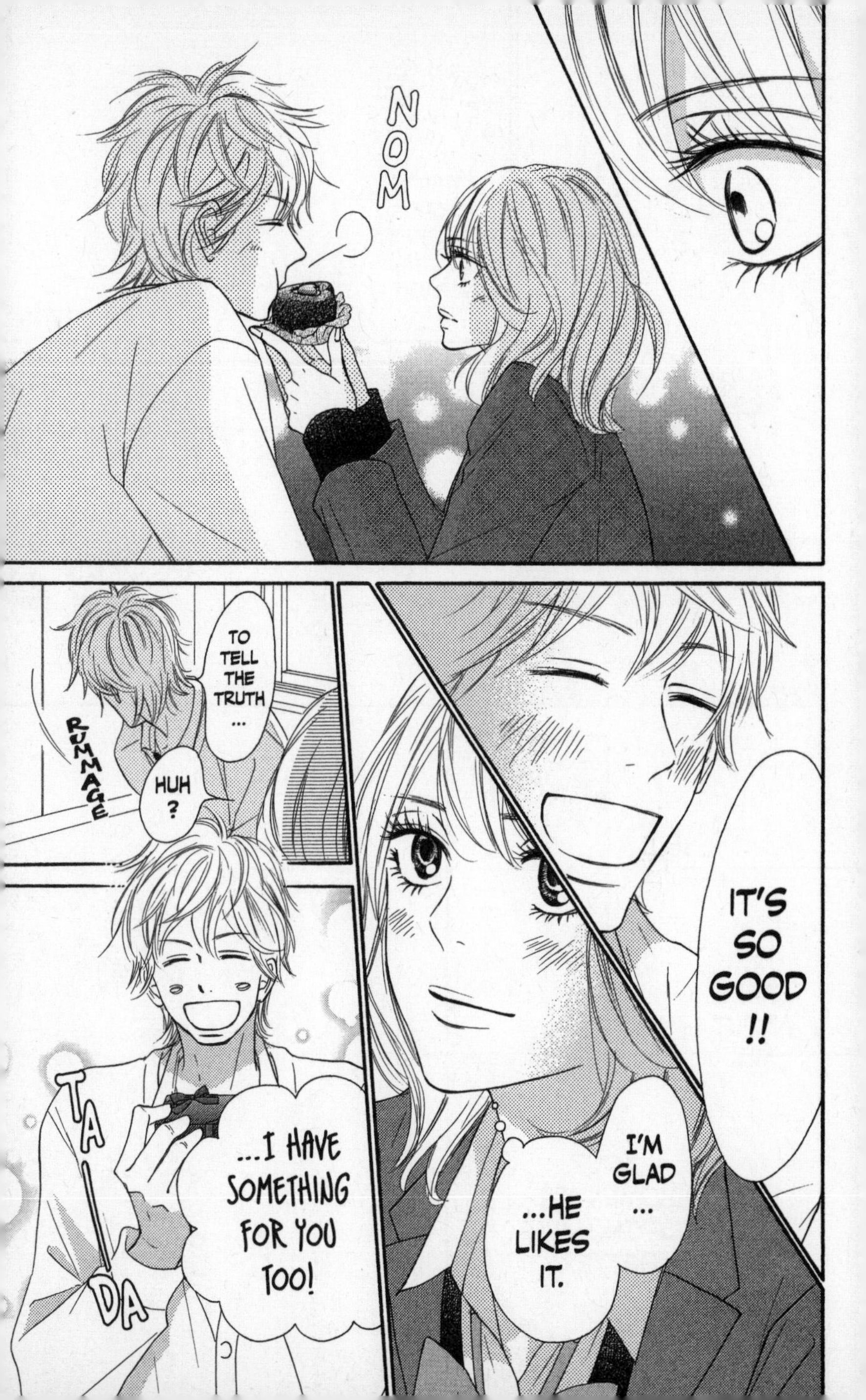
NOM
IT'S SO GOOD!!
I'M GLAD...
...HE LIKES IT.
TO TELL THE TRUTH...
RUMMAGE
HUH?
TA-DA
...I HAVE SOMETHING FOR YOU TOO!

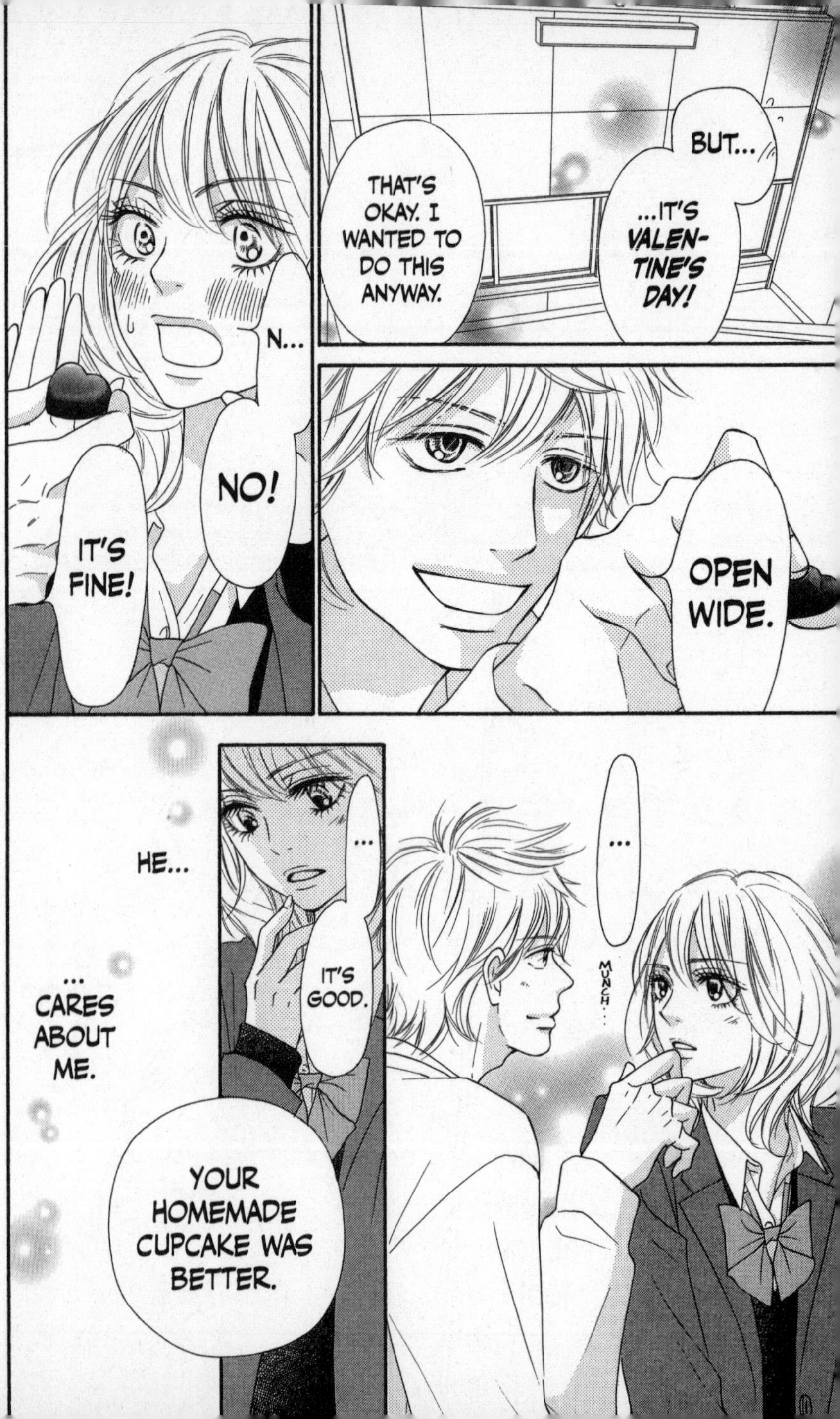
BUT...
...IT'S VALEN-TINE'S DAY!
THAT'S OKAY. I WANTED TO DO THIS ANYWAY.
OPEN WIDE.
N...
NO!
IT'S FINE!
...
MUNCH...
...
IT'S GOOD.
YOUR HOMEMADE CUPCAKE WAS BETTER.
HE...
...CARES ABOUT ME.

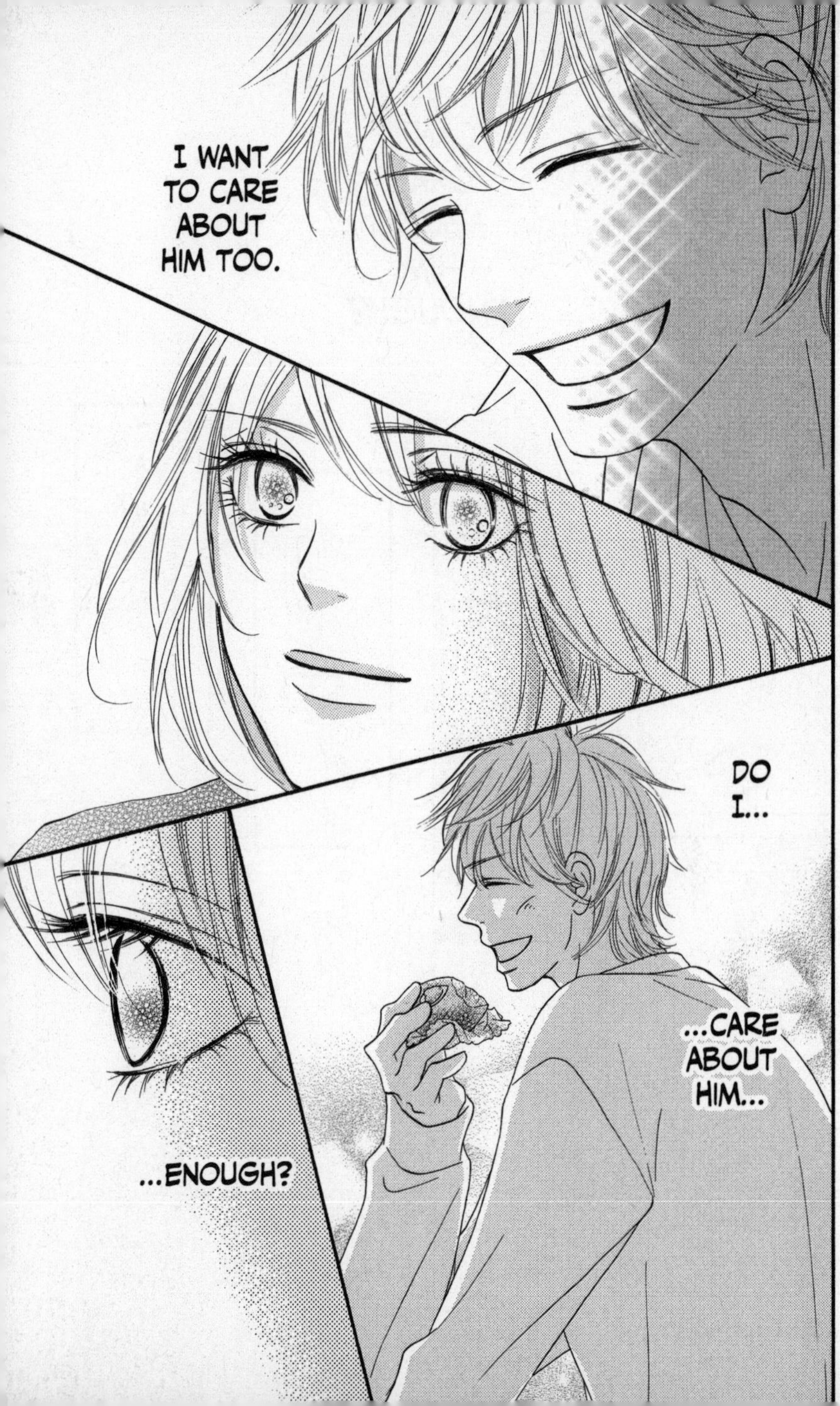
I WANT TO CARE ABOUT HIM TOO.
DO I...
...CARE ABOUT HIM...
...ENOUGH?

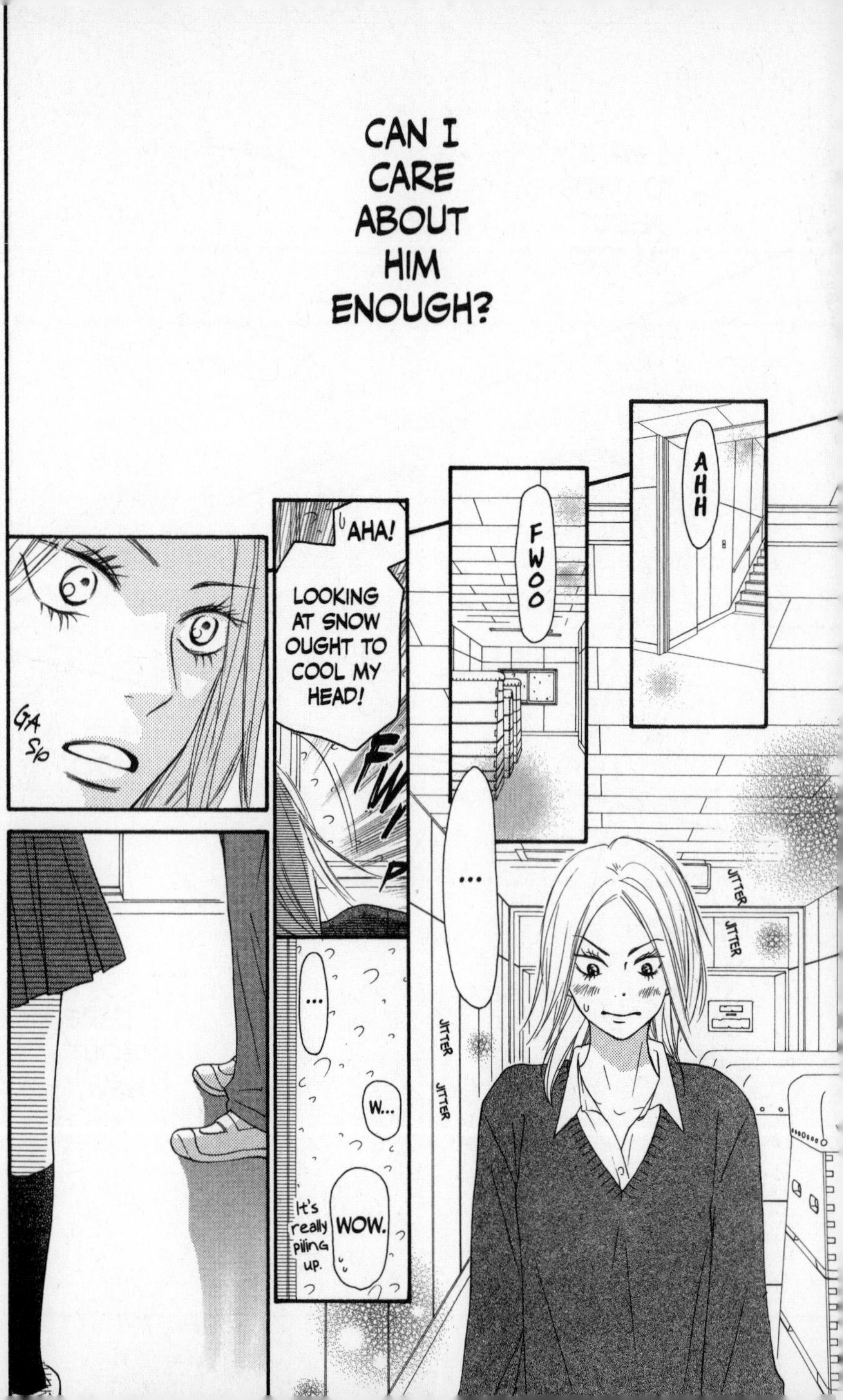
CAN I CARE ABOUT HIM ENOUGH?
AHH
FWOO
AHA!
LOOKING AT SNOW OUGHT TO COOL MY HEAD!
FWIP
GASP
...
JITTER
JITTER
JITTER
JITTER
...
W...
WOW.
It's really piling up.

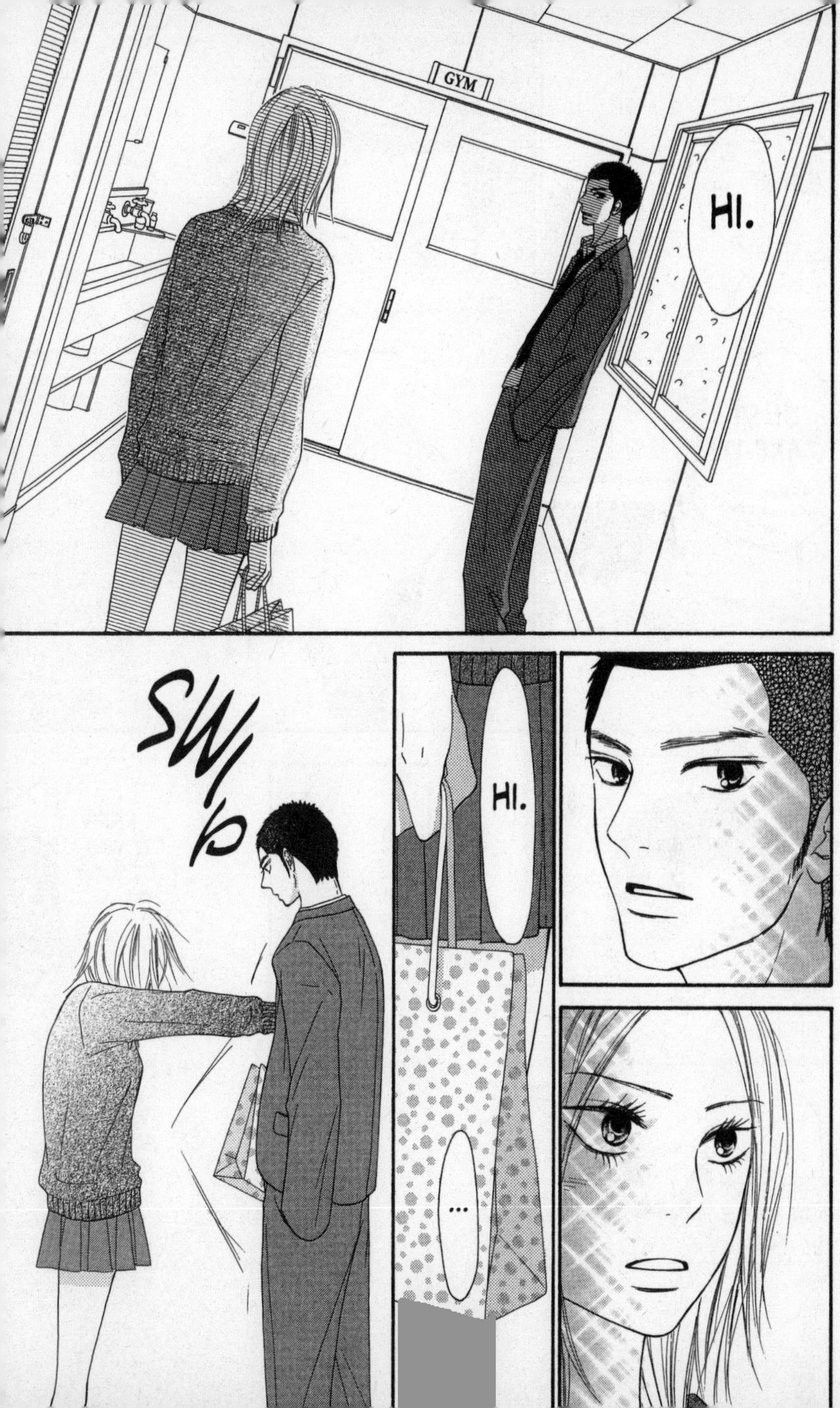
GYM
HI.
HI.
...
SWIP

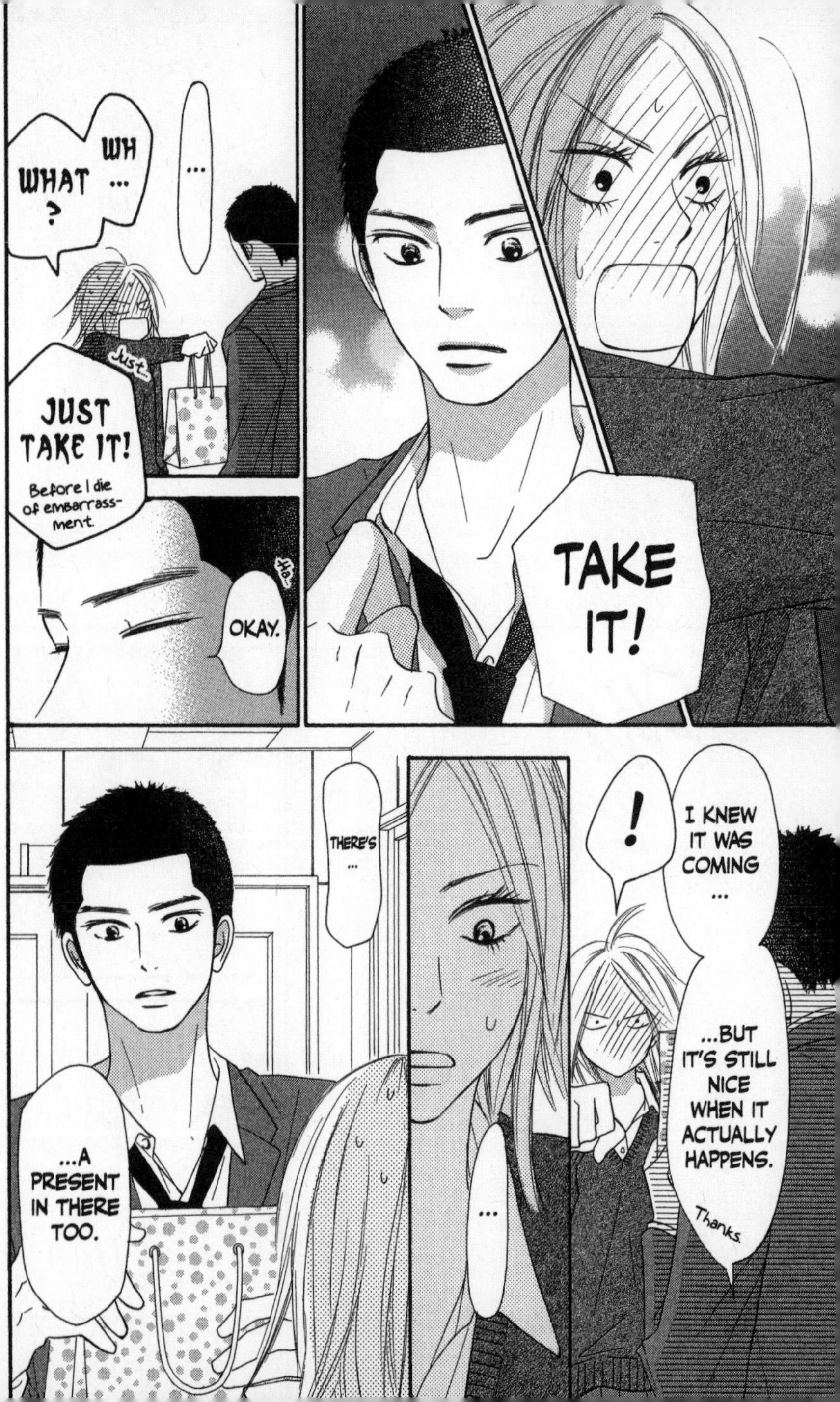
TAKE IT!
...
WH...
WHAT?
Just...
JUST TAKE IT!
Before I die of embarrassment.
Ha...
OKAY.
!
I KNEW IT WAS COMING...
...BUT IT'S STILL NICE WHEN IT ACTUALLY HAPPENS.
Thanks.
...
THERE'S...
...A PRESENT IN THERE TOO.

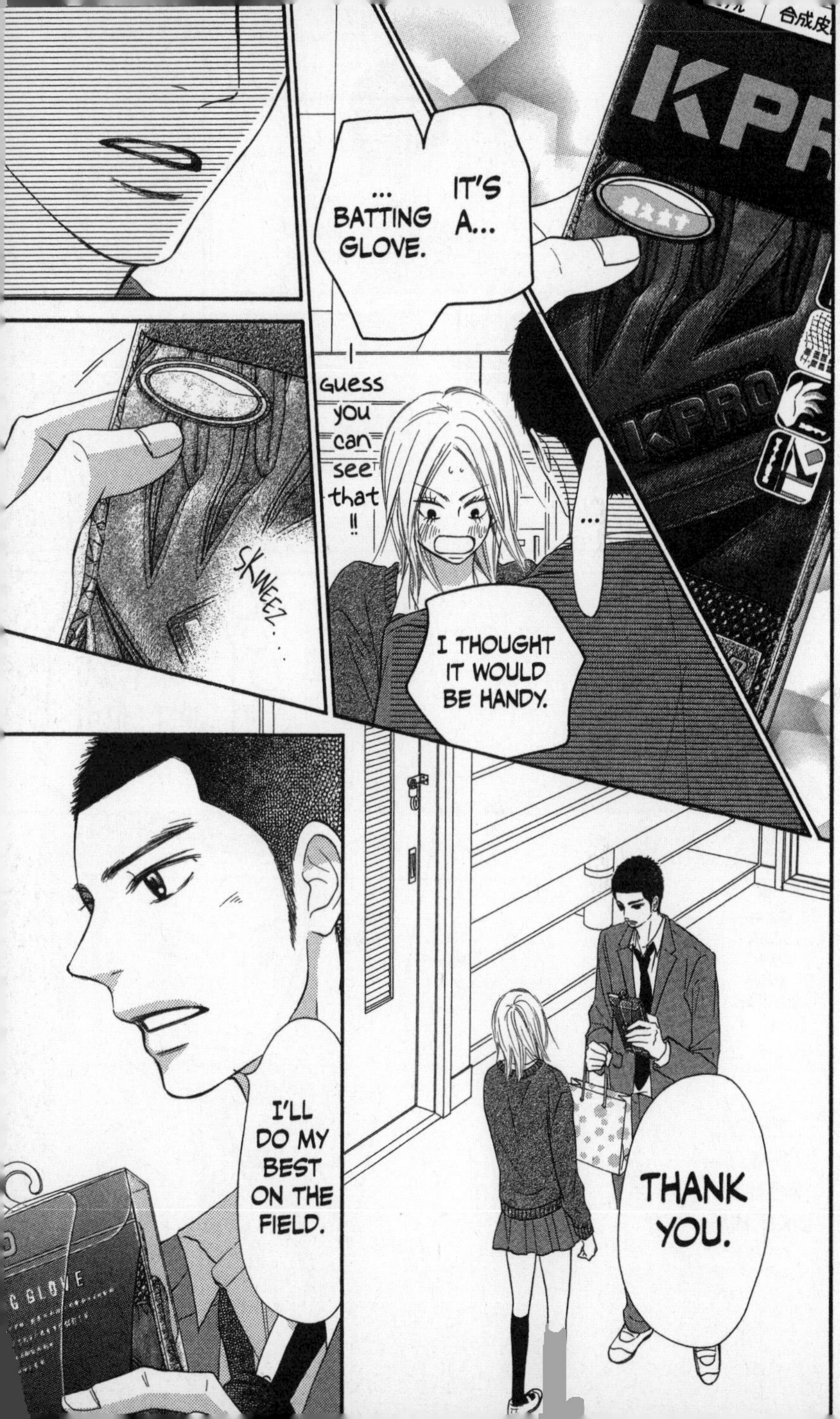
合成皮
KPR
IT'S A... ...BATTING GLOVE.
KPRO
I guess you can see that!!
...
I THOUGHT IT WOULD BE HANDY.
SKWEEZ
THANK YOU.
I'LL DO MY BEST ON THE FIELD.
G GLOVE

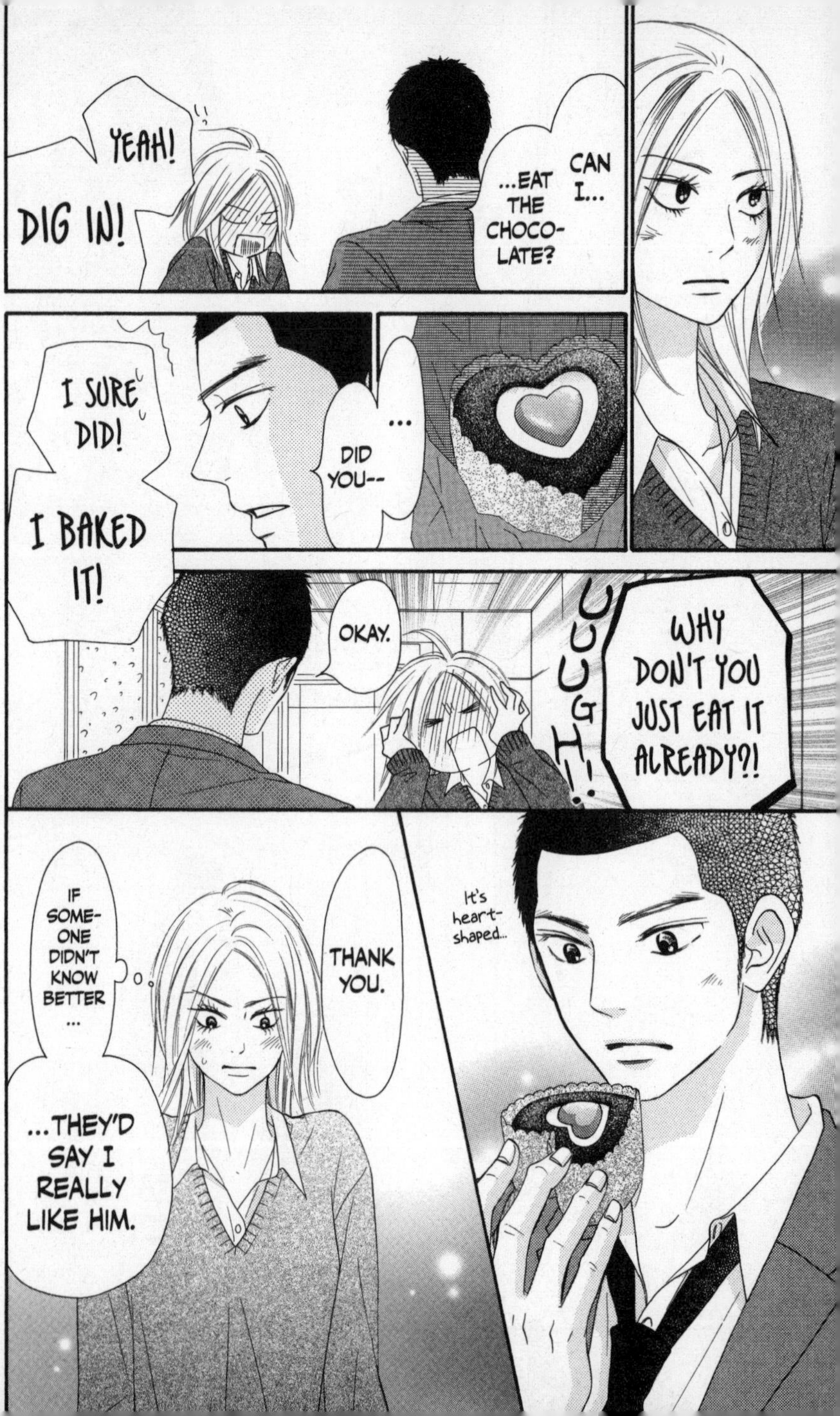
CAN I... ...EAT THE CHOCOLATE?
YEAH!
DIG IN!
... DID YOU--
I SURE DID!
I BAKED IT!
WHY DON'T YOU JUST EAT IT ALREADY?!
UUUGH!!
OKAY.
It's heart-shaped...
THANK YOU.
IF SOMEONE DIDN'T KNOW BETTER...
...THEY'D SAY I REALLY LIKE HIM.

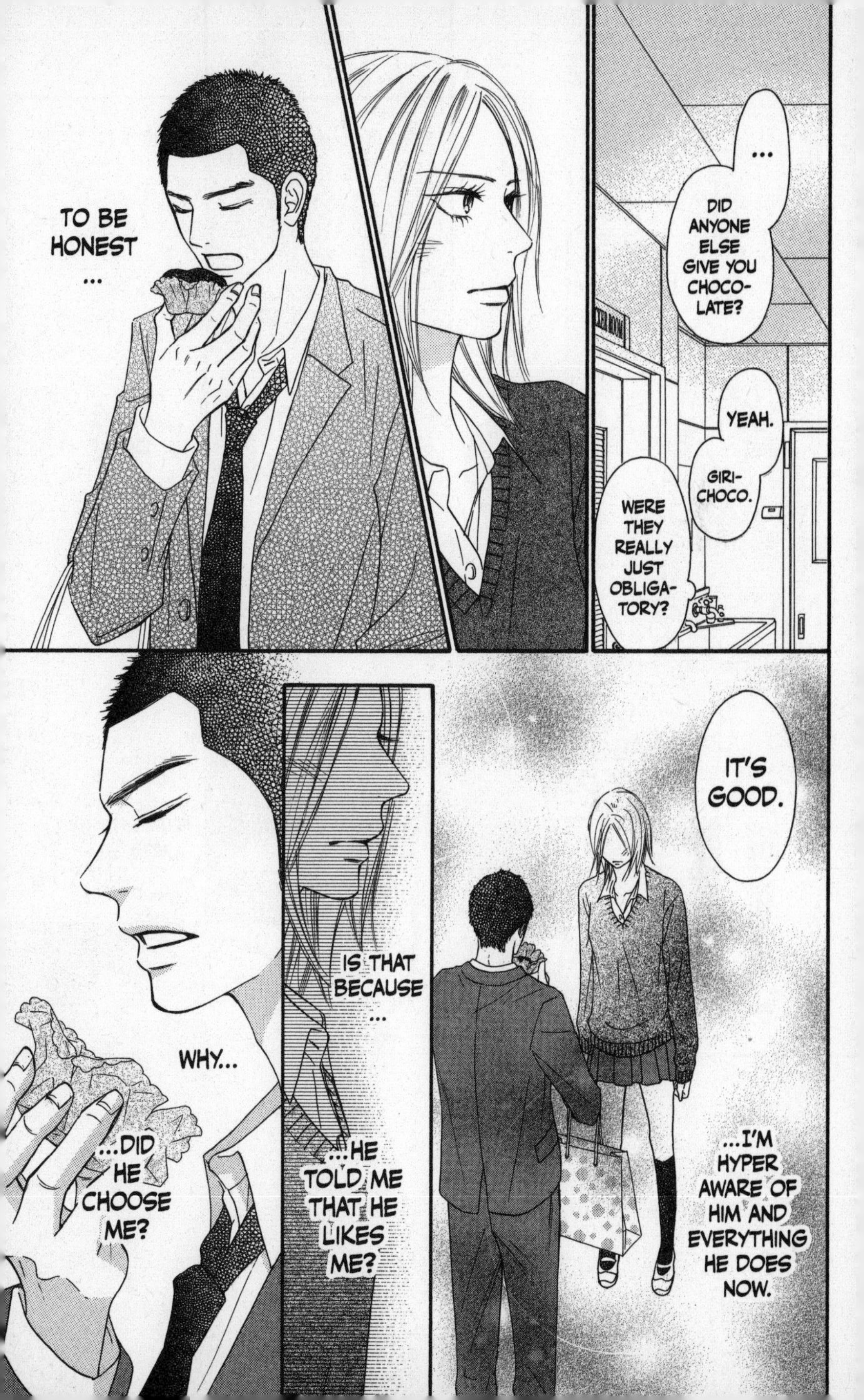
...
DID ANYONE ELSE GIVE YOU CHOCO-LATE?
YEAH.
GIRI-CHOCO.
WERE THEY REALLY JUST OBLIGA-TORY?
TO BE HONEST ...
IT'S GOOD.
...I'M HYPER AWARE OF HIM AND EVERYTHING HE DOES NOW.
IS THAT BECAUSE ...
...HE TOLD ME THAT HE LIKES ME?
WHY...
...DID HE CHOOSE ME?

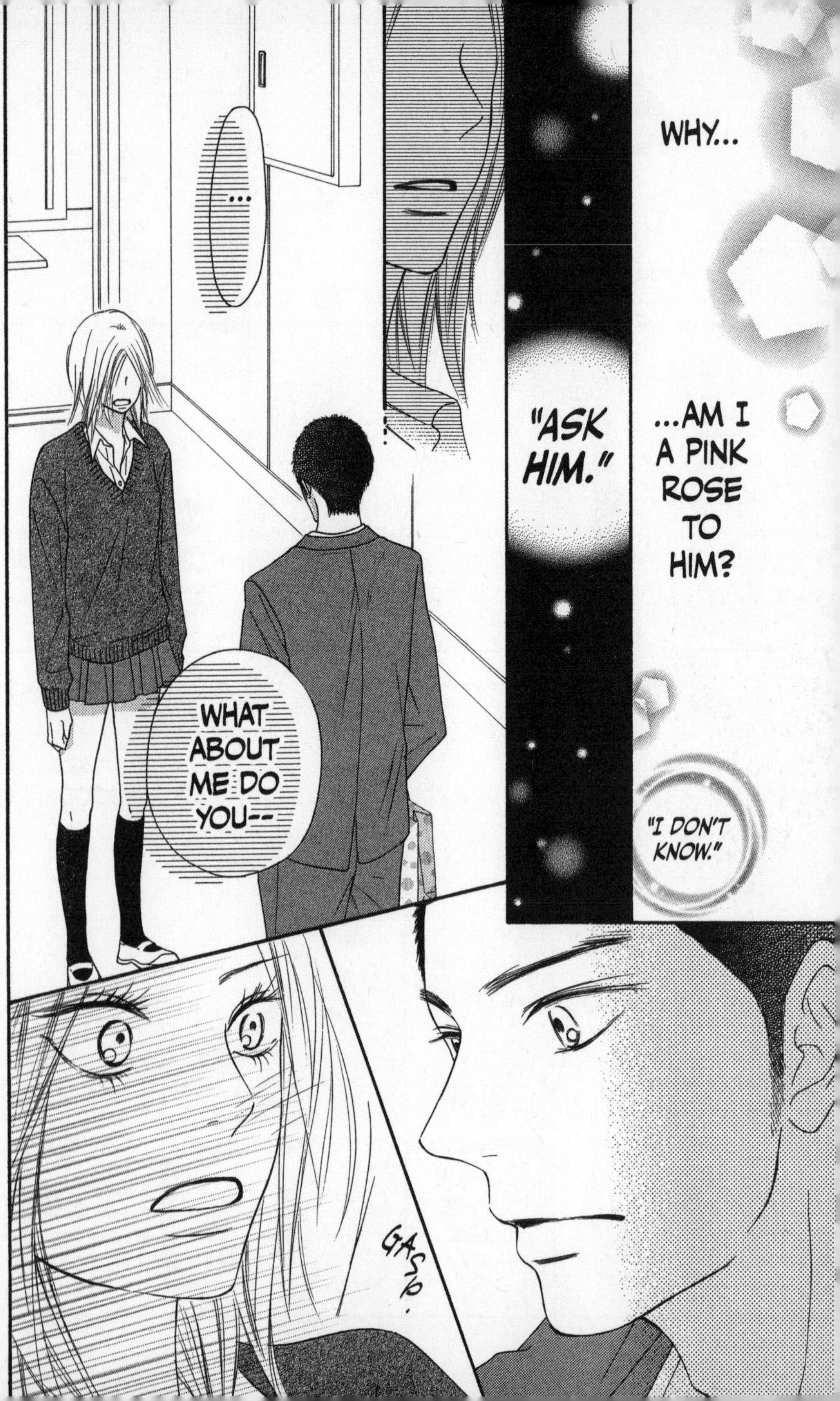
WHY...
...AM I A PINK ROSE TO HIM?
"I DON'T KNOW."
"ASK HIM."
...
WHAT ABOUT ME DO YOU--
GASP.

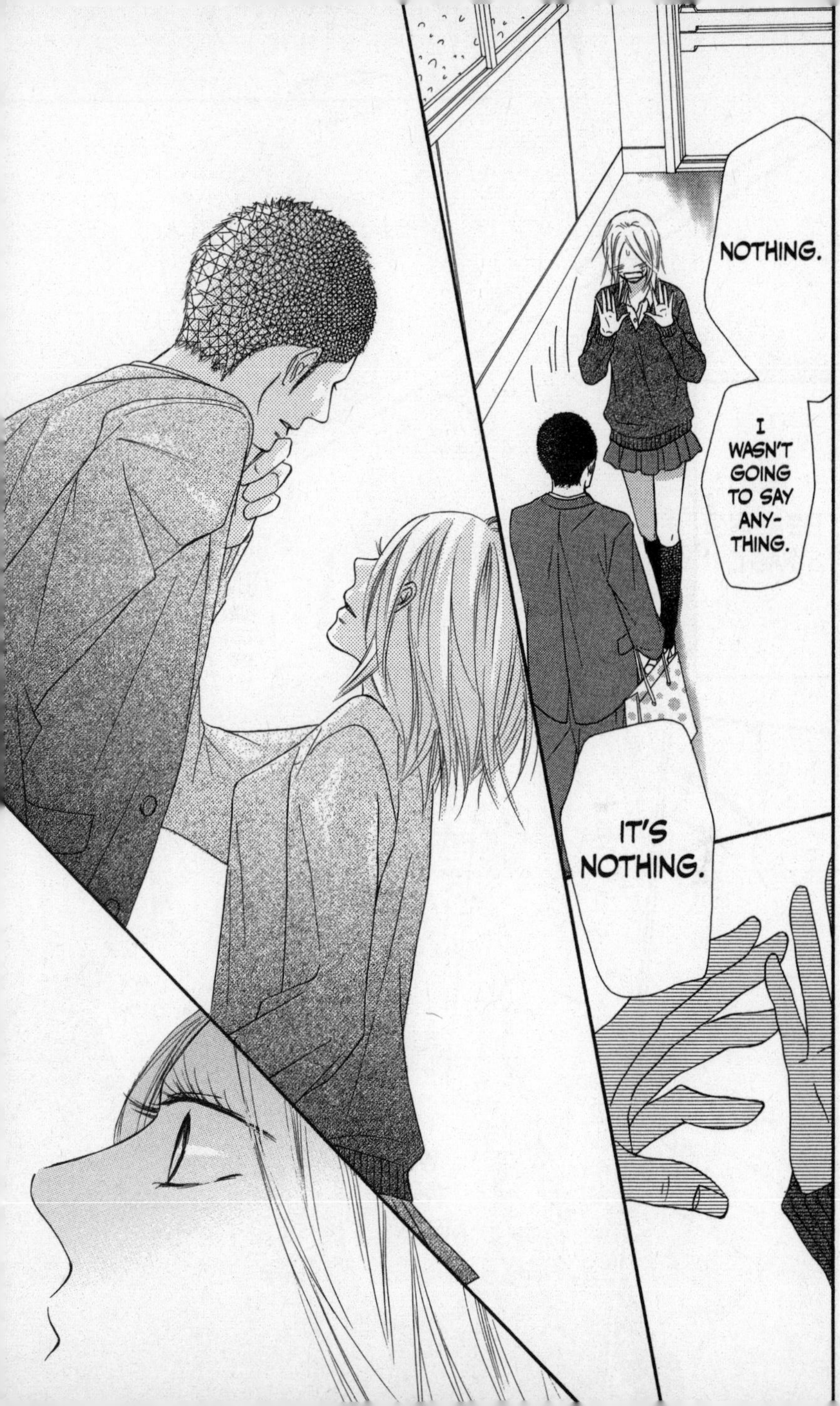
NOTHING.
I WASN'T GOING TO SAY ANY-THING.
IT'S NOTHING.

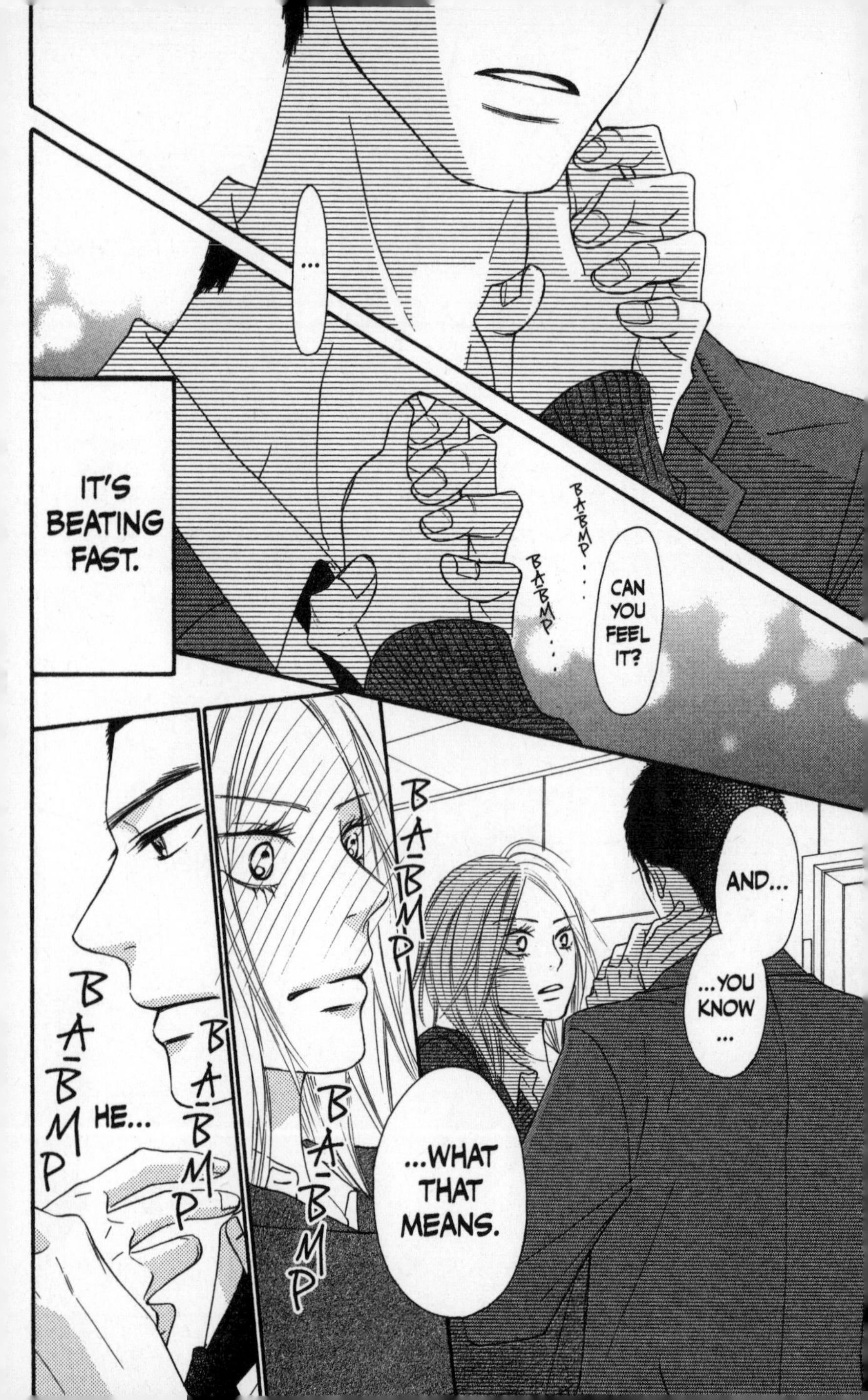
...
BA-BMP...
BA-BMP...
CAN YOU FEEL IT?
IT'S BEATING FAST.
AND...
...YOU KNOW...
...WHAT THAT MEANS.
BA-BMP
BA-BMP
BA-BMP
HE...
BA-BMP

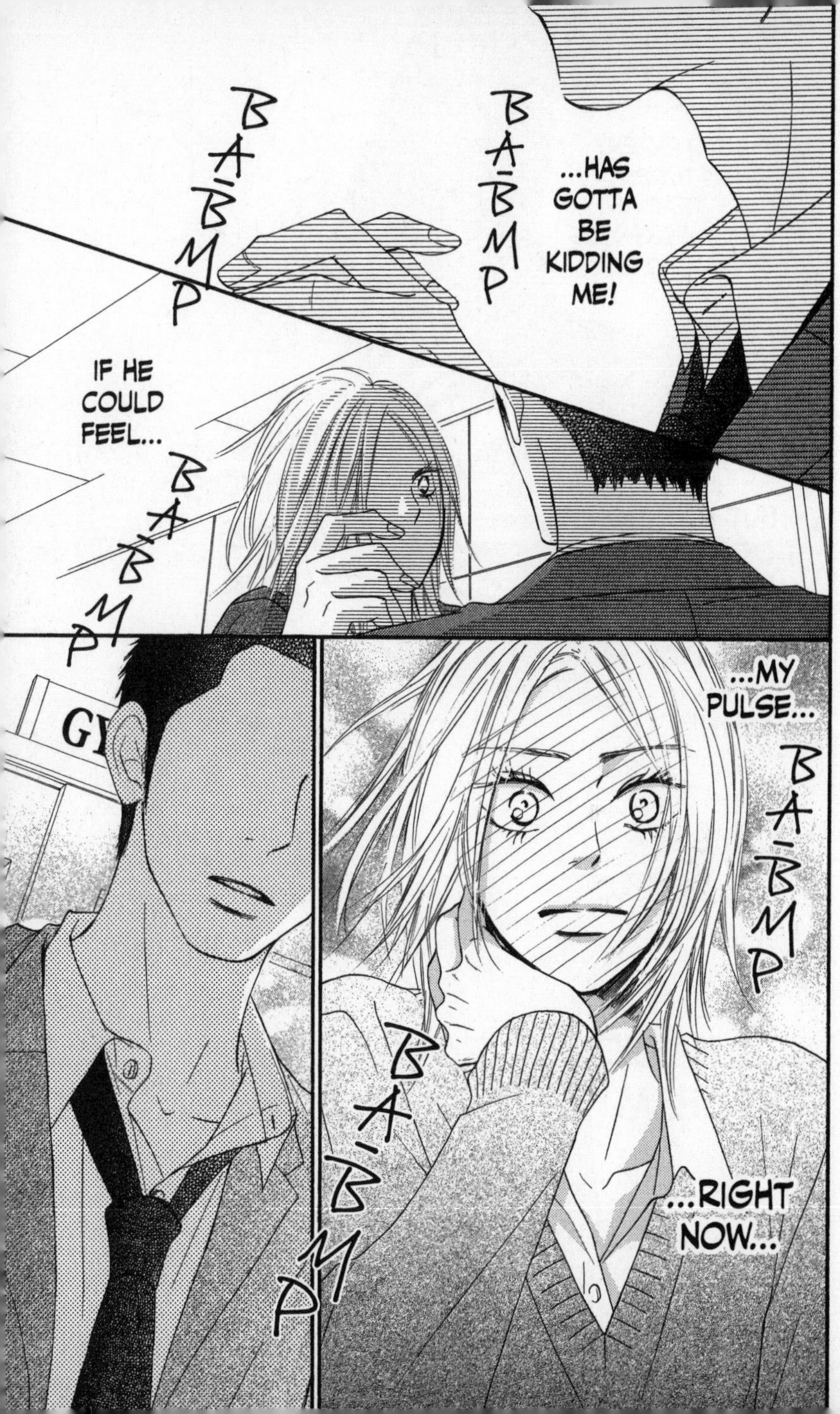
BA-BMP
...HAS GOTTA BE KIDDING ME!
BA-BMP
IF HE COULD FEEL...
BA-BMP
...MY PULSE...
BA-BMP
...RIGHT NOW...
BA-BMP

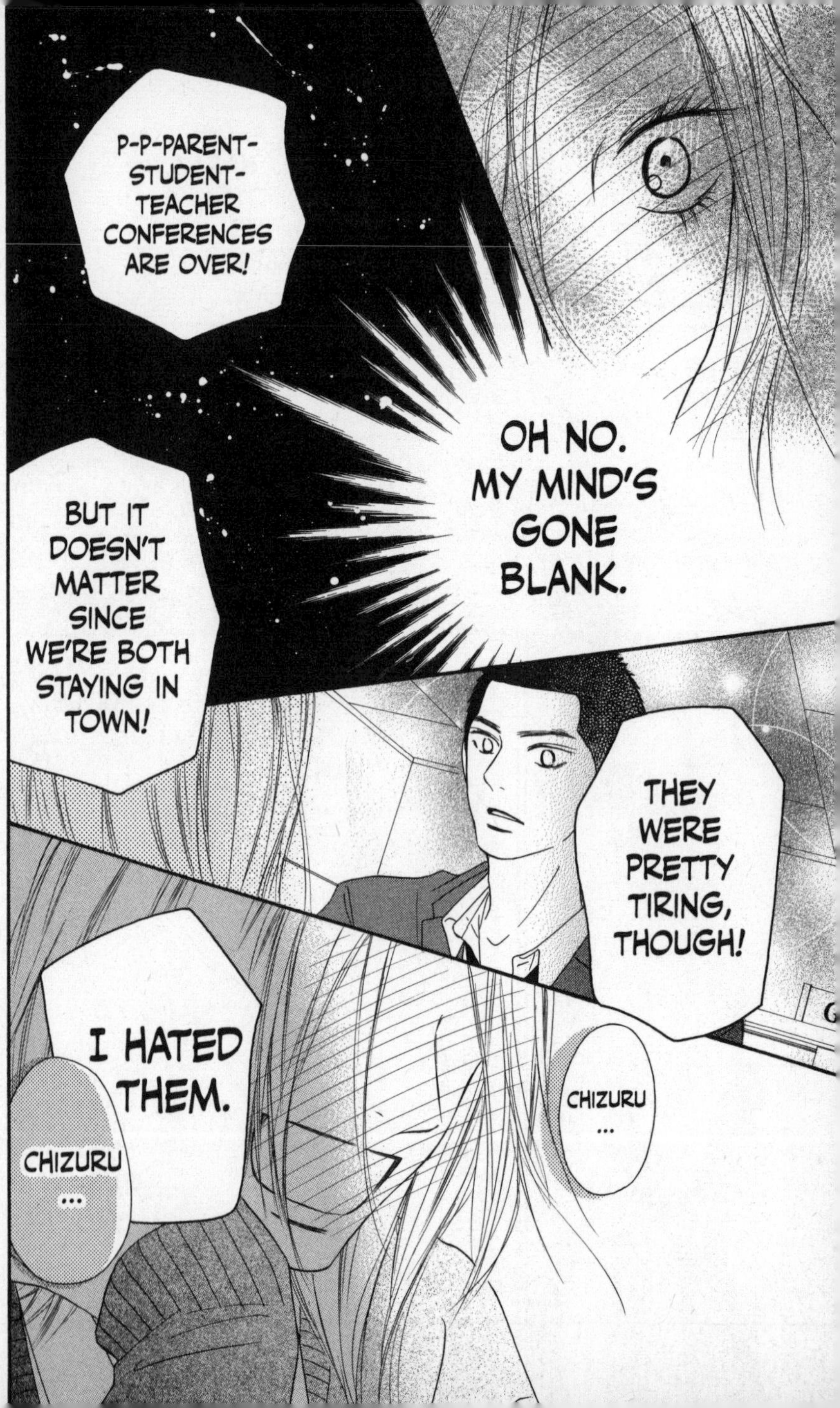
P-P-PARENT-STUDENT-TEACHER CONFERENCES ARE OVER!
BUT IT DOESN'T MATTER SINCE WE'RE BOTH STAYING IN TOWN!
OH NO. MY MIND'S GONE BLANK.
THEY WERE PRETTY TIRING, THOUGH!
CHIZURU ...
I HATED THEM.
CHIZURU ...

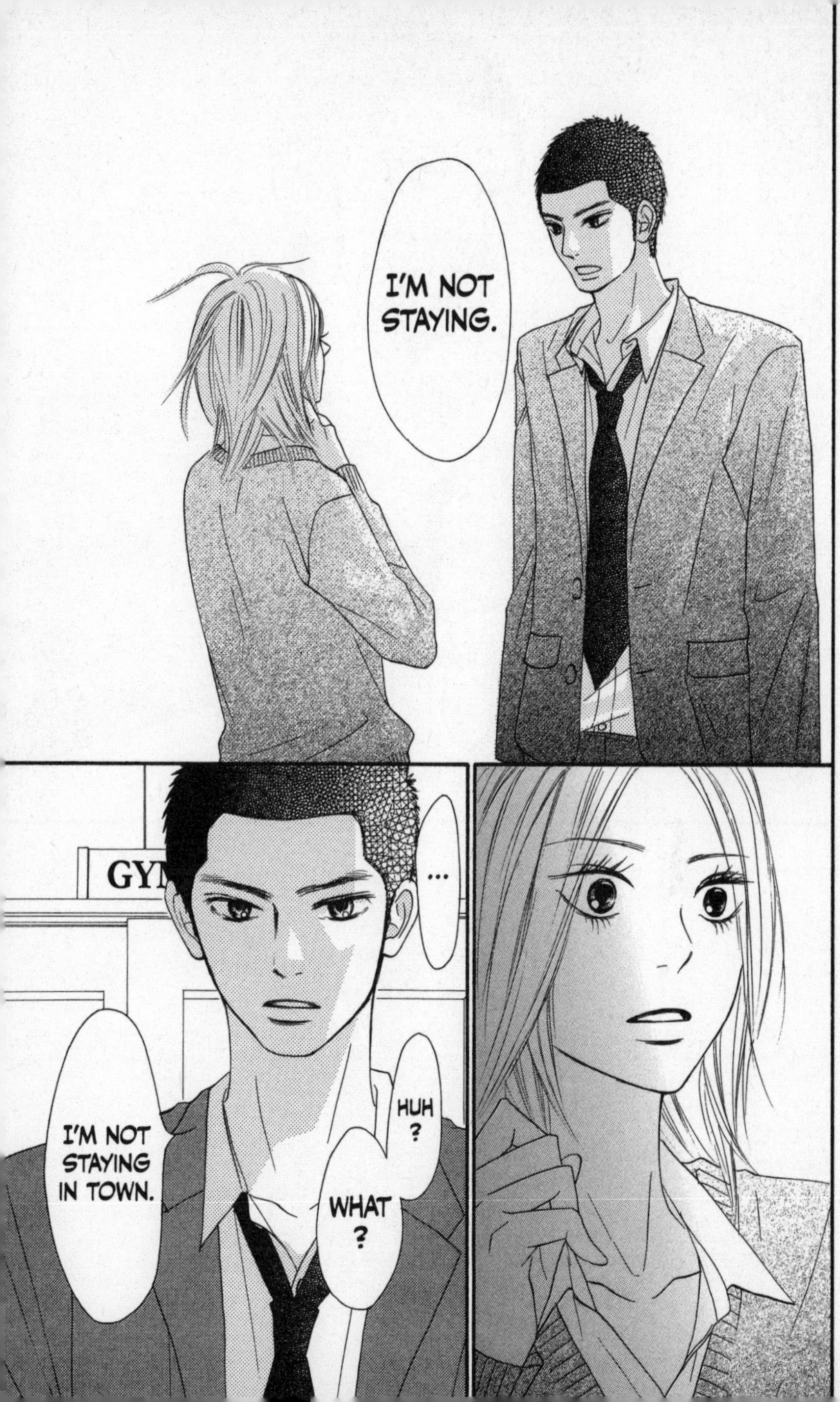
I'M NOT STAYING.
...
I'M NOT STAYING IN TOWN.
HUH?
WHAT?

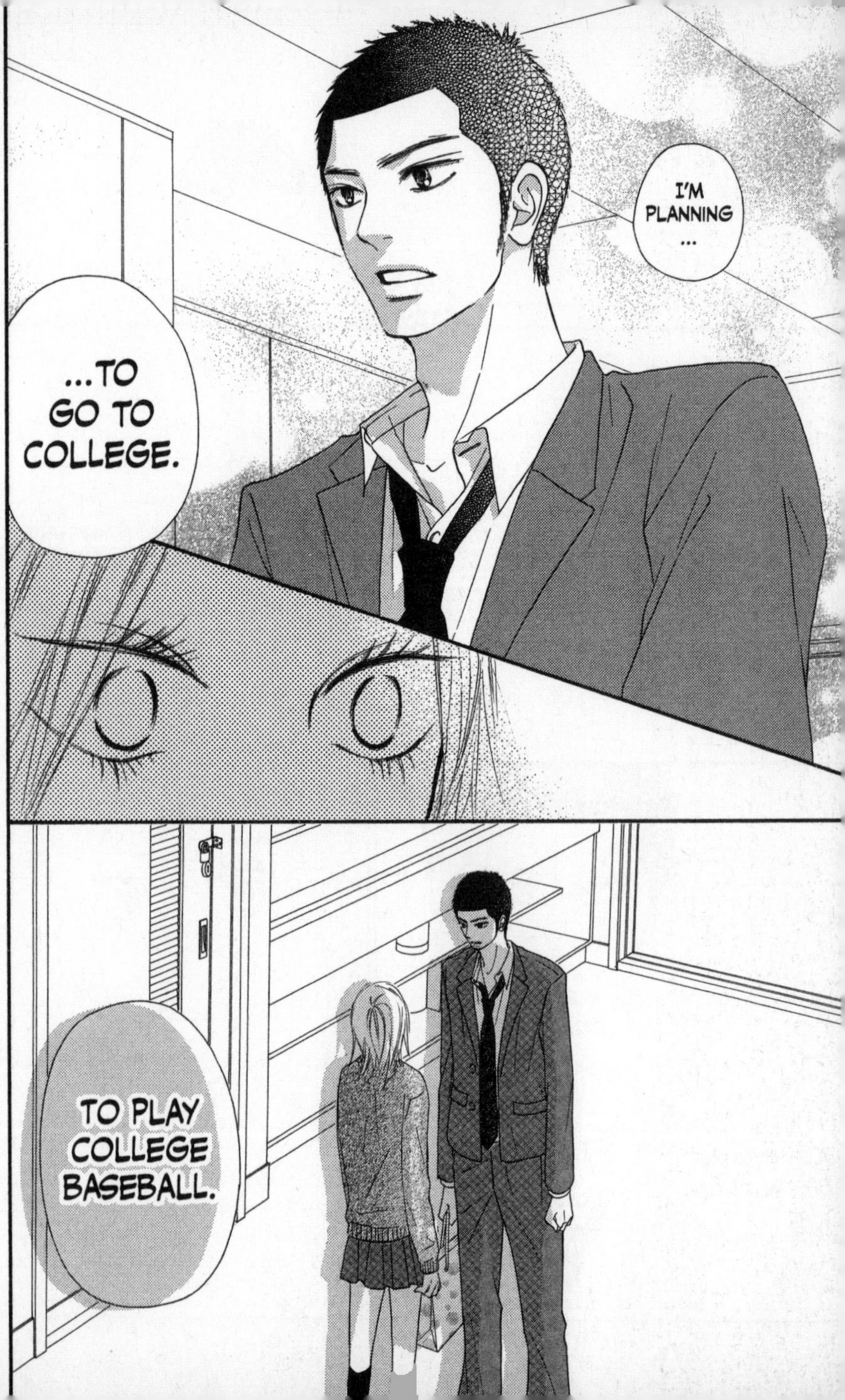
I'M PLANNING ...
...TO GO TO COLLEGE.
TO PLAY COLLEGE BASEBALL.

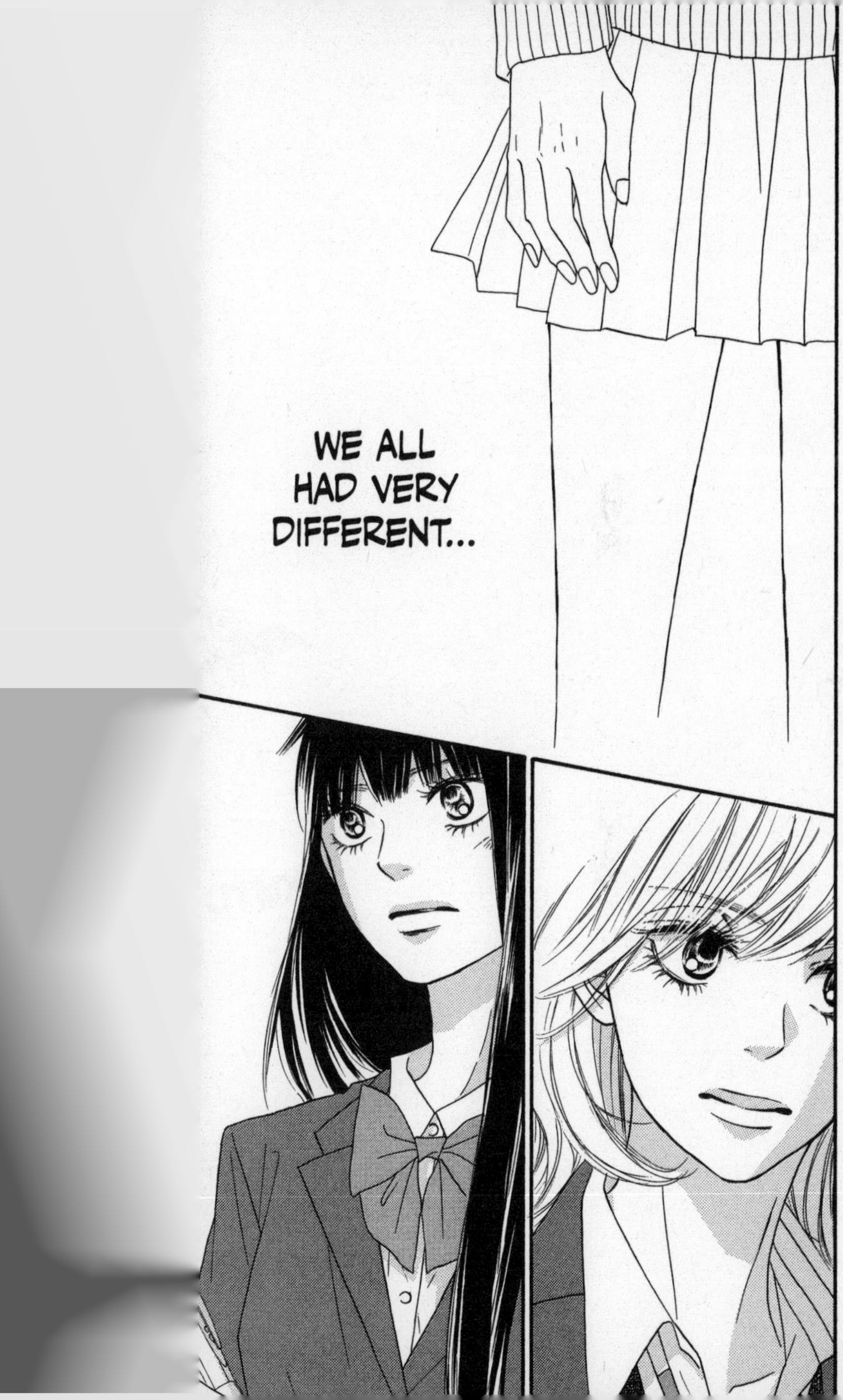
WE ALL HAD VERY DIFFERENT...

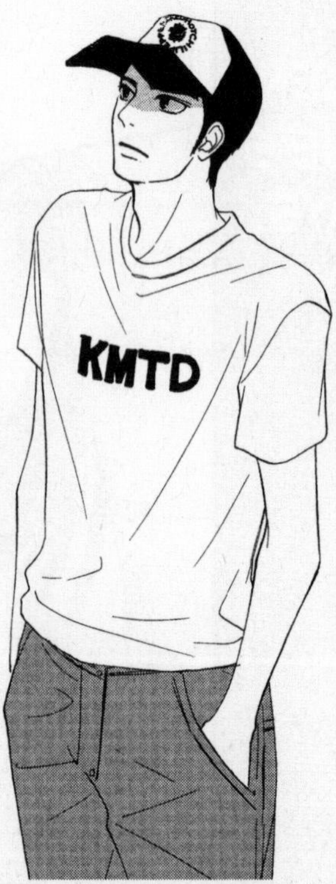
KMTD

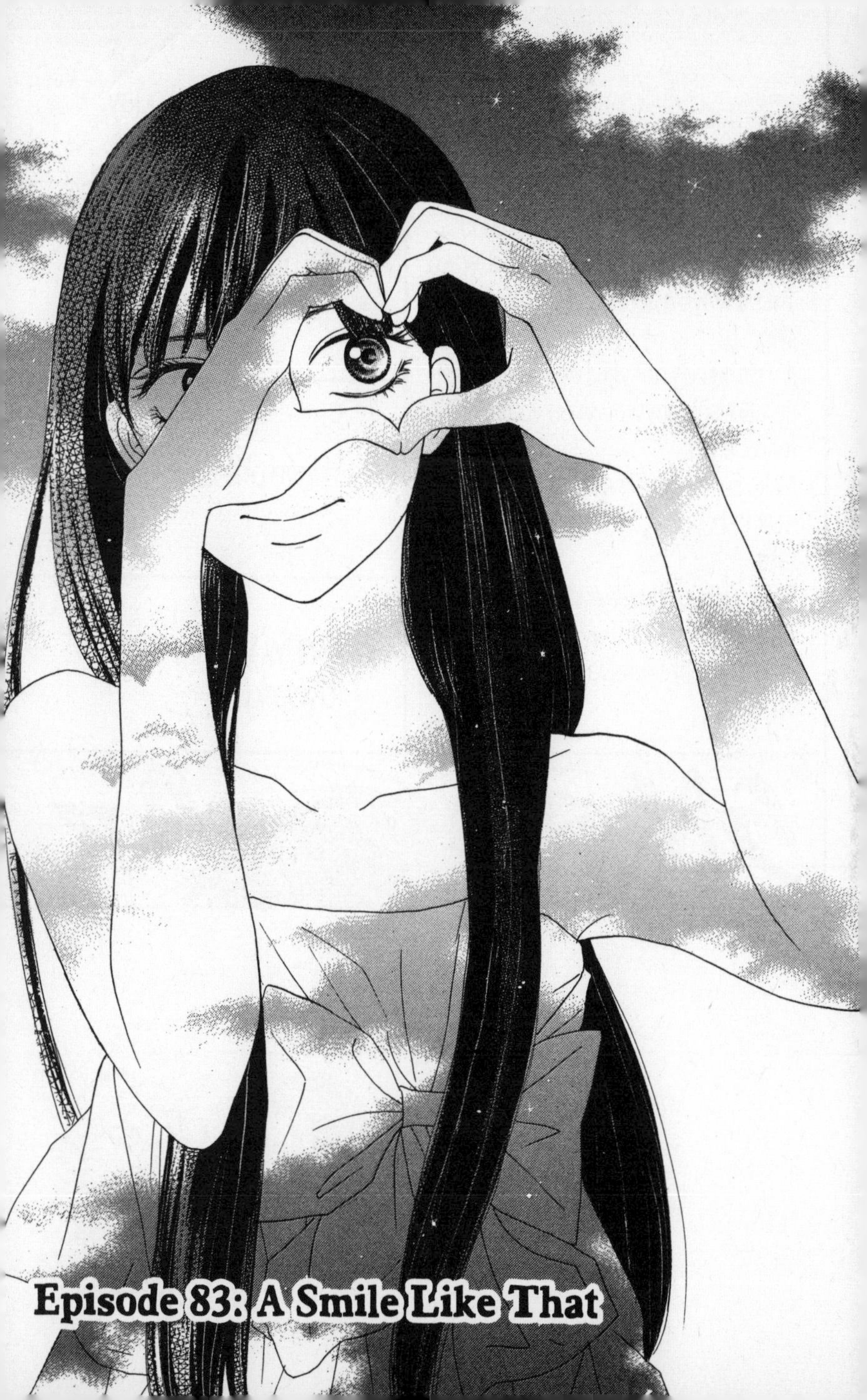
Episode 83: A Smile Like That

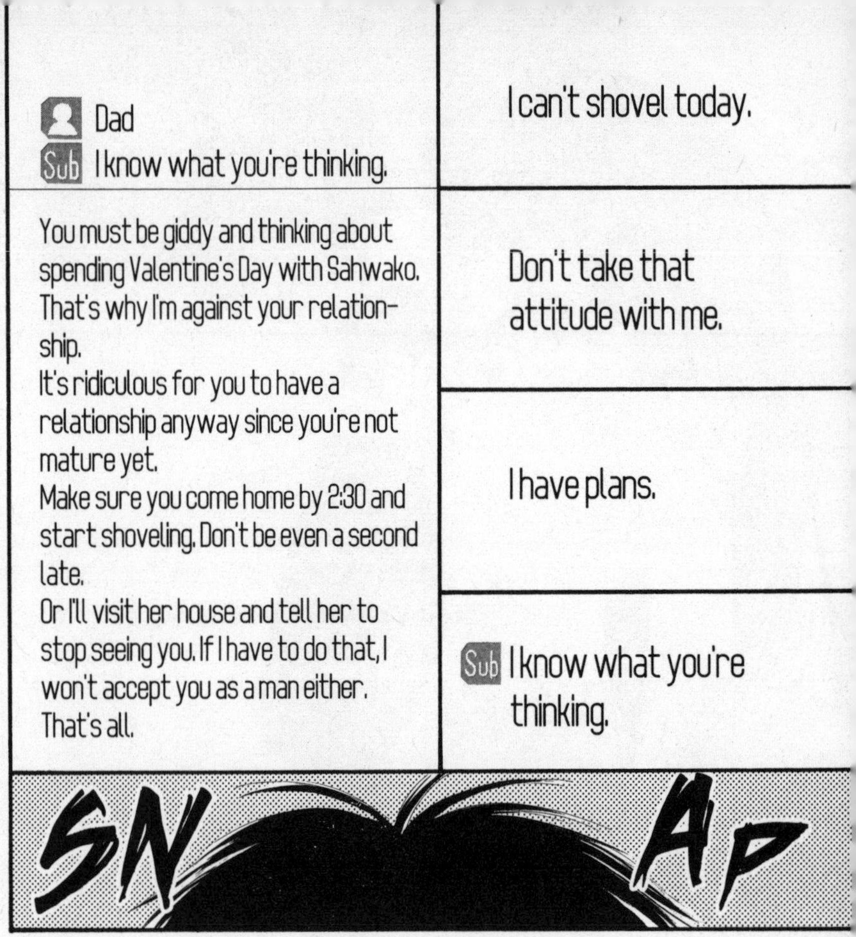
I can't shovel today.
Dad
Sub I know what you're thinking.
Don't take that attitude with me.
I have plans.
Sub I know what you're thinking.
You must be giddy and thinking about spending Valentine's Day with Sahwako. That's why I'm against your relationship.
It's ridiculous for you to have a relationship anyway since you're not mature yet.
Make sure you come home by 2:30 and start shoveling. Don't be even a second late.
Or I'll visit her house and tell her to stop seeing you. If I have to do that, I won't accept you as a man either.
That's all.
SNAP

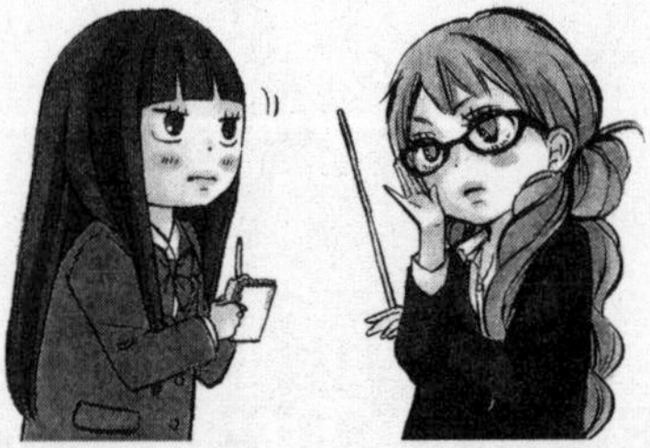

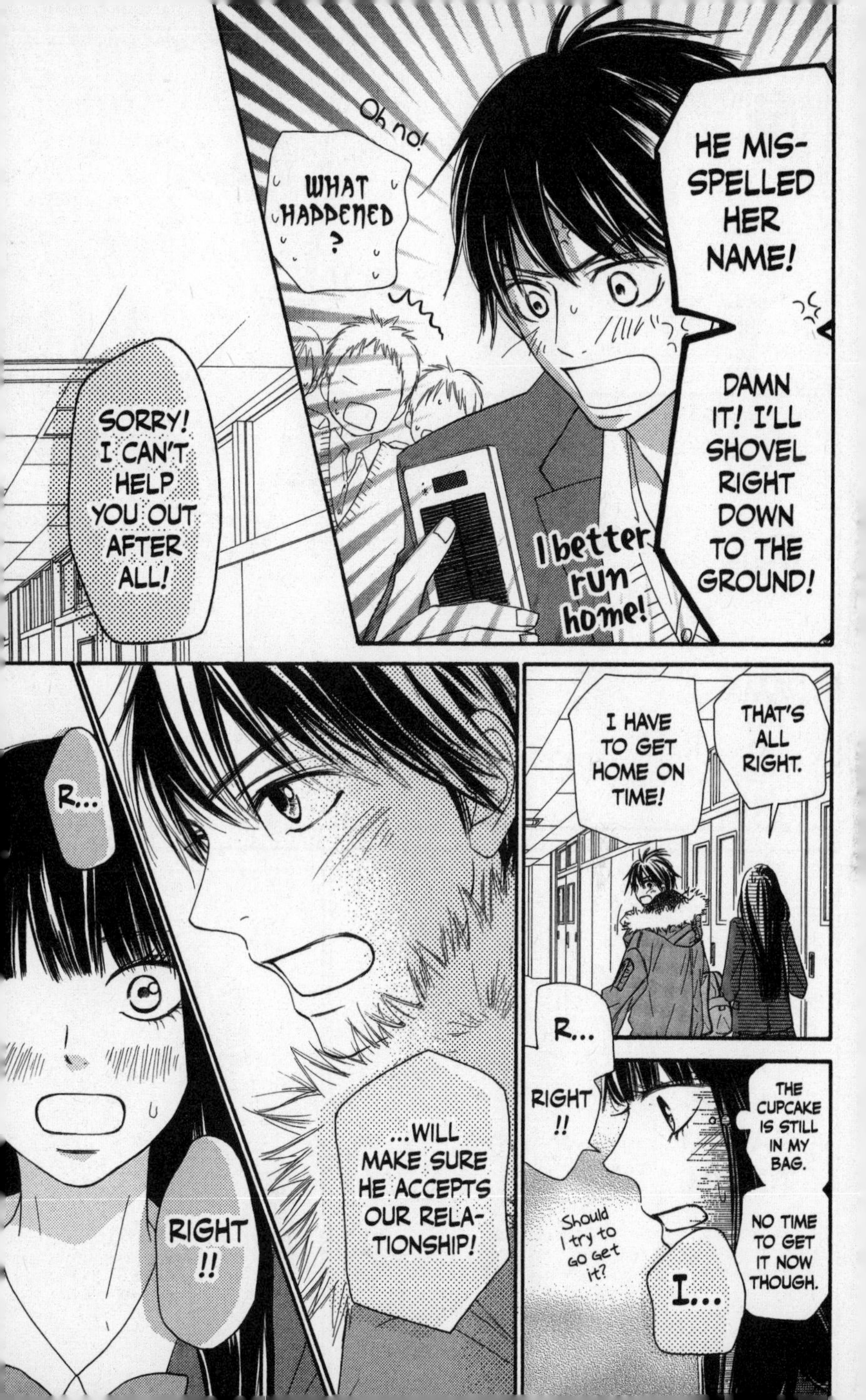
HE MIS-SPELLED HER NAME!
DAMN IT! I'LL SHOVEL RIGHT DOWN TO THE GROUND!
I better run home!
Oh no!
WHAT HAPPENED?
SORRY! I CAN'T HELP YOU OUT AFTER ALL!
THAT'S ALL RIGHT.
I HAVE TO GET HOME ON TIME!
R...
RIGHT!!
THE CUPCAKE IS STILL IN MY BAG.
NO TIME TO GET IT NOW THOUGH.
Should I try to go get it?
I...
...WILL MAKE SURE HE ACCEPTS OUR RELATIONSHIP!
R...
RIGHT!!

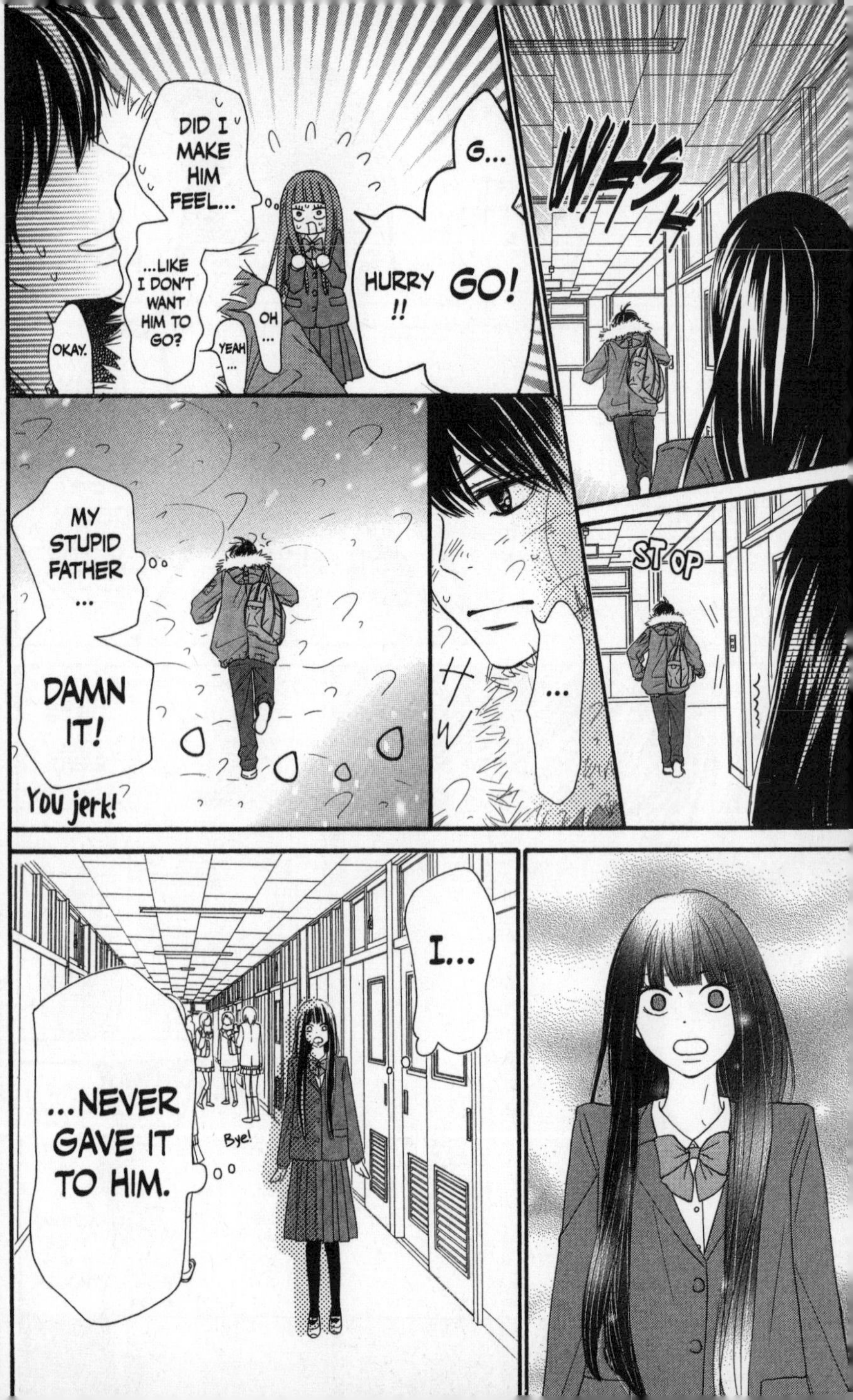
WHSH
G...
GO!
HURRY !!
DID I MAKE HIM FEEL...
...LIKE I DON'T WANT HIM TO GO?
OH ...
YEAH ...
OKAY.
STOP
...
MY STUPID FATHER ...
DAMN IT!
You jerk!
I...
...NEVER GAVE IT TO HIM.
Bye!

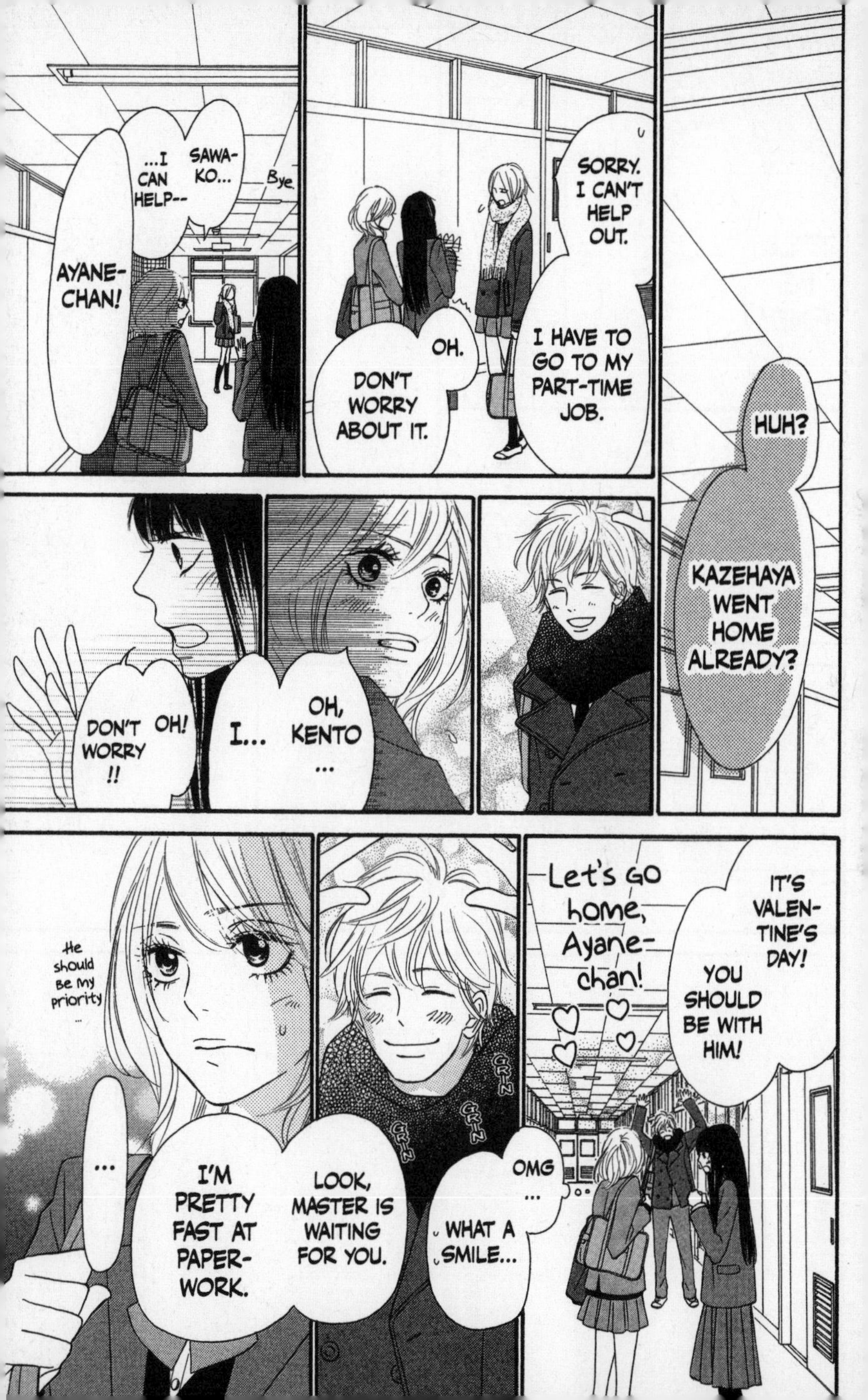
HUH?
KAZEHAYA WENT HOME ALREADY?
SORRY. I CAN'T HELP OUT.
I HAVE TO GO TO MY PART-TIME JOB.
OH.
DON'T WORRY ABOUT IT.
SAWAKO...
...I CAN HELP--
Bye.
AYANE-CHAN!
OH, KENTO...
I...
OH!
DON'T WORRY!!
IT'S VALENTINE'S DAY!
YOU SHOULD BE WITH HIM!
Let's GO home, Ayane-chan!
OMG...
WHAT A SMILE...
GRIN
GRIN
LOOK, MASTER IS WAITING FOR YOU.
I'M PRETTY FAST AT PAPER-WORK.
...
He should be my priority...

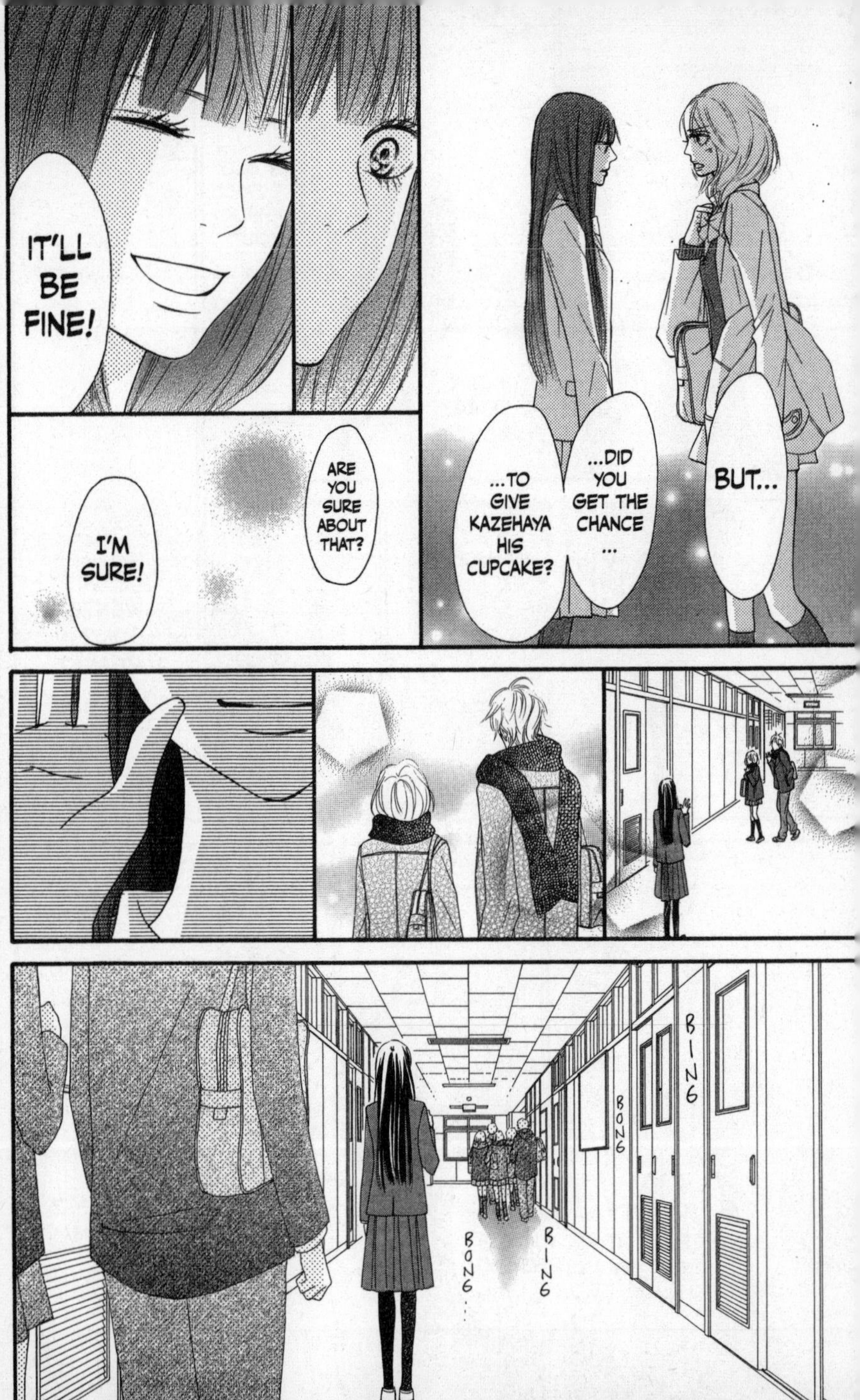
BUT...
...DID YOU GET THE CHANCE ...
...TO GIVE KAZEHAYA HIS CUPCAKE?
IT'LL BE FINE!
ARE YOU SURE ABOUT THAT?
I'M SURE!
BING
BONG
BING
BONG...

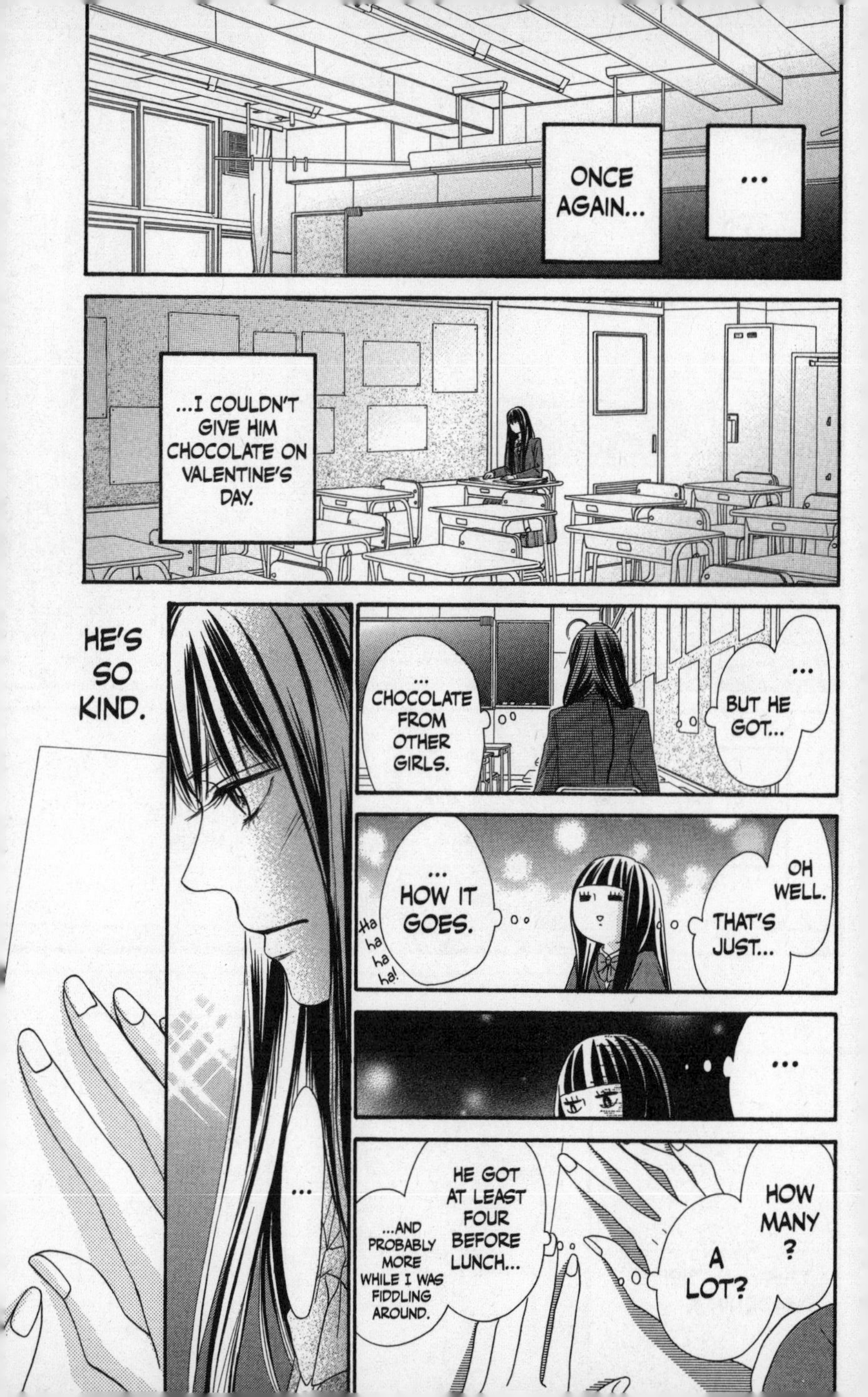
...
ONCE AGAIN...
...I COULDN'T GIVE HIM CHOCOLATE ON VALENTINE'S DAY.
... BUT HE GOT...
... CHOCOLATE FROM OTHER GIRLS.
OH WELL. THAT'S JUST...
... HOW IT GOES.
Ha ha ha ha!
...
HOW MANY? A LOT?
HE GOT AT LEAST FOUR BEFORE LUNCH...
...AND PROBABLY MORE WHILE I WAS FIDDLING AROUND.
...
HE'S SO KIND.

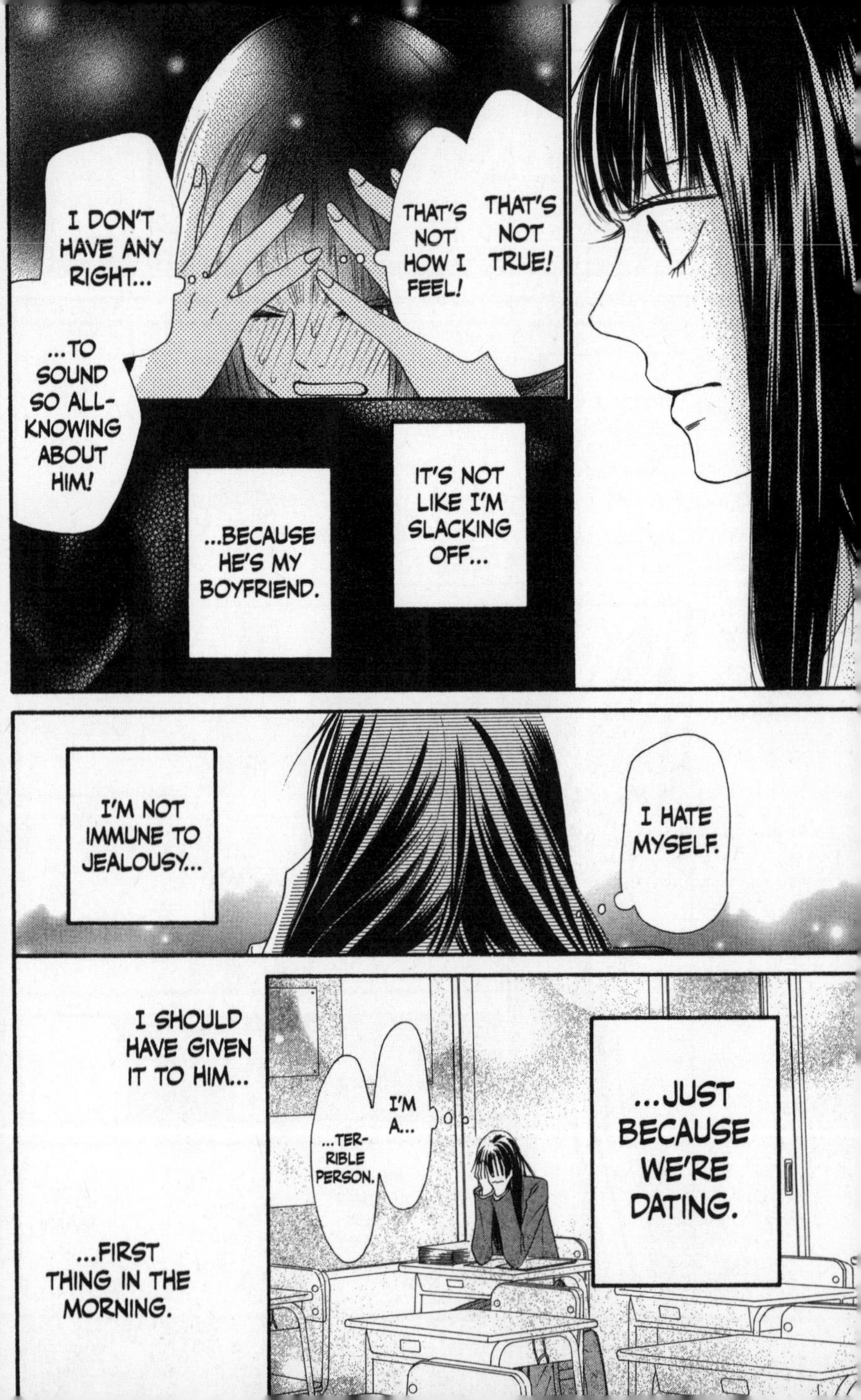
THAT'S NOT TRUE!
THAT'S NOT HOW I FEEL!
I DON'T HAVE ANY RIGHT...
...TO SOUND SO ALL-KNOWING ABOUT HIM!
IT'S NOT LIKE I'M SLACKING OFF...
...BECAUSE HE'S MY BOYFRIEND.
I HATE MYSELF.
I'M NOT IMMUNE TO JEALOUSY...
...JUST BECAUSE WE'RE DATING.
I'M A...
...TER-RIBLE PERSON.
I SHOULD HAVE GIVEN IT TO HIM...
...FIRST THING IN THE MORNING.

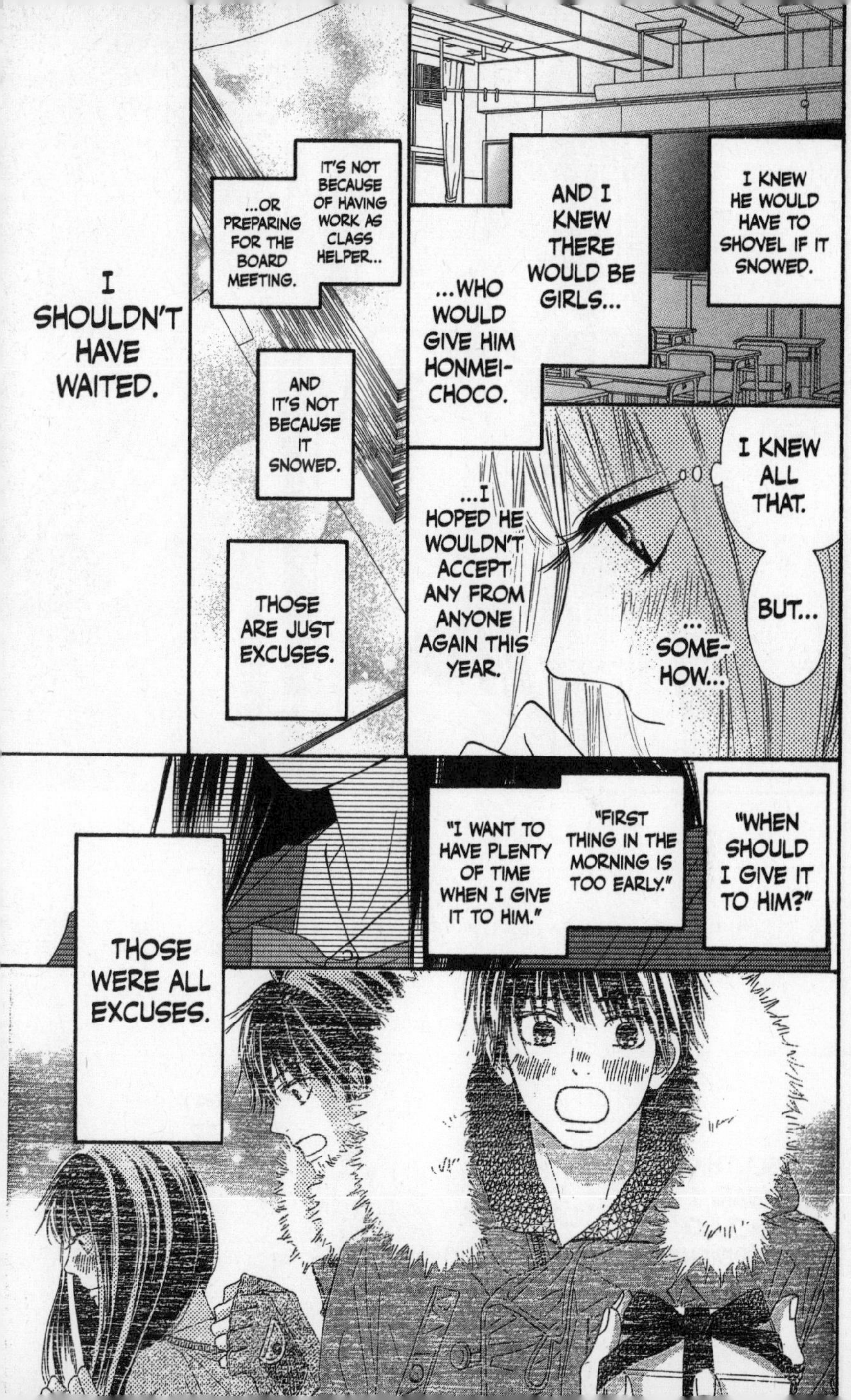
I KNEW HE WOULD HAVE TO SHOVEL IF IT SNOWED.
AND I KNEW THERE WOULD BE GIRLS...
...WHO WOULD GIVE HIM HONMEI-CHOCO.
I KNEW ALL THAT.
BUT...
...SOMEHOW...
...I HOPED HE WOULDN'T ACCEPT ANY FROM ANYONE AGAIN THIS YEAR.
IT'S NOT BECAUSE OF HAVING WORK AS CLASS HELPER...
...OR PREPARING FOR THE BOARD MEETING.
AND IT'S NOT BECAUSE IT SNOWED.
THOSE ARE JUST EXCUSES.
I SHOULDN'T HAVE WAITED.
"WHEN SHOULD I GIVE IT TO HIM?"
"FIRST THING IN THE MORNING IS TOO EARLY."
"I WANT TO HAVE PLENTY OF TIME WHEN I GIVE IT TO HIM."
THOSE WERE ALL EXCUSES.

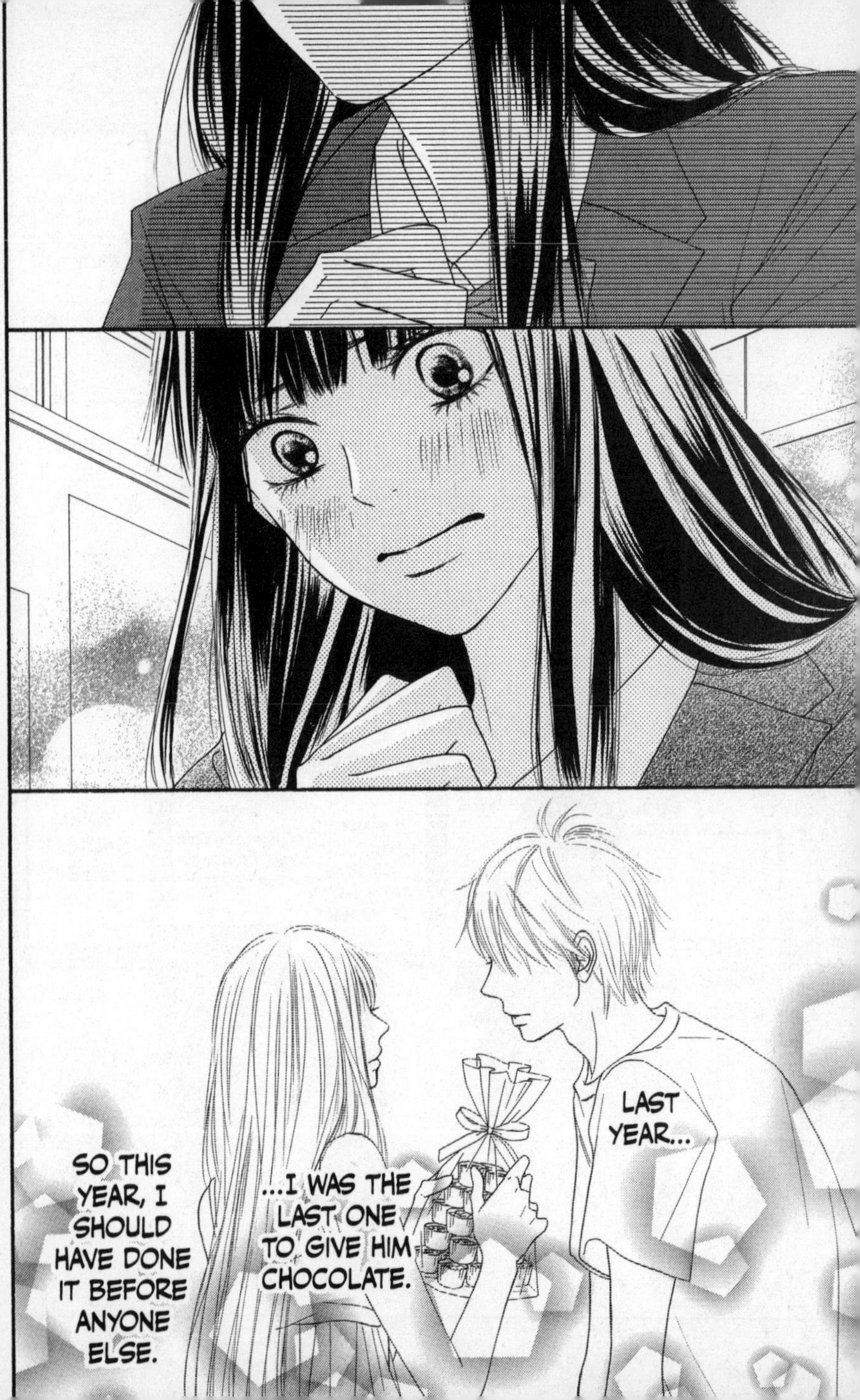
LAST YEAR...
...I WAS THE LAST ONE TO GIVE HIM CHOCOLATE.
SO THIS YEAR, I SHOULD HAVE DONE IT BEFORE ANYONE ELSE.

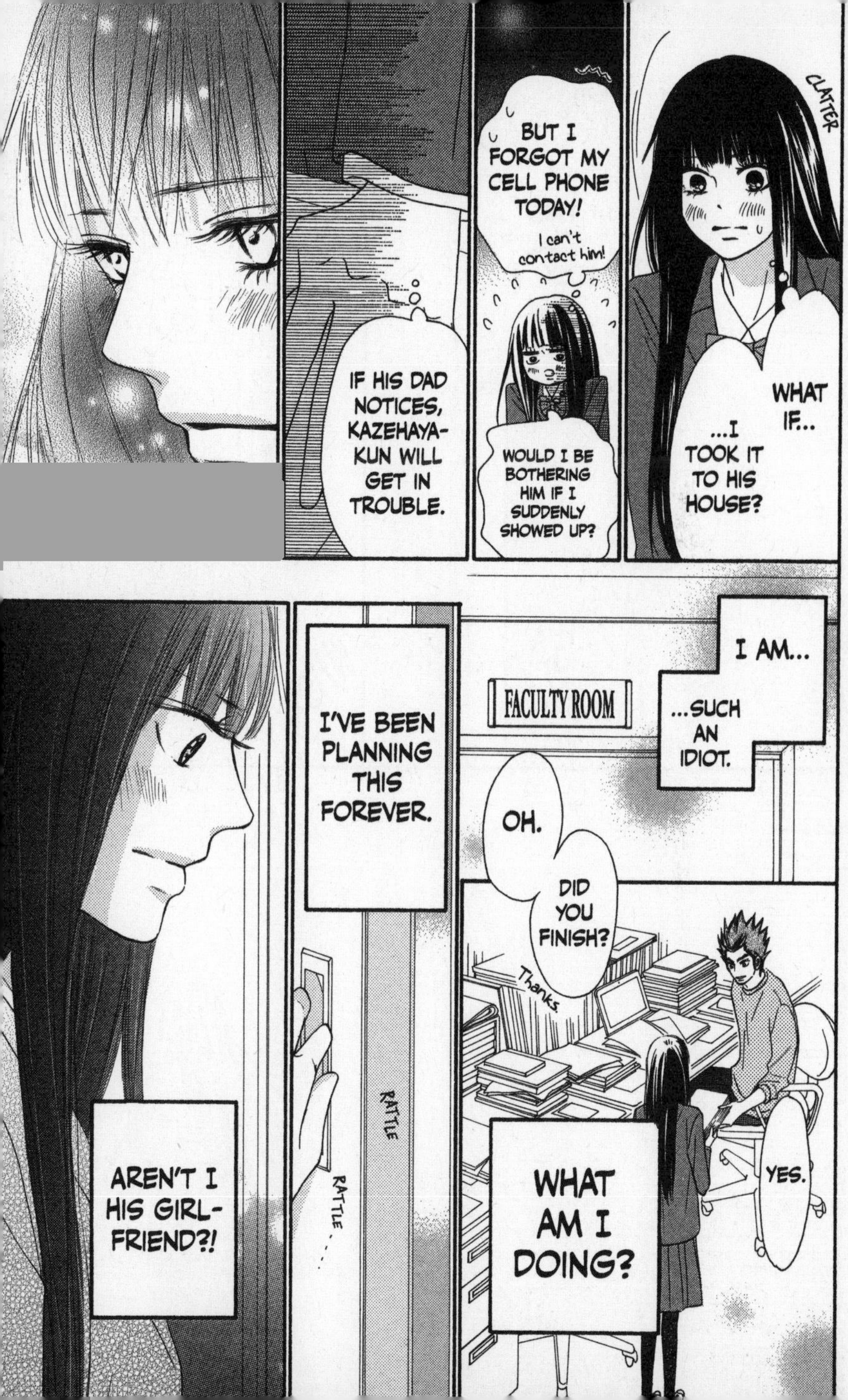

CLATTER
WHAT IF...
...I TOOK IT TO HIS HOUSE?
BUT I FORGOT MY CELL PHONE TODAY!
I can't contact him!
WOULD I BE BOTHERING HIM IF I SUDDENLY SHOWED UP?
IF HIS DAD NOTICES, KAZEHAYA-KUN WILL GET IN TROUBLE.
I AM...
...SUCH AN IDIOT.
FACULTY ROOM
OH.
DID YOU FINISH?
Thanks.
YES.
WHAT AM I DOING?
I'VE BEEN PLANNING THIS FOREVER.
RATTLE
RATTLE...
AREN'T I HIS GIRL-FRIEND?!

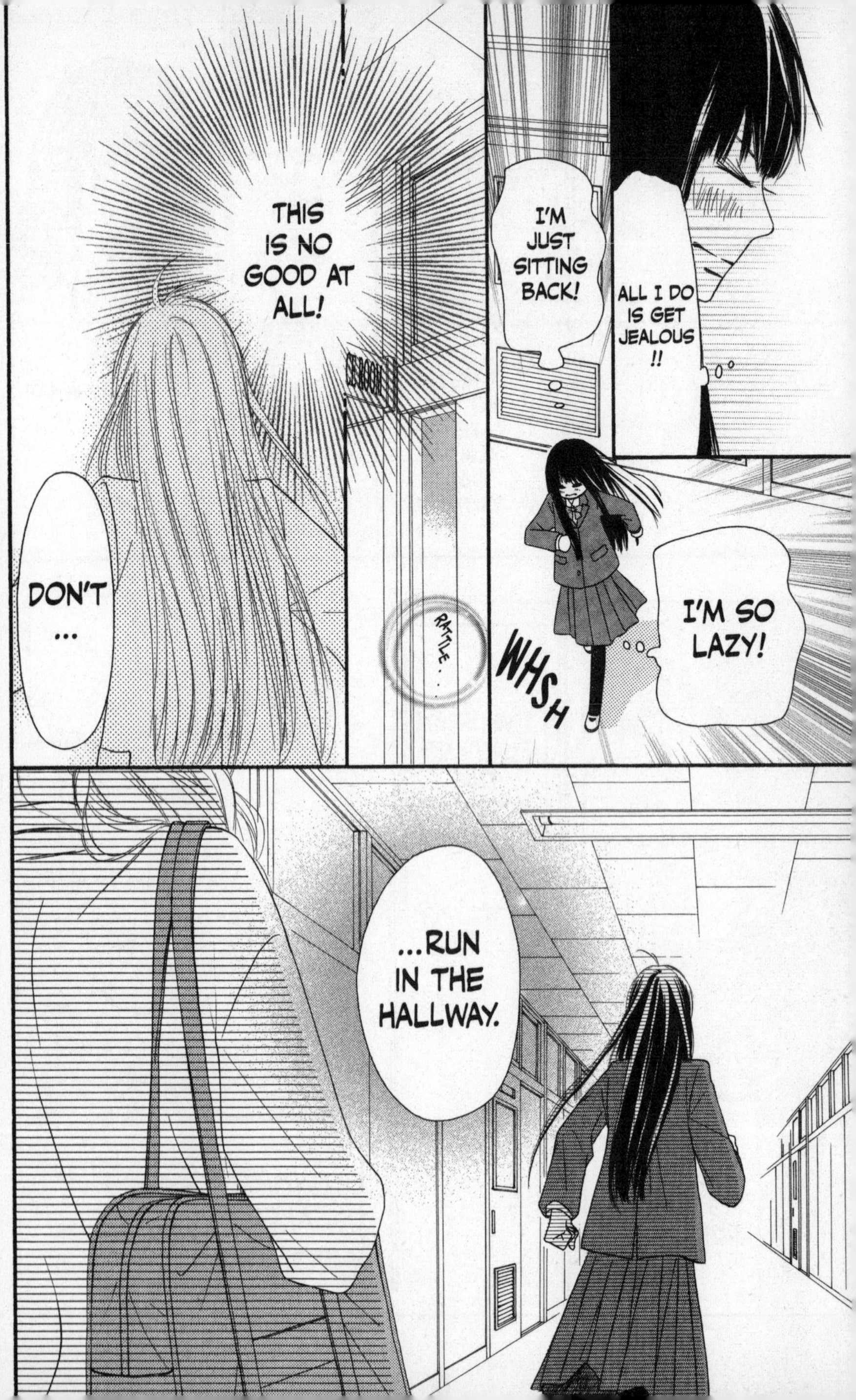
ALL I DO IS GET JEALOUS!!
I'M JUST SITTING BACK!
I'M SO LAZY!
WHSH
THIS IS NO GOOD AT ALL!
RATTLE..
DON'T ...
...RUN IN THE HALLWAY.

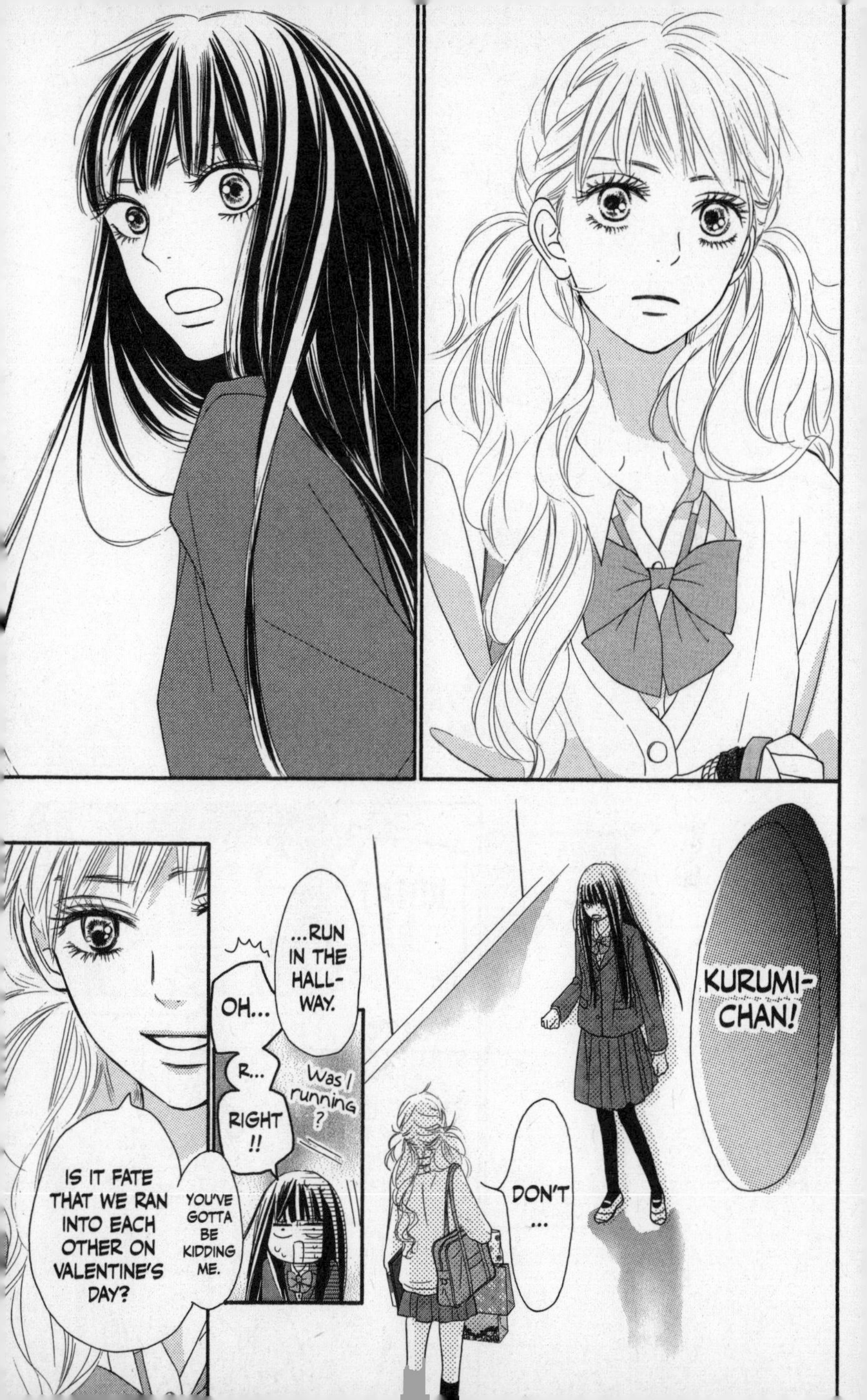
KURUMI-CHAN!
DON'T ...
...RUN IN THE HALL-WAY.
OH...
R...
RIGHT !!
Was I running ?
YOU'VE GOTTA BE KIDDING ME.
IS IT FATE THAT WE RAN INTO EACH OTHER ON VALENTINE'S DAY?

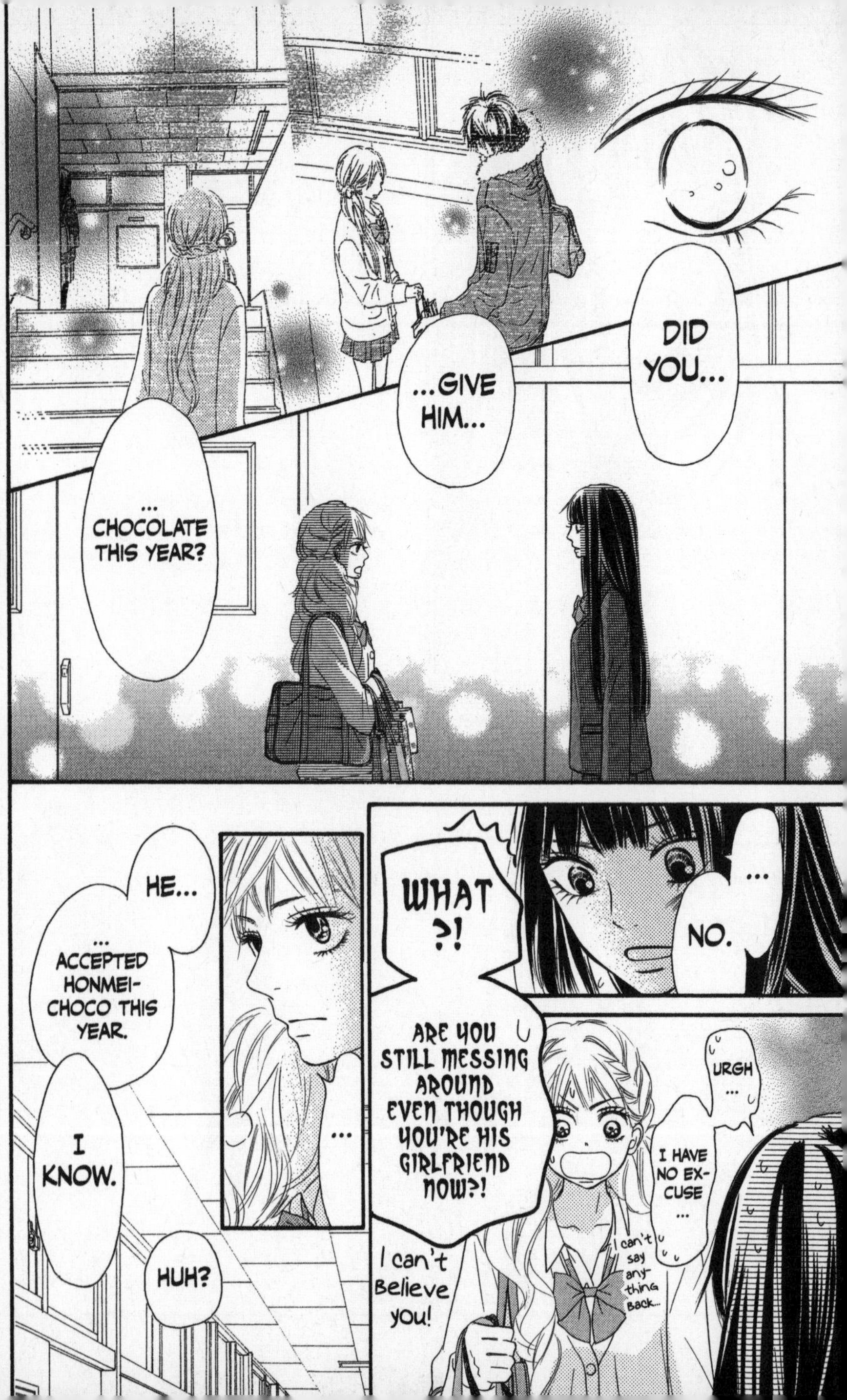
DID YOU...
...GIVE HIM...
... CHOCOLATE THIS YEAR?
... NO.
WHAT?!
ARE YOU STILL MESSING AROUND EVEN THOUGH YOU'RE HIS GIRLFRIEND NOW?!
URGH...
I HAVE NO EXCUSE...
I can't say anything back...
I can't believe you!
...
HE... ... ACCEPTED HONMEI-CHOCO THIS YEAR.
I KNOW.
HUH?

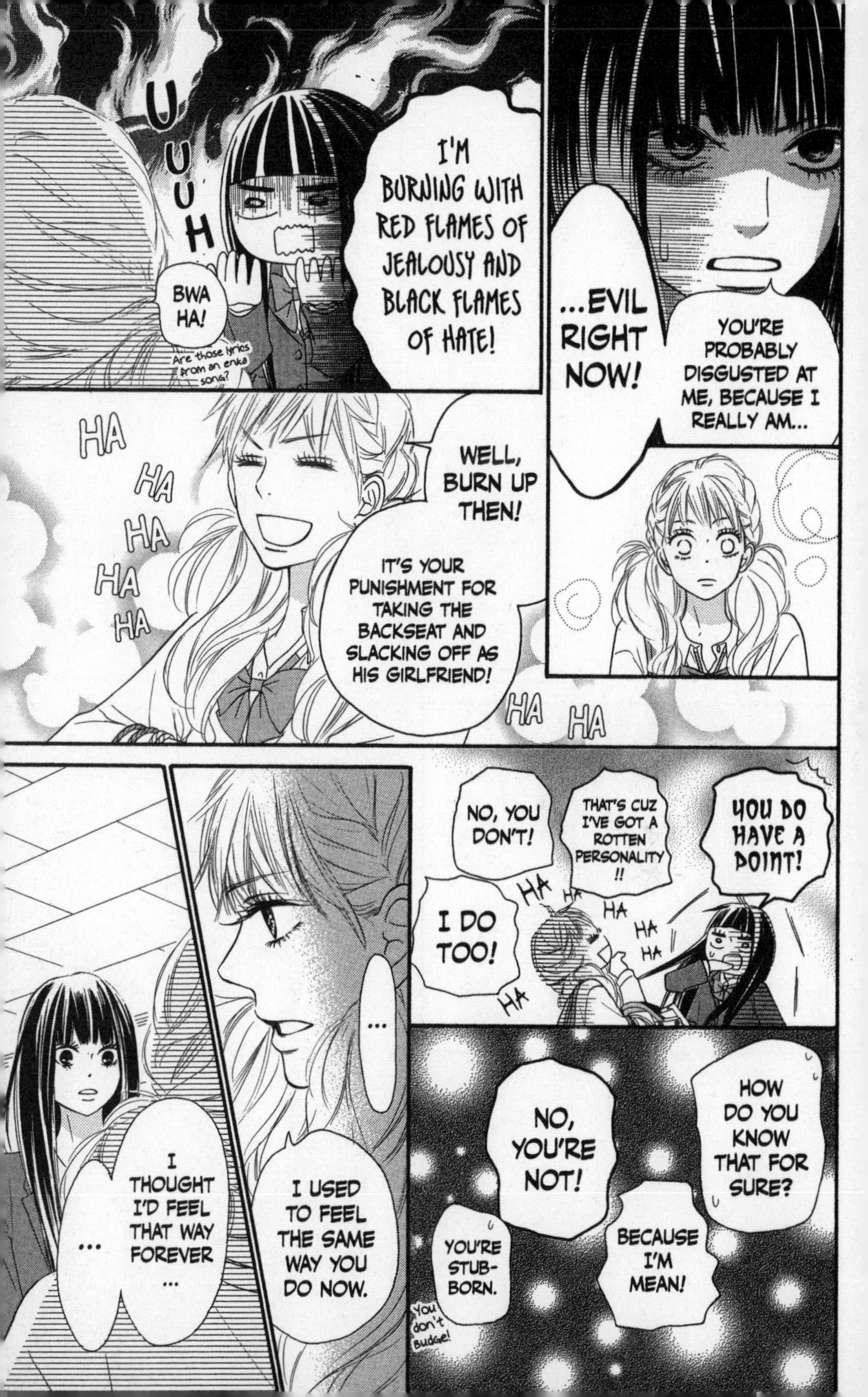
YOU'RE PROBABLY DISGUSTED AT ME, BECAUSE I REALLY AM...
...EVIL RIGHT NOW!
UUUH
I'M BURNING WITH RED FLAMES OF JEALOUSY AND BLACK FLAMES OF HATE!
BWA HA!
Are those lyrics from an enka song?
WELL, BURN UP THEN!
IT'S YOUR PUNISHMENT FOR TAKING THE BACKSEAT AND SLACKING OFF AS HIS GIRLFRIEND!
HA HA HA HA HA
HA HA
YOU DO HAVE A POINT!
THAT'S CUZ I'VE GOT A ROTTEN PERSONALITY !!
NO, YOU DON'T!
I DO TOO!
HA HA HA HA HA HA
HOW DO YOU KNOW THAT FOR SURE?
NO, YOU'RE NOT!
BECAUSE I'M MEAN!
YOU'RE STUB-BORN.
You don't Budge!
...
I USED TO FEEL THE SAME WAY YOU DO NOW.
I THOUGHT I'D FEEL THAT WAY FOREVER ...
...

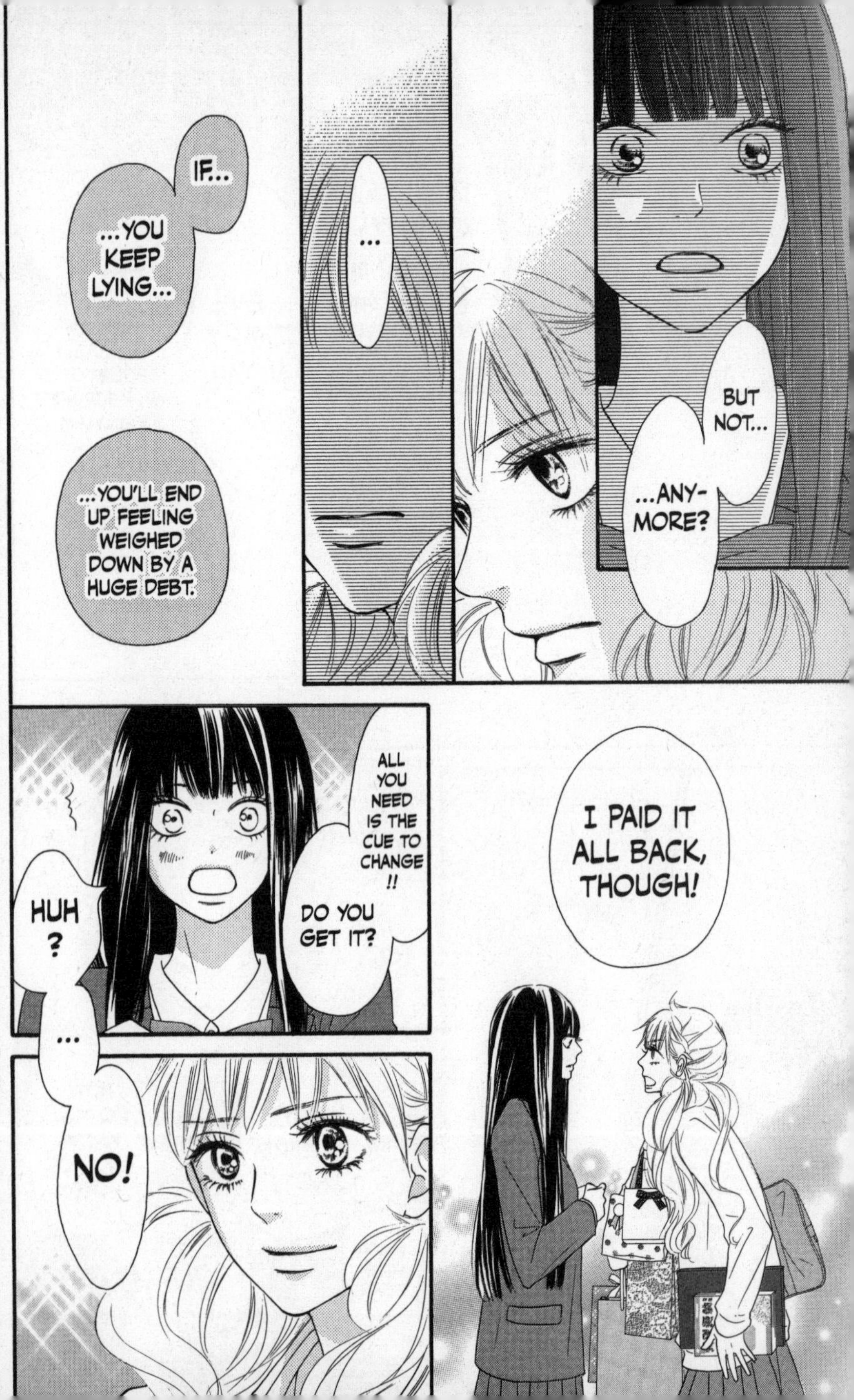
BUT NOT...
...ANY-MORE?
...
IF...
...YOU KEEP LYING...
...YOU'LL END UP FEELING WEIGHED DOWN BY A HUGE DEBT.
I PAID IT ALL BACK, THOUGH!
ALL YOU NEED IS THE CUE TO CHANGE !!
DO YOU GET IT?
HUH ?
...
NO!

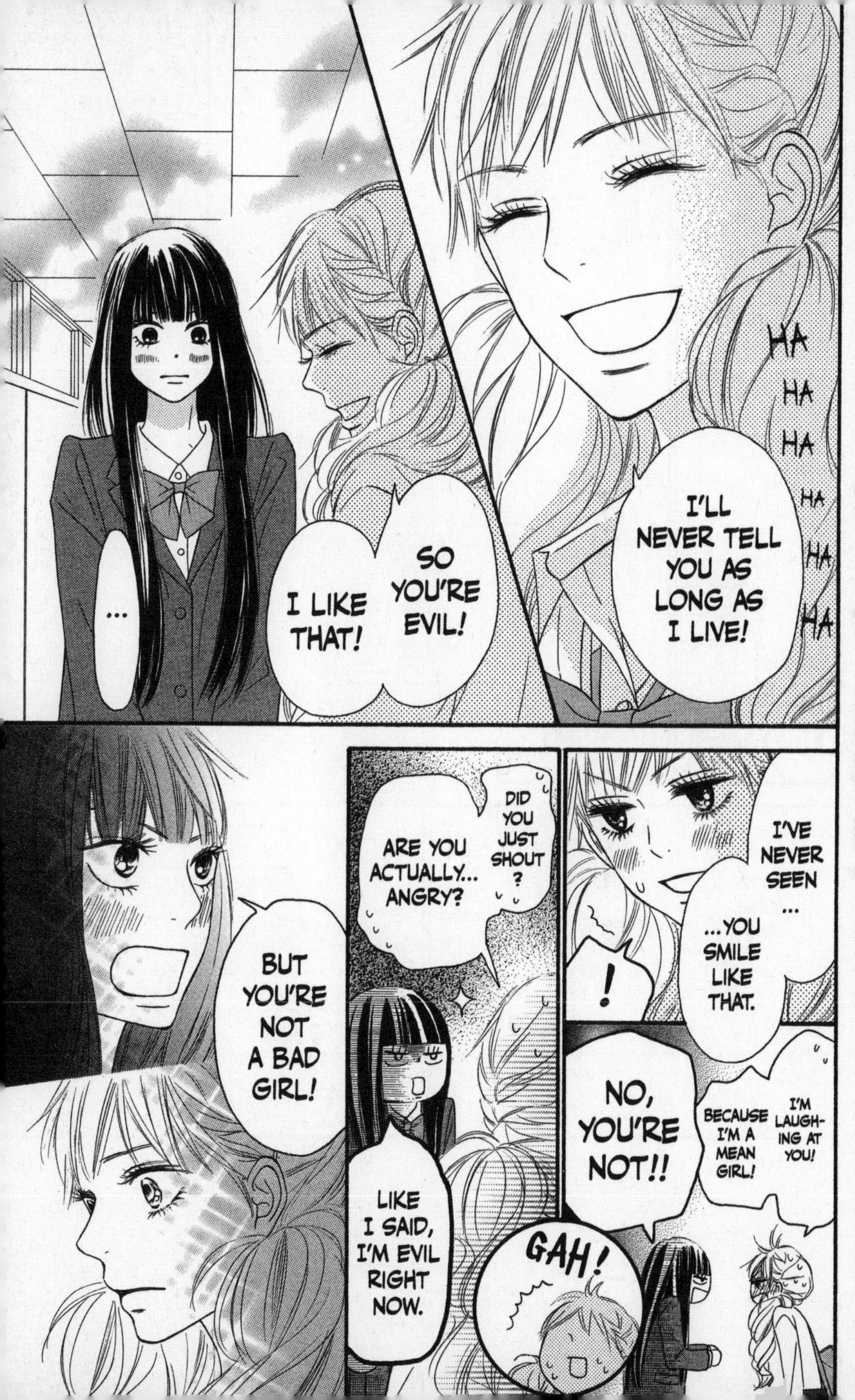

HA HA HA HA HA HA
I'LL NEVER TELL YOU AS LONG AS I LIVE!
SO YOU'RE EVIL!
I LIKE THAT!
...
I'VE NEVER SEEN ...
...YOU SMILE LIKE THAT.
!
I'M LAUGHING AT YOU!
BECAUSE I'M A MEAN GIRL!
NO, YOU'RE NOT!!
GAH!
DID YOU JUST SHOUT?
ARE YOU ACTUALLY... ANGRY?
LIKE I SAID, I'M EVIL RIGHT NOW.
BUT YOU'RE NOT A BAD GIRL!

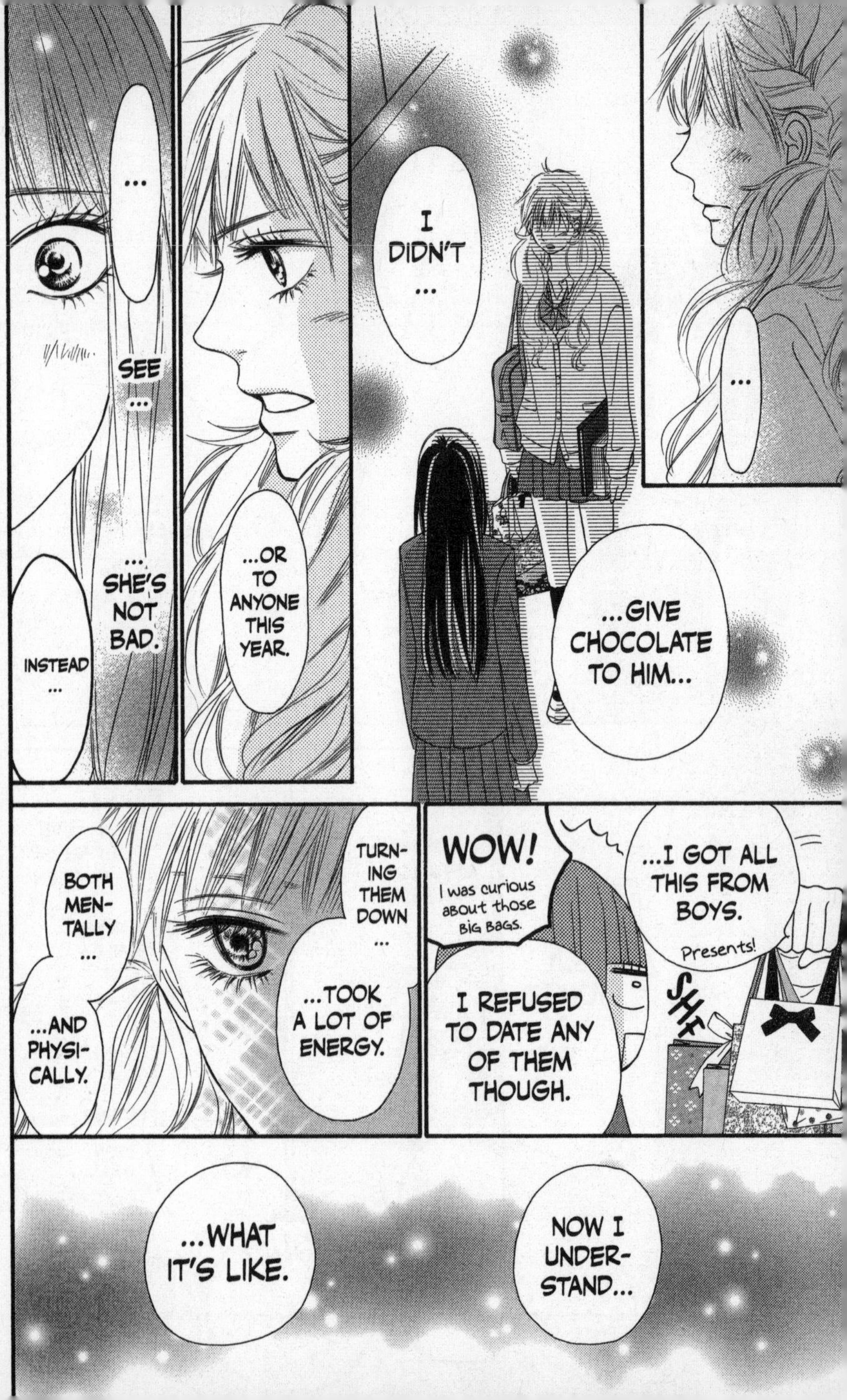
...
I DIDN'T ...
...GIVE CHOCOLATE TO HIM...
...OR TO ANYONE THIS YEAR.
...
SEE ...
... SHE'S NOT BAD.
INSTEAD ...
...I GOT ALL THIS FROM BOYS.
Presents!
WOW!
I was curious about those BIG BAGS.
SHF
I REFUSED TO DATE ANY OF THEM THOUGH.
TURN-ING THEM DOWN ...
...TOOK A LOT OF ENERGY.
BOTH MEN-TALLY ...
...AND PHYSI-CALLY.
NOW I UNDER-STAND...
...WHAT IT'S LIKE.

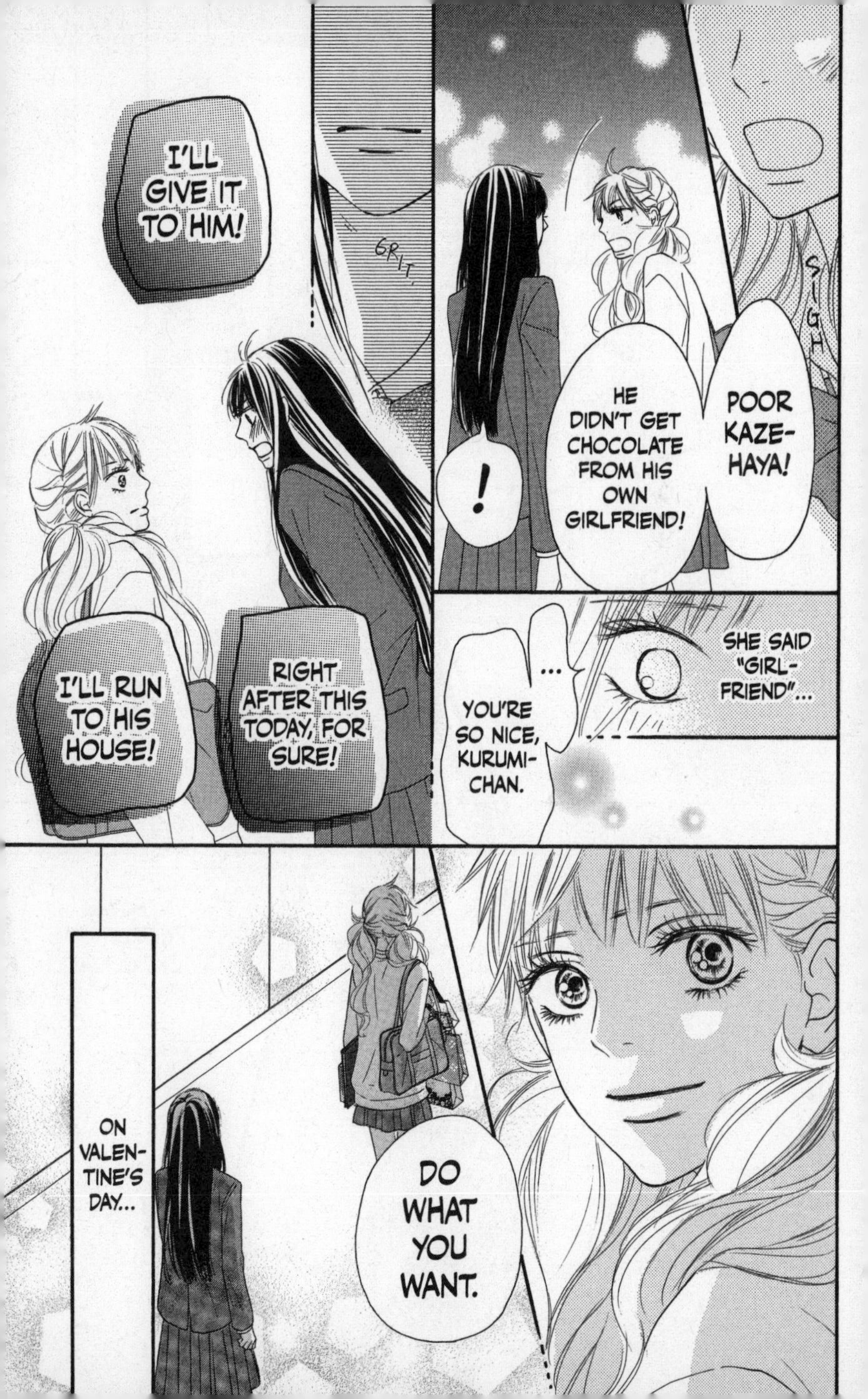
SIGH
POOR KAZE-HAYA!
HE DIDN'T GET CHOCOLATE FROM HIS OWN GIRLFRIEND!
!
SHE SAID "GIRLFRIEND"...
...
YOU'RE SO NICE, KURUMI-CHAN.
GRIT
I'LL GIVE IT TO HIM!
RIGHT AFTER THIS TODAY, FOR SURE!
I'LL RUN TO HIS HOUSE!
DO WHAT YOU WANT.
ON VALENTINE'S DAY...

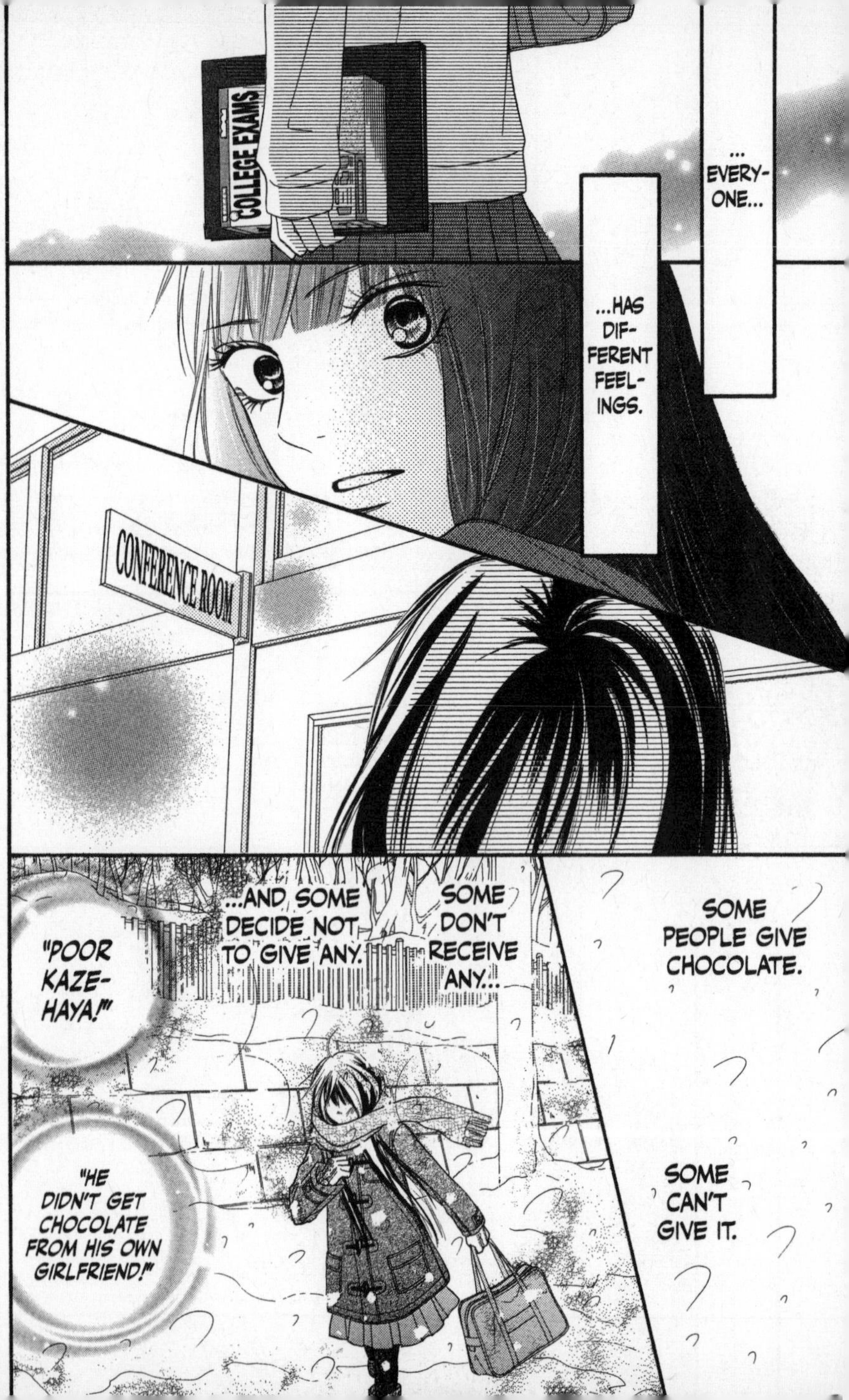

...EVERYONE...
COLLEGE EXAMS
...HAS DIFFERENT FEELINGS.
CONFERENCE ROOM
SOME PEOPLE GIVE CHOCOLATE.
SOME CAN'T GIVE IT.
SOME DON'T RECEIVE ANY...
...AND SOME DECIDE NOT TO GIVE ANY.
"POOR KAZEHAYA!"
"HE DIDN'T GET CHOCOLATE FROM HIS OWN GIRLFRIEND!"

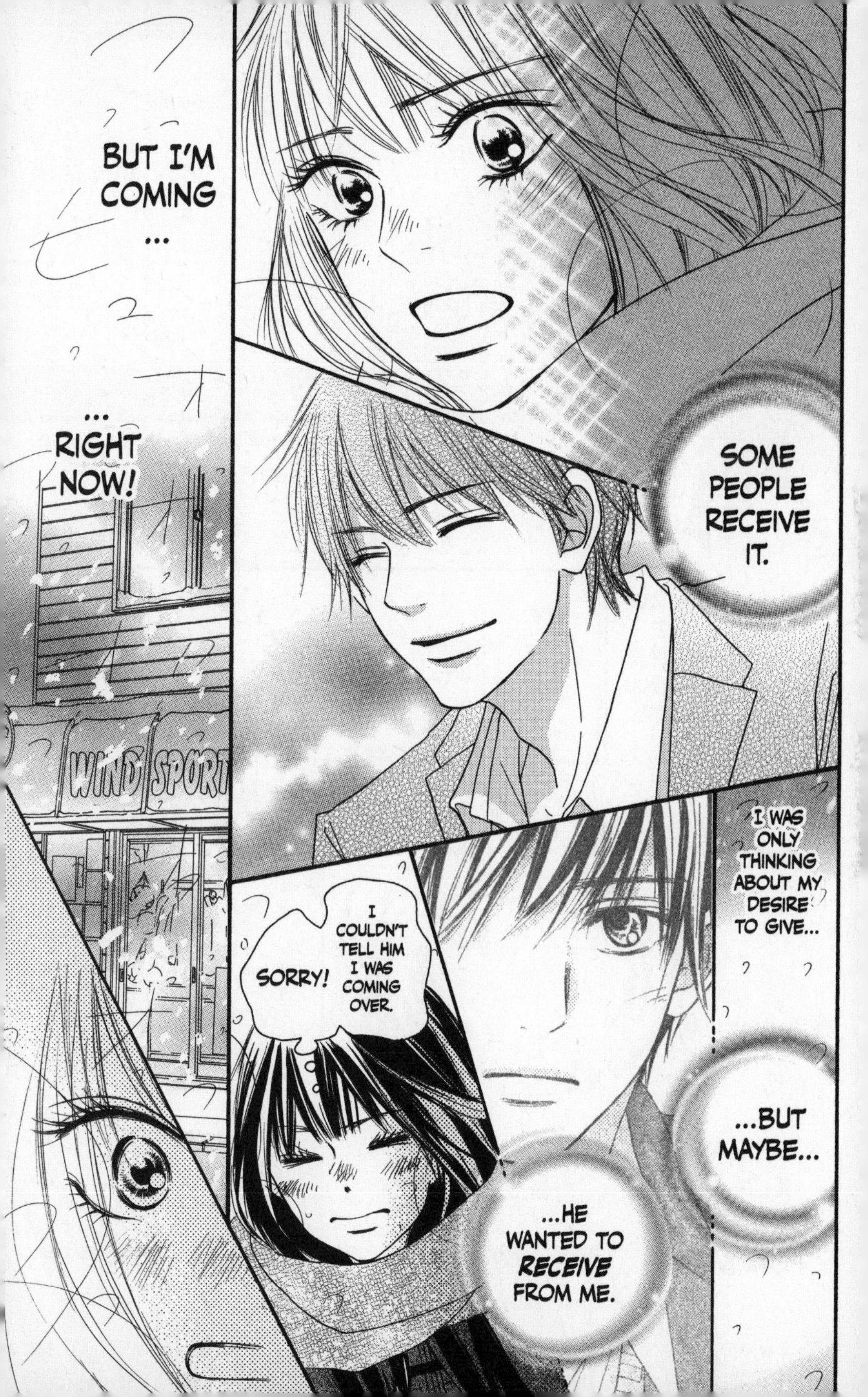
SOME PEOPLE RECEIVE IT.
I WAS ONLY THINKING ABOUT MY DESIRE TO GIVE...
...BUT MAYBE...
...HE WANTED TO *RECEIVE* FROM ME.
I COULDN'T TELL HIM I WAS COMING OVER.
SORRY!
BUT I'M COMING ...
... RIGHT NOW!
WIND SPORT

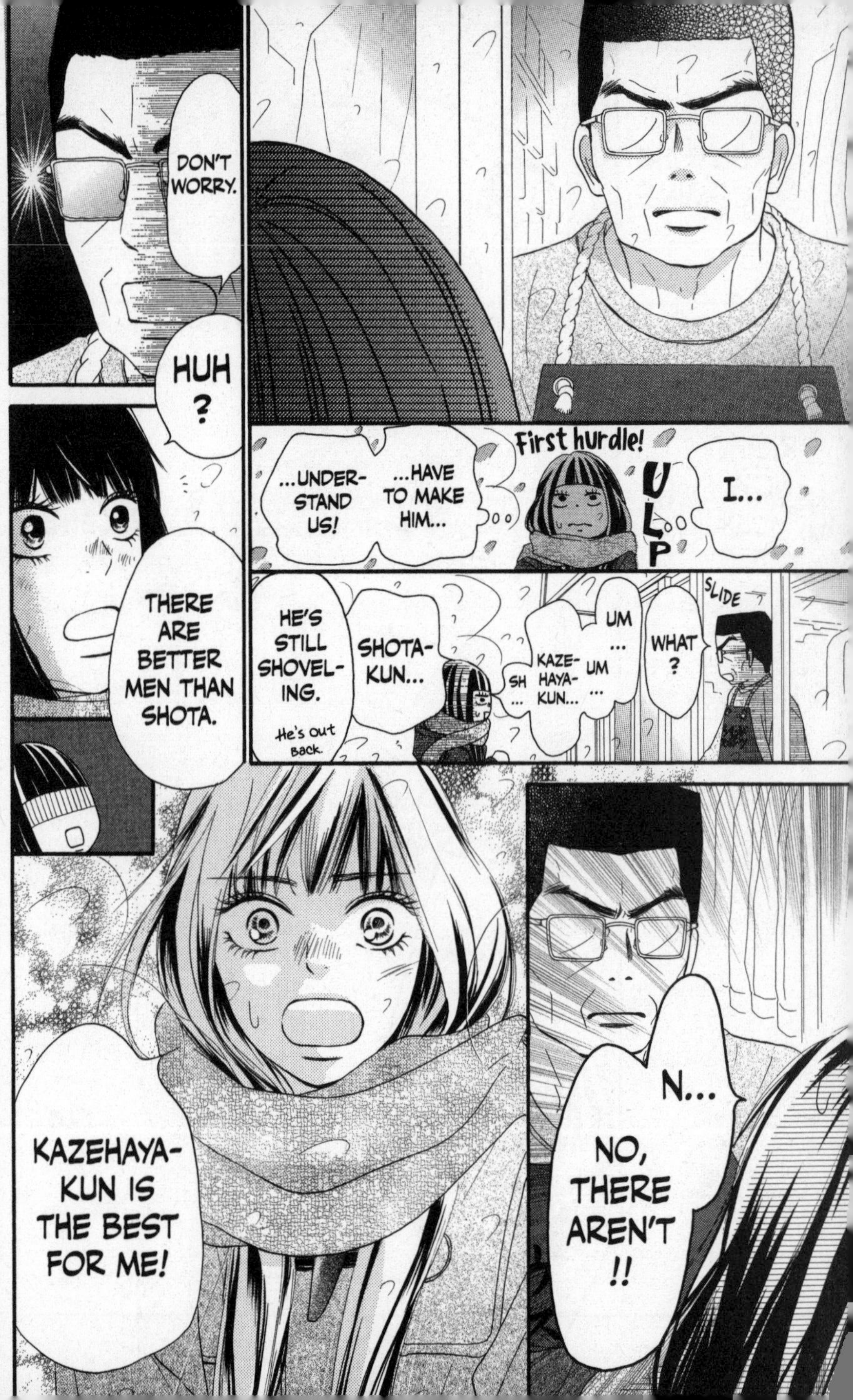
I...
ULP
First hurdle!
...HAVE TO MAKE HIM...
...UNDER-STAND US!
SLIDE
WHAT?
UM... UM...
KAZE-HAYA-KUN...
SH...
SHOTA-KUN...
HE'S STILL SHOVEL-ING.
He's out back.
DON'T WORRY.
HUH?
THERE ARE BETTER MEN THAN SHOTA.
N...
NO, THERE AREN'T!!
KAZEHAYA-KUN IS THE BEST FOR ME!

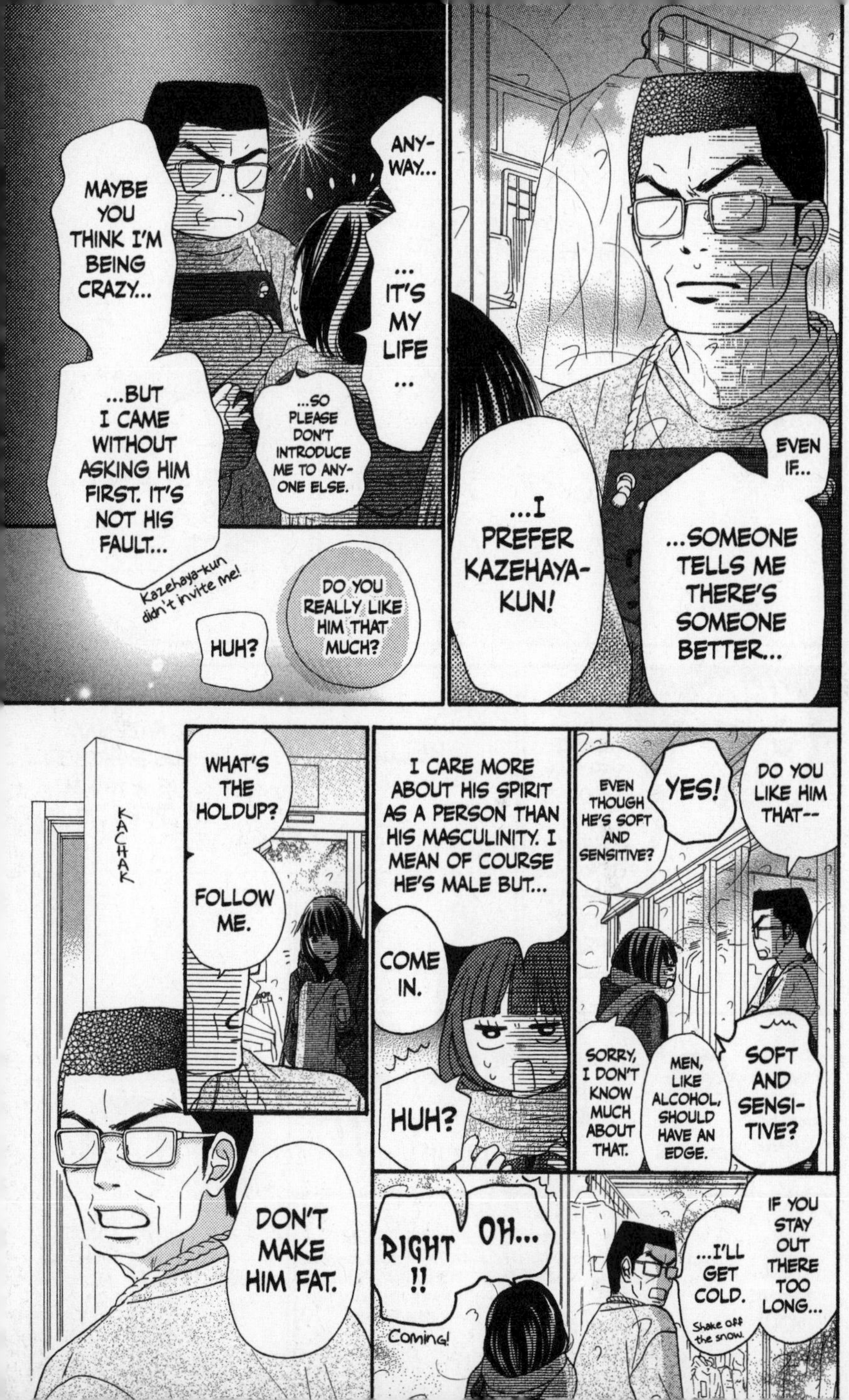

EVEN IF...
...SOMEONE TELLS ME THERE'S SOMEONE BETTER...
...I PREFER KAZEHAYA-KUN!
ANY-WAY...
...IT'S MY LIFE...
...SO PLEASE DON'T INTRODUCE ME TO ANY-ONE ELSE.
MAYBE YOU THINK I'M BEING CRAZY...
...BUT I CAME WITHOUT ASKING HIM FIRST. IT'S NOT HIS FAULT...
Kazehaya-kun didn't invite me!
DO YOU REALLY LIKE HIM THAT MUCH?
HUH?
DO YOU LIKE HIM THAT--
YES!
EVEN THOUGH HE'S SOFT AND SENSITIVE?
SOFT AND SENSI-TIVE?
MEN, LIKE ALCOHOL, SHOULD HAVE AN EDGE.
SORRY, I DON'T KNOW MUCH ABOUT THAT.
I CARE MORE ABOUT HIS SPIRIT AS A PERSON THAN HIS MASCULINITY. I MEAN OF COURSE HE'S MALE BUT...
COME IN.
HUH?
IF YOU STAY OUT THERE TOO LONG...
...I'LL GET COLD.
Shake off the snow.
OH...
RIGHT!!
Coming!
WHAT'S THE HOLDUP?
FOLLOW ME.
DON'T MAKE HIM FAT.
KACHAK

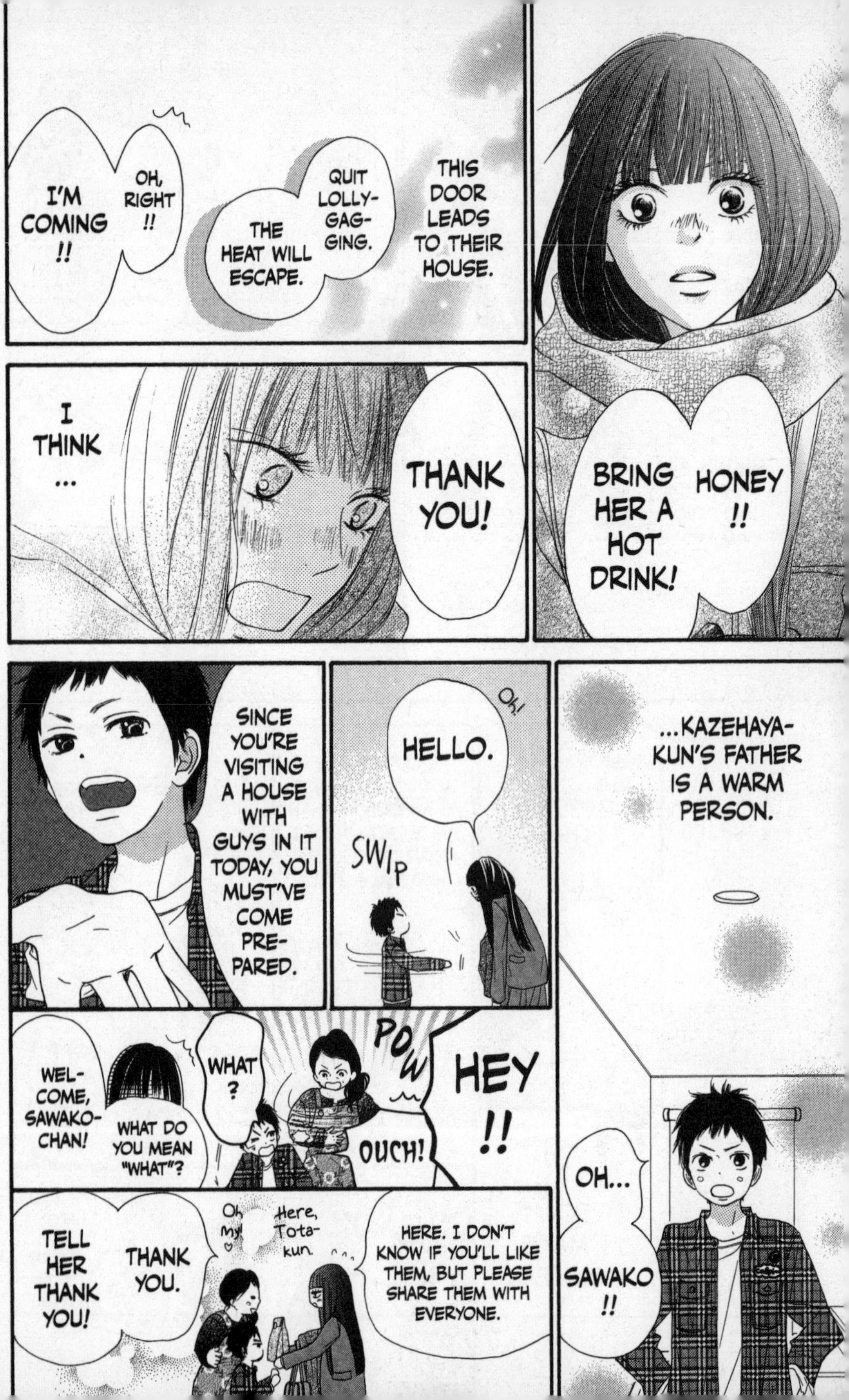
HONEY!!
BRING HER A HOT DRINK!
THIS DOOR LEADS TO THEIR HOUSE.
QUIT LOLLY-GAG-GING.
THE HEAT WILL ESCAPE.
OH, RIGHT!!
I'M COMING!!
THANK YOU!
I THINK...
...KAZEHAYA-KUN'S FATHER IS A WARM PERSON.
OH...
SAWAKO!!
Oh!
HELLO.
SWIP
SINCE YOU'RE VISITING A HOUSE WITH GUYS IN IT TODAY, YOU MUST'VE COME PRE-PARED.
HEY!!
POW
OUCH!
WHAT?
WHAT DO YOU MEAN "WHAT"?
WEL-COME, SAWAKO-CHAN!
HERE. I DON'T KNOW IF YOU'LL LIKE THEM, BUT PLEASE SHARE THEM WITH EVERYONE.
Here, Tota-kun.
Oh, My!
THANK YOU.
TELL HER THANK YOU!

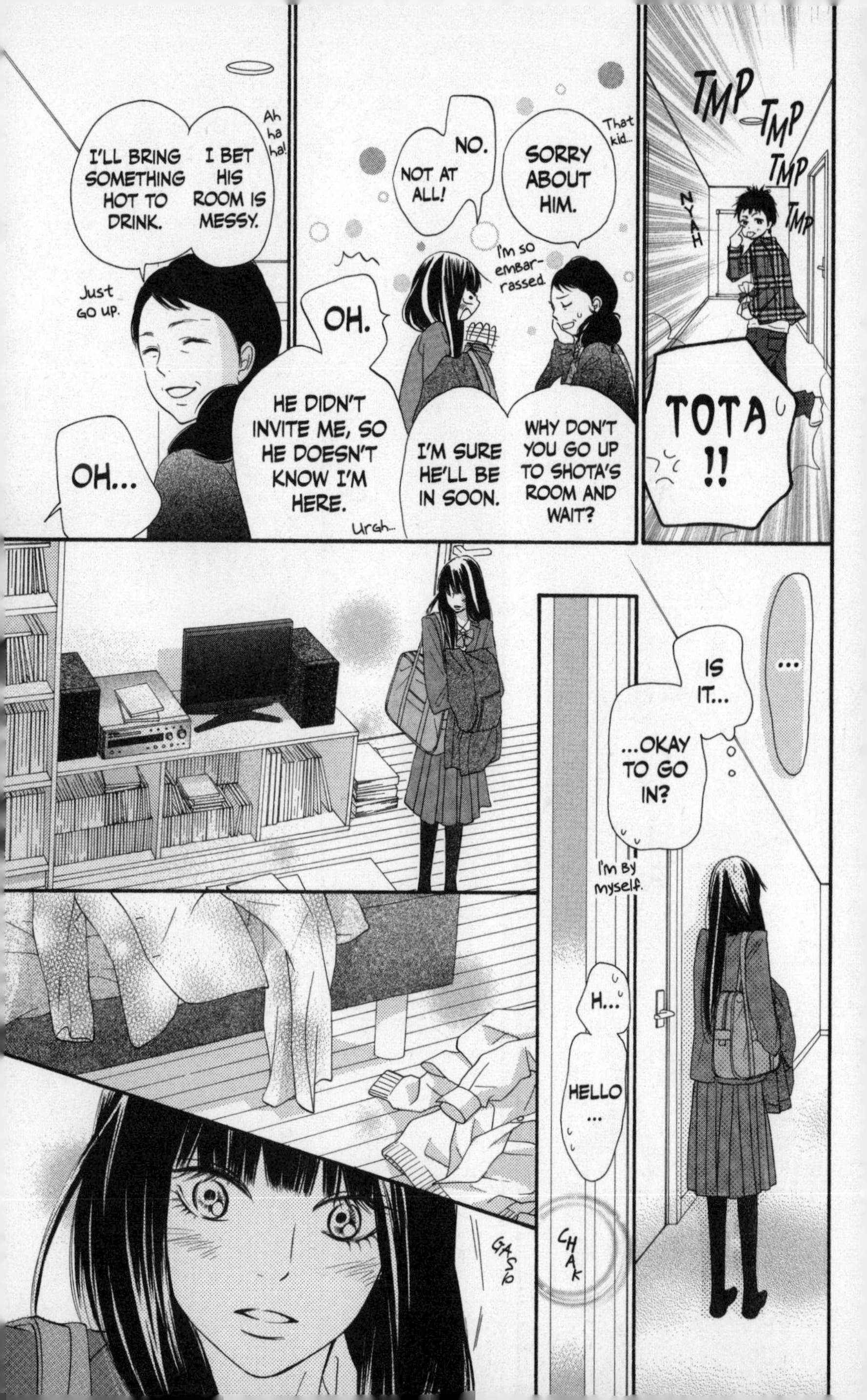
TMP TMP TMP TMP
NYAH
TOTA !!
SORRY ABOUT HIM.
That kid...
NO.
NOT AT ALL!
I'm so embarrassed.
OH.
WHY DON'T YOU GO UP TO SHOTA'S ROOM AND WAIT?
I'M SURE HE'LL BE IN SOON.
HE DIDN'T INVITE ME, SO HE DOESN'T KNOW I'M HERE.
Urgh...
I BET HIS ROOM IS MESSY.
Ah ha ha!
I'LL BRING SOMETHING HOT TO DRINK.
Just go up.
OH...
...
IS IT...
...OKAY TO GO IN?
I'm by myself.
H...
HELLO...
CHAK
GASP

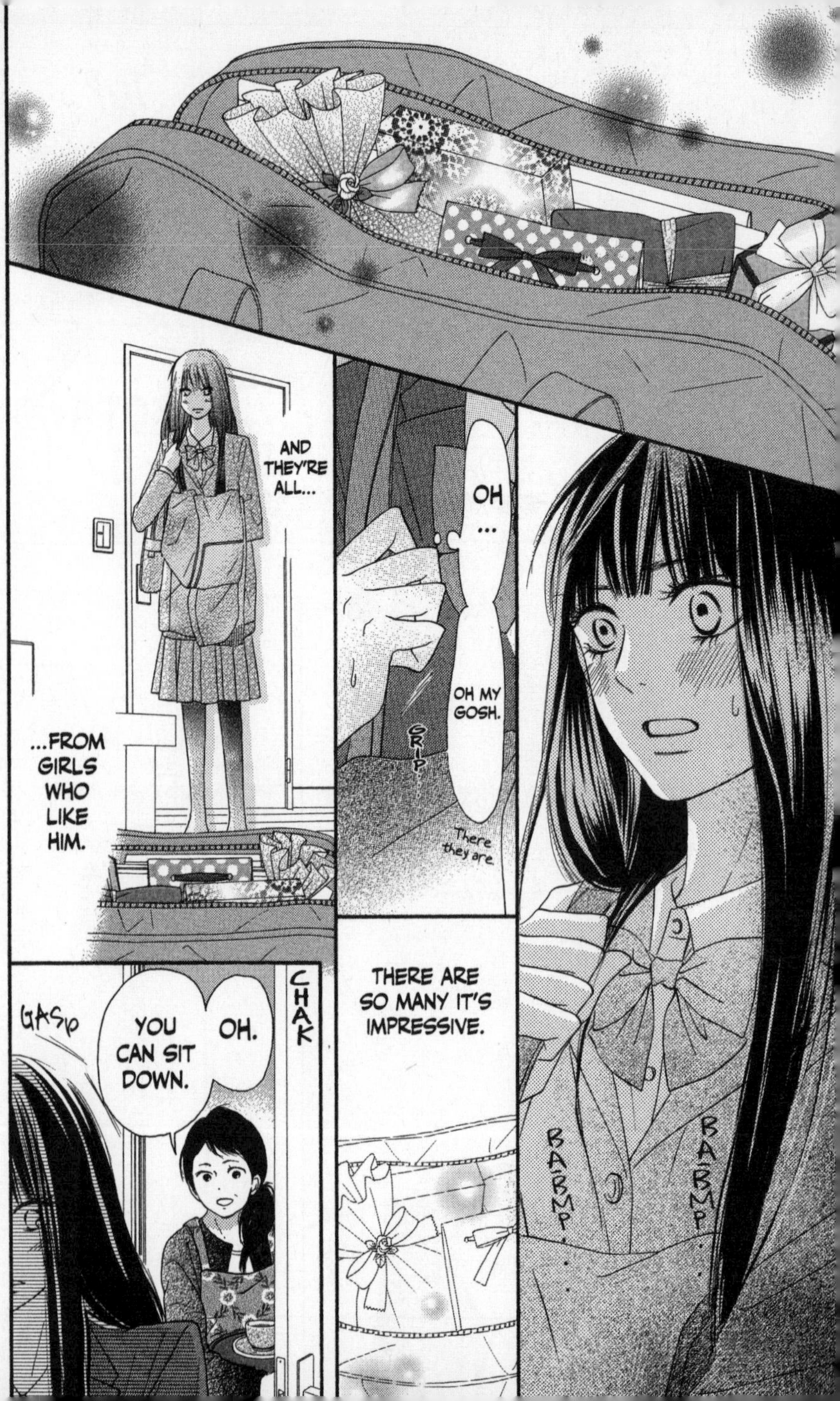
BA-BMP
BA-BMP
OH ...
OH MY GOSH.
GRIP
There they are
AND THEY'RE ALL...
...FROM GIRLS WHO LIKE HIM.
THERE ARE SO MANY IT'S IMPRESSIVE.
CHAK
OH.
YOU CAN SIT DOWN.
GASP

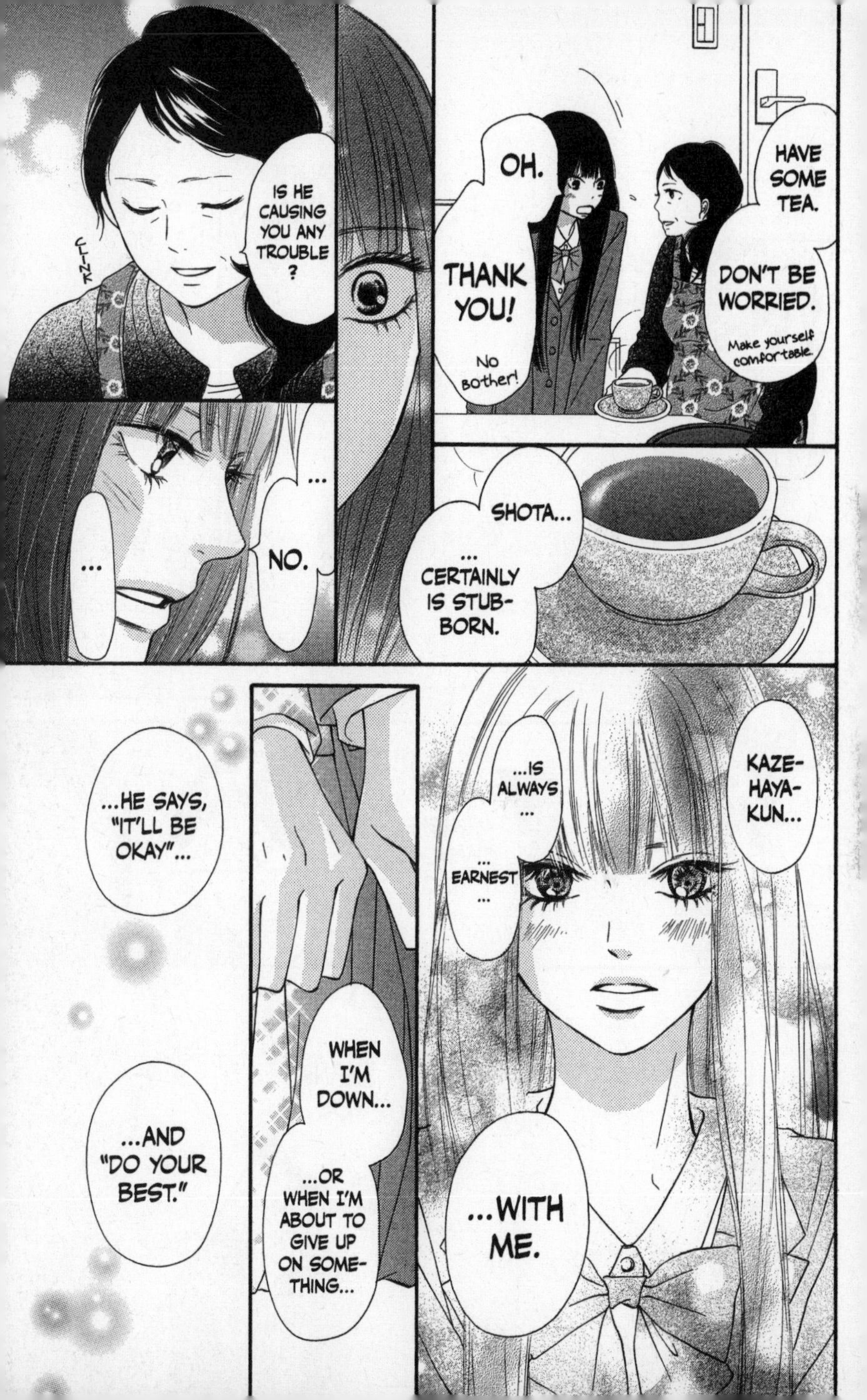
HAVE SOME TEA.
OH.
DON'T BE WORRIED.
Make yourself comfortable.
THANK YOU!
No bother!
SHOTA...
...CERTAINLY IS STUB-BORN.
IS HE CAUSING YOU ANY TROUBLE?
CLINK
...
NO.
...
KAZE-HAYA-KUN...
...IS ALWAYS...
...EARNEST...
...WITH ME.
WHEN I'M DOWN...
...OR WHEN I'M ABOUT TO GIVE UP ON SOME-THING...
...HE SAYS, "IT'LL BE OKAY"...
...AND "DO YOUR BEST."

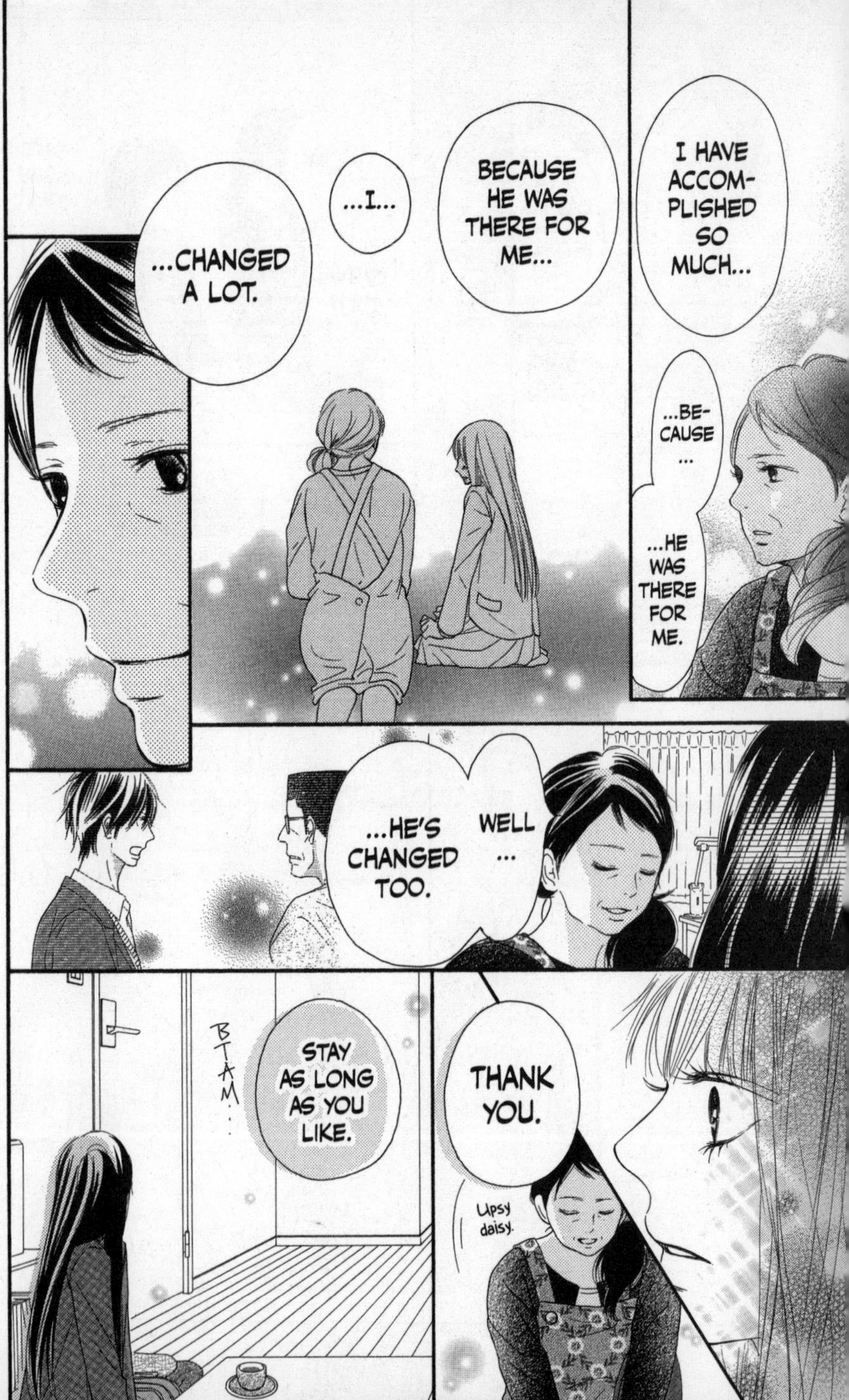
I HAVE ACCOMPLISHED SO MUCH...
...BECAUSE ...
...HE WAS THERE FOR ME.
BECAUSE HE WAS THERE FOR ME...
...I...
...CHANGED A LOT.
WELL ...
...HE'S CHANGED TOO.
THANK YOU.
Upsy daisy.
STAY AS LONG AS YOU LIKE.
BTAM...

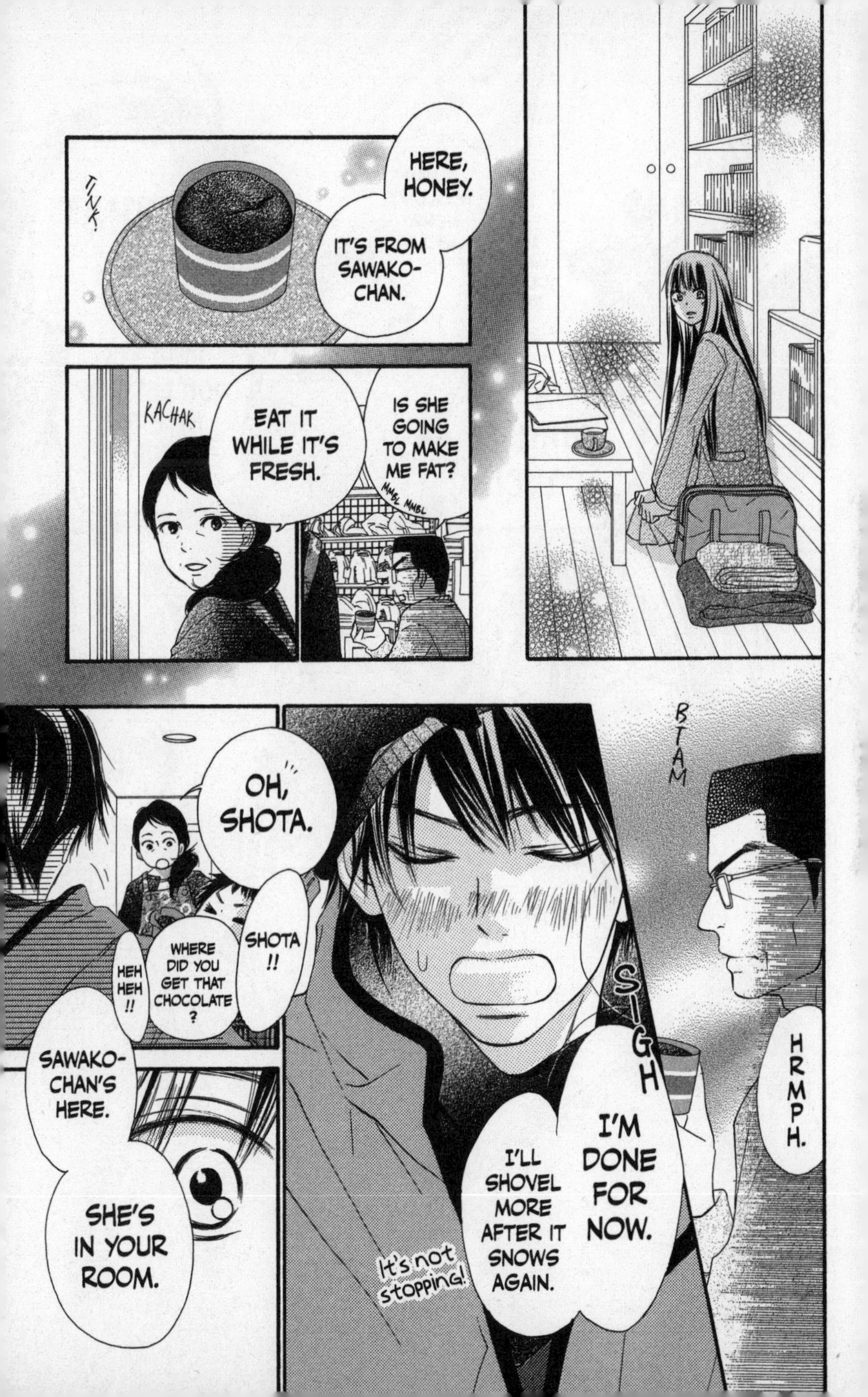
TINK
HERE, HONEY.
IT'S FROM SAWAKO-CHAN.
IS SHE GOING TO MAKE ME FAT?
MMBL MMBL
EAT IT WHILE IT'S FRESH.
KACHAK
BTAM
HRMPH.
SIGH
I'M DONE FOR NOW.
I'LL SHOVEL MORE AFTER IT SNOWS AGAIN.
It's not stopping!
OH, SHOTA.
SHOTA!!
WHERE DID YOU GET THAT CHOCOLATE?
HEH HEH!!
SAWAKO-CHAN'S HERE.
SHE'S IN YOUR ROOM.

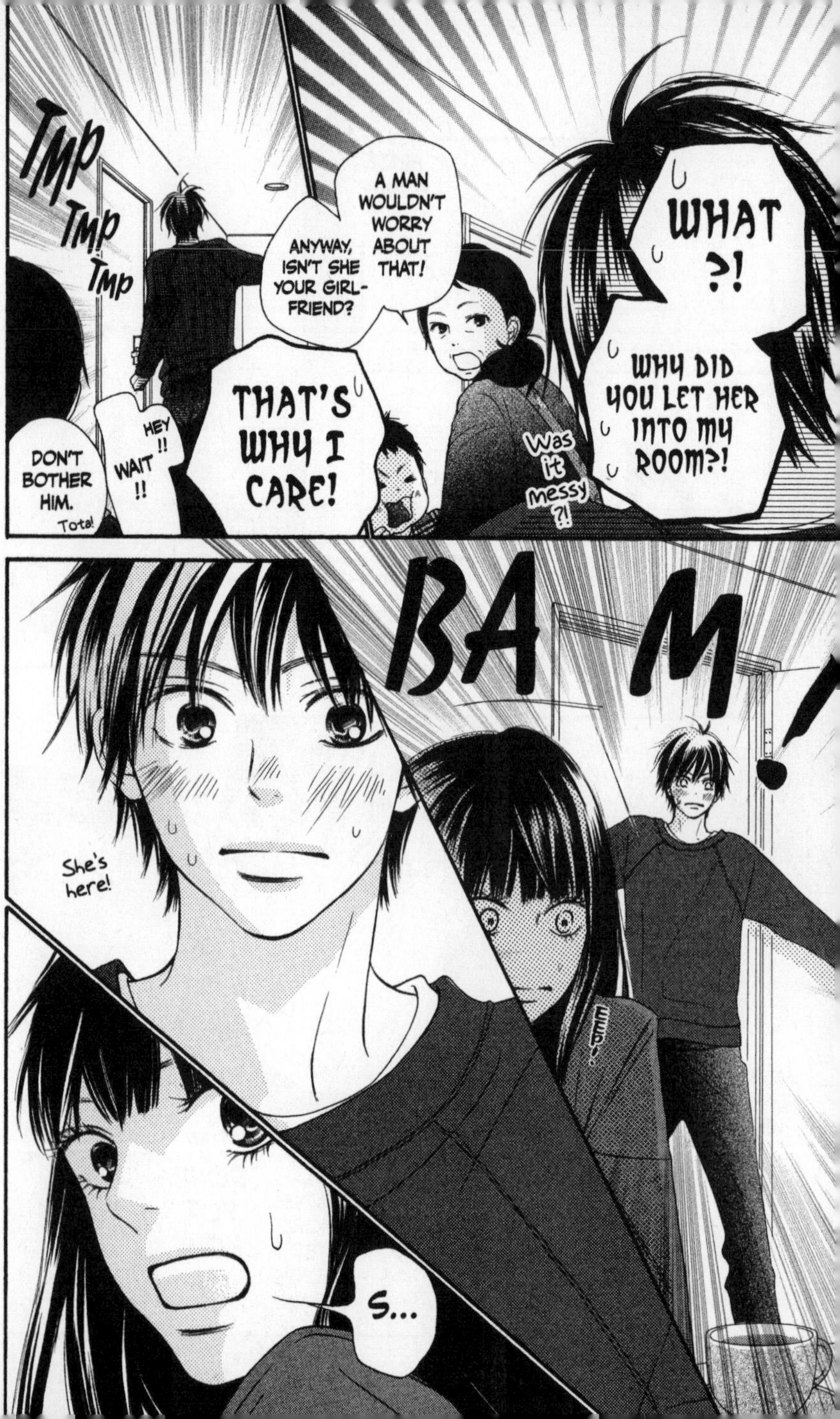
WHAT ?!
WHY DID YOU LET HER INTO MY ROOM?!
Was it messy ?!
A MAN WOULDN'T WORRY ABOUT THAT!
ANYWAY, ISN'T SHE YOUR GIRL-FRIEND?
THAT'S WHY I CARE!
HEY !! WAIT !!
DON'T BOTHER HIM.
Tota!
Tmp Tmp Tmp
BAM!
EEP!
She's here!
S...

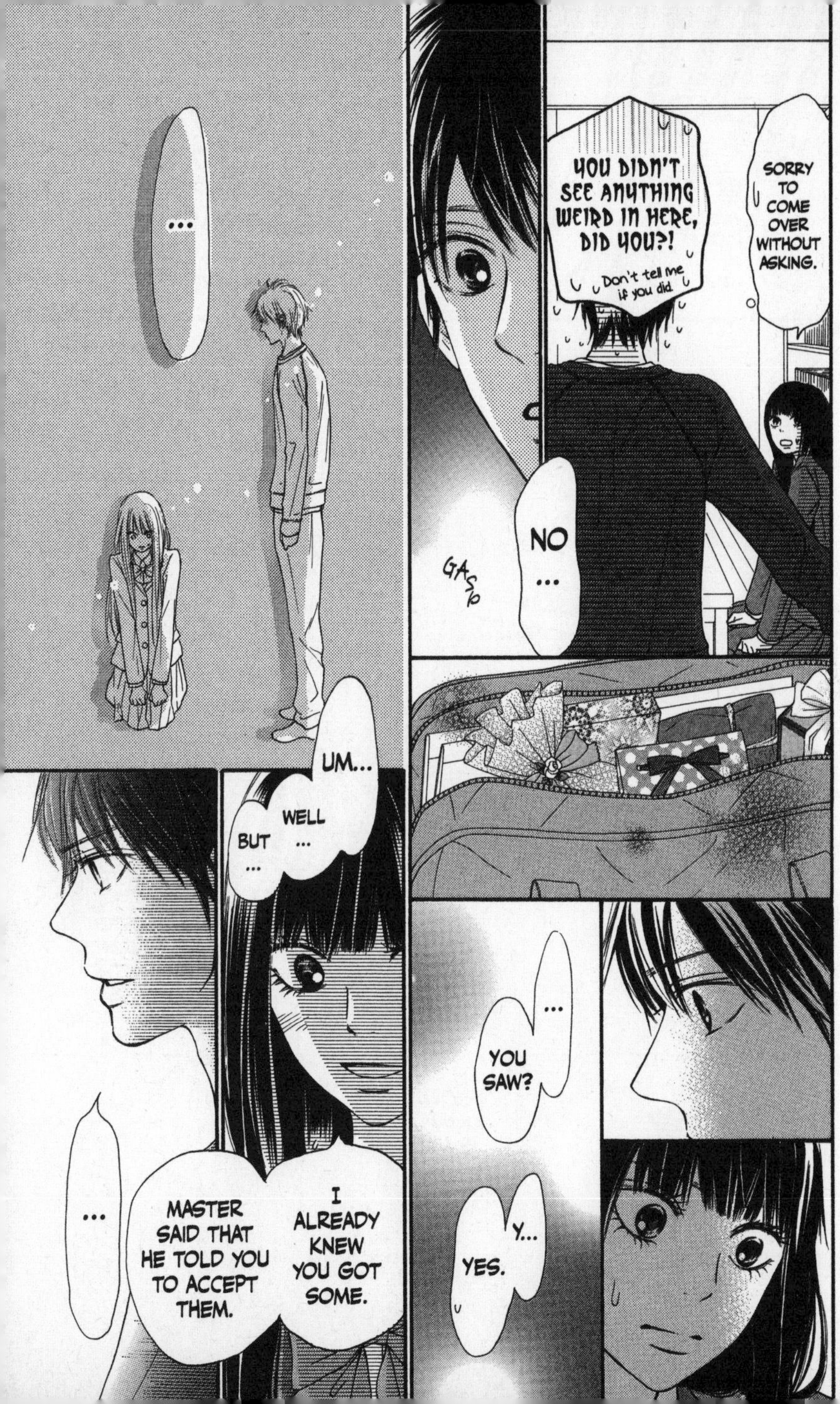
SORRY TO COME OVER WITHOUT ASKING.
YOU DIDN'T SEE ANYTHING WEIRD IN HERE, DID YOU?!
Don't tell me if you did.
NO ...
GASP
... YOU SAW?
Y... YES.
...
UM...
WELL ...
BUT ...
I ALREADY KNEW YOU GOT SOME.
MASTER SAID THAT HE TOLD YOU TO ACCEPT THEM.
...

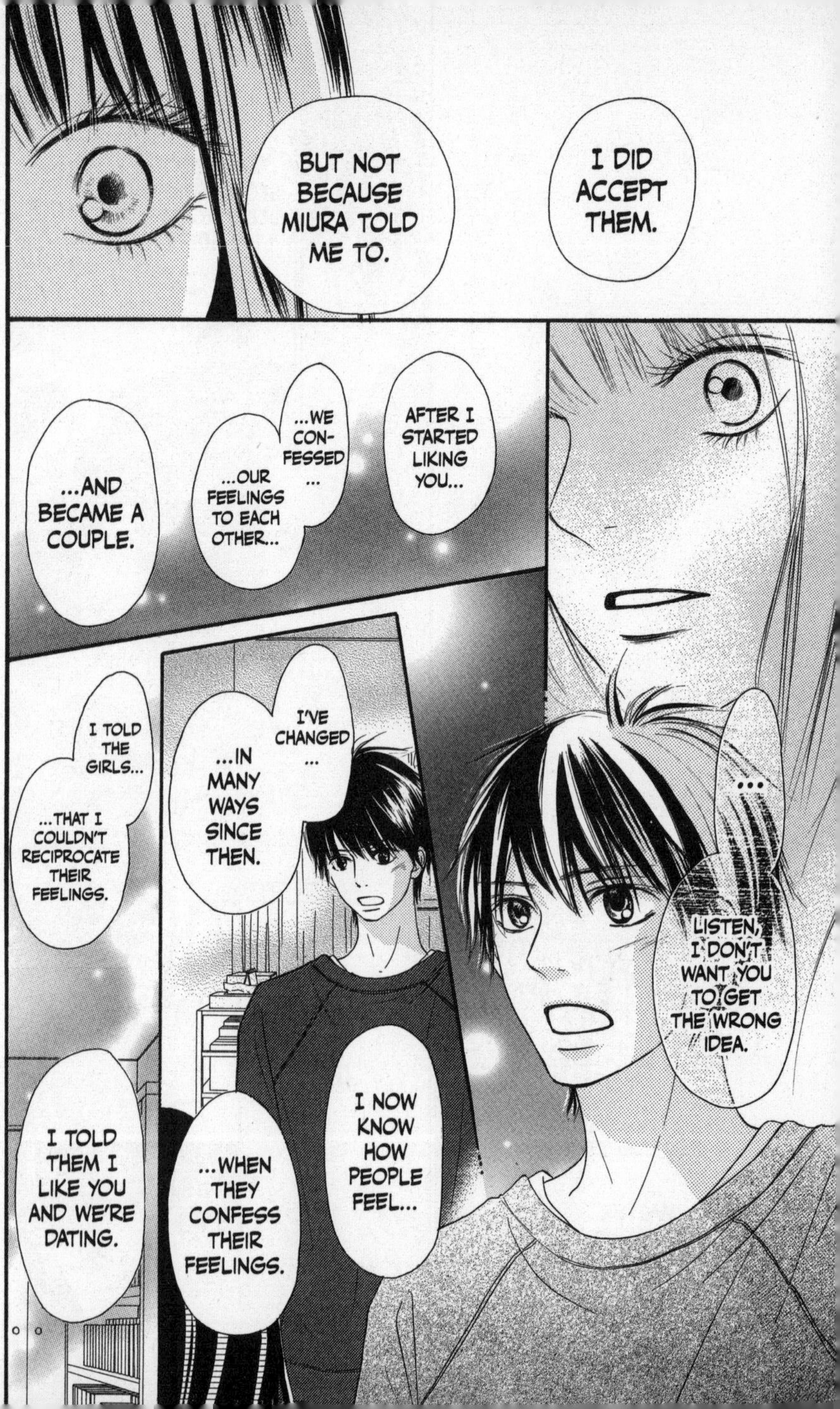
I DID ACCEPT THEM.
BUT NOT BECAUSE MIURA TOLD ME TO.
AFTER I STARTED LIKING YOU...
...WE CON-FESSED...
...OUR FEELINGS TO EACH OTHER...
...AND BECAME A COUPLE.
...
LISTEN, I DON'T WANT YOU TO GET THE WRONG IDEA.
I'VE CHANGED...
...IN MANY WAYS SINCE THEN.
I NOW KNOW HOW PEOPLE FEEL...
...WHEN THEY CONFESS THEIR FEELINGS.
I TOLD THE GIRLS...
...THAT I COULDN'T RECIPROCATE THEIR FEELINGS.
I TOLD THEM I LIKE YOU AND WE'RE DATING.

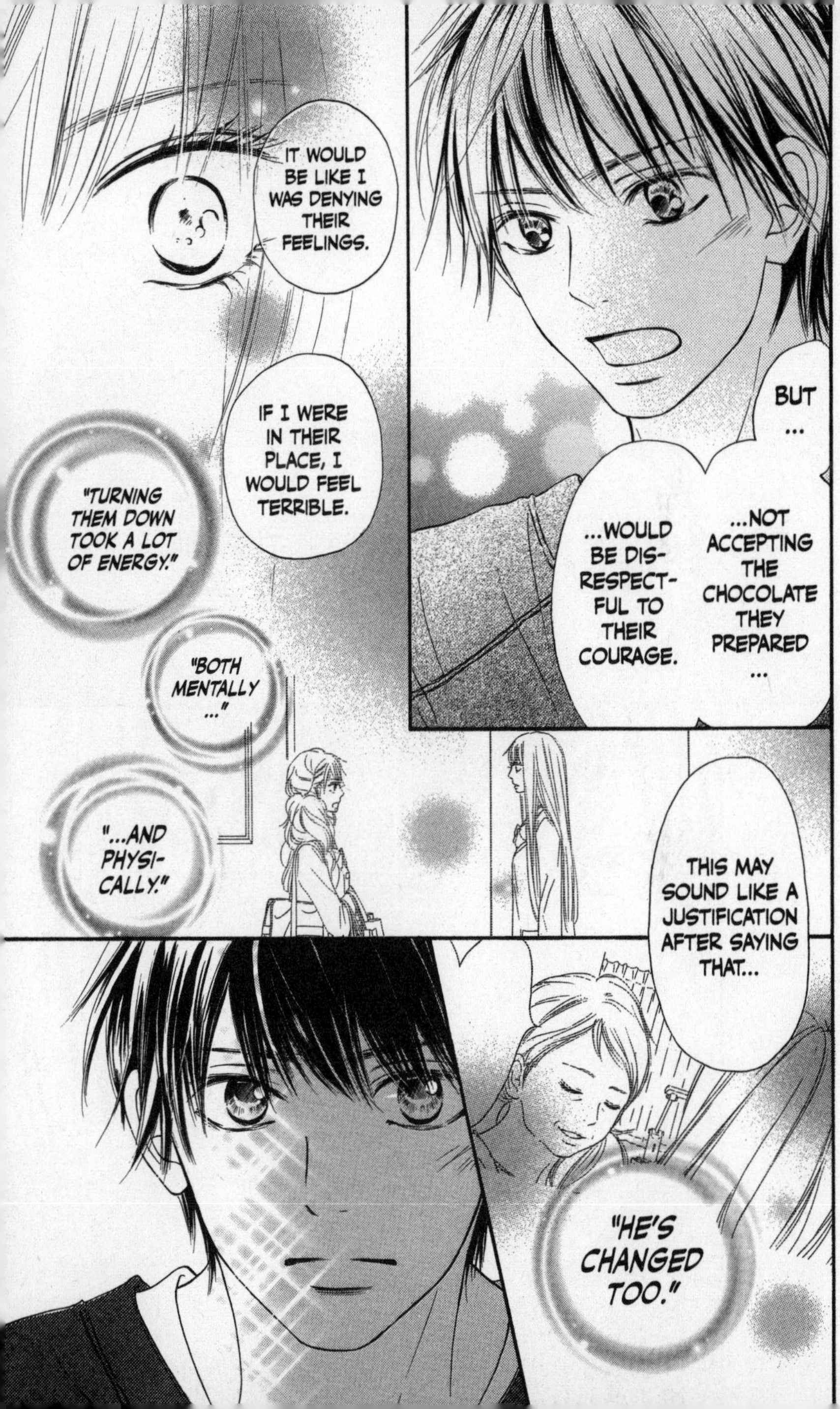
BUT ...
...NOT ACCEPTING THE CHOCOLATE THEY PREPARED ...
...WOULD BE DISRESPECTFUL TO THEIR COURAGE.
IT WOULD BE LIKE I WAS DENYING THEIR FEELINGS.
IF I WERE IN THEIR PLACE, I WOULD FEEL TERRIBLE.
"TURNING THEM DOWN TOOK A LOT OF ENERGY."
"BOTH MENTALLY ..."
"...AND PHYSICALLY."
THIS MAY SOUND LIKE A JUSTIFICATION AFTER SAYING THAT...
"HE'S CHANGED TOO."

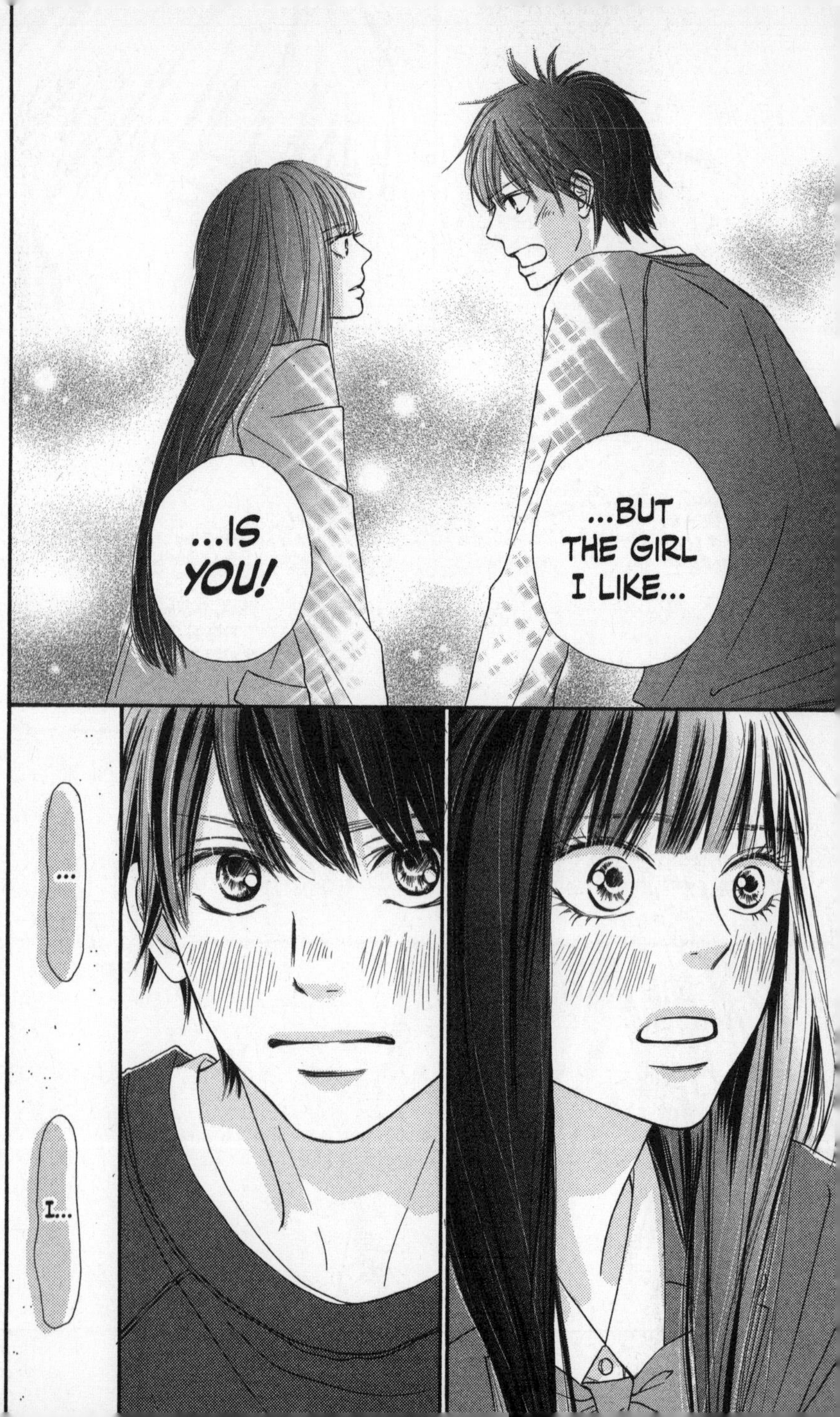
...BUT THE GIRL I LIKE...
...IS YOU!
...
I...

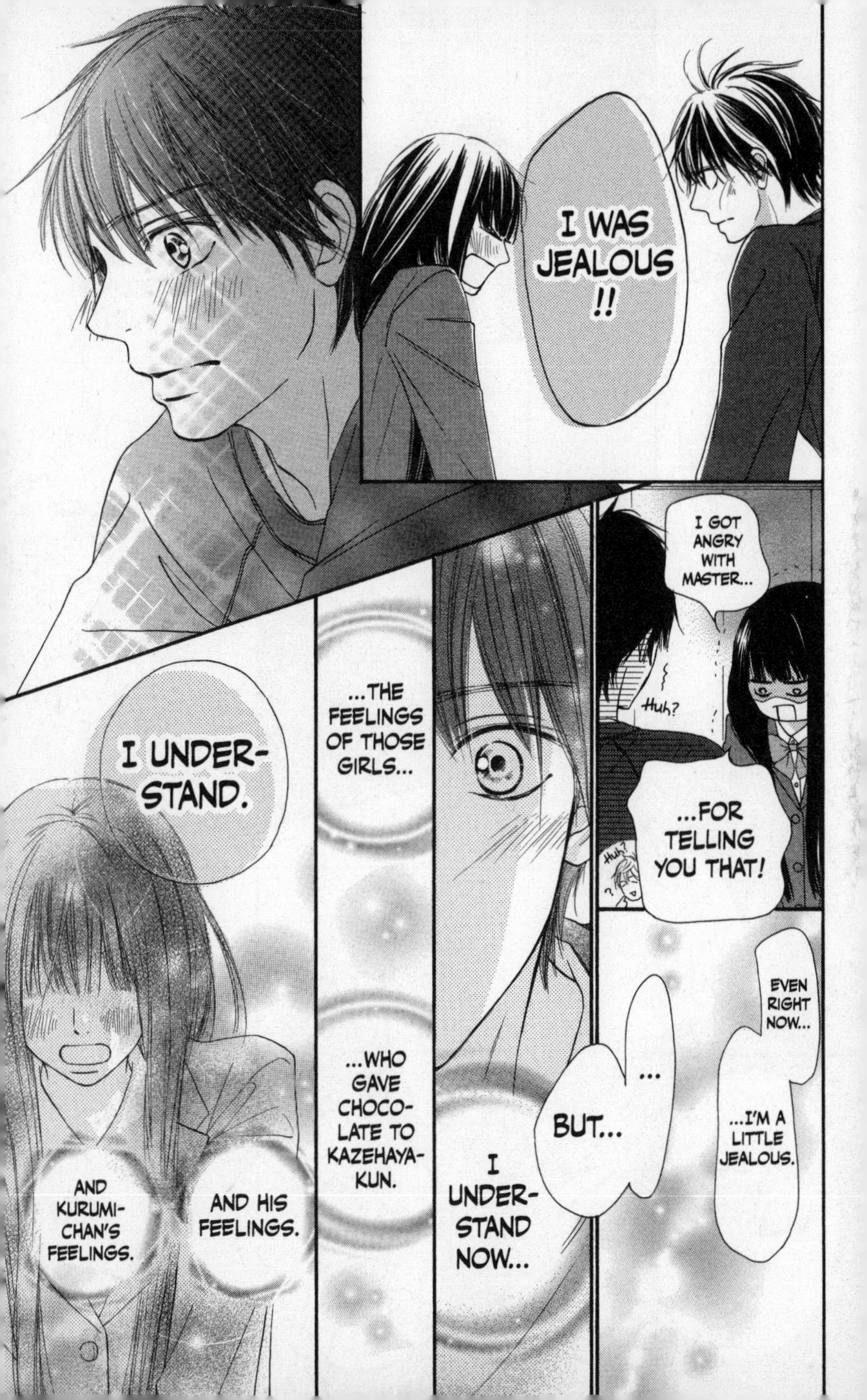
I WAS JEALOUS!!
I GOT ANGRY WITH MASTER...
Huh?
...FOR TELLING YOU THAT!
Huh?
EVEN RIGHT NOW...
...I'M A LITTLE JEALOUS.
...
BUT...
I UNDER-STAND NOW...
...THE FEELINGS OF THOSE GIRLS...
...WHO GAVE CHOCO-LATE TO KAZEHAYA-KUN.
I UNDER-STAND.
AND HIS FEELINGS.
AND KURUMI-CHAN'S FEELINGS.

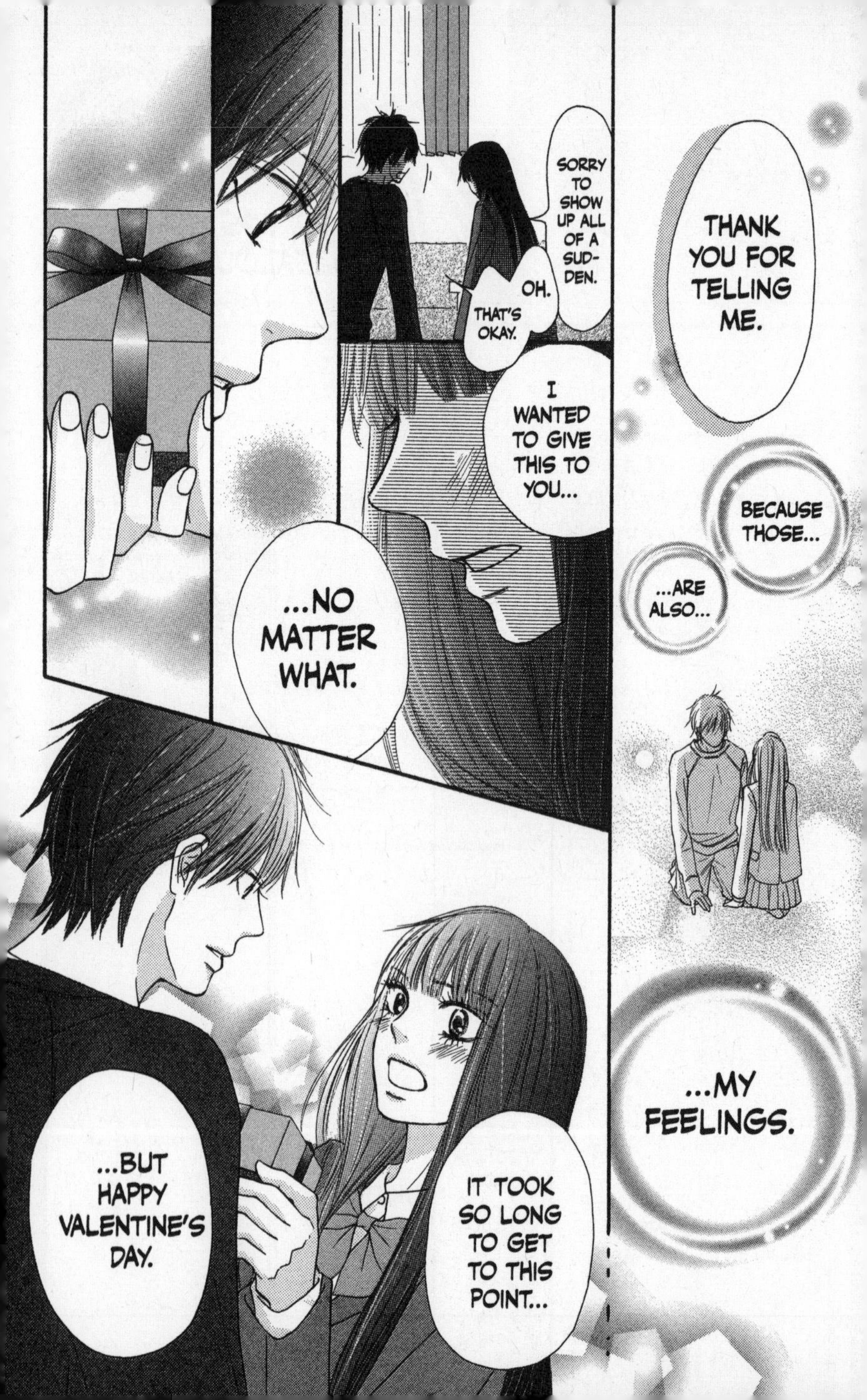
THANK YOU FOR TELLING ME.
BECAUSE THOSE...
...ARE ALSO...
...MY FEELINGS.
SORRY TO SHOW UP ALL OF A SUD-DEN.
OH.
THAT'S OKAY.
I WANTED TO GIVE THIS TO YOU...
...NO MATTER WHAT.
IT TOOK SO LONG TO GET TO THIS POINT...
...BUT HAPPY VALENTINE'S DAY.

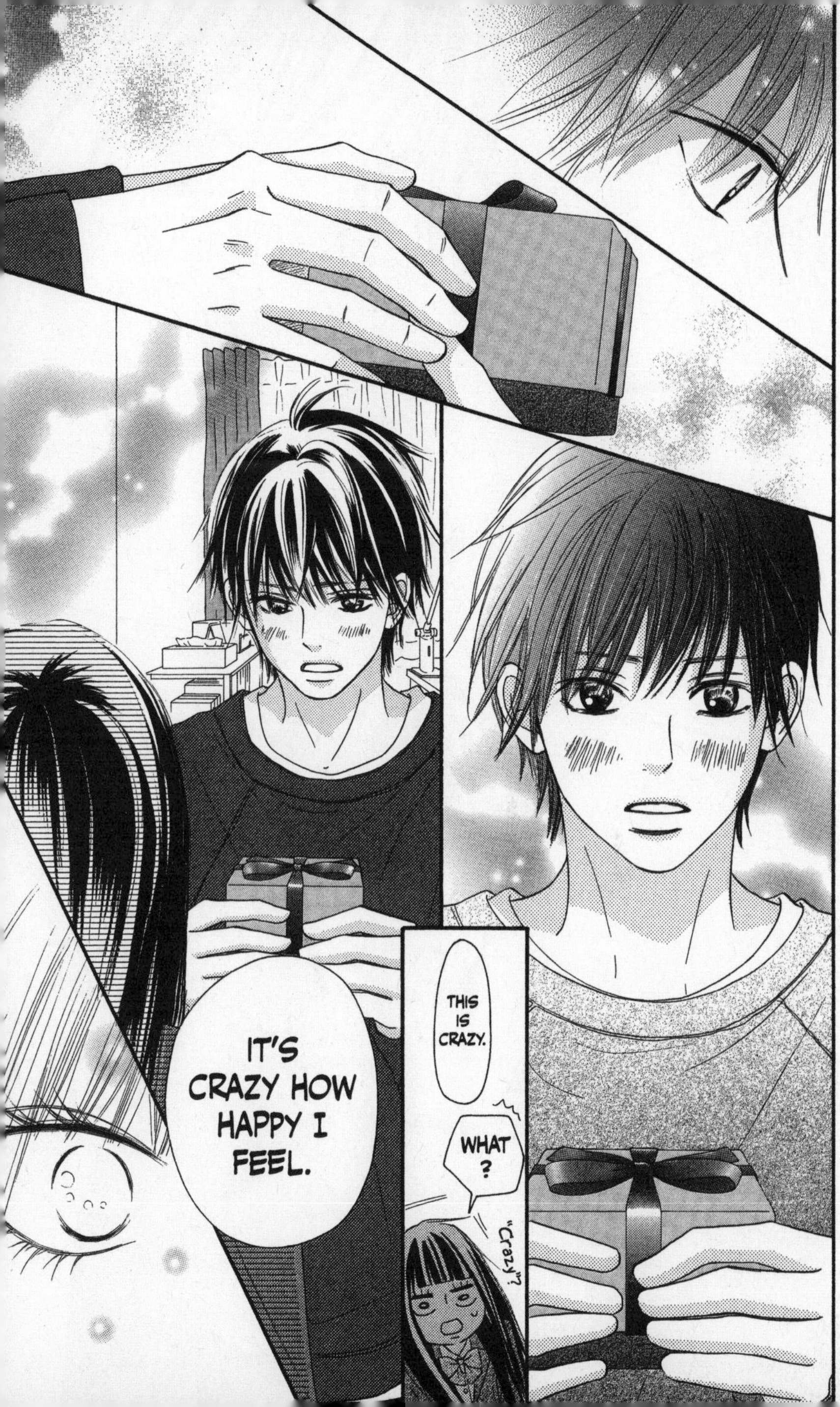
THIS IS CRAZY.
WHAT?
"Crazy"?
IT'S CRAZY HOW HAPPY I FEEL.

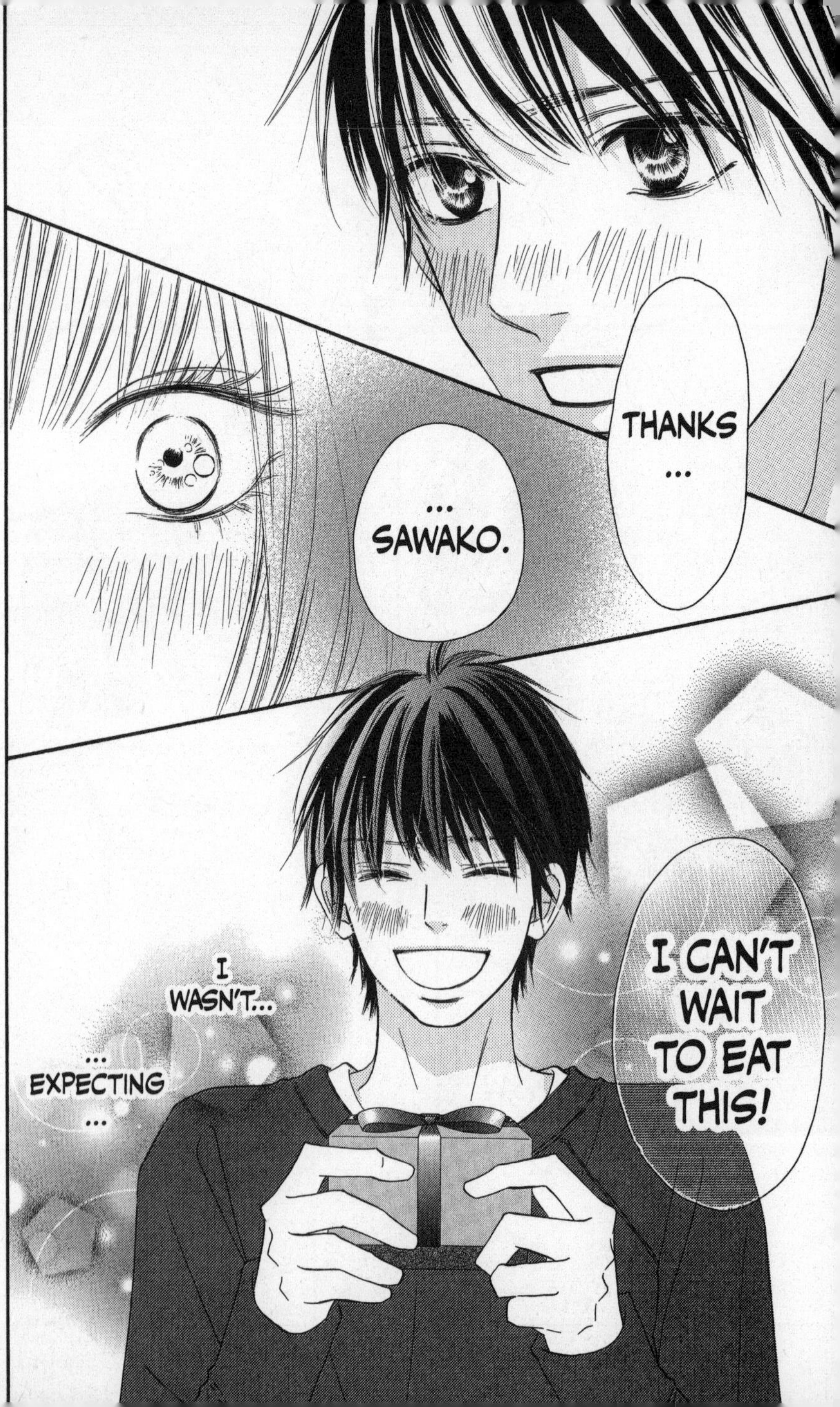
THANKS ...
... SAWAKO.
I CAN'T WAIT TO EAT THIS!
I WASN'T...
... EXPECTING ...

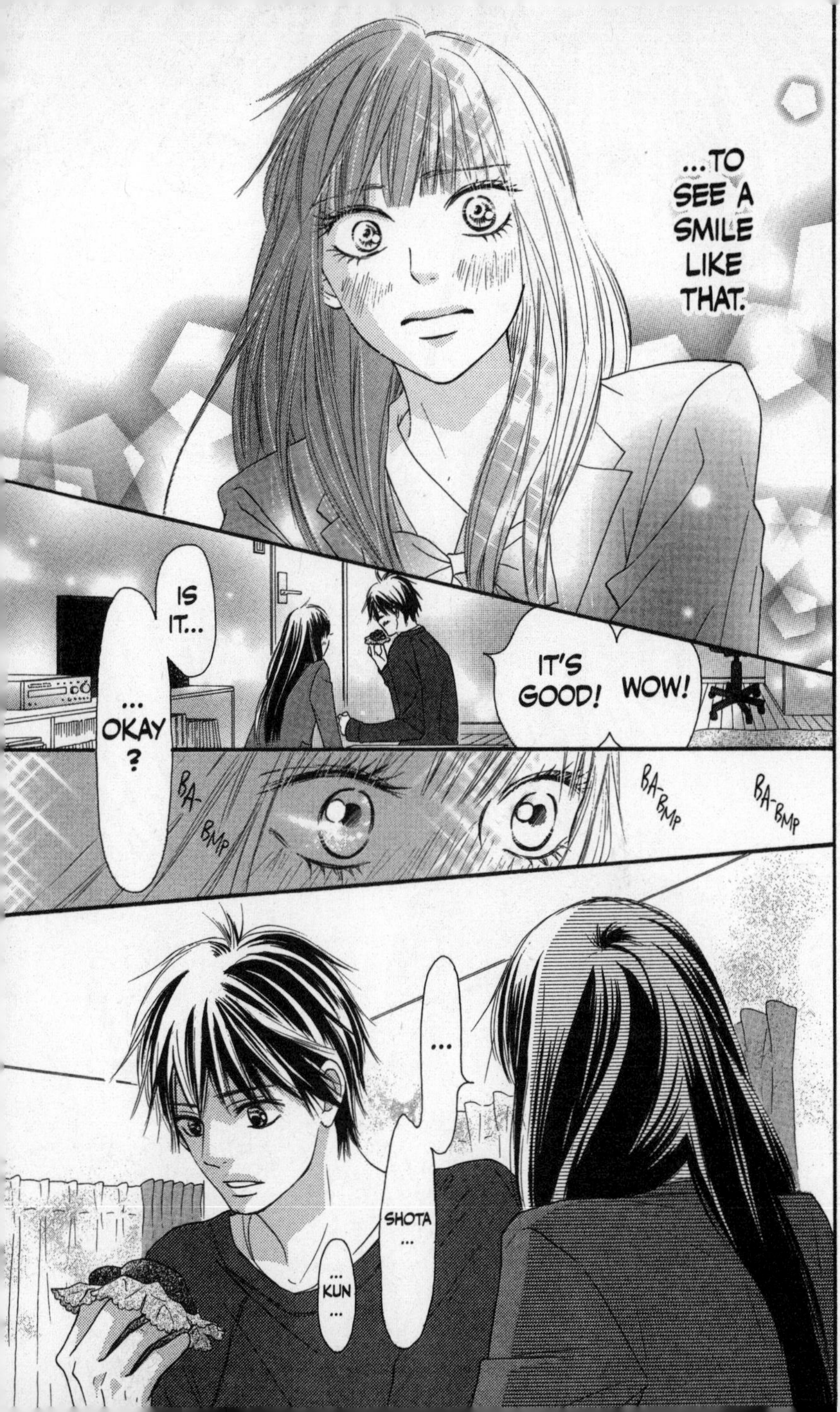
...TO SEE A SMILE LIKE THAT.
WOW!
IT'S GOOD!
IS IT... ...OKAY?
BA-BMP
BA-BMP
BA-BMP
...
SHOTA...
...KUN...

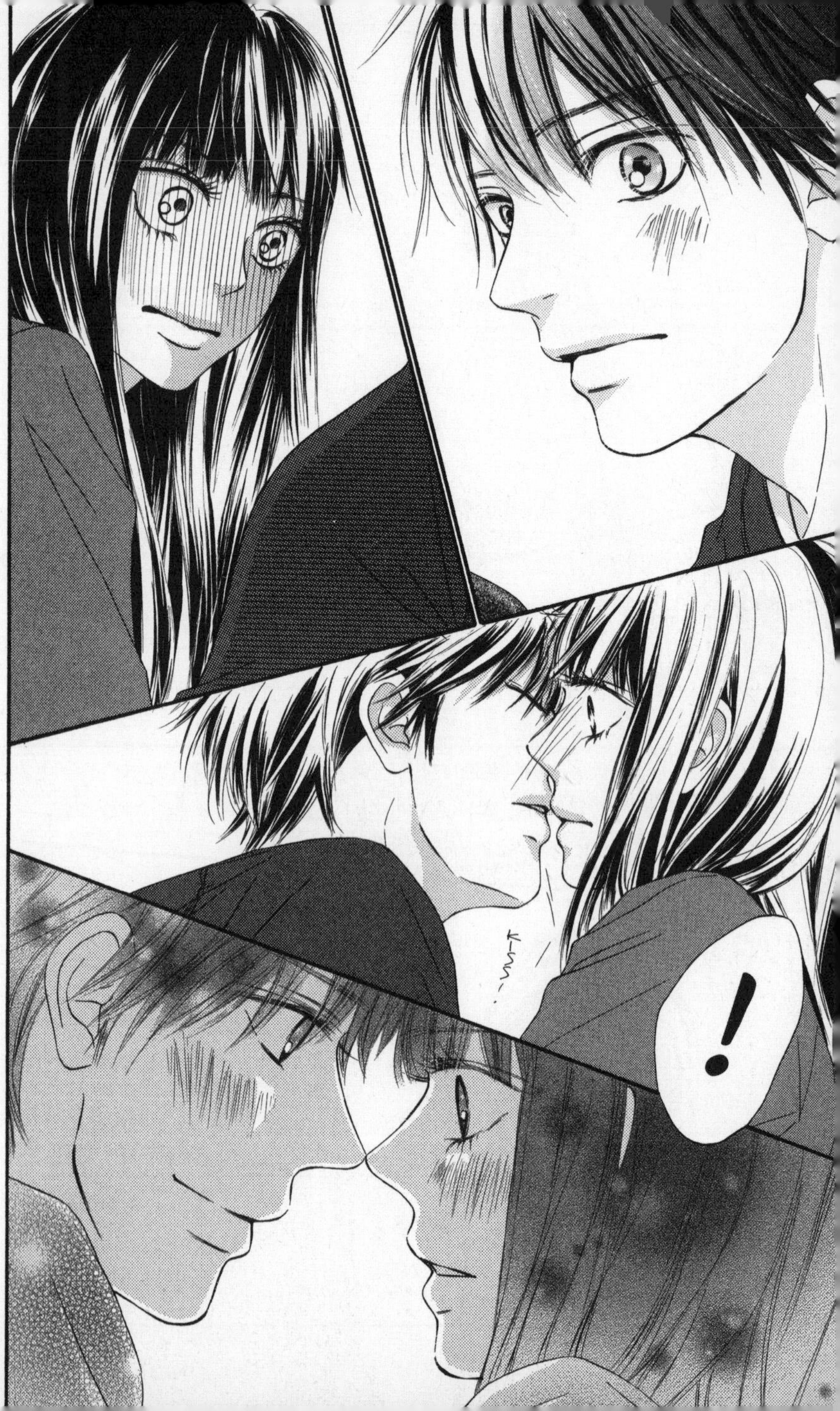
KISS!
!

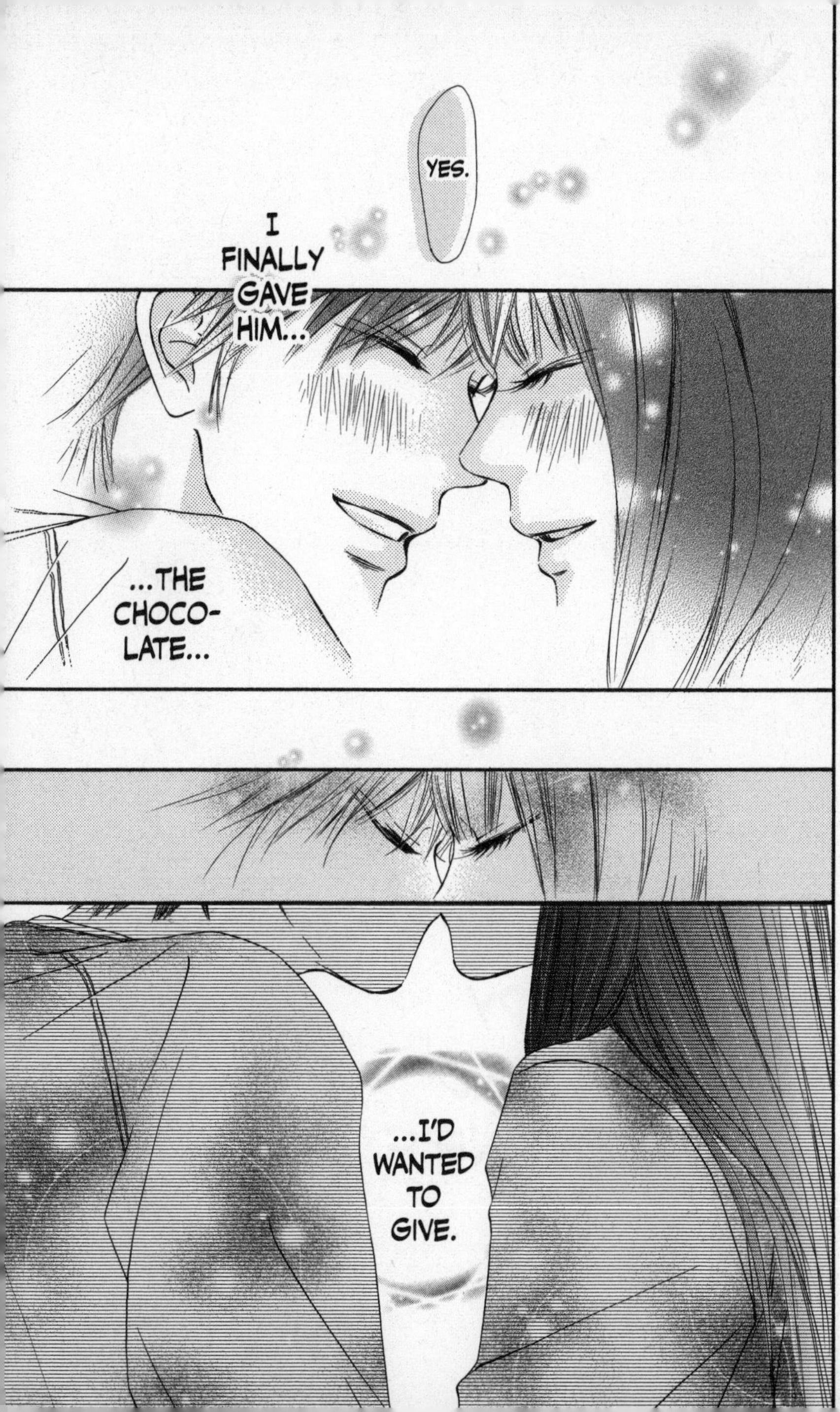
YES.
I FINALLY GAVE HIM...
...THE CHOCO-LATE...
...I'D WANTED TO GIVE.

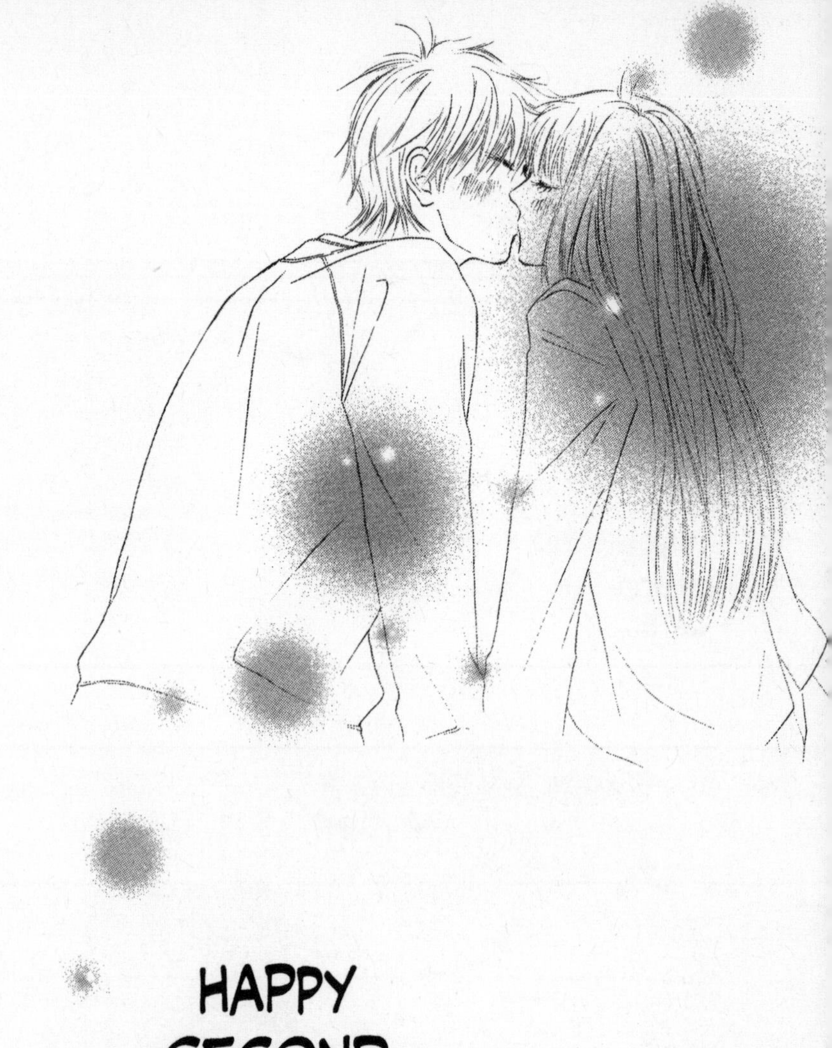
HAPPY SECOND VALENTINE'S DAY.

Vol. 20 End

From me (the editor) to you (the reader).

Here are some Japanese culture explanations that will help you better understand the references in the *Kimi ni Todoke* world.

Honorifics:

When saying someone's name in Japanese, a suffix is often attached to indicate how familiar the speaker is with the person. Some are more polite and respectful, while others are endearing. Calling someone by just their first name is the most informal.

-kun is used for young men or boys, usually someone you are familiar with.

-chan is used for young women, girls or young children and can be used as a term of endearment.

-san is used for someone you respect or are not close to, or to be polite.

Page 50, "welcome":

Mr. Sanada tries to pronounce the English "welcome," with results similar to his son's earlier attempt to pronounce "preverved" (preserved) in volume 17.

Page 58, *Sadako 3D*:

One of many sequels to the horror movie featuring the heroine Sawako is nicknamed after.

Page 63, grin:

A play on words. The sound of Chizu's grotesque smile is *ni*, which Ayane calls *nihirisumu* (nihilistic).

Page 67, Valentine's chocolates:

On Valentine's Day in Japan, girls give chocolates to boys and for the most part do not receive anything for themselves. Tirol-Choco is a company known for their small, inexpensive chocolates.

Page 74, Takahashi Meijin:

"Master" Takahashi, a gamer known for his fast fingers.

Page 90, giri-choco:

"Obligation chocolate," given to a girl's male classmates, friends and associates with no romantic intentions.

Page 91, honmei-choco:

"True feeling chocolate," given to someone with romantic feelings.

Page 135, Sawako:

Kazehaya's father uses different kanji that could also be pronounced "Sawako."

Page 147, enka:

A popular Japanese music genre with traditional Japanese elements.

This is volume 20! The series is getting long! Since I've been writing about winter for so long, I've started longing for blue skies and sunlight filtering through the trees, so Valentine's Day wraps up in this volume. I'm happy to have a warm season coming up in the manga!

--Karuho Shiina

Karuho Shiina was born and raised in Hokkaido, Japan. Though *Kimi ni Todoke* is only her second series following many one-shot stories, it has already racked up accolades from various "Best Manga of the Year" lists. Winner of the 2008 Kodansha Manga Award for the shojo category, *Kimi ni Todoke* also placed fifth in the first-ever Manga Taisho (Cartoon Grand Prize) contest in 2008. In Japan, an animated TV series debuted in October 2009, and a live-action film was released in 2010.

Kimi ni Todoke
VOL. 20

Shojo Beat Edition

STORY AND ART BY
KARUHO SHIINA

Translation/Ari Yasuda, HC Language Solutions, Inc.
Touch-up Art & Lettering/Vanessa Satone
Design/Nozomi Akashi
Editor/Hope Donovan

KIMI NI TODOKE © 2005 by Karuho Shiina
All rights reserved. First published in Japan in 2005 by SHUEISHA Inc.,
Tokyo. English translation rights arranged by SHUEISHA Inc.

Printed in the U.S.A.

Published by VIZ Media, LLC
P.O. Box 77010
San Francisco, CA 94107

10 9 8 7 6 5 4 3 2 1
First printing, December 2014

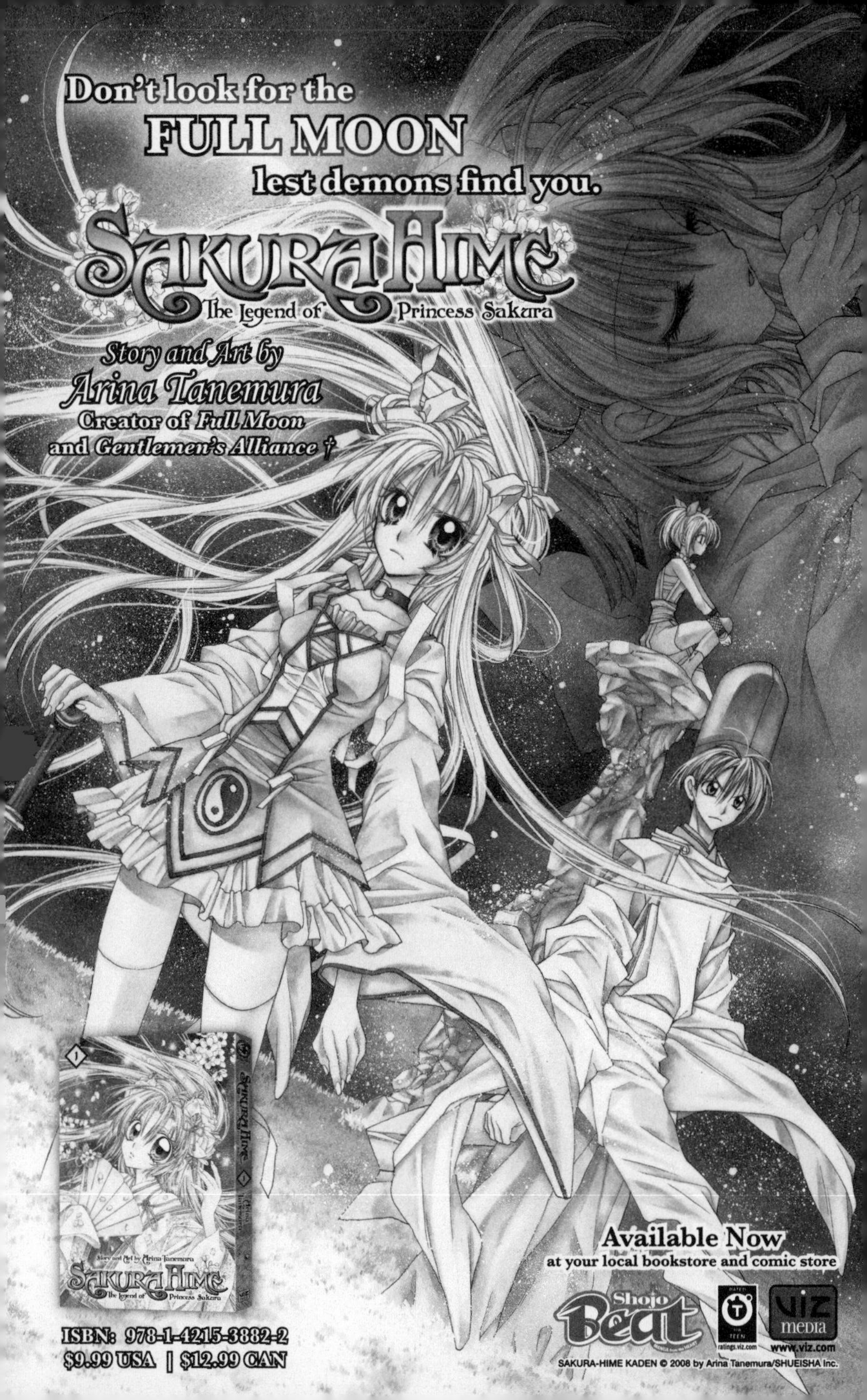
Don't look for the
FULL MOON
lest demons find you.
SAKURA HIME
The Legend of Princess Sakura
Story and Art by
Arina Tanemura
Creator of Full Moon
and Gentlemen's Alliance †
Available Now
at your local bookstore and comic store
ISBN: 978-1-4215-3882-2
$9.99 USA | $12.99 CAN
Shojo Beat
VIZ media
www.viz.com
SAKURA-HIME KADEN © 2008 by Arina Tanemura/SHUEISHA Inc.

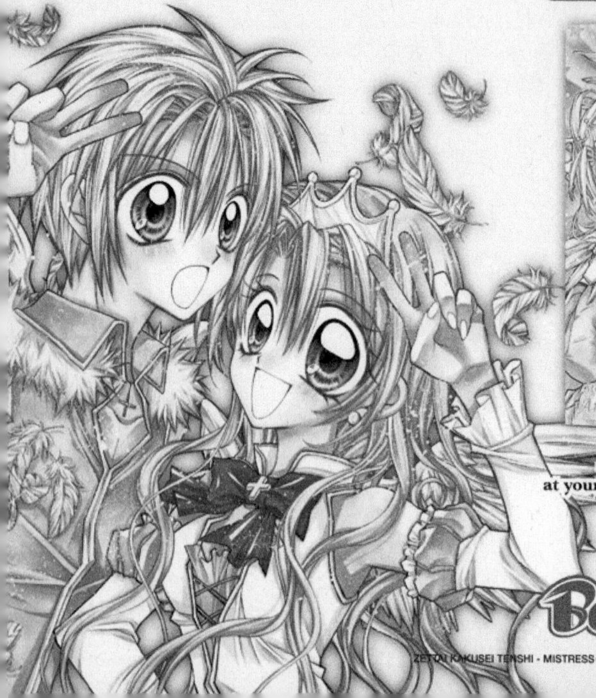

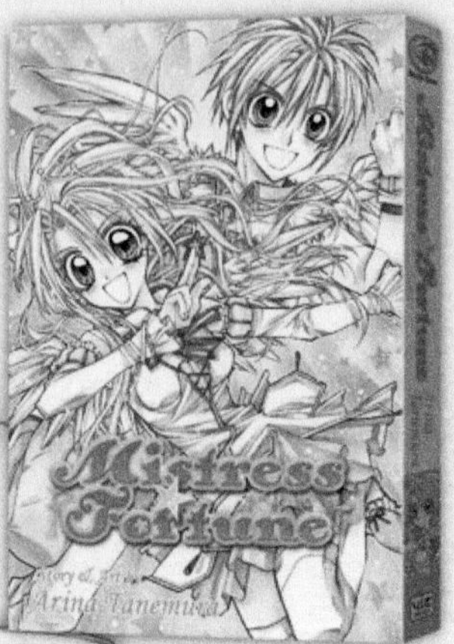
Mistress Fortune
Story & Art
Arina Tanemura

ISBN: 978-1-4215-3881-5
$9.99 USA | $12.99 CAN

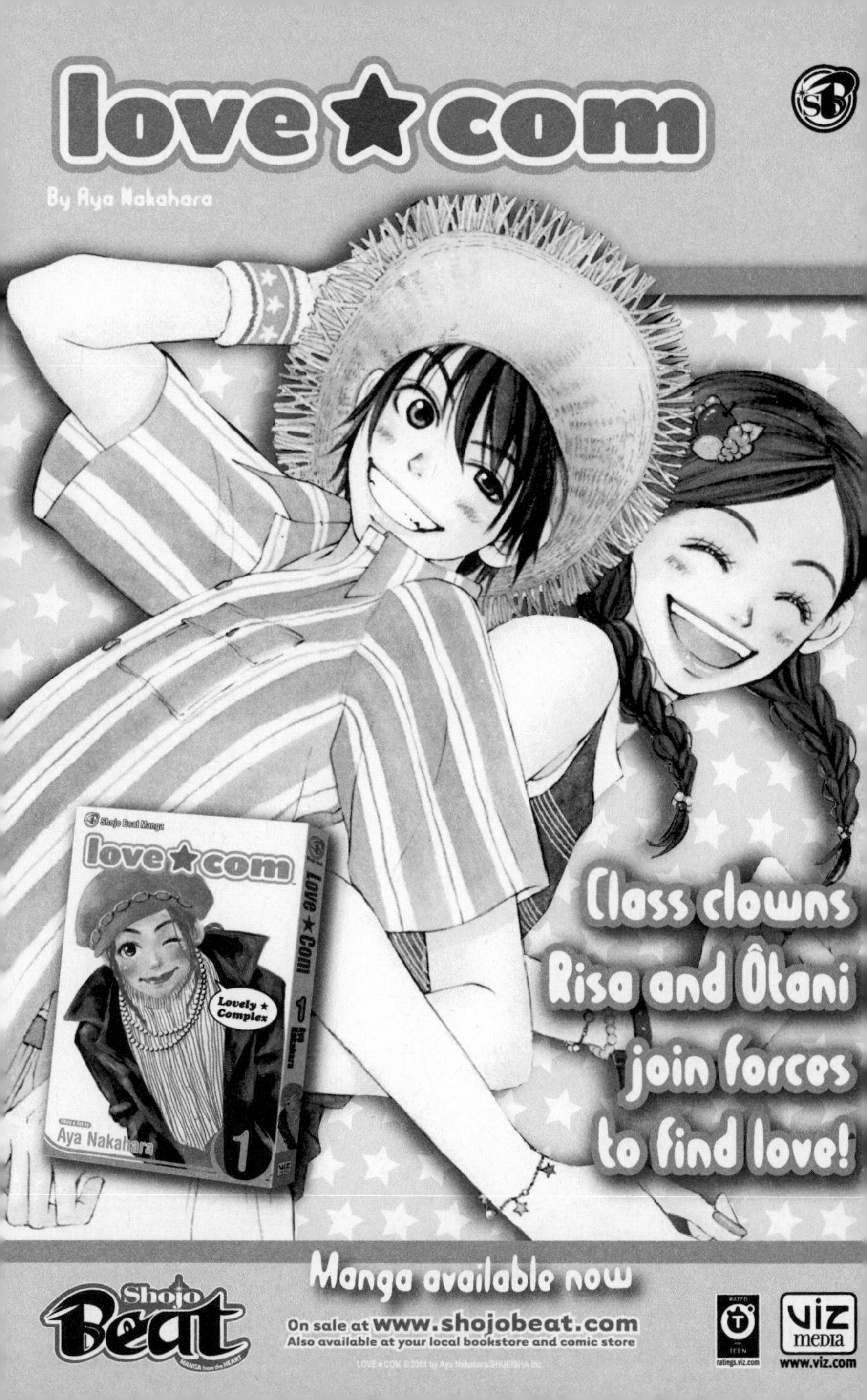

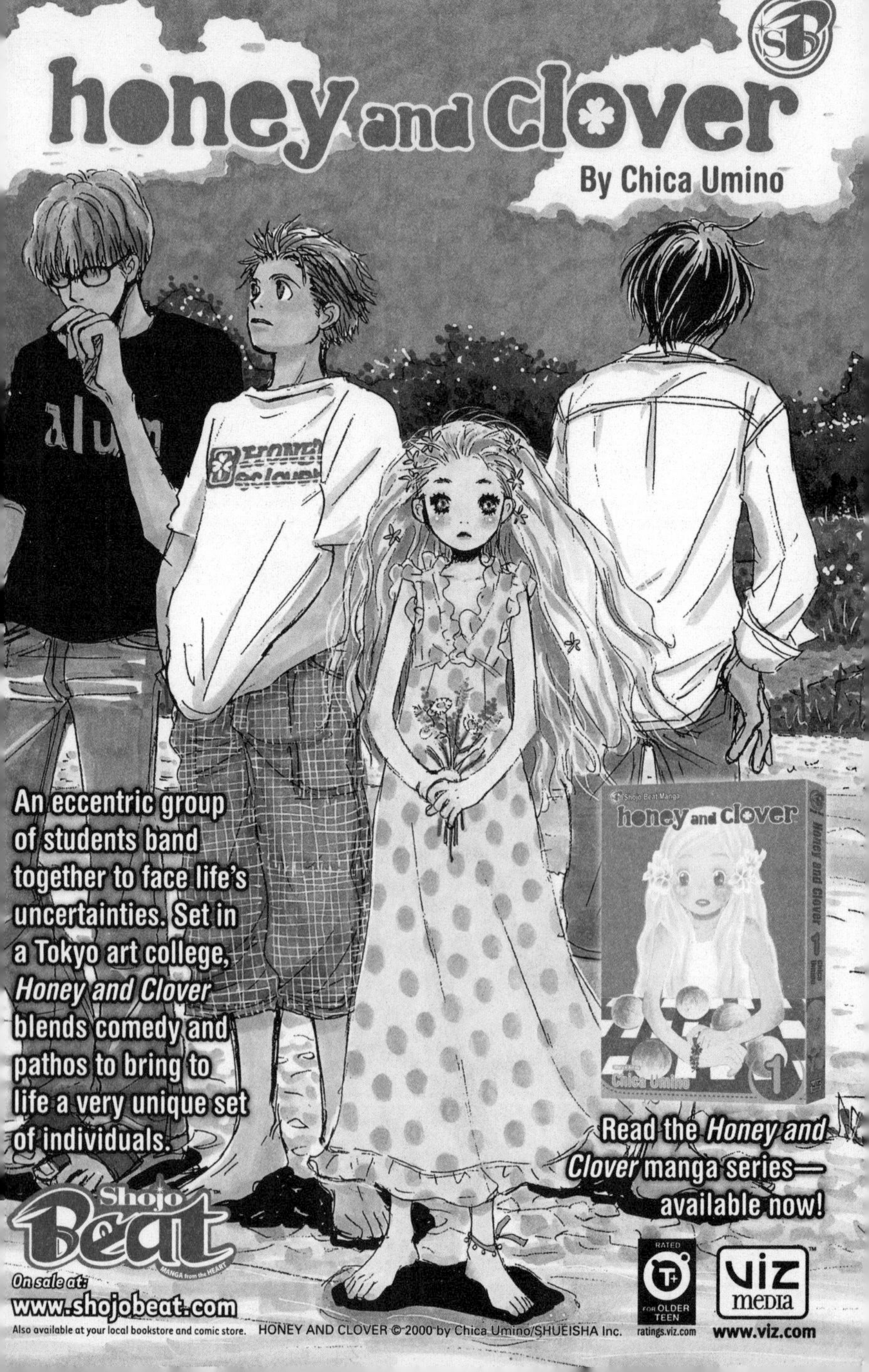
honey and clover
By Chica Umino
An eccentric group of students band together to face life's uncertainties. Set in a Tokyo art college, *Honey and Clover* blends comedy and pathos to bring to life a very unique set of individuals.
Shojo Beat Manga
honey and clover
Chica Umino
1
Read the *Honey and Clover* manga series—available now!
Shojo Beat
MANGA from the HEART
On sale at:
www.shojobeat.com
Also available at your local bookstore and comic store.
HONEY AND CLOVER © 2000 by Chica Umino/SHUEISHA Inc.
RATED
T+
FOR OLDER TEEN
ratings.viz.com
VIZ media
www.viz.com

Surprise!

You may be reading the wrong way!

It's true: In keeping with the original
Japanese comic format, this book reads
from right to left—so action, sound effects,
and word balloons are completely reversed.
This preserves the orientation of the
original artwork—plus, it's fun!
Check out the diagram shown here
to get the hang of things, and
then turn to the other side of
the book to get started!

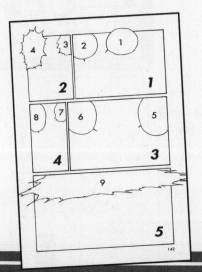